HISTORY OF INDIA DOWN TO THE END OF THE REIGN OF QUEEN VICTORIA

MACMILLAN AND CO., LIMITED
LONDON · BOMBAY · CALCUTTA
MELBOURNE

THE MACMILLAN COMPANY
NEW YORK · BOSTON · CHICAGO
DALLAS · SAN FRANCISCO

THE MACMILLAN CO. OF CANADA, LTD
TORONTO

BUDDHA.

From the Stupa at Mirpur Khas, Sind.

HISTORY OF INDIA

DOWN TO THE END OF THE REIGN OF QUEEN VICTORIA

BY

M. PROTHERO, M.A.

INDIAN EDUCATIONAL SERVICE (RETIRED)
FELLOW OF ROYAL HISTORICAL SOCIETY, LONDON, AND
EXAMINER IN INDIAN HISTORY TO THE CIVIL SERVICE COMMISSIONERS

AND

MAHAMAHOPADHYAYA
SATIS CHANDRA VIDYABHUSANA, M.A., PH.D.

PRINCIPAL, SANSKRIT COLLEGE, CALCUTTA

Low Price Publications

2011

First Published 1915

Reprinted in **LPP**
1993, 1996, 2011

ISBN 10: 81-85557-80-2
ISBN 13: 978-81-85557-80-9

Published by
Low Price Publications
A-6, Second Floor, Nimri Commercial Centre,
Ashok Vihar Phase-IV, Delhi 110 052 (INDIA)
Tel.: +91 11 27302453 Fax.: +91 11 47061936
E-mail: info@Lppindia.com
Website: www.Lppindia.com

Printed at
IIP Printers
Delhi

PRINTED IN INDIA

PREFACE.

THIS work is intended to provide the main facts of Indian History in sufficient detail for students going up for the B.A. Examinations of the various Indian Universities in the subject.

LONDON,
1st October, 1915.

CONTENTS.

BOOK I.

PRE-MUSALMAN INDIA.

BOOK II.

MEDIAEVAL INDIA.

BOOK III.

MODERN INDIA.

BOOK I.

PRE-MUSALMAN INDIA.

CHAPTER I.

PHYSICAL CONFIGURATION AND RACES OF INDIA.

INDIA is the name of a large country in Asia. This name has become familiar to the world since the advent of the British. The name India is derived from "Sindhu," the Sanscrit word for the sea. It was first applied to the Indus, which appeared to the Aryan invaders of the Panjab as large as the open sea, and afterwards to Sind, the country through which the Indus flowed. It is mentioned in the Avesta and in the Behistun inscriptions of Darius as including the Persian provinces west of the Indus. In Sanscrit the country was called Bharatavarsha, while to European geographers it is known as Hindustan. The term Hindustan is never used in India to describe the whole continent; it is confined to the country north of the Narbada, or still more narrowly to the northern portion of the basins of the Ganges and Jumna. The name "East Indies," as applied to the country, dates from the dawn of maritime discovery, and still lingers in certain parliamentary papers.

The name "India."

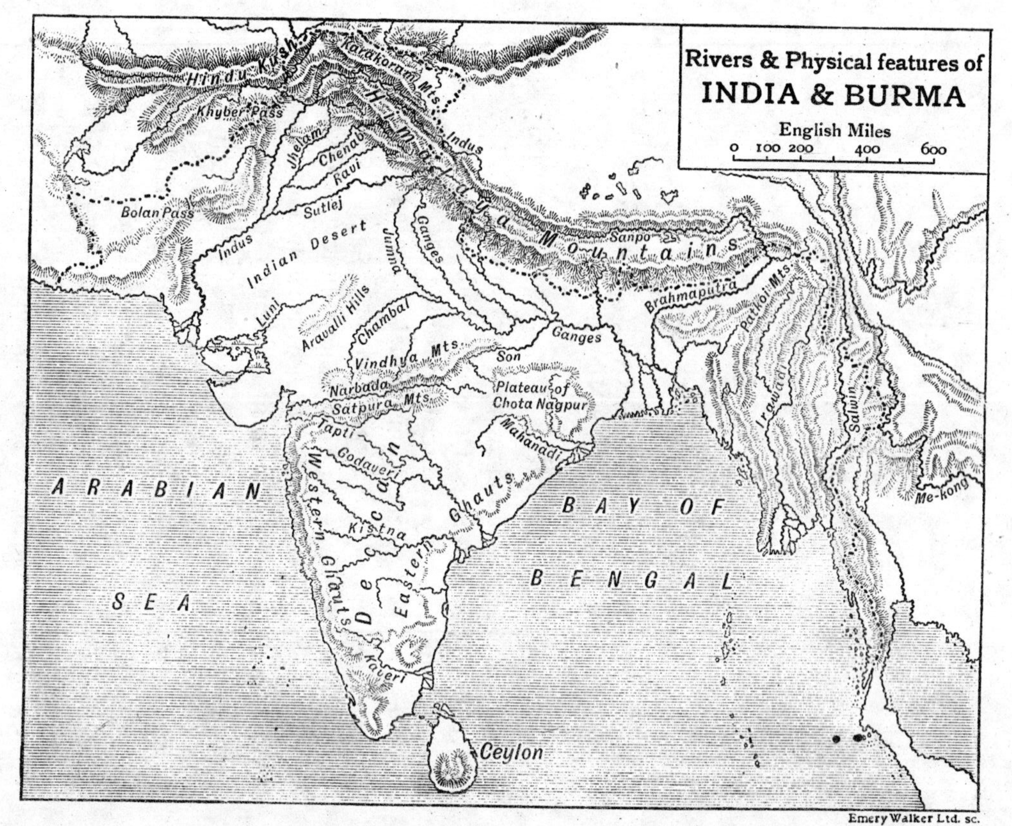
Rivers & Physical features of
INDIA & BURMA
English Miles
0 100 200 400 600
Hindu Kush
Karakoram Mts.
Himalaya Mountains
Khyber Pass
Bolan Pass
Indus
Jhelam
Chenab
Ravi
Sutlej
Indian Desert
Luni
Aravalli Hills
Chambal
Jumna
Ganges
Son
Vindhya Mts.
Narbada
Satpura Mts.
Plateau of Chota Nagpur
Mahanadi
Tapti
Godaveri
Kistna
Kaveri
Deccan
Western Ghauts
Eastern Ghauts
Sanpo
Brahmaputra
Patkoi Mts.
Irawadi
Salwin
Me-kong
Ceylon
ARABIAN SEA
BAY OF BENGAL
Emery Walker Ltd. sc.

THE GREAT SNOWY WALL OF THE HIMALAYAS.

(The word Himalaya is derived from two Sanscrit words meaning "the abode of snow.")

Shape of India.

India is the central of the three peninsulas extending out into the Indian Ocean. It is rhomboidal in shape. Its north-eastern face, from the head of the Bay of Bengal to the north-western extremity, measures about 1400 miles, its north-western face, from Kashmir to Karachi, measures about 1200. Its eastern coast line is 1750 miles long, and its western coast 1300. The chief characteristic of the coasts is their unbroken outline. The Runn of Cutch and the Gulf of Cambay on the west, the Gulf of Manaar between India and Ceylon, and the Gulf of Martaban in Burma, are the only important indentations.

Assam forms an acute-angled triangle, extending 550 miles to the north-east, from the north-eastern face of the main rhomboid. Burma is also triangular in shape, its base being the south-eastern face of the triangle of Assam. It stretches about 1200 miles to the south-east, and narrows to a point about two degrees north of Cape Comorin.

Area.

The area of India is 1,802,657 square miles, of which 1,093,074 square miles belong to British India and 709,583 square miles to Native States.

Population.

The total population according to the census of 1911, was 315,156,396, of which 244,367,542, or 77·5 per cent., belong to British India, and 70,888,854, or 25 per cent., to the Native States.

Divisions of India.

The Indian Empire is divisible into four well-marked regions—the Himalayas, Northern India or the Indo-Gangetic plain, Southern India or the Indian Peninsula, and Burma.

The Himalayas.

The Himalayas lie to the south-east of the Pamir plateau, "the roof of the world," in Central Asia, and form a curved double wall running along all

Northern India for some 1500 miles, and the average distance from its southern to its northern edge is over 500 miles. The Himalayan chain is really the southern buttress of the Thibetan plateau, and answers to the Kuen Lun mountains, which bound this plateau on the north. At its north-western angle (35° north latitude, 74° east longitude) the mountain chain curves to the south, forming the Sufed Koh immediately to the north of Peshawar, and the Sulaiman ranges, which separate India from Afghanistan, and the Hala or Khirthar hills, which separate it from Beluchistan.

Similarly, at its north-eastern angle (28° north latitude, 97° east longitude) it sends out spurs to the south-east, which form the Patkoi, Naga, and Lushai hills, and eventually run southwards as the Arracan Yoma mountains, and terminate in Cape Negrais. Parallel to the Arracan Yomas, which are broken into two parts by the bend of the Irrawadi near Mandalay, are the Pegu Yomas. Parallel again to the Pegu Yomas is the Runglung range. South of the Himalayas and separated from them by valleys, known as the Dun near Mussoorie, and the Mari in Nepal, is the low range of the Siwaliks. On the north-western frontier, the Himalayas are pierced in places by passes or depressions between the mountains. The Khyber leads from Kabul down the valley of the Kabul river to Peshawar. The Kuram river flows from Afghanistan into the Bannu district through the Kuram pass, and then falls into the Indus. The Tochi valley leads from Ghazni into British territory; through it flows the Tochi river, which rises on the slopes of the Waziristan mountains and is a tributary of the Kuram.

Passes in the Himalayas.

The Gomal lies between Afghanistan and Dera Ismail Khan. The Bolan lies between Shikarpur in Sind and Kandahar, and is commanded by the fortress of Quetta. One or other of these gateways has always been the route followed by invaders of India by land. On the north-eastern frontier, the Jelap, the Natu, and the Donkia passes lead from Sikhim into Thibet, but, being much higher, much less traffic passes through them than through the north-western passes.

River system of the Himalayas.

There is a lake called Manasarowar in south-western Thibet, near which is Kailas, the mountain sacred to Siva. From near this lake the Indus and Brahmaputra take their rise, and within a short radius from it the Sutlej and the Ghagra, which joins the Ganges at Revelganj in Bihar, rise. The Indus at first flows north-east dividing the Mustagh and Karakorum ranges from the Himalayas. Near its junction with the Gilgit river it takes a bend to the south-west, and thenceforward its course is almost due south to the Arabian Sea.

The Tsanpu, which is believed to be continuous with the Brahmaputra, flows eastward through Thibet for 500 miles, and bends abruptly to the south-east through unknown hills in the north-eastern corner of Assam. The river known as the Dihang is the link between the river always known as the Brahmaputra and the Tsanpu, which is believed to be the upper waters of the same river, but its course is unexplored, and whether the river descends from the plateau of Thibet by one large cataract, or a series of rapids, is as yet unknown. The Brahmaputra joins the Ganges at Goalando, and the united stream subsequently receives the waters of the Surma and

Kusiara from southern Assam, which combine to form the Barak. The river Meghna, which flows into the Bay of Bengal, is composed of the united waters of the Ganges, Brahmaputra, and Barak.

Drainage of the Himalayas by the three great rivers of India.

The Indus and the Brahmaputra receive the drainage of the western and eastern extremities of the Himalayas respectively. The Ganges drains their southern slopes. The smaller rivers of the Panjab lie between the Sutlej and the Indus. The Sutlej pierces the central Himalayas, and afterwards joins the Beas, and their united waters flow into the Indus. The Jhelum rises in the heart of Kashmir, and the Chenab and Ravi in the hill state of Chumba. Seventy miles north-east of Multan the Ravi and the Jhelum unite with the Chenab, which then joins the Sutlej. The Ravi, Jhelum, Chenab and Sutlej combined, take on the name of the Panjnad, and flow into the Indus at Mittendakot, 108 miles below Multan.

The Bhagirathi, the reputed head stream of the Ganges, issues from an ice cave in a glacier at Gangotri in the central chain of the Himalayas, but the Alaknanda, a much larger tributary, has its source in the glaciers of Badrinath and Nandadevi. The Jumna, the principal tributary of the Ganges, rises at Jumnotri near Gangotri, and joins the Ganges at Allahabad. The Gandak and Kusi rivers, which are Himalayan in origin, join the Ganges on its left bank.

Indo-Gangetic plain.

Northern India or Hindustan proper is the Indo-Gangetic plain, and is divided into the regions drained by the Indus on the west and the Ganges and Brahmaputra on the east. The basin of the Indus includes the Panjab, the native state of Bhawalpur, Rajputana, and Sind, and the basin of the Ganges and

Brahmaputra includes the United Provinces of Agra and Oudh, Bengal and Assam. The Indo-Gangetic plain was once a sea, in which the Aravalli range, which now forms the watershed between the two basins, alone appeared above the waters. This sea has been filled up by the silt brought down by the two rivers.

The Peninsula of India.

The Peninsula of India is an elevated diamond-shaped plateau having Delhi at its northern end. It has two short sides running northwards into the plain of northern India, and two long sides constituting the western and eastern coasts, south of the Vindhya mountains.

The term Deccan.

The term Deccan or Southern India is applied to this tract in two senses, in the more general sense it includes all India south of the Vindhyas, in the more limited sense it is confined to the tract between the Vindhya and Nilgiri mountains, and does not extend south of Palghat.

Mountain system of the Peninsula.

The Vindhya mountains run east and west across India from Gujrat, and enclose the Narbada valley on the north. Parallel to them runs the Satpura range forming the watershed between the Narbada and the Tapti. Towards the centre of India the Vindhyas and Satpuras converge to form the highlands of the Central Provinces, which are continued still further east in the Kaimur and Rajmehal hills in Bengal.

The shores of the Peninsula have two ranges of mountains running along their whole extent. These are called the Western or Sahyadri and the Eastern Ghats, because the occasional defiles which pierce them look like "ghats" or landing-places from the sea. The most important of these are the Thal Ghat north of Bombay, up which the railway runs to Igatpuri, the Por Ghat south of Bombay leading to Poona, the ghat between Belgaum and the coast at Vingorla, and the Pal Ghat or Coimbatore Gap south of the Nilgiris. The Western Ghats have an elevation of 3000 feet, rising to over 8000 feet in the Nilgiri and Anamalai hills, the highest summits being Dodabetta, which overhangs Ootacamand and the Anaimudi peak in the Anamalai hills.

Where the Western Ghats meet the Eastern, they culminate in the Nilgiris, south of which their almost uninterrupted line is broken by a depression known as Palghat, which permits of communication between the Malabar and Coromandel coasts. They have a narrow, densely forested tract, called the Konkan, between their eastern face and the Arabian sea.

South of Pal Ghat, the Western Ghats are continued by the Anamalai, the Pulni, and the Cardamum hills. These ranges recede from the coast, and leave level areas on the west and east. To the west, lie the native states of Travancore and Cochin, and the British districts of Malabar and South Canara.

On the east coast of the Bay of Bengal, between the Eastern Ghats and the sea, and extending as far as Orissa, is a narrow coast tract which widens out, between the Kaveri and Kistna rivers, to form the plains of the Carnatic. The Eastern Ghats are much lower than the Western in elevation, and are broken by valleys cut in them by rivers flowing into the Bay of Bengal.

Comparison of the rivers of Northern and Southern India.

The rivers of Northern differ from those of Southern India, as the former derive their water supply from the melting of the snow of the Himalayas, but the latter are chiefly fed by the monsoon rains. The former are much less dependent on the seasons, and have a fairly constant water supply all the year round. The latter are in heavy flood during the monsoons, and almost dry at other seasons. The channels of the Ganges and Jumna are level with the general surface of the country, and they are therefore centres of extensive irrigation systems.

The rivers of the south run in deep valleys, so that their water cannot be easily raised for irrigation till they approach the coast and begin to form deltas. The levels of the channels of the Indus and Ganges do not alter much after they debouch from the Himalayas on to the plains; they have therefore always been great highways of navigation and commerce from the sea into the interior. The rivers of the south are useless for navigation on account of the narrow gorges, through which they flow from the central plateau on to the coastal plains, and the rapids formed by the consequent fall in the level of the channel.

The river system of the Peninsula.

The Narbada rises in the Amarkantak mountains at the southernmost point of the Rewah state, and the Sone, a tributary of the Ganges, rises near. The valleys of these two rivers form a trough stretching right across India from Broach to Patna, and dividing the north from the south. The Narbada and the Tapti drain the southern slopes of the Vindhyas and the Satpuras into the Gulf of Cambay, and they are the only rivers of the peninsula not flowing from west to east. North of this line the drainage is from the centre to the sea on the west by the Indus, and on the east by the Ganges.

South of this line the general slope of the country is from west to east, and the rivers rise on the eastern side of the Western Ghats, and flow for some distance through the Deccan highlands, and finally fall into the Bay of Bengal. The Mahanadi rises on the southern slopes of the elevated plateau which culminates in Amarkantak. The Mahanadi and the Brahmini combined drain the eastern portion of the Central Provinces, Chota Nagpur, and Orissa.

The Godaveri rises near Nasik on the Western Ghats within 50 miles of the sea. Its most important tributary is the Pranhita, which contains the united waters of three streams—the Painganga, the Wardah, which rises in Amarkantak, and the Wainganga, which rises near Jabalpur. A fourth tributary, the Indravati, rises 50 miles from the east coast north of Vizianagram. The Kistna carries with it to the sea the waters of the Bhima from the north, and the Tungabhadra from the south-west. The Kaveri rises in Coorg near the west coast ; for about three-quarters of its course it runs through the south-western districts of Mysore plateau. It forms rapids as it passes, through a range of hills, on to the Carnatic plain.

Burma.

Burma is divisible into :

Divisions of Burma.

1. Western Burma or Arracan, separated from Central Burma by the Arracan Yoma mountains, and from the Chittagong district of Bengal by the river Naf.

2. Central Burma, or the basin of the Irrawadi.
3. The Shan States, or the basin of the Salwin, divided from the Irrawadi by the Runglung range.
4. The eastern coast strip, including Tenasserim and Martaban, separated from Siam by a continuation of the Runglung range.

Central Burma is a succession of parallel valleys separated by ranges of mountains running north and south commencing with that of the Chindwin, which flows into the Irrawadi at Myingyan. The Pegu Yomas separate the valleys of the Irrawadi and the Chindwin on the north, and those of the Irrawadi and the Sittang on the south. The Salwin basin lies east of the Irrawadi basin. The basin of the Sittang, which rises in the Pegu Yomas, and flows into the Gulf of Martaban, lies between the basins of the Salwin and the Irrawadi.

The Salwin, the Mekong, and the Yang-tse-kiang rise in eastern Thibet, and run in narrow valleys roughly parallel to each other through the Chinese province of Szechuen. The Irrawadi rises in a mass of mountains near the bend of the Brahmaputra in north-eastern Assam. It is formed by the junction of the Mali-kha and the N'mai-kha (kha means stream) in the district of Myitkina.

The eastern boundary of Burma is the frontier of China running north and south. For a short space, where the Shan States are conterminous with the French dependency of Annam, the river Mekong is the eastern boundary, and in the south of Burma, the river Salwin, which flows into the sea at Moulmein, is the eastern boundary.

Ceylon is a pear-shaped island separated from the mainland of India by Palk's Strait, in the narrowest part of which lies the island of Ramessaram. The Paumben passage lies between Ramessaram and India, and the Manaar passage between Ramessaram and Ceylon. Ceylon is 271 miles long from north to south, and its greatest width is 137 miles. The mountains lie in the south, with scattered hills at Mihintale and Sigri. The chief river is the Mahaveliganga, which rises in the Pidurutagalla mountain, and, after a course of about 200 miles, falls into the sea at Trincomalee. The western and southern coasts are low, the eastern precipitous. **Ceylon.**

On the north, the unbroken line of the Himalayas guards India from invasion. On the west, deserts, and on the east, almost impenetrable forests, form additional barriers. **Effect of physical conditions on political divisions.**

On the west coast, the line of the Western Ghats, and on the east coast, the want of harbours, the shallow depth of water along the coast, and the cruel surf, are obstacles to intercourse with foreign countries. The consequence is that Northern India to a great extent, and Southern India almost entirely, have been free to work out their own destinies without outside interference. Northern India has been several times invaded through the north-western passes, but only at long intervals, and, the invasions once made, their results have not been much modified by repeated large immigrations from Central Asia. The Himalayas once passed, the plains of Northern India present no barrier to the establishment of an empire, and to the crushing out thereby of racial distinctions. Racial distinctions could only survive on isolated hill **Survival of racial distinctions.**

ranges or plateaus, access to which was guarded by fever-haunted forests. Kolarian and Dravidian tribes in the Sonthal Pergunnahs, in the hills and forests of Central India, and on the Nilgiris have so survived.

Effect of internal barriers.

The empire of Northern India was limited by the forests of Central India (Mahakantara) and the Vindhya and Satpura mountains. Separated by these, the Deccan had its own indigenous race, history, and civilisation, and has played but a secondary part in Indian history.

The Tamil kingdoms of the furthest south, throughout their whole history, never saw more than mere forays for plunder on the part of the Mahomedans. The Anamalai, Pulni, and Cardamum hills isolated the kingdom of Kerala, which in modern times developed into the native states of Cochin and Travancore. This isolation has continued to the present day. Hence the survival of polyandry, and the matriarchal system of inheritance of landed property, by which a man's heir is his sister's son. The internal barriers have prevented the organisation of one strong centralised state. No ruler of the Northern Plains, except Asoka and the British Government, has ever more than temporarily extended his sovereignty over the Deccan.

Artificiality of British Provincial boundaries.

British Provincial boundaries are in many cases purely artificial, though the Repartition of Bengal has remedied the principal grievance urged against the creation of the province of Eastern Bengal and Assam, that the solidarity of the Bengali race was thereby broken. In some cases the boundaries of race and language overlap provincial boundaries. There are Uriyas under Behar and Orissa and Madras,

Canarese under Bombay and Madras, and Mahrattas under the Central Provinces and Bombay.

Effect of the physical conditions upon the national character.

The effect of the external barriers is seen in the mental exclusiveness and absorption in their own concerns characteristic of the people. Alberuni, who wrote in the eleventh century, speaks of their isolation and want of sympathy with foreigners: "They are by nature niggardly in communicating that which they know, and they take the greatest possible care to withhold it from men of another caste among their own people, still much more, of course, from any foreigners. According to their belief, there is no other country on earth but theirs, and no other created beings besides them have any knowledge of science whatever. Their haughtiness is such that if you tell them of any science or scholar in Persia or Khorasan, they will think you both an ignoramus and a liar. If they travelled and mixed with other nations, they would soon change their minds, for their ancestors were not so narrow-minded as this generation." [1]

The general fertility of the soil makes unnecessary that severe labour in the fields which hardens the body, and the hot climate has so enervated the Indians that they have always succumbed to Pathan, Moghal, or European invaders bred in more temperate regions. The Indians of the plains are naturally averse to active exertion and devoted to philosophic contemplation, and the climate appears to have acted as a forcing-house upon the acuteness of their mental powers.

Interaction between Mahomedanism and Hinduism.

The mountains and deserts acted as breakwaters against the first flood-tides of Mahomedanism which

[1] Alberuni (Trubner), I, I, 23.

gradually spent their force. The Mahomedan supremacy was eventually established by fresh inroads from Central Asia, but its tenure of power was precarious, and it could not crush Hinduism out of existence, as it did Zoroastrianism in Persia. The Mahomedans disorganised Hinduism, without being able to erect in its place any strong religious organisation of their own.

Influence of physical conditions on population.

Physical conditions largely influence civilisation, which cannot exist without a fairly dense population to permit of division of labour. In a country where from 50 to 80 per cent. of the population depend for their living upon agriculture, population depends upon fertility of soil, and fertility of soil upon rainfall, and rainfall upon the prevalent winds and the distribution of the mountains. The density of population is greatest in Bengal and least in Beluchistan, Sind, and the Jaisalmer State of Rajputana. Where the rainfall is small, a high rate of density of population is only rendered possible by irrigation. In the Chenab Canal Colony in the Panjab, irrigation has made a desert to " blossom like a rose," and has vastly increased the numbers gaining their living from the land.

The races of India.

The races of the Indian Empire can be divided according to (1) language, (2) race.

According to language, they are divisible into (1) the Indo-Chinese or Mongoloid family, subdivided into the Mon-Khmer, Thibeto-Burman, and Siamese-Chinese sub-families; (2) the Munda or Kolarian family; (3) the Dravidian family; (4) the Indo-European family.

Indo-Chinese family.

1. The Mon-Khmer sub-family contains the language

of the Khassis spoken round Shillong in the Assam hills, and that of the Mons or Talaings on the coast of Pegu. The Thibeto-Burman sub-family contains the languages spoken by the Thibetans of Sikhim, Almora and Garhwal, the Bhutias of Bhutan, the Daflas, Abor-Miris and Mishmis of northern Assam, the Bodos, or Kochs, or Kacharis of Nowgong, Kamrup, Goalpara and Cooch-Behar, the Garos of the western end of the Assam hills, the Kuki-Chins from the Naga hills to Sandoway in Burma, the Kachins or Singphos on the upper waters of the Chindwin and Irrawadi, and the Burmese. The Chinese-Siamese sub-family contains the languages spoken by the Karens and the Tai, or people of the Shan States in eastern Burma.

Munda or Kolarian family.

2. The Munda or Kolarian family of languages is spoken by the hunting tribes living in the north-east of the central plateau of India, the Sonthal Pergunnahs, Chota Nagpur, Orissa, the Chattisgarh division of the Central Provinces, and north-east Madras.

Under this head are included the Sonthals and Mundas, the Korkus of the Pachmarhi hills, and the Betul district at the junction of the Central Provinces and Berar, the Kols of the Jabalpur and Mandla districts, and the Chattisgarh division of the Central Provinces, the Juangs of the Orissa Tributary States of Keonjhar and Dhenkanal, and the Korwas of the Central Provinces Tributary States of Sirguja and Jashpur, and the Mirzapur district in the United Provinces south of the Sone.

Dravidian family.

3. The term Dravidian includes the languages spoken by the inhabitants of the southern part of

the Central Provinces and the greatest part of the Madras Presidency. They were the original tree and serpent worshippers, whom the invading Aryans found in possession of the plains of the Jumna and Ganges. They were probably the aborigines of the Deccan, whence they spread over all India. Another

KOLS.

hypothesis about them is, that they invaded India from the north-west through Mekran, Beluchistan, and Sind. The presence of the Brahuis ("ba rohi" people of the hills) in Beluchistan, from Khelat to the sea, supports this view. The Brahuis speak a language akin to the Dravidian, but, being of Iranian descent, have no racial affinity with the Dravidians of southern India.

When the Dravidians were pushed to the south, they left behind them certain kindred races in Northern India, such as the Mal and Sauria Paharias of the Rajmehal hills, the Uraons of Chota Nagpur, the

TODAS OF THE NILGIRIS.

Bhuiyas of the Sonthal Pergunnahs, the Bhumij tribe of Orissa, the Gondhs of the native states of Jaipur near Vizianagram (subordinate to Madras) and Jagdalpur or Bustar in the hills skirting the Indravati river (subordinate to the Central Provinces), and the Kandhs of Orissa and the Tributary States.

The Dravidian family is subdivided into Tamil and Telegu on the east coast, and Canarese, Malayalam, and Tulu on the west coast, and the Toda and Kota languages on the Nilgiris.

Tamil is the language of south-eastern India and Ceylon north of a line drawn from Colombo to Trincomalee, and of the Nilgiri Irulas. Its northern boundary may be taken roughly as the Venkati hills or the town of Tirupathi north of Madras. Telegu is spoken in what was called the Andhra country in Sanscrit times and Telingana in Mahomedan. It lies between a line drawn from Chicacole in Ganjam to Chandra in the Central Provinces, and the Tamil country on the south. North of Chicacole Uriya is spoken, and north of Chanda Hindi.

Canarese is an offshoot of Tamil, and is the language of Mysore and South Canara. The Nilgiri Kurumbas and Badagas speak a dialect of Canarese. Malayalam is the language of Malabar, and is an offshoot of Tamil dating from about the ninth century A.D. Tulu is a language spoken in South Canara between the Chandragiri and Kalyanpur rivers.

4. The Indo-European or Aryan family of languages is divided into the Iranian and Indo-Aryan sub-families. The Iranian sub-family contains the Beluchee and Pushtoo languages. The Indo-Aryan sub-family is subdivided into those languages which are, and which are not derived from Old Sanscrit.

Indo-European or Aryan family.

The main branch of the Aryans crossed the western passes of the Hindu Kush and entered the Panjab through Eastern Afghanistan. A smaller body probably passed from the head waters of the Oxus through Gilgit, Chitral, Swat, and Bajaur into the Panjab.

Hence the languages of Gilgit, Chitral, and Kafiristan west of Chitral, are Indo-Aryan, but not derived from the Old Sanscrit, which was spoken in Eastern Afghanistan. This second swarm pushed the Aryans whom they found already in occupation outwards.

Two branches of Aryan immigration.

The Aryans, or the race to which the inhabitants of modern Europe, the Hindus and the Persians belong, had their original home in the western part of Central Asia, between the Caspian and the Sea of Aral. The word Aryan means honourable, others connect it with a root meaning to plough. By noticing the words common to the Sanscrit and Zend or ancient Persian on the one hand, and the European languages on the other, we can judge how far our ancient forefathers had progressed in civilisation before they separated, Europeans to the west, the Persians to the south-west, and the Hindus to the south-east. They lived in houses, were acquainted with the use of iron, and knew how to sail boats, and how to domesticate the horse, the cow, and the dog. The Aryan influence must have stretched far even in the earliest times. The cuneiform inscriptions tell us that the kings of Mitanni, a branch of the Hittites in the district of Malatia in Asia Minor, had Aryan names and worshipped Indra, Varuna, Mitra, the Asvins (under Vedic name of Nasatya) in the fourteenth and fifteenth centuries B.C.

The Aryans.

The separation of the Persians and the Hindus took place " within sight of the Indus and its tributaries," where " the undivided South-Eastern Aryans spoke a language more primitive than the Sanscrit or Zend." That the union between the two sections was close is proved by their common deities Ahura-Mazda,

Long connection between the Vedic and Iranian Aryans.

who may be compared with the Varuna Asura of the Vedas, Yama the god of the Dead, and Mitra (Persian Mithra). Both nations knew the use of the Soma plant, called in the Zend Avesta, Homa, both venerated fire, both worshipped the cow. The Hindus worshipped the Devas; the ancient Persians Ahuras (Asuras), *e.g.* Ahura-Mazda. In the Rig Veda the word Asura means strong or powerful, and is usually applied to the gods. In the Brahmanas the meaning of the word has altogether changed, and it is used to designate the enemies of the gods.

Development of the Aryan language.

In the earliest times, Sanscrit, the "accurately made" or "polished" language of the Rig Veda, was spoken by the invaders, who called themselves Aryans or men of good family, in Southern Afghanistan, the North-Western Frontier Province, and the Panjab, in contradistinction to their indigenous enemies, whom they called "Dasas" or "Dasyus." In the times described in the Mahabharat and Ramayan, when the Aryans had penetrated south-east to the plains of the Jumna and Ganges, the spoken language was the prose Sanscrit of the Brahmanas and Aranyakas. After 1000 B.C., the common people spoke the language of the edicts of Asoka, or Pali, a language closely approximating to Sanscrit, from which the modern Singhalese has been developed. Still later, the Prakrit "derived," "natural" or "common" dialects were evolved, which Vararuchi divided into four: Mahrashtra now Mahratta; Sauraseni, corresponding to the Braj Bhasha; Magadhi now Bihari; and Paisachi, a term for the dialect with the greatest mixture of non-Aryan words.

These dialects were modified into Hindi, meaning by this term the language of the United Provinces, Gujrat, and the Panjab written in the Devanagari character. Hindi is more akin to the Sanscrit, than the languages of those Aryans who were forced outwards from their original home, and betook themselves to Western Kashmir, Sind, the Mahratta country, Central India, Orissa, Behar, Bengal, and Assam, which are much more intermixed with Dravidian or Mongoloid elements. The Bhils of the Aravalli hills between Guzrat and Rajputana, Indore, and Khandesh were formerly classed as Mundas, but the Linguistic Survey considers their language a connecting link between the languages of Gujrat and Rajputana.

The Urdu language is a mixture of Persian, Turki, and other Central Asian languages with the vernaculars of India, and the unifying process commenced from the time of the first invasions of India from the north. Mir Amman, author of the Bagh-o-Behar, thus describes the origin of Urdu: "By the arrival and stay of the Amir Timur, the camp or bazaar of the Army was introduced into the city (of Delhi), whence the city bazaar was called Urdu, a Tartar word signifying camp. When Akbar ascended the throne, various races from all quarters, on hearing the kind patronage and bounty of that incomparable house, came and assembled in the royal presence, but the speech and dialect of each was different. From their being collected together, and owing to the trade, traffic, and intercourse which they carried on with one another, a single language, Urdu or Hindustani, was established." When this language was applied to poetical purposes, it was called "rekta" (*i.e.* mixed). Besides Urdu, Mahomedans throughout India speak Persian and Arabic.

Affinity of language not always a safe guide to affinity of race.

Affinity of language is not always a safe argument to prove affinity of race. The Brahuis of Beluchistan speak a language akin to Dravidian, but are not Dravidian in type. The Raj-bansis of north-eastern Bengal belong to the Koch, a Mongoloid race, but they speak Bengali, as do the Bhumij tribe in Orissa, who are Dravidians.

Race distinctions.

The best criteria on which to establish distinctions of race are based on anthropological peculiarities.

1. The proportion of the maximum breadth to the maximum length of the skull.
2. The projection of the teeth and jaws beyond a line drawn from the forehead.
3. The proportion of the breadth of the nose to the height, and the height of the root of the nose above the level of the eye-sockets.

The ratio of the breadth of the skulls of the Aryan type in the United Provinces to the length is below 75 per cent., and their teeth and jaws do not project much beyond a line drawn from the forehead, and their noses are finely cut with a breadth less than 70 per cent. of the height. Their complexions are light.

The Dravidian type has a skull, the ratio of the breadth of which to the length is over 80 per cent., and a nose, the breadth of which is over 85 per cent. of the height, and a very dark complexion. The Mongoloid type is also broad-headed, but its peculiarity is that the root of the nose rises much less above the level of the eye-sockets than in other races. The eye is oblique and prominent, the cheek bones high, the nose short and flat, and the complexion olive in colour.

The Indian Census of 1901 divides the races of India under the following heads:

Races of India divisible into eight types.

Turko-Iranian, in Beluchistan and the North-west Frontier Province, including the Beluchs, Brahuis, and Pathans.

Indo-Aryan, including Rajputana, the Panjab, and Kashmir.

Aryo-Dravidian, in the United Provinces, Behar, and Ceylon south of a line drawn from Colombo to Trincomalee. The highest strain is the Hindustani Brahman, and the lowest the Chamar.

Scytho-Dravidian in the Bombay Presidency and Coorg. The census of 1901 rejects the common idea that the Jats of the Panjab show intermixture of Scythian blood.

Mongolo-Dravidian, in Bengal and Orissa. The Bengal Brahmans and Kayasthas come under this head; the Mongoloid element is strongest in Eastern, and the Dravidian in Western Bengal. There is also a strain of Aryan blood, whence the legend of the importation of Brahmans from Kanauj by Adisur has originated.

Mongoloid, in Nepal, Sikhim, Bhutan, Assam, and Burma, including the Limbus Murmis and Gurungs of Nepal, the Bodo or Kacharis of Assam, and the Burmese.

All the other races of India may be classed under the term Dravidian, including those hunting tribes of Central India who speak Munda or Kolarian languages.

The term Hindu.

The term Hindu includes Rajputs, Sikhs, Mahrattas, Hindi-speaking Hindus, Guzratis, Bengalees, Uriyas, and Assamese. These races differ much in mental qualities, bodily physique, and social customs, but they all have this in common, that they follow Hinduism and maintain the caste system.

Definition of Hinduism.

Sir Alfred Lyall defines Hinduism as "the collection of rites, worships, beliefs, traditions, and mythologies that are sanctioned by the sacred books and ordinances of the Brahmans, and are propagated by the Brahmanic scriptures."[1] As the Madras Census Report for 1881 puts it, Hinduism "serves fairly well as a socio-political classification, since it treats as a whole the people who recognise caste, and who are governed by one form or other of Hindu Law." It is not necessary to be of Aryan descent to be classed as a Hindu. The Sudras represent the original inhabitants of Northern India who have been incorporated among Hindus, but upon terms imposed by their conquerors. The Dravidians of Southern India, and the Mongoloid Assamese, are also Hindus in the sense of professing the Hindu religion.

Receptivity of Hinduism.

"Brahmanism is essentially a religion of compromise. It reconciles itself with ancient forms of worship, and with new ones, when they are become sufficiently prevalent by taking them up into itself, and accepting the fashionable divinity as an incarnation of Vishnu or Siva."[2]

[1] Rede Lectures.

[2] Sir Henry Maine's 'Village Communities,' p. 217.

Sir Herbert Risley thus described this power of proselytising, which has enabled it to assimilate many aboriginal tribes: "Siva and Krishna drove out the tribal gods, as surely as grey shirtings displace the less elegant but more durable handwoven cloth."[1]

Mahomedans.

There are four classes of Mahomedans: Moghals, Afghans, Saids or descendants of Mahomed, who are called Ashraf or Sharif, meaning noble, and Sheikhs, who are called Aglaf, meaning wretches. There are a large number of Arabs in Hyderabad, on the south-east Coromandel, and on the Malabar coasts. Those on the Coromandel coast are called Labbays, and those on the Malabar coast Moplahs. Both Labbays and Moplahs are sailors by trade.

In the Bombay Presidency, the majority of the Mahomedans go by the name of Memons in Sind, Bohras in Guzrat, and Khojas on the island of Bombay.

[1] Sir Herbert Risley's 'The People of India,' p. 209.

CHAPTER II.

INDO-EUROPEAN OR ARYAN CIVILISATION. SOCIAL AND ECONOMIC CONDITIONS. CASTE.

Materials for Indian History.

1. Religious literature of the Brahmans, Jains, and Buddhists.

2. Inscriptions on stone or copper, coins, and seals.

3. Accounts of Greek, Latin, and Chinese writers.

The religious literature is only indirectly of historical value. It contains lists of dynasties, mention of castes, allusions to customs, which throw light upon the history of society. The Aitareya Brahmana, which gives the story of Sunahsepa, is evidence for the prevalence of human sacrifices. The eighth book of the same Brahmana speaks of the coronation ceremonies of kings, and thus provides evidence for the extension of the power of the Brahmans. The same book mentions the races inhabiting Southern India. The Tandya Brahmana mentions the "*bratya-stomas,*" sacrifices performed when certain tribes of Aryan origin were received within the pale of Brahmanism. We infer from this that there were other tribes who remained outside the pale. The Satapatha Brahmana describes the Aryan penetration into Kosala and Videha. It is also interesting as containing the

Buddhist terms *arhat* and *sramana*. It exemplifies the tendency of religion to become mechanical and unintelligent. The Jatakas or Birth-stories of Buddha teem with historical allusions. The historical value of inscriptions, coins, and the accounts of foreign writers will be alluded to in their proper places.

Vedic age. We learn the nature of the earliest stage of Aryan civilisation from the Rig Veda, a collection of 1017 hymns to various deities compiled between 2000 and 1400 B.C., by various Rishis, who were, in the earliest times, either Brahmans or Kshatriyas. It is a collection of the hymnals of various Vedic families. Out of the ten Books, seven are the hymnals of families bearing the names of Gritsamada, Vishvamitra, Vamadeva, Atri, Bharadvaja, Vasistha, and Kanva. Of the 1017 hymns, 226 are in honour of Indra, 187 in honour of Agni, and 115 in honour of Soma the moon god. **Aryans.** The name Aryans is used in the Rig Veda to distinguish the invaders from the aborigines of India, who are called Dasas or Dasyus.

The Vedas. The oldest Sanscrit Sacred Books were called Vedas, from a word meaning " to know." The Vedas are " sruti." " They are the eternal voice of Divine Knowledge, heard by certain holy men called Rishis, and by them orally transmitted ; or if committed to writing, then written down exactly as heard without any intervention of human authorship." There were four Vedas—the Rig Veda, the Yajur Veda (the white and black), the Sama Veda, and the Atharva Veda. The Vedas were specially arranged for different classes of priests, the Rig Veda for the Hotri priests, the Yajur Veda for the Adhyaryu priests, the Sama Veda for the Udgatri priests, and the Atharva Veda for the priests called Brahmans. The Rig Veda, the most ancient religious book of the Hindus, shows us how their ideas on religion originated. "The Aryans in India worshipped first as they feared; then as they admired; and finally as they reasoned." This is the key to the characteristics of the Hindu religion in the Vedic, Epic, and Puranic ages. First the awe-inspiring powers of nature strike the mind, next those that are bright and beautiful, and finally, in a more intellectually advanced epoch, men delight in philosophising on matters of religion. Each Veda is divided into three parts: Mantra (Sanhita) or collection of hymns; Brahmana or prose part, treating of religious ceremonies; and Sutra, or compendious statement of the contents of the Brahmanas made to assist the memory and to facilitate explanation. The Rig Veda has the Aitareya Brahmana, the Yajur the Satapatha, the Sama the Tandya, and the Atharva the Gopatha. The Brahmanas contain sacrificial directions (vidhi), explanations (arthavada), legends accounting for the history of different ceremonies of the sacrifice, and philosophical speculations on the nature of things. The last portion of each Brahmana is called Aranyaka, because on account of its mysterious nature it should be taught in the forest. The Aranyakas generally contain the Upanishads or philosophic speculations as to the nature of the Supreme Being. Upanishad, which literally means "sitting near," is a part of the Veda, which was learnt by disciples sitting near their teacher secretly in the forest. In the Upanishads, knowledge is considered of more importance than the correct performance of sacrifices. The Upanishads are the Isa, Katha, Chandogya, Mandaka, and Brihadaranyaka.

There is another class of literature called Sutras, from siv, a root meaning to sew, implying that they are written on palm leaves with a string through them, which are explanations of ritual, tradition, and speculations made as concise as possible, bearing mostly on the matters treated of in the Brahmanas. The style of the Sutras is so compressed that the work of Panini, though dealing with all Sanscrit grammar, can be contained in thirty-five small octavo pages. The Sutras are of two kinds : Srauta, those relating to Vedic rites, and Smarta, those dealing with domestic rites. The Srauta Sutras include those of Asvalayana and Sankhayana for the Rig Veda ; by Katyayana for the White Yajur Veda ; by Apastambha, Baudhayana and the Manavas for the Black Yajur Veda ; by Latyayana, Drahyayana, Masaka and Gobhila for the Ṣama Veda ; and by Kusika for the Atharva Veda. The Smarta Sutras include the Grihya Sutras and Dharma Sutras, which form the basis of the later Dharma Sastras or Law books attributed to Manu, Yajnavalkya, Parasara, and others. **Sutras.**

There were also, in later times, the Vedangas or treatises on the sciences subsidiary to the study of the Vedas. These were Siksha (Phonetics), Vyakarana (Grammar), Nirukta (Etymology), Chhandas (Metre), Jyotish (Astronomy), and Kalpa (Ceremonials). The Upavedas are said to include Ayurveda (Medicine), Gandharva-veda (Music), Dhanur veda (Military science), and Silpa or Stapatya-veda (Mechanical arts and architecture). The Vedas were compiled in their present form by a great sage **Vedangas.**

(or Rishi), Vyasa, to whom the Mahabharat is also attributed.

Sanscrit philosophy.

The Hindus in all ages have been philosophical thinkers, and the essence of the Sanscrit philosophy is deducible from the Vedas, especially the Upanishads. "The Hindu enters this world as a stranger; all his thoughts are directed to another world; he takes no part in it, even where he is driven to act, and when he sacrifices his life, it is but to be delivered from it. No wonder that a nation like the Indian cared so little for history; no wonder that the political and social virtues have been so little cultivated; and the ideas of the useful and beautiful scarcely known to them."[1] The doctrine of Karma, that a man is punished for his sins in one life, by rebirth in a lower condition of existence in another, imposes upon philosophers the problem of discovery how to attain salvation by getting rid of transmigration, and the various kinds of misery connected with it. It provides an explanation of a man's misfortune or prosperity, when these cannot be considered as caused by anything he has done in this present life. The political and social order is the result of Karma, for a man's station and duties depend upon the class in which he is born, and the class in which he is born depends upon the accumulated effect of his deeds in previous states of existence.

The six principal schools of Hindu philosophy.

There were six principal schools of Hindu philosophy, viz. the Sankhya, Yoga, Nyaya, Vaisesika, Mimamsa and Vedanta.

Sankhya philosophy.

The Sankhya philosophy was founded by a sage named Kapila. His pupils put the tenets of his

[1] Max Müller, 'History of Ancient Sanscrit Literature,' p. 18.

philosophy into verses called *Karika*. It derives its name from its enumeration of the number (twenty-five) of the Categories (Tattva) of human knowledge.

The twenty-five Tattvas are the following :

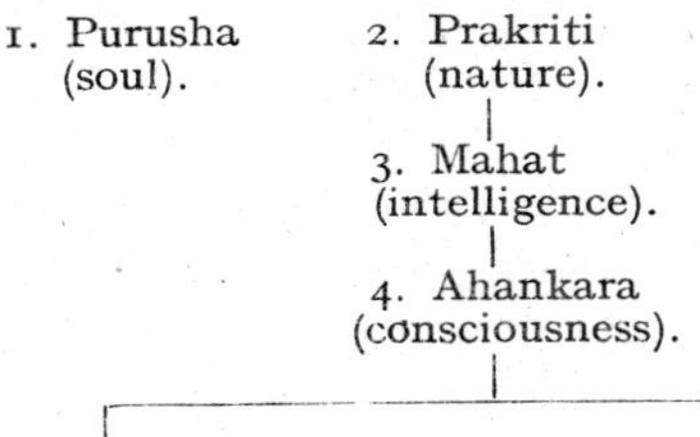

Prakriti has existed from all eternity independently of a creator, and has become developed by evolution into all the forms of the phenomenal universe. It consists of three different constituents (*Guna*), viz. *Sattva* (illuminating), *Rajas* (moving) and *Tamas* (enveloping), and, by combination of these in different proportions, everything has been created. Though Purusha is pure consciousness and Prakriti an inactive principle, the connection between the two gives rise to the universe as manifested through the successive stages of Mahat, Ahankara, etc., thus bringing about the Purusha's bondage to the world. This bondage can only be ended and salvation attained, if the distinction between Purusha and Prakriti is realised through a true knowledge of the twenty-five Tattvas enumerated above.

The Purusha produces nothing, and is like a mirror, which receives all images without itself undergoing any change. There is no Supreme Being, either material or spiritual, to whose will the creation of the universe can be attributed. When the creative powers (Guna) are transferred to matter itself, then God becomes superfluous, and the ancient Trinity God, the Universe, and the Soul, which the Vedantists understand as different manifestations of one and the same thing, is resolved into the Sankya Dualism of Purusha and Prakriti.

Yoga philosophy.

The Yoga philosophy, founded by Patanjali, added to the twenty-five categories of the Sankhya system, a twenty-sixth, the Nirguna Purusha, or self devoid of qualities, *i.e.* God. Salvation, according to the Yoga system, consists in concentration or Yoga, *i.e.* yoking of the mind to God. The Yogi has to practise eight Angas, Yama or discipline (abstention from five acts), Niyama or self-restraint (the performance of five positive duties), Asanam, correct posture, Pratyahara, suppression of the organs of sense, Dharana, concentration of the attention, Dhyânam, meditation on the syllable Om, Samadhi, absorption, and Nirakatvam, sleeplessness. The Atman is unknowable, for such knowledge presupposes a knowing subject and a known object. The Atman is an absolute all-comprehending unity, and can only be known by suppression of the organs of sense by Yoga. The Yogi by diet, posture, breathing, intellectual concentration and moral discipline, enters into the condition called Samadhi, and " comes face to facts which no instinct or reason can ever know. He learns that the mind itself has a higher state of existence beyond reason, a superconscious state, and when the mind gets to that higher state, then this knowledge beyond reasoning comes." The Bhagavadgita gives the following sketch of a Yogi: " He is a recluse of subdued mind and spirit, free from hope and free from perception. He planteth his own feet firmly on a spot that is undefiled, neither too high or too low, and sitteth upon the grass which is called Kusa, covered with a skin and a cloth. There he, whose business is the restraining of his passions, should sit with his mind fixed on one object alone, on the exercise of his devotion for the purification of his soul; keeping his head, his neck, his body steady without motion, his eyes fixed on the point of his nose looking at no other place around."

The mental attitude after which the Yogi is to strive is thus described by Krishna to Arjun:

> " Who fixed in faith on me
> dotes upon none, scorns none; rejoices not
> and grieves not, letting good or evil hap
> light when it will, and when it will depart,
> That man I love. Who, unto friend and foe
> keeping an equal heart, with equal mind
> bears shame and glory; with an equal peace
> takes heat and cold, pleasure and pain abides,
> quit of desires, hears praise and calumny
> in passionless restraint, unmoved by each;
> linked by two ties to earth, steadfast in me,
> That man I love."[1]

The Nyaya philosophy founded by Aksapada-Gotama

[1] 'Bhagavadgita,' translated by Edwin Arnold, book xii.

classifies objects of knowledge under sixteen categories (Padartha), and is primarily a system of Logic. The sixteen categories are: means of right knowledge, object of right knowledge, doubt, purpose, familiar instance, established tenet, members of syllogism, confutation, ascertainment, discussion, wrangling, cavil, fallacy, quibble, futility, and occasion for rebuke.

Nyaya philosophy.

Vaisesika philosophy.

Kanāda, the founder of the Vaisesika school, considers all material substances to be made up of atoms (Anu) which are eternal. These atoms are ultimate simple substances, or units of space, eternal, unchangeable, and only characterised by particularity (Vishesha). Individual or Living Souls (Jiv-Atman) are distinguished from the Universal Soul (Paramatman), which is the seat of eternal knowledge and the maker and ruler of all things. He classifies objects of knowledge under six categories, viz. substance, quality, action, generality, particularity, and intimate connection.

Vedanta philosophy.

The Mimamsa, or rather the Purva Mimamsa, founded by Jaimini, insists that in due performance of the Vedic ritual lies our duty, which begets merit. The Vedanta, designated also as Uttara Mimamsa, was founded by Badarayana Vyasa. It is called Vedanta, because it is founded upon the Upanishads, which close the period of Vedic instruction. It considers Brahma as the Universal Soul from which all has issued, and into which all will be resolved.

"The Brahma, the power which presents itself to us materialised in all existing things, which creates, sustains, preserves, and receives back into itself all worlds, is identical with the Atman, with that which after stripping off everything external, we discover in ourselves as our real, most essential being, our individual self, the soul." [1]

"That in truth out of which these beings arise, by which they, when they have arisen, live, into which they again enter, that seek to know, that is Brahman." [2]

"The creation (Sristhi) of the Universe is an emergence from Brahma. He deliberated how can this (human frame) exist apart from me? And he deliberated—in what way shall I enter into it? Accordingly he split open the crown of the head, and entered by this door." [3]

The Atman is the knowing subject within us, and, as the knowing subject, is itself unknowable. It is *Satcitananda*, pure existence (*Sat*, purity; *cit*, consciousness, *ananda*, bliss). It is the sole reality, "*ekam eva advitiyam.*" The Atman doctrine was the protest of the Kshatriyas against the sacrificial cult, and the animistic polytheism of the later Vedas. The Individual Soul is identical with the Universal Soul; this is expressed in the phrases, "*tat tvam asi*" and "*aham Brahma.*" The real ego is no mere part or emanation of the All-Soul, but is actually the All-Soul entire and indivisible. Brahma is the *Ishvara* or Supreme God, he alone exists; the Vedanta system is therefore called the doctrine of *Advaita-vada* or Monism. Brahma, in conjunction with Maya (illusion), is the cause of the Universe that seems to exist, but does not really exist. Maya is possessed of two powers, Envelopment (*Avarana*) and Projection (*Vikshepa*). The former conceals from the soul its

[1] Deussen, 'The Religion and Philosophy of India,' p. 39.
[2] 'Taittiriya Upanishad,' iii. 1.
[3] 'Aitareya Brahmana,' i. 3. 11.

identity with God ; the latter makes the mind imagine the appearance of the external world. There is no such thing as substance, and substances only appear real because of the illusion of the mind. "The power of Projection is such, that just as ignorance regarding a rope by its own power raises up the form of a snake on the rope which is covered by it, so ignorance, too, by its projective power, raises upon self, which is covered by it, ether and the whole universe." [1]

The aim of Vedantism is summed up by Deussen: "Salvation comes of recognition. When the soul has recognised itself as Brahman, redemption immediately ensues. Recognition of identity with Brahman, and identification with the soul of the universe follow simultaneously." [2]

Materialism. In addition to the six recognised Schools of Sanscrit Philosophy, there was a discredited band of materialists called *Charvakas* or *Lokayatas*, who held that the supreme good lay in the gratification of the senses.

Divisions of Northern India. The Rig Veda [3] speaks of the Sapta Sindhu, meaning thereby the five rivers of the Panjab with the Kabul and Swat rivers, and the Saraswati between the Indus and the Jumna is worshipped as a protecting barrier, so the territory first occupied by the Aryans probably lay between the Indus and the Saraswati. Manu gives the names of *Brahmavarta*, *Brahmarsidesa*, *Madhyadesa*, and *Aryavarta* to the tracts conquered by the Aryans in Northern India. Brahmavarta lay between the Saraswati and the Drishadvati

1 'Vedanta Sara.'

2 Deussen, 'System of the Vedanta,' p. 510.

3 Rig Veda, x. 75.

(Ghagra); Brahmarsidesa included Kurukshetra (Delhi), the country of the Matsyas (west of the Jumna answering to the Cis-Sutlej or Phulkian Sikh States), of the Panchalas (Gangetic Doab and Rohilkhand), and of the Surasenas (round Mathura). The Mahabharat tells us: "Those who dwell in Kurukshetra, to the south of the Sarasvati and the north of the Drishadvati, dwell in heaven." Madhyadesa extended from the Himalayas on the north to the Vindhyas on the south, and from Kurukshetra on the west to Prayag (Allahabad) on the east. Aryavarta was the whole of Northern India between the Himalayas and the Vindhyas, with the Indus as its western and the Bay of Bengal as its eastern boundaries. Other Aryan tribes were the Kurus near Delhi, the Kosalas in Oudh, the Videhas in Behar, the Kasis near Benares.

Caste non-existent in the earliest times.

In the beginning, there were no castes. The word "varna," meaning caste in later Sanscrit, in the Rig Veda merely distinguishes Aryans from non-Aryans, and the word "bipra," the name for the priestly caste in later Sanscrit, means simply "wise" in the Rig Veda. The unit of society was the family.

How society combined.

War and emigration combined families into villages, villages into settlements, and settlements into tribes. The chief was elected by the tribal assembly to lead the host in war, and his office tended to become hereditary. There was at first no separation of occupations.

Position of women.

Women chose their own husbands at the ceremony of Swayambhara. They were honoured, and were not secluded from the public gaze; they shared in the studies of men. The wife's participation in the worship of the fire on the hearth was essential. The second marriage of widows was expressly authorised.

Manners.

They had all the manners of a northern people, ate horse-flesh and beef, and drank fermented liquor made of the juice of the soma plant, which they held to be the "amrita," or nectar of the gods.

Metals and the Arts.

In the Rig Veda the metals are gold and bronze. A piece of gold of a specified weight under the name of "nishka" was used as money. The red "ayas" mentioned in the Vedas is said to be copper. Silver and iron are mentioned later in the Atharva Veda. The Aryans had some knowledge of working in metals, and of the arts of spinning and weaving. Day and night are compared to "two famous weavers, intertwining the extended thread."[1]

Agriculture.

The Aryans possessed teams of horses and oxen. Their agriculture was rude, burning the forests was known as "shaving the earth." The solar deity Pushan was the tutelary deity of agriculture.

Warfare.

They were constantly fighting with other "non-sacrificing" Aryans or with the Dasyus. They wore armour, and fought from chariots or on horseback. Hymns are composed in honour of the war-horse under the name of Dadhikra. Their weapons were bows and arrows, spears, and swords made of wood, bone, stone, or metal.

Ships.

They appear to have known the use of ships. It is said of Varuna, the god of the enveloping heaven: "He knows the path of birds through the air, and, sovereign of the sea, he knows the ships that are thereon."[2] "Merchants," for gain, "are said to frequent every part of the sea."[3] When Bhujyu

[1] Rig Veda, ii. 3. [2] *Ibid.* i. 25. [3] *Ibid.* vi. 56. 2.

the son of Tughra is shipwrecked, he is saved by the Asvins in their hundred-oared galley.[1] They had a system of Marine Insurance, and the Laws of Manu lay down that "whatever interest or price of the risk shall be settled between the parties by men acquainted with sea voyages or journeys by land, with times and places, such interest shall have legal force."[2]

Religion. Personification of the powers of nature. They personified and worshipped the powers of Nature. A verse of the Rig Veda enumerates thirty-three gods. "Gods who are eleven on earth, eleven dwelling in glory in mid-air, and who are eleven in heaven, may ye be pleased with this our sacrifice."

Agni. Agni, god of fire, is chief of the gods of the earth. He is the friend of all men, and is especially worshipped on the domestic hearth. He is generated by the friction of two pieces of the sacred fig-tree. Agni was brought down from the sky by the Atharvan or fire-priest. "Thee Agni from out the sky Atharvan twirled."[3]

Indra. The aid of Indra, god of the atmosphere, chief of the gods of mid-air, is invoked against the aborigines. "Indra, the destroyer of cities, has scattered the black-skinned servile host."[4] He is addressed as Parjanya, sender of rain. "When the clever Tvashtar had turned the well-made, golden, thousand-edged thunderbolt, Indra takes it to perform his manly deeds; he slew Vritra (the cloud demon); he forced out the stream of water."

Surjya. Surjya, the chief of the gods of the air, is addressed in the Gayatri: "Let us meditate on the excellent glory of the divine vivifier; may he enlighten our

[1] Rig Veda, i. 116. 3.
[2] *Ibid.* viii. 156-157.
[3] *Ibid.* vi. 16. 13.
[4] *Ibid.* ii. 20.

understandings."[1] The most famous existing temples of this deity are Martand in Kashmir, the Black Pagoda of Kanarak in Orissa, Osia in the Jodhpur State, and Mudhera in Gujrat. The Sauras, a subsection of the Vaishnavas, still worship Vishnu as Surjya-Narayan.

There was an early triad of Agni, Vayu (the wind) and Surjya, and Agni sometimes takes the place of Vayu.

Vedic religion is Henotheistic, that is, the god who happens to be addressed at the moment is considered the one and only god. A vague conception of a supreme deity was current: "In the beginning death was not, nor immortality; the distinction between day and night was not. There was only one who lived, and breathed, without the help of air, supported by himself. Nothing was except him."[2] The various deities were looked upon as manifestations of one supreme God, whose energy was immanent in every object in the Universe. "They (the priests) speak of him as Indra, Mitra, Varuna, Agni, that which is but one they call variously."[3]

Deification of men.

They deified men, whose bodily or intellectual powers were out of the common, *e.g.* Yama.

"To great King Yama homage pay
Who was the first of men that died
That crossed the mighty gulf, and spied
For mortals out the heavenly way."[4]

[1] Sir Monier Williams, 'Indian Wisdom,' p. 20.

[2] Rig Veda, x. 129.

[3] *Ibid.* i. 164. 46; *Ibid.* viii. 58. 2.

[4] Muir, O.S.T., 327.

They also offered Pindas or balls of rice and flour, and water to the Pitris or Manes of their ancestor at stated periods. Those authorised to offer these pindas were all connected by the bond of agnatic relationship and called "*sapindas.*" A man's property after his death devolved upon his *sapindas* in order of nearness of relationship. A man was believed to have two bodies—a subtle body (*sukhsma sarir*), which enclosed a portion of the universal spirit, constituting a personal individual soul, and a gross body (*sthula sarir*). The gross body was of three kinds, divine, earthly and intermediate. The intermediate body clothes the soul in the world of spirits (*pitri loka*). If it were not for the intermediate body, which is believed to be formed by the funeral offerings of the kindred, the soul would be an impure and unquiet ghost (*preta*).

Cult of ancestors. Descent of property connected with ancestral rites.

The chief idea of the Vedic religion is that a personal union between man and the higher powers is secured by sacrifice, the word for which is "*yajna.*" The ideas of the transmigration of the soul, and of gaining religious merit by penance are not yet found. Religious rites can be performed by any father of a family and anywhere. There were as yet no special priests, nor temples, nor images.

The Epic Age.

The Epic Age may be reckoned from B.C. 1400 to 1000; in it the Sama, Yajur and Atharva Vedas were compiled, and the Brahmanas and Aranyakas and earlier recensions of the Mahabharat and Ramayan composed. Within this period the Aryans passed into the Madhyadesa (plains of the Jumna and Ganges as far as Tirhut).

Reciters of the Epics.

The epics appear to have been kept alive in the

memory of the people by a class of professional reciters (akyayika) in much the same way as the Greek Rhapsodists recited the Homeric poems. These reciters relied on an elaborate mnemonic system, by which the number of letters in each word and syllable was counted.

The great Epics or Itihasas. The Mahabharat.

The Mahabharat is attributed to Krishna Dwaipayani, its Vyasa or arranger. The name Vyasa is at the present day given to the public reciters of slokas at Benares. The scene is laid in Upper India, which is one reason for regarding it as older than the Ramayan, the scene of which travels to the Deccan and Ceylon. The original poem describes the war between the Pandavas, a polyandrous wild tribe, and the Kurus, who belonged to the original Aryan settlers, and lived near Delhi. The Pandavas were successful, and were received into Hinduism.

The Interpolations in the Mahabharat and its relation to Krishna worship.

This nucleus does not amount to more than between a quarter and a fifth of the present poem. The Mahabharat includes the Bhagavadgita, a philosophical and religious poem in eighteen cantos recited by Krishna to Arjun. The teaching of this poem is that of Hinduism in its purest and most elevated form. Both epics deal with the deification of heroes, by which personal deities sympathising with human joys and sorrows were provided to replace the shadowy entities of the Vedas.

The interpolations in the Mahabharat originated thus. Every prominent race in Northern India was eager to have its ancestors mentioned as taking some part in the war. Every new religious preacher wished to appeal to passages in the Mahabharat as sanctioning his doctrines. Passages from legal and moral codes were incorporated, because they appealed to the people more effectively in this form, than if they formed part of a dry code. Caste rules and rules about the different stages of life were included for the same reason. All the stories, traditions, legends and myths, that were circulating among the people, were included in the epic.

Krishna worship, after the decline of Buddhism, became the chief religion in India, and the Mahabharat, reflecting the ideas of the time, is a strong advocate of this cult. Krishna (he who attracts or draws) is first represented as a hero and Prince of Dwarka, next as a demigod acknowledging the greatness of Siva, in later legends he appears as an incarnation of Vishnu, and finally in the Bhagavadgita he is the Supreme God. The original idea of the poem was thus lost in a vast mass of other material superimposed upon it. The Book of Peace (Santi parva), the Book of Laws (Anusasana parva), the genealogy of Krishna, the legends of Siva, the mention of the Yavanas, Sakas, and Pahlavas, as allies of the Kurus, and also as produced by Vasistha's Cow of Plenty from her own limbs to drive out Vishvamitra from his kingdom, and the allusions to Hindu temples and Buddhist stupas are some of the more obvious interpolations.

Date of the Mahabharat.

The earliest mention of the Epics by an Indian writer is in the Grihya Sutra by Asvalayana, B.C. 350. Dion Chrysostom, A.D. 80, has the following passage: "Even among the Indians, they say Homer's poetry is sung, having been translated by them into their own dialect and tongue, and the Indians are well acquainted with the sufferings of Priam, and the lamentations and wails of Andromache and Hecuba, and the prowess of Achilles and Hector." Weber understands this passage to refer to the Mahabharat, of which Megasthenes, who was in India about B.C. 315, says nothing. Weber places the date of the original form of the Mahabharat half-way between B.C. 315 and the time of Dion, but defers the date of the final redaction of the entire work in its present shape, to some centuries after the commencement of the Christian era. We may, without great risk of error, say that it took place during the literary revival of the Gupta period about A.D. 400. Arjun's banner bore a figure of Hanuman. This is one of the few references in the Mahabharat to the Ramayan Though the Mahabharat as a whole is older than the Ramayan, it is possible that some episodes in the latter date from earlier times than the former.

The Ramayan.

The Ramayan by Valmiki has a clear and coherent plot, but it refers to a later stage of society than the Mahabharat, as its kings acknowledge the supremacy of the Brahmans, *e.g.* Janak, king of the Videhas, who was as learned as any Brahman, was the obedient servant of the priests. In the Mahabharat, the kings of the Lunar race at Hastinapur and Dwarka carry on war without reference to the Brahmans. In the Ramayan the kings of the Ikshwaku or Solar race reign in the orderly fashion laid down in the Laws of Manu. The penetration of the Aryans beyond the Vindhya mountains had hardly commenced, as Janasthana on the upper waters of the Godavery is the furthest settlement towards the south mentioned in the Ramayan. Sita, Rama's wife, was found by her father Janak in a plough furrow, so some authors interpret the poem as an allegory, the subject of which is the protection of Aryan agriculture against predatory aborigines. Others take it to refer to an Ayran invasion of Southern India and Ceylon, in alliance with some Dravidian tribes. There are two versions of the Ramayan, the northern text is the purer, and the Bengal text the more corrupt. It has few interpolations, one being Rama's denunciation of Buddha as a thief, in his answer to Javali.

Division of labour and beginning of caste.

As civilisation advanced, it became advisable to set apart special classes for special occupations. Only a priest, who had made a professional study of the hymns, could teach their correct use at sacrifices, and his services were the more important, as it was believed that the slightest mistake in pronunciation would incur divine anger. *Parishads* or settlements for the encouragement of Brahmanic learning fostered the corporate feeling of the priests.

Degradation of religion.

In the Yajur as compared with the Rig Veda, the degradation of religion commenced. The moral yielded entirely to the ceremonial. Sacrifice became the all-important part of religion. It was primarily a thank-offering for bounties received, and was intended to strengthen the gods in supporting the burden of the universe. It could be used as a means of wresting boons from the gods, and finally it was an instrument for obtaining superhuman powers. Elphinstone says: "the most singular anomaly in the Hindu religion is the power of sacrifices and austerities. Through them a religious ascetic can inflict the most severe calamities even on a deity by his curse; and the most wicked and impious of mankind may acquire such ascendancy over the gods as to render them the passive instruments of his ambition, and even force them to submit their heavens and themselves to his sovereignty."[1]

Snake worship appears for the first time in the Yajur Veda, and was presumably borrowed from the religious system of the aboriginal non-Aryans.

The Atharva Veda.

Mr. Barnett describes the Atharva Veda as "an immensely intricate web of ritual, often of the most gruesome and butchery kind, which was spun round the whole web of Indian life, with the avowed object of forcing from the powers of nature, the gifts of worldly welfare which were theirs to bestow, and the ghostly power of the Brahmans became supreme in the land." It is full of incantations which breathe a spirit, not of love towards a beneficent deity, but of homage to a malevolent power to avert harm. The Brahmans naturally magnified the power of sacrifice, as they alone knew how it should be performed, with the result that they were looked upon as almost divine. "Verily there are two kinds of Gods, for the Gods are the Gods, and the Bràhmans, who have studied and teach sacred lore, are the human gods. With oblations one gratifies the Gods, and with gifts to the priests (one gratifies) the human gods. Both these kinds of Gods, when gratified, place him (man) in a state of bliss."[2]

"The entire world depends upon the Gods, the gods depend upon the religious formulas, the religious formulas depend upon the Brahmans, the Brahmans are my Gods."[3]

[1] 'History of India,' 5th edition, pp. 104, 105

[2] Satapatha Brahmana, ii. 22. 6

[3] Proverb quoted in Barth's 'Religions of India,' p. 88.

The word Brahmă used in the Rig Veda, at first impersonally in the sense of prayer, was identified with Brihaspati or Brahmanaspati, the deity who personifies the magic power inherent in every prayer, or with the Father-God Prajapati, the eternal boundless power on which the whole world is based. The Brahman came to be considered as the visible embodiment of prayer and holiness, and the almighty power of prayer was recognised by its identification with the personal Brahmā, the creator, the first person of the Puranic Trinity. The Brahmans made full use of their power, as Purohits or private chaplains, to inculcate upon the Kshatriyas the religious duty of enriching the Brahmans.

Philosophic or Rationalistic Age.

The Philosophic or Rationalistic Age, from 1000 to 250 B.C., owes its title to the sceptical philosophy of Kapila. The Upanishads, the Sutras which give the essence of the Upanishads in aphorisms, and the present recast of the Laws of Manu, belong to this period. The root idea of the Upanishads is the Atman, which was the protest of the Kshatriyas against the sacrificial cult of the Brahmans.

Pantheism of the Kshatriyas.

The Vedas taught the existence of gods, the Brahmanas taught the existence of a Father-God above the gods, in Prajapati or Visvakarman, "who produced the earth and disclosed the sky," the Upanishads taught the existence of a Supreme Soul, with which the individual soul of each man was identical. This pantheism was the Kshatriya answer to the animistic polytheism of the Vedas. Both Gautama and Vardhamana were Kshatriyas, so it is reasonable to suppose that a desire to escape from the supremacy of the

Brahmans was an additional motive leading the Kshatriyas to strive for religious reform. Meditation and bodily mortification made sacrifice, and therefore the aid of the Brahmans, unnecessary. The ideas of the transmigration of souls, and of the automatic retribution by which a man was born again in a higher or lower grade in the world, according as his deeds in his former life were good or bad, originated from the Kshatriyas.

Other religious ideas of the Kshatriyas.

Certain Kshatriyas acknowledged as Rishis.

The word "Rajarshi" shows that many Kshatriyas were equal to Brahmans in learning, and instructed them, and that such persons were recognised as Rishis. Visvamitra, a Kshatriya by birth, and the great opponent of the Brahman, Vasistha, was elevated to Brahmanic rank on account of his holiness and learning, and was the ancestor of the Kaushika Brahmans. Another Rishi, Ikshvaku, was a Kshatriya by birth. The Brahmans compromised the dispute, the bitterness of which is shown by Parasuram's attack upon the Kshatriyas, the comparison in R.V. VII. 103 of the Brahmans, after imbibing Soma, to frogs in a marsh, and the jealousy manifested against Arjun at Draupadi's *Swayambhara*, by adopting the Kshatriya philosophy and granting the Kshatriyas precedence next themselves.

Dispute between the Kshatriyas and Brahmans, and its settlement by the Brahmans.

Kingdoms of Aryavarta.

The tribes were consolidated into the powerful kingdoms of Magadha, capitals Rajgriha and afterwards Pataliputra; Anga, capital Champa, near Bhagalpur; Kosala, capital Savathi; Avanti, capital Kausambi, and the Vajjians, a confederation of eight clans including the Lichchavis of Vaisali, and the Videhas of Mithila or Behar.

Baudayana, who lived in the sixth century B.C., divided the Hindu world into three circles :

Baudayana's divisions of the Hindu world.

1. Aryavarta, "that which lies between the two mountain ranges (Himalaya and Vindhya) and from the eastern to the western ocean, the wise know as Aryavarta. Where the black antelope naturally roams about, that land should be known as the land suitable for sacrifice ; what lies beyond that is the country of the Mlechchas (foreigners)."
2. In the southern Panjab, Sind, Gujrat, Malwa, the Deccan, South and East Behar, the people are said to be of mixed descent.
3. If a man travel in the third or outer circle comprising part of the Panjab and southern India, eastern and northern Bengal, and Orissa, he has to perform an expiatory sacrifice.

This recognition that the Aryans were not all of equal purity of descent illustrates what is said in the section on Indian races.

Western influences.

This historical period includes the conquest of Afghanistan and part of North-western India by Darius Hystaspes, and the inclusion of these territories among the Persian satrapies, and the invasion of India by Alexander the Great. Chandragupta greatly extended the boundaries of Magadha, and Megasthenes, the Greek resident ambassador of Seleucus, king of Syria, has left us a contemporary account of his court at Pataliputra, from which Arrian also quoted. Seleucus ceded to Chandragupta the Greek possessions west of the Indus for a yearly tribute of 500 elephants, B.C. 312. India was thus for the first time brought under western influences.

It was also the period when the customs of the country were codified, and it came for the first time under a settled system of law. The Laws of Manu are a versified redaction of older Dharmasutras, but they probably furnish an accurate picture of society as it existed when the Dharma Sutras were compiled. The law of the time depended upon custom, and therefore was more or less fixed. There was no idea that it should change and adapt itself to the improved moral sense and mental ideals of the people. The rules of the Laws of Manu fall under four heads :

The Laws of Manu.

1. Achara, " immemorial practices."
2. Vyavahara, " practices of law and government."
3. Prayaschita, " expiation."
4. Karmạ-phala, " consequences of acts."

The first six books of the Laws of Manu deal with the duties of Brahmans to study, teach, sacrifice, officiate at another's sacrifices, to make and receive gifts, and to live by inheritance, occupancy, lawful gleaning and gathering or receipt of what is given unasked. In default, they may become soldiers, or till the ground, or tend cattle. After their student stage, Brahmans are to marry and beget sons. After a certain interval passed as householders, when they have paid the three debts, to the Rishis (in the study of the Vedas), to the Manes of their ancestors (by begetting a son), and to the gods (by the performance of sacrifice), they should retire to the forest, and devote themselves to holy studies, and subsist on herbs and roots and the alms of the twice-born.

Special privileges of the Brahmans in the Laws of Manu.

The Laws of Manu give special privileges to Brahmans. "Let every man according to his ability give wealth to Brahmans; such a giver shall attain heaven after this life."[1] "He who merely assails a Brahman with intent to kill him will continue in hell for a hundred years, and he who actually slays him for a thousand years."[2]

Sentence of death cannot be pronounced on a Brahman for any crime, he can but be banished; and his property must remain untouched, and his body unhurt.[3] Brahmans cannot be taxed. "Let not the king, though fallen into the greatest distress through deficiency of revenue, provoke a Brahman to anger by taking revenue from him, for he, if once outraged, could instantly destroy him with his army and retinue."[4]

Royal power.

The Kshatriya is to govern, and fight, and make conquests, to learn the management of chariots and the use of the bow, to stand firm in battle and not to turn back, to protect the people, to abstain from sensual pleasures, and to pay obedience to Brahmans. The royal power was not confined to Kshatriyas, some of the greatest Indian sovereigns, *e.g.* Chandragupta, were Sudras, but inauguration by Brahmans was indispensable.

"A king, even though a mere child, must not be treated with contempt, as if he were a mortal; he is a great divinity in human shape."[5] "Hunting, gaming, sleeping by day, singing, dancing, useless travel, a king must shun; because he only, who has

[1] Manu, xi. 6.
[2] *Ibid.* xi. 206.
[3] *Ibid.* viii. 380-81.
[4] *Ibid.* ix. 15, 16.
[5] *Ibid.* vii. 8.

victory over his own organs, can keep his people firm in their duty."[1] He is to give audience freely to his subjects, and to take counsel with his ministers in a lonely place unobserved by the public.[2] The king is the fountain of justice. "Where three Brahmans versed in Vedas, and the learned judge appointed by the king, they call that the court of Brahma."[3] "As a leech, the sucking calf, and the bee take their food little by little, so must the king draw from his dominions an annual revenue."[4]

In every town there was a spy to give the king information about the conduct of his officers. We are told such spies "were necessary, for the servants of the king, who were appointed to protect the people, generally became knaves, who seized the property of others; let him protect his subjects against such men."[5]

The king is to settle prices for sale and purchase, and to test weights and measures.[6]

Mechanism of Exchange.

The mention of Sale and Purchase presupposes a mechanism of exchange. If goods were not exchanged by simple barter, money was used which consisted of copper coins with marks punched upon them in proof of their purity and of their being up to the required weight. These marks were usually placed upon the coins by the goldsmiths who issued them. Coinage properly so

PUNCH-MARKED COIN.

[1] Manu, vii. 44, 45.
[2] *Ibid.* vii. 145, 147.
[3] *Ibid.* viii. 10, 11.
[4] *Ibid.* vii. 129.
[5] *Ibid.* vii. 115-123.
[6] *Ibid.* viii. 401, 402.

called was introduced from Babylon in about the seventh century B.C.

The eighth book deals with Criminal, and the ninth with Civil Law. Civil and Criminal Law are both mixed up together, and there is no distinction between the Law of Persons and the Law of Things.

Position of woman.

The position of woman was altered for the worse since the Vedic epoch. She was always dependent on father, brother, or husband, and "neither by sale nor desertion can she be released." [1]

The Vaisyas.

The tenth book treats of Vaisyas and Sudras. The Vaisyas are to tend cattle, to lend money, and to cultivate the land. The Brahmans, Kshatriyas, and Vaisyas are said to be born again after investiture with the sacred thread. They are therefore termed "twice-born." The "twice-born" classes are connected by the ceremonies at various occasions in life called Sanskara, and laid down in the Grihya Sutras. Max Müller traces another connection between them: "The high forehead, stout build, and light copper colour of the Brahmans and other castes allied to them, contrast with the somewhat low and wide heads, slight make and dark bronze colour of the lower castes." [2]

The "Twice-born" Castes.

The Sudras.

The Sudra, who represents the conquered non-Aryan races, is to serve the other three castes. "No superfluous collection of wealth must be made by a Sudra, even though he has the power to make it; since a servile man, who has amassed wealth, becomes proud; and by his insolence or neglect gives pain even to Brahmans." [3]

[1] Manu, ix. 85.
[2] 'Chips from a German Workshop,' ii. 27.
[3] Manu, x. 129.

Difference between the rules of caste as laid down in the Laws of Manu and those at present in force.

The rules of caste as laid down in the Laws of Manu differ from the present rules :

1. Marriages between men and women of different castes were recognised, and rules laid down for determining the status of the children of such marriages.
2. Eating with men of another caste or eating food prepared by men of another caste does not seem to have necessitated caste degradation, of which it is now the most frequent cause.
3. Few secondary or mixed castes were as yet developed, as the industrial and mechanical arts were hitherto unimportant.

Brahmanic account of the development of caste.

The Brahmanic account of the origin of caste is purely fanciful. It derives the castes from the limbs of the primeval man. " From him called Purusha was born Viraj (the primeval female), and from Viraj was Purusha produced, whom gods and holy men made their oblation. With Purusha as victim they performed a sacrifice. When they divided him, how did they cut him up ? What was his mouth ? What were his arms and what his thighs and feet ? The Brahman was his mouth, the kingly soldier was made his arms, the husbandmen his thighs, the servile Sudra issued from his feet." [1]

Profession theory.

Sir Henry Maine traced the development of caste to community of occupation. Trades and crafts were usually hereditary, and were organised in guilds (srenya), each with their headmen (pramukha). Caste denotes the practices of each group of Hindu society, by which its members worship special gods, eat

[1] Purusha Sukta, Rig Veda, x.

together, inter-marry, generally have the same occupation, and trace their descent to a common ancestor. There are two characteristics of caste. There is no entry into it except by birth, and marriage outside the caste is strictly forbidden. The disintegrating effect of caste on any feeling of nationality is therefore very great.

The Brahmans were first separated from the mass of the people by their sanctity, and their accurate acquaintance with the elaborate sacrificial rites, which were coming into fashion, and they became a caste by ceasing to marry women of other classes, or to give their daughters in marriage to men of other classes, or to eat with them. It was essential to Brahmans to know the Vedas. Vasistha said "an elephant made of wood, an antelope made of leather, and a Brahman ignorant of the Vedas, these three have nothing but the name of their kind."

The exaltation of the royal power and the belief that kings were a race apart produced a similar separation of the Kshatriya class. The Vaisyas followed a number of trades and professions which all became differentiated into separate castes. The Kayasthas were a profession caste whose duties were to be clerks in the public offices and tax-collectors, as Yajnavalka's injunction to kings to protect their subjects against Kayasthas probably refers to tax-collectors. The Vaidyas, who are included by Yajnavalka in his list of mixed castes, were also a profession caste distinguished by their practice of medicine.

Race theory.

Sir Herbert Risley, on the other hand, finds the origin of caste in the conflict of fair and dark races, and in the subjection into which the dark races eventually fell. Nasal index (the proportion of the breadth to the height of the nasal bones and of the nasal opening) if below a certain percentage, causes the person to be classed as lepto-rhine or fine-nosed. A fine nose is a distinguishing mark of Aryan descent. If this proportion is above a certain percentage, the person is classed as platy-rhine or broad-nosed. A broad nose is an unfailing sign of Dravidian descent or low caste. " It is scarcely a paradox to lay down as a law of the caste organisation, that the social status of the members of a particular group varies in inverse ratio to the mean relative width of their noses." [1]

Other types of caste.

Other types of caste are :

1. Tribal castes, *e.g.* the Bhumij of Chota Nagpur, the Koch of North Bengal, the Jat of the Panjab, and the Koli of Bombay.
2. Functional castes, *e.g.* the Nayars of Malabar and the Khandait of Orissa, who were originally military bodies, and castes such as Dhobi, Barhi, Nai.
3. Sectarian, caused by differences of religion, such as Vaishnavas, or the Lingayets of Southern India, or the Saraks of Orissa.
4. Castes formed by the crossing of races, such as the Khas of Nepal or the Dogras of Kashmir, who are the children of Brahmans or Rajputs by Mongolian women of the country.

[1] 'The People of India,' p. 28.

5. Castes formed by migrations such as the Nambudri Brahmans of Malabar, or the Saurashtra silk weavers of Madura, who originally came from Gujrat.
6. Castes formed by deviation from the customary caste occupation. The Babhans or Bhuinhars of Behar are Brahmans who have taken to agriculture.

Case for caste.

Mr. Sidney Owen thus sums up the case for caste: "The caste organisation is to the Hindu his club, his trades union, his benefit society, his philanthropic society. The obligation to provide for kinsfolk and friends in distress is universally acknowledged, nor can it be questioned that it is due to that recognition of the strength of family ties, and of the bonds created by association and common pursuits, which is fostered by the caste principle. An Indian, without caste, as things stand at present, is not quite easy to imagine." [1]

Eleventh and Twelfth Books of the Laws of Manu.

The eleventh book of the Laws of Manu deals with the expiation of sin, and the twelfth with the future recompenses or consequences good or bad of actions done in this life.

Asramas or stages of life.

As the people were divided into castes, so the lives of individuals, especially of Brahmans, were divided into asramas or stages, viz. Brahmacharjya, or student-life; Garhastha, or the life of a householder; Vanaprastha, or the life of a recluse in a forest, and Bhikshu, or the life of a mendicant ascetic.

Aryan organisation.

The tribe (Jana) was split up into settlements (Vis), and the settlements were aggregations of villages (Grama). The chief was elected by the tribal assembly of freemen (Samiti).

[1] 'Vision of India,' p. 263.

Village community.

Connected with the caste system is the Village Community, which is first mentioned in the Laws of Manu, and has proved the most permanent institution in India. The village headman, whose appointment was hereditary or conferred by the village council itself, settled with the king the revenue to be paid by the village and apportioned it among the villagers. The headman was the judge in all village disputes. The village community may be looked at in two ways; as a group of families united by the assumption of a common kinship, or a company of persons exercising joint ownership over land. It is generally the result of a clan settlement of waste land, or a clearing in the forest made by persons of non-Aryan race who were reduced to the position of slaves and menials. The community divide the arable land, and the waste land is used as pasture in common.

Certain village officers (the watchman, accountant, priest, schoolmaster, doctor, barber, astrologer) had allotments in the village land, and certain artisans who worked for the villagers were given doles at harvest time. These artisans included the blacksmith, harness-maker, shoemaker, and potter.

The grain dealer did not belong to the community, and there were always men of other trades, closely connected with the village, but not belonging to it, who live outside it. Such are the Mahars, who are scavengers, gate-keepers, and watchmen in the Mahratta country, and the Pariahs, who are forced to dwell in the " parcherries " outside the boundaries of the village in Southern India. The Village Community was kept together by a common resistance to oppression. Under British rule, no one is able to oppress it, so the community tends to disintegrate. Industrial causes have contributed also to this result. Artisans have given up their ancestral trade in favour of agriculture, and "the old days when each village was a self-sufficient unit replete with the industries, trades and professions necessary for its modest requirements, are over."[1] In Southern India the villages sometimes had general assemblies, or Sabhas, sufficiently organised to become trustees of temple funds, to undertake the collection of the revenue, and to transact many other duties connected with rural administration.

[1] 'Government of India Census Report, 1911,' p. 409.

CHAPTER III.

BUDDHISM AND JAINISM. FOUNDATION OF POWER OF MAGADHA.

Buddha. BUDDHISM was founded by Sidhartha, better known as Gautama in Southern, or Sakya Sinha in Northern India, son of Suddhodana, a principal member of the aristocratic republic of the Sakyas, who occupied the southern border of Nepal, and the north-eastern part of Oudh, between the rivers Irawati (modern, Rapti) on the west and south, the Rohini (modern, Kohana) on the west, and the Himalayas on the north. Suddhodana's capital was Kapilavastu, which has been identified with a place called Nigliva in the Nepal Terai. Sidhartha's birth, about B.C. 577, is said to have been miraculous. One of the commonest scenes in Buddhist sculpture is that of the dream of his mother Maya, who saw the celestial white elephant known as Chhadanta carrying a lotus in his trunk enter her side to be born as her son. Suddhodana endeavoured to conceal from his son the ills the human flesh is heir to, and shut him up in a palace with his fair young wife Yasodhara, daughter of the Raja of Koli. The people objected that Sidhartha was becoming a mere voluptuary, and would be unfit to lead them in war. He demanded a

The Feet of Gautama's Horse Kanthaka are miraculously held up by the Earth Spirits at the time of the Great Renunciation, so that the noise of his departure from Kapilavastu should not be heard.
(From the Amaravati Stupa.)

trial, and proved superior in martial exercises to all his contemporaries. One day it chanced that he saw

Gautama says Farewell to his Sleeping Wife Yasodhara, from Cave XVI. Ajanta.

with his own eyes sickness, old age, and death, and, filled with pity, he took a silent farewell of his sleeping wife and his young son Rahula, on hearing of whose birth he pathetically remarked: "This is a new and strong tie which I shall have to break." He summoned his charioteer Channa to prepare his horse and accompany him. They went together to the river Anoma, the boundary of the territory of Koli, and there Sidhartha divested himself of his royal ornaments, cut off his long flowing hair with his sword, and gave his horse and ornaments to Channa to take back to the palace. He himself took the road to Rajgriha on the hills between Patna and Gya. This departure of Sidhartha from Kapilavastu is known as the "Great Renunciation." While at Rajgriha he attached himself to two Brahmans named Alāra and Udraka, from whom he learnt all that Hindu philosophy had to teach, and gave himself to mortification of the flesh.

Still unsatisfied, he wandered to the jungle of Uruvela on the banks of the river Nairanjanā in Gaya, where, under the shade of a large pipul tree, he remained for six years meditating on the true nature of the world. He overcame all temptations and acquired the true knowledge of self and the world. Thenceforth he assumed the title of "Buddha" or "the Enlightened One," and the tree was known from that time as the sacred Bo tree or the tree of wisdom. Thereafter he proceeded to Benares and delivered his first sermon to five Brahmans in the Deer Park (Sarnath). For full forty-five years he preached his religion in various parts of India, notably at Sravasti on the Rapti (Sahet Mahet in the Gonda district of Oudh) and Vaisali (modern Besarh in the district of Muzaffarpore).

In the course of his wanderings, he revisited Kapilavastu, and could not be dissuaded by any remonstrance from asking alms with his begging-bowl at the palace. On this occasion Buddha had an interview with his wife, Yasodhara, who was the first to seek admission into the order of Buddhist nuns (*Bhikshunis*). His chief disciples, Ananda his cousin, Sariputra, Mogallana, Upali, and Kasyapa, joined him on various occasions during his long ministry. Buddha died at Kusinagara (Kasia in the Gorakhpur district) about

Buddha's last words.

B.C. 477 at the age of eighty years. His last words to his disciples were: "Beloved, that which causes life causes also decay and death. Never forget this; let your minds be filled with this truth." Like Jesus

Buddha, "the friend of publicans and sinners."

Christ, Buddha was "the friend of publicans and sinners," and all sorts and conditions of men were included among his converts. As Jesus Christ converted Mary Magdalene from the error of her ways, so Buddha numbered a notorious courtesan among his converts, and allowed her to entertain him at banquets. All classes of society tried to honour his memory. Cities contended for the possession of some part of his remains or of things that had belonged to him during his lifetime as sacred relics. The merchant Anathapindaka bought the garden Jetavana at Sravasti, in which Buddha used to preach, by covering it with as much bullion as could be spread over its surface, and after Buddha's death he built in it a monastery, in which were two famous shrines, Gandakuti and Kosambakuti.

Buddha was the friend of kings. Early in his missionary career he converted Prasenajit, king of Kasala. Bimbisara and Ajatasatru, kings of Magadha, of the Saisunaga dynasty, both became converts to Buddhism. Bimbisara gave to Buddha the garden

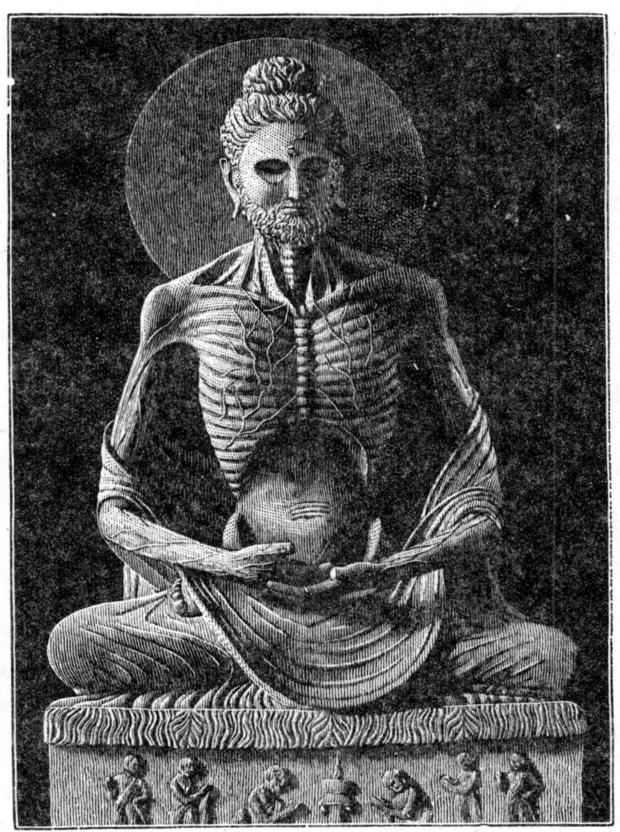

THE FASTING BUDDHA.
From Sikri near Hoti Mardan.

Veluvana or the Bamboo Grave, at Rajgriha, and Ajatasatru frequently visited him to discuss how he could obtain relief from the remorse he felt for poisoning his father Bimbisara. We may perhaps find in the character of Buddha severe monasticism on the one hand, combined with infinite compassion on the other, the model in accordance with which the character of Siva was conceived. His character has been said to represent to the world "the power of goodness or the Sattvic aspect of Ishvara."

Buddhism, Hinduism, and Jainism mutually tolerant.

For about seven hundred and fifty years after the end of the Philosophic or Rationalistic Age, Buddhism replaced Hinduism as the state religion of India, but both sects, as well as Jainism, were mutually tolerant, and interchanged pupils. Hiouen Thsang, in his description of the convocations held by Harsha-vardhana at Kanauj and Allahabad, said that the kings honoured Buddhists and Brahmans equally, and that half the people held one doctrine and half the other. The Buddhist drama Nagananda invokes Buddha in its Nandi or opening prayer, and in the Malati Madhava, a Buddhist female ascetic and her attendant are two of the chief dramatis personae. Both these dramas are proofs of the mutual tolerance between Buddhism and Brahmanism. Buddhism is as adoptive of other forms of religion as Hinduism. The snake canopies to Buddha's statues at Bodh-Gaya and elsewhere illustrate this statement.

Caste equality.

Buddhism benefited considerably from its recognition of caste equality. Many of the kings were Sudras, who were naturally inclined to support a religion which abolished their ceremonial impurity under the caste system. The Brahmans only taught pupils of their own caste and in their own *maths*, the Buddhist taught everybody and everywhere. The

Universal Teaching.

Buddhists had no esoteric doctrines reserved only for the privileged few. "In the matter of the Law, the

OLD INDIAN CLAY SEAL.
From Bodh-Gaya, showing the sacred Bo-tree. Original in Berlin Museum.

Tathagata has never had the closed fist of the teacher who withholds some doctrines and communicates

Buddhism favourable to nationality.

others."[1] Buddhism also fostered the growth of the ideas necessary to make India a nation by preaching the common rights of all men, whatever their birth, and so prepared the way for the empire of Asoka.

Future life ignored.

Buddhism avoids all reference to the future life. After he had discovered the emptiness of ceremonials and asceticism, Buddha preached the doctrine of the Middle Path—the duty of avoiding sensuality on the one hand and asceticism on the other. "Not nakedness, nor plaited hair, not dirt nor fasting, nor lying on the ground, nor rubbing with dust, nor sitting motionless can purify a man who has not overcome desire."[2]

Doctrine of the Middle Path.

Four noble truths.

Buddhism is a system of morality based upon the Four Noble Truths, that life is suffering, that thirst after life is the cause of suffering, that the conquest of this thirst causes cessation of suffering, and that self-culture is the means to conquer thirst after life.

The Eight Points.

Self-culture is attained by being right on the Eight Points, in belief and in resolution, in speech and in act, in livelihood and in training, in reflection and in mental concentration. Buddha denied the existence of any invisible self or ego, distinct from the material body, called the soul, therefore he disbelieved in the transmigration of souls, but he adopted from the Upanishads the doctrine of Karma. "All that we are is the result of what we have thought; it is founded on our thoughts, it is made up of our thoughts. If a man speaks or acts with an evil thought, pain

[1] Mahaparinibbana sutta, ii. 32, translated by Rhys Davids.
[2] Vasetta Sutta, Sutta Nipata, 57.

follows him as the wheel follows the foot of the ox that draws the carriage. If a man speaks or acts with a pure thought, happiness follows him like a shadow."[1] "He, whose conduct has been good, quickly attains some good embodiment, as a Brahman, Kshatriya or Vaisya. He whose conduct has been bad assumes an inferior embodiment, as a dog, a hog, or a Chandala."[2] Only by purity of life and cessation of desire is it possible to attain release from the chain of rebirths. Purity of life is attained by keeping the commandments not to kill, not to take what is not given, not to lie, not to drink intoxicating drinks, not to have unchaste sexual intercourse. These precepts are binding on laymen, who are also bidden dutifully to maintain their parents. Monks are also not to eat at forbidden times, not to wear garlands or ornaments, nor to use perfumes, not to lie on a high or broad bed, not to dance nor sing, nor enjoy music nor stage plays, and not to use gold or silver.[3]

Karma.

"Better even than a harmless sacrifice (without slaughter of animals) is liberality; better than liberality is faith, and kindness, and truth; better than faith, kindness and truth is renunciation of the world and the search for peace; best of all the highest sacrifice and the greatest good is when one enters Nirvana, saying I shall not return to earth."[4]

Buddha's confession of faith.

The release from the chain of rebirths and absorption in the primal essence is Nirvana, from Nir-va, to be extinguished, used with reference to a flame, and

Nirvana.

[1] Dhammapada, I. I.

[2] Chandogya Upanishad, v. 10. 7.

[3] Dhammika Sutta, Sutta Nipata.

[4] Kutadanta Sutta, Oldenberg, p. 175.

then metaphorically with reference to life. Nirvana is attained when impressions and knowledge, and therefore desire, cease. It is "a condition in which nothing remains of that which constitutes existence. As a flame blown about by the wind goes out and

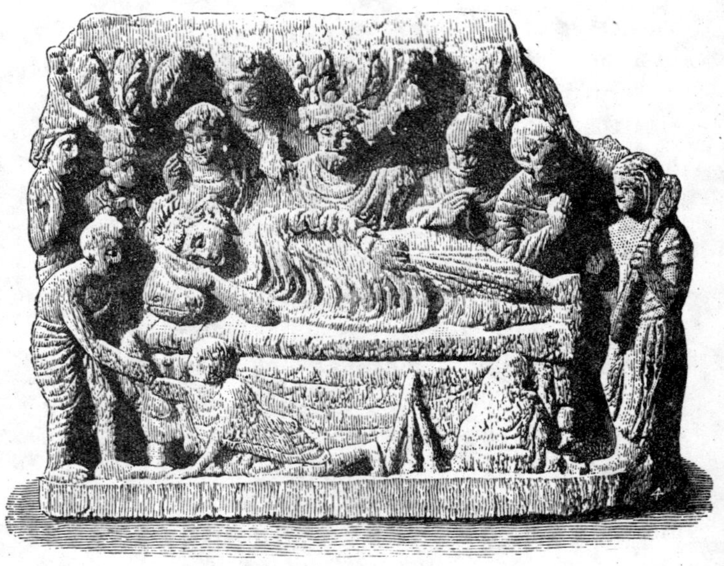

THE PARI-NIRVANA OF BUDDHA.
From the Yusufzai country.

cannot be reckoned as existing, so a sage, delivered from mind and body, disappears and cannot be reckoned as existing."[1]

It is the special peculiarity of Buddhism that a man can work out his own salvation. It ignored the soul, and "for the first time in the history of the world, proclaimed a salvation which every man could

[1] Upasiva Manavapuccha.

gain *for himself*, and *by himself, in this world and during this life*, without the least reference to God or gods, either great or small." [1]

Mahavira.

Jainism made its appearance a little before Buddhism: the derivation of the word is from "Jina," a conquering saint, one who has vanquished self and desire. Its founder Mahavira, also called Vardhamana or Jnatiputra, came of the Jnata section of the Kshatriyas, who dwelt near Vaisali, the capital of Videha. Mahavira was born at Vaisali about 599 B.C., and died about 527 B.C. His followers were first called Nirgranthas (without a bond), who afterwards became known as Jains. They were subsequently subdivided about 80 A.D. into Svetambaras, who wore white garments, and the Digambaras (literally sky-clothed), who wore no garments at all. The Digambaras migrated into Southern India about 350 B.C. under Bhadrabahu, and practised stricter asceticism than the Svetambaras. The Jains revere the Tirthankaras, of whom twenty-four are born in every cycle of time. Adinath was the first Tirthankara, while the last three were Nemnath, Parasnath and Mahavira. The Tirthankaras are the "makers" of the passage or ford over the river of transmigrations to the spiritual life in the mansions of the blessed.

Parasnath or Parswanath, who immediately preceded Mahavira, was born at Benares two centuries before Gautama. He was the son of king Aswasena; he married the daughter of the king of Kosala, and, like Gautama, left her to lead the life of an ascetic. At the age of one hundred years he attained Nirvana

[1] Rhys Davids, Hibbert Lectures, 1881.

at Parasnath in Bengal, which is also called Saumat Sikhar or the Hill of Bliss.

Jainism.

The Mahabratas, or great duties of the Jain moral code, are refraining from injury to life, which involves a revolt against the sacrificial cult of the Brahmans, and the practice of truth, honesty, chastity and freedom from worldly desire. Its four Dharmas or Merits are: liberality, gentleness, piety, and penance, and its three restraints are: government of the tongue, mind, and person. The Jain Sacred Books are divided into forty-five *Siddhantas* or *Agamas*, and eleven or twelve *Angas* and twelve *Upangas*. The teachings of Mahavira, as represented in these Agamas, are said to have been collected by a disciple of his called Indrabhuti. They were handed down by oral tradition until, in A.D. 453, they were codified in writing by Devardhigani, otherwise known as Ksamāsramana, at a council held at Valabhi.

Points of similarity with Hinduism and Buddhism.

The Jain householders observe caste, and obey the Hindu rules on ceremonial purification and marriage. They follow the tenets of the sanctity of animal life, the worship of deified saints, and the practice of the five-fold virtues of self-culture, self-control, truthfulness, honesty, and kindness. Like the Buddhists, they refuse to acknowledge that God created the world or that He exercises any personal and providential control over it.

Points of difference from Buddhism.

Jainism is an aggregate of opinions (*pannattis*) on various subjects, with no fundamental ideas to give them cohesion. It has no ethical basis like Buddhism. The Jains differ from the Buddhists in receiving laymen into communion with the order; the conduct of laymen was regulated by vows and rules, and devotional services were held for them. The Buddhist lay adherents, on the other hand, had no share in the monastic organisation. The Jains reject Nirvana; when the soul is delivered from the trammels of successive existences, it begins a spiritual life in some mansion of the blessed. The Tirthankaras have attained this spiritual life.

Another great difference between the Jains and Buddhists is the great importance attached by the former to the mortification of the body. "Through mortification arises the severance of Karma," and the Jain is therefore called on to forgo all the joys of the senses.

The Jains hold that not only all breathing animals and the whole vegetable kingdom, but also every particle of matter included in the category of the prime elements, earth, air, fire, and water, have individual souls endowed with self-consciousness and knowledge of surrounding things, and are subject to all the changes of soul life.

Differences between Hinduism and Buddhism.

Brahmanism is not congregational. The Hindu caste observances have to be carried out by the individual, and sacrifices are offered by the priest for the individual, or, at the most, for the family. Buddhism introduced the element of the Sangha (congregation) for the first time. Other differences are the denial of caste, and of a personal deity.

Jainism an offshoot of Buddhism.

Hiouen Thsang regarded Jainism as an offshoot of Buddhism. "The laws of their founder are mostly filched from the books of Buddha. The figure of their sacred master (Mahavira) they stealthily class with that of Tathagata (Buddha); it differs only in point of clothing, the points of beauty are the same." The truth is Jainism is nearer Brahmanism than Buddhism. Whether belonging to the Svetambar or Digambar or Dhundia sections, all Jains fall into two classes—Sravakas or laymen, and Yatis or monks, who have taken perpetual vows.

DILWARA TEMPLES, MOUNT ABU.

Jain temples.

The most famous temples of the Jains are those of Vimala Shah, Tejupala, and Bastupala on Mount Abu in Rajputana, and on the mountain called Parasnath in Bengal. The caves in the rock, on which the Fort of Gwalior is built, preserve many Jain sculptures and carvings. Other sites of temples and sacred places of the Jains are: Mathura; Satrunjaya hill in the Palitana State, and Girnar in the Junagadh

Modern Jain Temple, Calcutta.

State in Kathiawar; the Indra and Jaganath Sabha caves, Ellora; Khajuraho in Central India, Gadag and Lakkundi in Dharwar, and Sravana Belgola in the Hassan district of Mysore. At Sravana Belgola there is a gigantic statue of Gomatesvara, with an inscription which describes a migration of Digambar Jains to Southern India, and contains the epitaph of the teacher Prabha Chandra. Other Jain colossi are found at Karkala and Venur in South Kanara. In the extreme south of India there was a famous resort of the Jains at the Alagiri rock, twelve miles north-west of Madura. The picture of the Jain temple at Calcutta shows the appearance of a Jain temple of modern date.

Spread of Buddhism.

Even during the lifetime of its founder Buddhism made many converts. Bimbisara and Ajatrasatru (Sanscrit, *Amitraghata*; Greek, *Amitrochates*, slayer of his foes), kings of Magadha of the Saisunaga dynasty, embraced the new religion, and in the reign of Asoka, grandson of Chandra Gupta, founder of the Maurya dynasty, it became the state religion of the country. It was preached in Ceylon by Mahinda and Sanghamitta, Asoka's son and daughter about 254. The name Sanghamitta (friend of the Buddhist Order) suggests that it has been coined, and throws doubt on her historical existence. By Mahinda's mission to Ceylon, Asoka unconsciously provided a memorial of himself and the history of Buddhism in the Pali Chronicles of Ceylon, which would never otherwise have existed. Strabo tells us that a Buddhist priest named Zarmana Chagos or Sramanacharjya, went, at the head of an embassy from Poros, who appears to have reigned over the Pandya kingdom in Southern India, to the court of Augustus Caesar at Rome about

B.C. 26, and burned himself at Athens. Another embassy arrived at Rome six years later.

Buddhist councils.

Asoka held the third great council of southern Buddhists at Pataliputra, about 254 B.C., the first having been held at Rajgriha just after the Master's

JAIN REMAINS AT GWALIOR.

death, B.C. 477, and the second at Vaisali, B.C. 377. The first council dealt with the question of the expulsion from the order of Tirthyas or heretics, the second decided against indulgences which relaxed the strictness of the former rules. These councils failed in their object of introducing unanimity in the Buddhist doctrines, but this very want of conformity to any fixed standard may have conduced to the spread of Buddhism. Asoka's council settled the canon of Buddhistic scriptures, especially the Sutta, Vinaya and Abhidamma Pitakas according to what is now known as the Hinayana (Southern Buddhist) School. The first Pitaka deals with the religious tenets and sermons of Buddha, and was drawn up by Ananda; the second with the discipline and confessional (*Patimokha*), and was drawn up by Upali; the third with the metaphysics of Buddhism, and was drawn up by Kasyapa.

Buddhism in the Further East.

Buddhism extended over Kashgar and Khotan, when Kanishka ruled his empire in Central Asia. The emperor Ming-ti, A.D. 58-76, had a dream, in which a golden man appeared to him, who was interpreted to be Gautama Buddha. In A.D. 65, the Chinese emperor sent a mission to Khotan, which returned after two years, bringing with it the Buddhist missionary Kasyapa-Matanga from Central India; he was followed shortly after by Gobharana. Of the numerous other Buddhist monks, who visited China and translated Sanscrit books into Chinese, the most famous is Kumarajiva, nineteenth of the Patriarchs of Western Buddhism, who arrived in China, with the famous sandal-wood image of Buddha, and took up his residence at the court of the emperor Yao-Hsing, A.D. 406. In A.D. 520 Buddhidharma, "the White Buddha," called by the Chinese Ta-mo, arrived at Canton, bringing with him the Sacred Bowl of the Buddhist Patriarchate, of which he was the last representative in the West and the first to hold office in the East. Jinagupta visited China, *via* Central Asia, about the middle of the sixth century A.D.

From China Buddhism spread to Corea A.D. 372. Java was converted between A.D. 413 and 431 by Gungavarman, crown prince of Kashmir, who renounced his rank to become a Buddhist monk, and died at Nankin A.D. 431. Buddhism was introduced into Burma by Budhaghosa 450, and reached Japan 552, and Siam 638. The Japanese Shintoism was adapted by turning the Shinto deities and demigods into Buddhisattvas, *e.g.* Kwannon, the Japanese goddess of mercy, was considered a female form of Avalokiteshvara.

Buddhism in Thibet.

Srong-tsan-ganpo, who was born in A.D. 617, was the first king of Thibet who embraced Buddhism. He also introduced Indian painting and wood-carving into Thibet from Nepal. His minister Thumi or Thonmi Sambhota designed the Thibetan alphabet from the Indian and added six new letters. Thumi translated into Thibetan the Tantric work Mani Kambum, describing the introduction of Buddhism into Thibet, and founded the yellow-capped sect of Lamas. Thibet was completely converted to Buddhism by the preacher Padma Sambhava, who arrived A.D. 747 in the country from Udyana or Dardistan (west of the Indus, and north of Peshawar). He was invited by king Khri-srong-de-tsan, and translated the Buddhist Northern Canon into Thibetan. From this translation, the Thibetan Scriptures—Kanjur (108 books), and Tanjur (225 books of commentaries)—originated.

Padma Sambhava favoured Saivism and sorcery, and founded the Red-capped sect of Lamas. Santa Rakshita, another Indian Buddhist monk, came from Bengal to visit Thibet. He became the first abbot of Samye, the first Buddhist monastery in Thibet. Dipankara Srijnana, better known as Atisa, who was prefect of the Buddhist university of Vikramasila in the Bhagalpur district, visited Thibet in A.D. 1038 to reform the Buddhist religion there.

Buddhism in Mongolia.

Mongolia became Buddhist after Jenghiz Khan, the Mongol emperor, conquered Thibet in 1207. Khublai Khan, 1259-94, made the abbot of the Buddhist monastery of Sakya in Thibet the temporal ruler of the country, and Buddhism hence became the religion of the country. It ousted Shamaism by adopting its deities as Buddhisattvas.

Rise of Magadha upon the ruin of the adjacent smaller states.

Ajatasatru, king of Magadha, annexed the little kingdom of Champa or Anga (modern Bhagalpur and Monghyr). The first capital of Magadha was Rajgriha, on the chain of hills between the Patna and Gaya districts. Bimbisara, king of Magadha, built a fort at the confluence of the Ganges and the Sone to restrain the inroads of the Licchavis of Vaisali. This fort was the nucleus of the city of Patna, the ancient name of which was Pataliputra (so called from Patali, the trumpet-flower or bignonia), in Greek Palibothra.

Persian invasion of India.

In the reign of Bimbisara occurred the first of the foreign invasions of India of which we have any record. Darius Hystaspes, king of Persia, conquered Afghanistan and a part of the Panjab, inhabited by the Ashvakas on the north and the Gandharas on the south of the Kabul river, about B.C. 500, and levied from this territory a large revenue in gold. The revenue of Darius from nineteen Satrapies was in modern money £2,964,000, but the twentieth, India (including Bactria and the west bank of the Indus) produced 360 talents of gold dust, or £1,290,000. The Indian gold-digging ants, of which Herodotus speaks, and the story of the Arimaspians, who fought with the Gryphons for the gold they guarded, are supposed to disguise a reference to the gold of Thibet guarded by mastiffs kept by the miners for the purpose. Pliny says a horn of a gold-digging ant was preserved in the temple of Hercules at Erythræ; this was probably a pick-axe made of the horns of a wild sheep mounted on a wooden handle. Darius also sent Skylax of Karyanda to explore the Indus. Herodotus tells us that this king subdued the "Northern Indians," and the same author describes the Indians in the army which Xerxes led against Greece as dressed in cotton clothes with cane bows and iron-tipped cane arrows.[1]

Alexander's invasion of India and the consequences thereof.

Alexander's Indian expedition has been described by Arrian in the Anabasis of Alexander, Quintus Curtius Rufus, Plutarch, and Justinus Frontinus 'On Philippic (Macedonian) History.' He spent three years in Central Asia and founded Herat Alexandra Ariorum in B.C. 330. He crossed the Hindu Kush mountains in B.C. 327 and founded in Afghanistan Alexandra ad Caucasum, on the plains of Bagram, twenty-five miles north of Kabul, and Kandahar, the name of which is the modern equivalent of Alexandra in Arachosia. Then he turned east and crossed the Panjkhora river. After this he besieged Mount Aornos (Mahaban), and protected his flank, preparatory to crossing the Indus, by subduing the tribesmen of Swat and Bajaur. When he was passing through the country between the Kabul river and the Indus

[1] 1 Herodotus, vii. 65; viii. 13; and ix. 91.

the city of Nysa, said to have been founded by Dionysos (the Greek god of wine), which was situated near the modern Jelalabad, surrendered to Alexander. The crossing of the Indus took place at Attock, near the junction of the Kabul river and the Indus, or else at Ohind, 18 miles up the river from Attock. After passing the Indus, Alexander received the submission of Omphis, Prince of Taxila, and ruler of the Doab between the Indus and the Jhelum, who is spoken of in the Greek writers under the territorial title of Taxiles. Taxila was a city 24 miles north-west of the modern Rawal Pindi, the name of which is either derived from Takshaka-sila, "the rock of Takshaka," the great Naga king, or from Takka-sila, the rock of the Takkas, a powerful tribe, who lived between the Indus and the Chenab. At Taxila, the Gymnosophists, or naked sages, who were probably Digambar Jains, were met with; Kalanos, a Digambar Jain, whose real name was Sphines, accompanied Alexander when he left India and burnt himself alive at Susa on being taken ill.

Paurava, "the prince of the Purus" who are mentioned in the Vedas, whom the Greeks called Porus, another prince whose dominions lay in the doab between the Chenab and the Jhelum, opposed him. Alexander defeated Porus on the Karri plain on the banks of the Jhelum (June, 326) after stealing a passage of the river some way further up. He then advanced to the Beas, after crossing the Chenab and the Ravi. On the Beas, his troops refused to follow him any further, and he had to retreat down the Jhelum as far as its confluence with the Indus. On the Jhelum, Alexander was nearly slain in the assault on the city of the Malli, which Mr. Vincent Smith identifies with Multan. When he reached Patala (Hyderabad, Sind), he sent his admiral Nearchus to sail down the Indus, which he took for the Upper Nile, to the mouth of the Euphrates. In Southern Sind Alexander met with and defeated a prince whom the Greeks called Sopeithes. At the mouth of the Indus the Greeks saw for the first time the phenomenon of the tides, which does not occur in the Mediterranean. From Patala, he returned (August, 325) with one division of his army through the deserts of Gedrosia (Mekran) to Susa in Persia, and another division returned to Persia by way of Kandahar. Alexander, on leaving India, left the Paropanisadae, or territory of the Indus, in charge of Oxyartes, father of his wife Roxana. The Panjab, including the territories of Omphis, prince of Taxila, and Porus and the country of the Malli, was placed under Philip, son of Machetas. Sind was entrusted to Peithon, son of Agenor, from which he was subsequently ousted by Porus.

Tides.

Alexander's invasion of India had the important consequence of acquainting the Indians that another, and in some respects, superior civilisation to their own existed in the West. "It had been the fond dream of Alexander to found an universal empire which should be held together, not merely by the unity of the government, but also by unity of language, customs, and civilisation. All the Oriental races were to be saturated with Hellenic culture, and to be bound together in one great whole by means of this intellectual force. All Western Asia, in fact, if not among the widespread masses of the population, yet

Alexander's policy.

certainly among the higher ranks of society, became thoroughly Hellenised." [1]

Rise of Chandra Gupta.

The story of Chandra Gupta's descent from an amour of the Queen of Mahapadma Nanda with a barber is told by both Quintus Curtius and Diodorus Siculus. Another tradition makes him the son of Mahapadma Nanda by a Sudra woman, Mura, after whom the dynasty he founded was called Maurya. After deposing Mahapadma Nanda, the reigning king of Magadha, Chandra Gupta, who was called by the Greeks Sandracottus, brought the whole of Northern India under one rule, and extended the kingdom of Magadha from Behar to the Panjab. His minister was the Brahman Chanakya (sometimes called Kautilya or Vishnugupta), author of the 'Arthasastra.' After Alexander's death in 323, his general Seleucus Nikator obtained as his share of the empire Syria, Bactria (Balkh), and the Greek conquests in India. After the failure of his attempt to invade India, he allied himself with Chandra Gupta, sent Megasthenes, and afterwards Deimachus, as ambassadors to his court, and gave Chandra Gupta his daughter in marriage. He also ceded the Greek possessions west of the Indus, comprising the provinces of the Paropanisadai (Hindu Kush), Aria (Herat), and Arachosia (Kandahar), in return for a tribute of 500 elephants (B.C. 312). Strabo tells us that Seleucus received the elephants from Sandracottus, and that he contracted "affinity" with him. From this it has been inferred that he gave him his daughter in marriage.

[1] Schurer, 'History of the Jews in the time of Jesus Christ,' vol. i. p. 194.

The kingdom of Bactria (Balkh), founded by Diodotus (B.C. 256), afterwards became independent of the descendants of Seleucus. Bactria consisted of two parts: (1) Old Bactria, capital Balkh, north of the Hindu Kush; (2) Bactria, south of the Hindu Kush, capital Alexandra ad Caucasum, called in Buddhist writers Alasadda, on the plains of Bagram, 25 miles north of Kabul. Bactria north of the Hindu Kush was conquered by Mithradates of Parthia, about B.C. 235. Bactria south of the Hindu Kush passed into the hands of Euthydemus, B.C. 230-195. In B.C. 206 Antiochus III. (the Great), king of Syria, endeavoured to reunite Bactria to his empire. He captured Kandahar and besieged Euthydemus in Balkh, but afterwards made a treaty with him. At the time when Demetrius, son of Euthydemus, conquered the Panjab and Sind, Euthydemus was dispossessed of Bactria south of the Hindu Kush by Eucratides, B.C. 175. There were thus two lines of Greek princes, one derived from Euthydemus ending B.C. 100, when it was dethroned by the Sakas, and one derived from Eucratides ending A.D. 25. The family of Eucratides reigned in Gandhara (capital Kapisa) and Kabul. A pillar inscription at Besnagar, near Bhilsa in the Gwalior state, mentions that Heliodorus, son of Dion, who had come as ambassador from Antialcidas, king of Bactria of the house of Eucratides, to Bhagabadra, who was one of the Sunga kings, had adapted an Indian faith. The last prince of this house was Hermæus, who was dethroned by Kadphises the Kushan, A.D. 25. The house of Euthydemus ruled north-western India, including Rajputana and Guzrat, as far as the Tapti and

Kingdom of Bactria and other Greek principalities in India.

Narbada. Their capital was Sakala (Sangla on the Ravi, or Sialkot). This house was overthrown by the Sakas, B.C. 100. In B.C. 155, Menander, of the family of Euthydemus, whose questions to the Buddhist sage Nagasena, and Nagasena's answers thereto, have come down to us in the 'Milindapanha,' crossed the Beas and conquered Malwa. He penetrated as far as Oudh and fought a battle there with the army of Pushyamitra Sunga.

Bactrian coins.

Bactrian coins mark the first introduction into India of double dies for minting, so that the coin could receive an impression on both sides at once.

The Parthians.

The Parthians, who invaded India, did not belong to the race which founded the Parthian empire, but to a subordinate branch established in Seistan, Kandahar, and North Beluchistan. There were two lines of Parthian princes, the family of Vonones in Seistan, Kandahar, and North Beluchistan, and that of Maues in the West Panjab and Sind. In the first quarter of the first century A.D. these two lines were united under Gondophares. He is known in early Christian legends as the king to whose court St. Thomas "the apostle of the Parthians," or the "apostle of the Indians," was sent. St. Thomas is said to have written to Gondophares, who was reigning at Peshawar between A.D. 25 and 45, a letter announcing his purpose of visiting India. According to tradition, Christianity in Malabar dates from A.D. 52, when St. Thomas is said to have landed at Cranganore and to have founded seven churches.

St. Thomas and Indian Christianity.

There was considerable Christian missionary activity in North-western India, and Christian communities, which may have been founded by St. Thomas, were in existence in the third century A.D. Eusebius speaks of the missionary labours in India of Pantœnus about A.D. 180. Thomas, a missionary bishop from Edessa,

1. Menander.

Obverse: Elephant head.

Reverse: Club.

2. Menander.

3. Antialkidas.

BACTRIAN AND PARTHIAN COINS.

landed in Malabar about A.D. 345, and founded the community of Nestorian Christians in subordination to the Patriarch of Antioch, which exists to this day. Kosmos Indikopleustes was an Egyptian monk, who wrote about the middle of the sixth century A.D. As a merchant, he visited Arabia, Persia, and India. After becoming a monk, he wrote 'Christian Topography,' which has many allusions to India and some account of Indian Christian communities.

4. Hermæus. Reverse: Zeus.

5. Maues. Reverse: Nike.

BACTRIAN AND PARTHIAN COINS.

The Greek influence.

The Greek influence was mainly æsthetic. It was not Macedonian, but Bactrian in origin, and lasted from the revolt of Diodotus, B.C. 250, to the deposition of Hermæus, A.D. 25. This influence is shown in sculpture and architectural ornament, and in the imitations of Greek models on the coins.

The Roman influence.

The Roman influence was chiefly political and commercial. The impression wrought upon India by the power of Rome is shown by the constant embassies despatched to Rome by Indian sovereigns to seek for her alliance. The closeness of the commercial connection between Rome and India is shown by the large finds of Roman coins discovered in India.

Chandra Gupta's army consisted of 600,000 foot, 30,000 cavalry and 8000 elephants, with a large number of war chariots, and was managed by a Board of thirty members, divided into six committees with five members each. Arrian thus describes the equipment of the soldiers: "The foot soldiers carry a bow made of equal length with the man who bears it. This they rest upon the ground, and pressing against it with their left foot thus discharge the arrow, having drawn the string far backwards; for the shaft they use is little short of being three yards long, and there is nothing which can resist an Indian archer's shot—neither shield, nor breastplate, nor any stronger defence if such there be. All wear a sword which is broad in the blade but not longer than three cubits; and this, when they engage in close fight (which they do with reluctance), they wield with both hands to fetch a lustier blow. The horsemen are equipped with two lances and a shorter buckler than that carried by the foot soldiers. But they do not put saddles on their horses, nor do they curb them with bits, but they fit on round the extremity of the horse's mouth a circular piece of stitched raw ox-hide studded with pricks of iron or brass pointing inwards, but not very sharp: if a man is rich he uses pricks made of ivory. Within the horse's mouth is put an iron prong like a skewer, to which the reins are attached. When the rider, then, pulls the reins, the prong controls the horse, and the pricks, which are attached to this thong, so goad the horse that it cannot but obey the reins." [1]

Means whereby the central administration was informed of the state of the provinces.

To keep the central administration informed of the state of the provinces, there appear to have been entertained news-writers or informers (the *pulisani* or *pativedaka* of the Rock Edicts, the *episkopoi* of Megasthenes, and the *akbari navis* of the Moghal emperors). Arrian, who lived about 150 A.D., and who was the pupil of Epictetus and the contemporary of Marcus Aurelius, speaks of these officers who sent reports to the kings or magistrates. Chandra Gupta was somewhat of a tyrant. Justinus Frontinus, who abridged the History of the Macedonian Empire by Trogus Pompeius, an author of the time of Augustus, and who is quoted by Mr. Vincent Smith in his book on Asoka, says that Chandra Gupta, "after his victory forfeited by his tyranny all title to the name of liberator, for he oppressed with servitude the very people whom he had emancipated from foreign thraldom."

Chandra Gupta somewhat of a tyrant.

Severe Criminal Law.

The Criminal Law was severe, false evidence being punished by mutilation, and any one who injured a workman of the royal retinue suffered the death penalty. Special care was taken to foster agriculture, the agricultural population was exempt from military service, an Irrigation Department was maintained, and the land revenue appears to have been limited to one-fourth of the gross produce. The inscription of the Satrap Rudradaman, A.D. 150, on the Girnar bridge in Kathiawar, the oldest inscription

Care to foster agriculture.

Inscription on Rudradaman's Bridge at Girnar.

[1] Indika xvi. translated in McCrindle's 'Ancient India.'

[2] Vincent Smith, 'Asoka, the Buddhist Emperor of India,' p. 83.

in pure Sanscrit known, is authority for the care bestowed by the Maurya dynasty upon irrigation. It records Rudradaman's repair of the Sudarsan irrigation lake at Girnar, originally "ordered to be made by the Vaisya Pushyagupta, the provincial governor of the Maurya king Chandra Gupta; and fitted with conduits for Asoka Maurya by the Yavana Raja Tushaspa during his rule.

Capital city of Pataliputra.

The capital city of Pataliputra was under the jurisdiction of a sort of Municipality of thirty members, and the same sort of government was introduced in other large towns. The city was in shape a long narrow parallelogram, nine miles in length, and a mile and a half in breadth; it stretched from modern Bankipore on the west, to beyond the present city of Patna on the east, and was placed on a long strip of high land some eight miles long north of the modern village of Kumrahar. The long streets ran east and west, the shorter north and south, an arrangement which admitted a free circulation of air. The capital was a mere aggregation of villages. Like the army, it was ruled by thirty commissioners divided into six committees of five each (an enlargement of the ordinary village panchayet). Asoka's palace was to the south of the city, between the mound called Choti Pahari and Kumrahar. To the north-west of it, was the hill called Bhikna Pahari, and, in its vicinity, the well called Agam Kuan.

The Greek historians.

The allusions to India made by Herodotus have been already mentioned. Ktesias (about B.C. 398) wrote the first Greek book specially dealing with India. 'Indika,' the book written by Megasthenes about India, has been lost, but its substance has been handed down by Diodorus Siculus, Strabo, and Arrian.

Other authorities for the history of Buddhistic India.

Arrian wrote an account of Alexander's expedition to India, called 'The Anabasis of Alexander.' His book on India is also called 'Indika.' The accounts left by Megasthenes and Arrian of the Prasii (inhabitants of Magadha), (Sanscrit, *prachya,* eastern), and the Gangaridae (inhabitants of Bengal) are, however, the earliest elaborate descriptions of India by European authors that we possess. Megasthenes mentions that the valley of the Ganges south of the Magadha territory to the sea was held by the Kalingae (people of Kalinga, Orissa) and the Andarae (Andhras). The Gangaridae were a branch of the Kalingae, and their capital was Parthalis, which has been conjecturally identified with Burdwan. The writers next in point of time were Pliny and Ptolemy. Their accounts, the travels of the Chinese pilgrims Fa Hian and Hiouen Thsang, and the Pali Chronicles, such as the Dipavamsa and the Mahavamsa, are our chief authorities for the history of Buddhist India.

The castes of India as enumerated by Megasthenes.

Megasthenes described the castes of India as consisting of:

1. The philosophers or sophists.
2. Agriculturists.
3. Herdsmen, shepherds and graziers.
4. Artisans and traders.
5. The Military.
6. The Overseers or spies.
7. The Counsellors.

The philosophers.

The "philosophers" referred to by Megasthenes were subdivided into Brahmans and Sramans (perhaps Buddhist) ascetics; the "counsellors" also were probably Brahmans. The Gymnosophists, of whom Megasthenes speaks, have been identified by some authors with the Digambar Jains. The second, third, fourth, and sixth castes of Megasthenes were probably Vaisyas or Sudras. The Brahmans "abstain from animal food and sensual pleasures, and spend their time listening to religious discourse, and in imparting their knowledge to such as will listen to them." The Sramans "live in the woods, where they subsist on the leaves of trees and wild fruits, and wear garments made from the bark of trees. They communicate with the kings, who consult them by messengers, regarding the causes of things, and who, through them, worship and supplicate the deity."

The agriculturists

The Agriculturists "devote the whole of their time to tillage, nor would an enemy, coming upon an husbandman at work on his land, do him any harm; for men of this class, being regarded as public benefactors, are protected from all injury. The land remaining thus unravaged, and producing heavy crops, supplies the inhabitants with all that is requisite to make life very enjoyable. They pay a land tribute to the king, because all India is the property of the crown, and no private person is permitted to own land. Besides the land tribute, they pay into the royal treasury a fourth part of the produce of the soil." In this account of the land tribute, Megasthenes is confirmed by Strabo, who wrote about A.D. 20.

The Indian people.

Megasthenes states that "No one is allowed to marry out of his own class or exercise any calling or art except his own." The only exception to this rule was made in favour of the philosophers. The people of India are thus described: "They live happily enough, being simple in their manners and frugal. They never drink wine except at sacrifices. Their beverage is a liquor composed from rice instead of barley, and their food is principally a rice pottage. The simplicity of their laws and contracts is proved by the fact that they seldom go to law. They have no suits about pledges and deposits, nor do they require seals and witnesses, but make their deposits and confide in each other. Their houses and property they generally leave unguarded. These things indicate that they possess sober sense. Truth and virtue they hold alike in esteem. Hence they accord no special privileges to the old unless they possess superior wisdom."

The Indians were "well skilled in the arts, as might be expected of men who inhale a pure air, and drink the very finest water. They love finery and ornament. Their robes are worked in gold and ornamented with precious stones, and they also wear flowered garments made of the finest muslin. Attendants walking behind hold up umbrellas over them; for they have a high regard for beauty, and avail themselves of every device to improve their looks."

Buddhist architecture. Viharas.

The history of early Indian Architecture deals very largely with the remains of various structures used for Buddhist religious worship. A Buddhist monastery called *Vihara* or *Sangharama* generally consisted, when complete, of seven divisions, viz. (1) *Kuti* or rooms for the high priest, and for the senior and junior priests; (2) *pannasala* or cells for the accommodation of monks or pupils; (3) *pratima-griha*, or temple in which there are images of Buddha and Buddhisattvas; (4) *grantha-griha*, or library, which is generally located on the upper story ; (5) *uposatha-griha*, or ordination house, in which meditation, etc., is practised ; (6) *stupa* or pagoda, in the inside of which there are relics of Buddha and Arhats

THE GREAT CHAITYA CAVE AT AJANTA, ENTRANCE.

or Buddhist saints ; and (7) *bodhi-tree*, which represents the famous tree under which Buddha attained supreme knowledge.

The Viharas were rectangular flat-roofed halls, having verandahs with a door and windows on each Viharas.

INTERIOR OF CHAITYA CAVE, AJANTA.

side in front, and cells in the end and side walls, with a frieze over their doors. In later times, the sides of the centre hall were surrounded by aisles, divided from it by rows of columns, and the cells opened into the aisles, not directly into the hall. In the front of the centre hall was a porch supported by pillars and pilasters. In the centre of the end aisle an antechamber was excavated, and beyond

INTERIOR VIEW OF KARLI CHAITYA.

this, with another doorway giving access to it, was a second chamber which, in earlier times, contained a relic receptacle, and, in examples of later date, a statue of Buddha seated.

The most famous Viharas were Nalanda (Baragaon, near Rajgriha) and Vikramasila (in the Bhagalpur district), those situated in the Udaygiri and Khandagiri hills in Orissa, those at Ajanta in the Nizam's dominions, fifty-five miles north-east of Aurungabad, at Nasik, and at Takt-i-Bahi near Hoti Mardan. The Ajanta remains are particularly noteworthy, as

View of Interior of a Vihara at Ajanta.

including examples of the plain simplicity of the Hinayana, as well as examples of the florid splendour of the Mahayana sect extravagantly ornamented and full of statues not only of Buddha, but also of the Hindu gods.

The *dhwaja-stambhas* or Vishnu standards in front of the Chaityas generally have *amalaka* (lotus fruit, sometimes called "cushion") capitals. At Karli only one *dhwaja-stambha* survives. The *amalaka* at Karli is placed within the four legs of the Vedic altar, at the Gautamiputra Vihara at Nasik the legs are carved into dwarf figures of *pisachas*. The so-called "horse-shoe" windows of the Chaityas were borrowed in shape from the thatched roofs of Bengal, which were constructed of bent bamboo. Chaityas.

The Chaityas were places for religious worship, mostly carved out of rock. The only *built* Chaitya is at Sanchi. The Chaitya was not quadrangular like the Vihara, but its length greatly exceeded its breadth. The entrance to the Chaitya was through a porch with three entrances; laymen came in by the door on the left, performed "*pradakshina*" round the relic shrine, and passed out by the door on the right. Religious persons came in through the centre door. There were three aisles in length twice the breadth of the Chaitya, and the central aisle terminated in a semi-circular apse or hollow with a dome, under which stood a relic-shrine.

The most famous Chaitya is that of Karli near Lanauli, between Bombay and Poona. Others are at Bhaja and Bedsa, both to the south of Lanauli. The ninth, tenth, nineteenth, twenty-sixth and twenty-eighth (unfinished) caves at Ajanta are also Chaityas.

The Stupas were mounds erected over the sacred relics of Buddha or on the spots sanctified by their association with his life. The Stupa at Sanchi in the state of Bhopal in Central India is the most important. Others are at Bharhut, C.P., at Sarnath, Stupas.

near Benares, called the Dhamek Stupa, and at Piprawa in the Basti district (United Provinces). The Amaravati Stupa in the Guntoor district on the Kistna, the Kesariya Stupa in the Chumparan district, and the Gandhara Stupas of Manikyala and Huta Murta or "the Body offering" between Rawal

Exterior of a Vihara, Ajanta.

Pindee and Jhilum, and Shah-ji-ki-deri near Peshawar, and the Mirpur-Khas Stupa should also be mentioned.

Mr. Vincent Smith thus describes the Stupa: "In Asoka's age, a stupa was a solid hemispherical mass of masonry springing from a plinth, which formed a perambulating path for the worshippers, and was flattened at the top to carry a square altar-shaped structure, surmounted by a series of stone umbrellas. The base was usually surmounted by

Sanchi Stupa, General View.

Ranihansapura Cave, Udaygiri.

a stone railing, of which the pillars, bars, and coping-stones were commonly, though not invariably, richly carved and decorated with elaborate sculptures in relief." [1]

The Stupa, with its procession path for *pradakshina*, was enclosed by the sculptured rail, and was divided by four entrances into northern, southern, eastern and western portions, each guarded by its appropriate *Lokapala* or Guardian of the Quarter. It was commonly ornamented by great open lotus flowers symbolising the rising sun. The northern, southern, eastern and western portions of the Stupa, with the pinnacle, were connected with the Five Elements earth, fire, water, air, and ether.

Development of the Lingam and Sikra.

The Stupas are also called Daghobas in Ceylon (from *deh*, a body, and the root *gup*, to hide, or from *dhatu*, a relic, and *gabhan*, a shrine). The Stupa was not a development of the sepulchral tumulus, which was conical, but was derived from the curved bamboo roof built over the primitive circular hut used as a shrine. The Lingam or emblem of Siva is said to have been developed from the Stupa. At first an image of Buddha was placed upon each of the four faces of the Stupa, then these were replaced by a four-headed image of Brahma, with the dome of the Stupa and its pinnacle remaining as the top of his *Mukuta* or Tiara. This dome was afterwards gradually modified into the Lingam. The Sikra or spire, characteristic of Indo-Aryan architecture, is also said to have been developed from the dome of the Stupa by increasing the height more than in proportion to the base, and leaving out four of the eight ribs.

[1] 'Asoka, the Buddhist Emperor of India,' p. 89.

The Stupa at Sanchi is dedicated to "the all respected Sramanas, who by deep meditation have subdued their passions." The edifice has survived to the present day with wonderfully little injury from man and almost unharmed by time. The central relic shrine is encircled by a sculptured rail in which are four gateways on the north, south, east and west. Sanchi.

MIRPUR KHAS STUPA, SIND.

The southern gateway is the earliest of the four, and dates from between 150 and 100 B.C. The carving is perfect, and gives a vivid idea of the everyday life of the people and an accurate picture of animal life. Buddha appears as prince Siddhartha, and in ascetic guise, but he has not yet attained to divine honours.

The Stupa at Bharhut was the work of the Sunga dynasty, which reigned at Magadha B.C. 184-72. Ferguson thus describes the art of which specimens Bharhut.

have been found at Bharhut: "It cannot be too strongly insisted that the art here displayed is

MODEL OF A STUPA AT AMARAVATI.

"Vidyadharas," or attendant spirits, are hovering round the summit, and worshippers in the centre scene are adoring a seat on which a headdress is placed.

perfectly indigenous. There is absolutely no trace of Egyptian influence; it is indeed in every detail antagonistic to that art. Neither is there any trace of classical art ; nor can it be affirmed that anything here could have been borrowed directly from Babylonia or Assyria. The capitals of the pillars do resemble somewhat those of Persepolis ; and the honeysuckle ornaments point in the same direction ; but barring that, everything else, especially the figure sculpture belonging to the rail, seems an art elaborated on the spot by Indians and by Indians only." [1] The Buddhism is still of the Hinayana school only. " Everything is Buddhist, but it is Buddhism without Buddha. He nowhere appears either as a heavenly person to be worshipped or even as an ascetic." [2]

The Bharhut sculptures are some of the oldest known existing examples of Indian art ; they embrace such subjects as the banker Anathapindaka purchasing the garden Jetavana at Sravasti, for the site of a Buddhist monastery, by covering its surface with pieces of gold, the processions of Ajatasatru and Prasenajit to visit Buddha, and the figure of the Sudarsana Yakshini.

Amaravati.

The great railing of the Stupa at Amaravati dates from the half century between A.D. 150 and 200, and all the sculptures of the railing and casing of the lower part of the Stupa belong to the century between A.D. 150 and 250. In these sculptures Buddha appears for the first time as a divine personage.

Daghobas Memorial Stupas.

In Ceylon stupas are called Daghobas (from *deh*, a body, and the root *gup*, to hide, or from *dhatu*, a relic, and *gabhan*, a shrine). In late times, a model of a stupa was often carved out of the solid rock in

[1] Ferguson, ' History of Indian Architecture,' page 89.
[2] *Ibid.*

honour of deceased persons. A large number of these miniature votive model stupas have been discovered at Sakharam in the Vizianagram district.

Jain Stupas.

The Jains also occasionally built stupas, such as the Kankali mound at Mathura, of which the temple railing and many Jain statues are preserved in the museum at Lucknow. A tablet with relief sculpture of a Jain Stupa has been unearthed at Mathura.

Ajanta.

Hinayana. Buddhism.

The caves of Ajanta belong both to the Hinayana and Mahayana schools of Buddhism. The Hinayana school forbade the worship of Buddha as a divinity, but allowed the veneration of the symbols which represented his life on earth or the principles of his teaching, such as his begging bowl, and the prints of his feet, and the Bodhi-tree under which he obtained enlightenment. It could not allow the worship of images, because the teaching of Buddha was agnostic, and denied the existence of a personal God.

Mahayana Buddhism.

Mahayana means the Great Vehicle, or boat, or raft which carries devout worshippers over the ocean of existence. It differs from the Hinayana school in recognising Buddha as a divinity and in permitting the use of images. The founder of the Mahayana school was Nagarjuna, author of one of the Mahayanist Scriptures called 'Prajnaparimita' or Perfected Wisdom, who lived about the middle of the first century A.D. Besides attributing divine honours to Buddha, he created a vast hierarchy of gods (Buddhisattvas), and gave a place in it to the Brahmanical deities: Brahma, Vishnu, Siva, Sarasvati, Ganesh, who were represented with an image of Buddha in their foreheads, and given the title of "Upasaka" or devotee. The Mahayana Buddhism

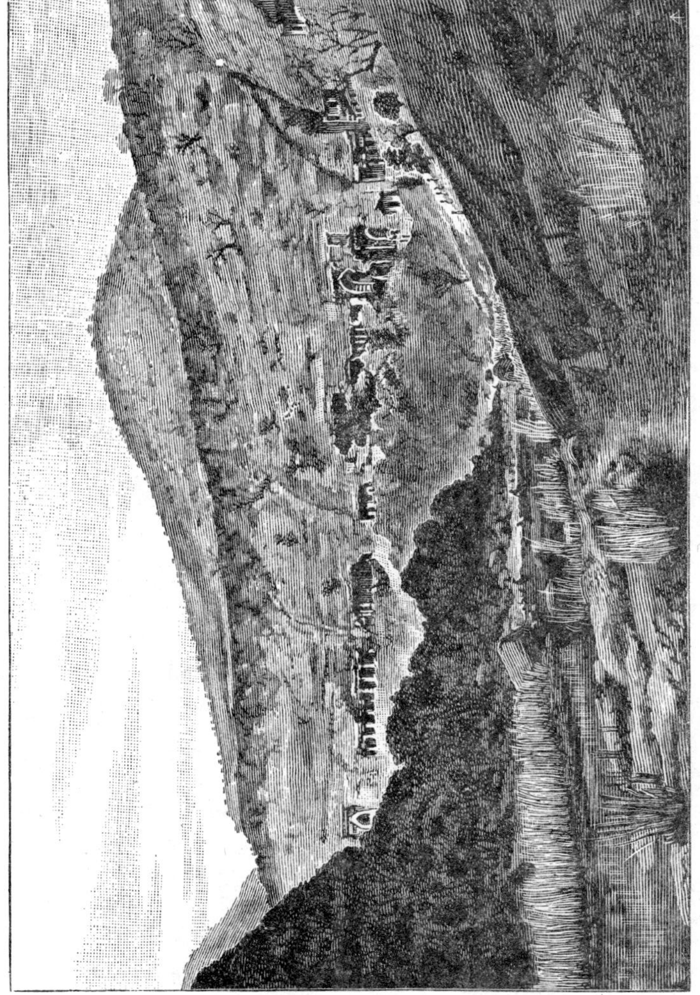

GENERAL VIEW OF AJANTA CAVES.

of Nagarjuna was based upon the philosophy of Yoga as expounded by Patanjali, which contained by implication the doctrine of Incarnation. If the soul within the human body could be joined with the Universal Soul by the spiritual exercises of the Yoga system, the Divinity itself could be manifested in the persons of the teachers of Yoga philosophy. When Buddhist philosophy admitted the possibility of a personal God, it could not acknowledge any other God than Buddha.

The worship of images was only a help and a preparation for those who were unable to understand the abstruse conceptions of Vedic philosophy. "The vulgar look for their gods in water; men of wider knowledge in celestial bodies; the ignorant in wood, clay, or stone; but the wisest men in the Universal Soul. Those who in their ignorance believe that Ishvara is (only) in images of clay or stone, or metal, or wood, merely trouble themselves by their 'tapas.' They can never attain liberation without knowledge. Yoga is the union of the embodied soul with the Supreme Soul. Puja is the union of the worshipper and the worshipped; but he who realises that all things are Brahman, for him there is neither Yoga nor Puja."[1]

At Ajanta, there are twenty-nine caves in all; they are excavated in the almost perpendicular rock, which, bending in a semi-circle, forms the northern side of the valley of the Waghora, a small torrent in the upper basin of the Tapti river.

The caves may be divided into three groups:

1. The first group in the order of age contains the caves numbered, commencing from the east, as VIII.

[1] 'Mahanirvana Tantra,' translated by Arthur Avalon, pp. 348-9.

CORONATION CEREMONY, FROM CAVE I.

The upper part of the panel shows the king on his throne being anointed with holy oil poured out of earthen vessels, and touching offerings made by his queen. In the vestibule other figures are bringing more offerings and oil. Beggars are to be seen outside. Below, women are presenting to a priest heads from human sacrifices.

XI. XII. and XIII. (Viharas), and IX. and X. (Chaityas). These are Hinayana, and date from the second and first centuries B.C. All the rest are Mahayana.

2. The second group contains the caves numbered as XIV. XV. XVI. XVII. and XVIII. (Viharas), and XIX. (Chaitya). These date from the second to the fifth centuries A.D. The date of XVI. XVII. and XVIII. is more clearly indicated by the fact that they were dedicated by the king of the Vatakatas, whose wife was a daughter of Chandragupta II.

3. The third group contains the caves numbered I. to VII. and XX. to XXV. (Viharas), and XXVI. (Chaitya). The great caves XXVII. and XXIX. are unfinished Viharas, and XXVIII. is a Chaitya, but unfinished.

In this group the pillars have the amalaka or lotus fruit capital, the base is square (*Brahma kanta*), above, the pillar is octagonal (*Vishnu kanta*), still higher up, it is circular or sixteen-sided (*Rudra kanta*). These pillars thus recall each of the three persons of the Brahmanic Trinity. The date of this group is approximately the seventh century A.D.

Sarnath. One of the most important relics found at Sarnath is a seated statue of Buddha dressed in a smooth, close-fitting robe, and with the head crowned by an elaborately ornamented aureole. Both these features point to the statue being late work. The top of the Lat or pillar found at Sarnath has also been preserved. Two lions, standing back to back, crowned the pillar, and the abacus or space under the two animals, sculptured on the top, is ornamented by figures of bulls and the Wheel of the Law.

Mathura. Mathura is remarkable for the statue of " Hercules

Temptation of Buddha by Mara. From Cave I, Ajanta.

and the Nemean lion," and for the so-called "Bacchanalian" images typical of a sensual form of popular Buddhism, which may have been associated with the worship of the Yakshas or sprites; of these the most remarkable is the "Stacy Silenus." The two lions

KAILASA TEMPLE AT ELLORA.

carved in red sandstone and covered with Kharosthi characters are evidence for the existence of a dynasty of Saka Satraps at Mathura.

At Ellora there are twelve Buddhist, fifteen Brahman, and five Jain caves and the Kailas temple. Of the Buddhist caves, the most remarkable is the Chaitya in the Viswakarma or Carpenter's Cave. Among the Brahman caves, the *Dumar Lena* or *Sitaki nahani* is a reproduction of Elephanta on a larger scale, and has carvings of Ravana shaking Kailasa, the Marriage of Siva and Parvati, and of Siva dancing the "*tandava*" dance. The Das Avatara has two other remarkable carvings of Siva in the form of Bhairava, and of Siva rescuing Markandeya from Yama.

Ellora, Buddhist and Brahman caves.

The Kailasa temple was built by the Rashtrakuta king Krishna I. about the middle of the eighth century, on the model of the temple of Virupaksha at Pattadakal. Like the Seven Raths of Mamallapuram or Mahabalipuram, near Chingleput, the temple is carved out of the solid rock. Another such temple is that of Kalugumalai in Tinnevelly. Hindus, when excavating temples in rock, which they did in imitation of the Buddhists, unlike them, cleared away all the surrounding stone, so as to allow the temple thus carved to be distinctly seen, as is done in the Kailasa temple at Ellora, and at Dhumnar in Rajputana.

The Kailasa temple.

The Kailasa temple was so called, because the hill on which it stands, and the streams and waterfalls near it, formed a copy in miniature of the mountain sacred to Siva in the Himalayas and of the mighty rivers which rise near by. To construct the temple, a pit 50 to 100 yards deep, 250 feet long, and 160 feet wide had to be quarried out of the side of the hill, and a double-storied temple, twice as large as that of Pattadakal, carved out of the rock thus separated off.

Forming the entrance, which faces west, like all Siva shrines, is a *Gopuram,* and connected with it by a bridge cut out of the rock is a two-storied shrine for Nandi Siva's *vahan.* On either side of the Nandi shrine are two *dhwaja-stambhas* surmounted by Siva's *trisul.* A second rock-bridge connects the Nandi shrine with the twelve-pillared *mandapam,* which has a fine porch. The *mandapam* has doors, on each side of the *Antarala* or Inner Chamber, by which worshippers can enter and depart, after performing *Pradakshina* round the *Garbha Griha,* or Holy of Holies. The *Vimana,* or Inner Shrine, rests on a plinth about 27 feet high, ornamented with a frieze of elephants. This basement provides a procession path round the *Garbha Griha,* and the procession path has shrines at the corners and in the middle of its three sides, with the *Garbha Griha* in the middle. On the north is the shrine of Ganesa, god of the reasoning faculties, who is always invoked on the commencement of any undertaking. On the north-east corner is the shrine of Bhairava (Siva in his destructive aspect). On the east is the shrine of Parvati. On the south-east is the shrine of the scavenging deity, Chanda. On the south is the shrine of the Seven Mothers of Creation.

The roof of the *Antarala* rises above that of the *mandapam,* and has a window in it, in which stands a statue of Siva as a Jogi, with his right hand raised in the attitude of teaching. The highest point of the temple is the tower of the *Garbha Griha,* which is crowned with a stupa dome, as is usual in Siva shrines. On the south, cut out of the solid rock, is the largest of the side chapels, called Lankesvara,

CHAPTER IV.

THE EMPIRE OF ASOKA, ANDHRA, SCYTHIAN, GUPTA, AND KSHATRAPA KINGS.

Asoka.

CHANDRA GUPTA deposed the last king of Magadha of the Nanda dynasty in B.C. 317, and reigned till B.C. 292. His son, Bindusara Amitraghata (slayer of foes, Greek, *Amitrachates*), reigned till 272. Bindusara's second son Asoka succeeded him, and reigned till his death in B.C. 218. Asoka's empire was the most successful attempt to bring all India "under one umbrella" that the country ever saw till it passed under English sway. We have seen that Darius Hystaspes included a portion of India in the Persian empire; we now see that an empire with its capital in India included extensive territories beyond Indian borders.

Indian and external civilisation begin to influence each other.

In both cases the result was the same: Indian and external civilisation began to influence each other. The missionary spirit of Buddhism spread the religious even beyond the political influence of India, and Sir Aurel Stein's recent discoveries in Chinese Turkestan show how widespread the religious influence of India was, and that the isolation of India was less complete in former times than it is now. Civilisation in Chinese Turkestan was extinguished by the drying up of the country, which was probably brought about by the sudden elevation of mountains, which blocked out the rain-bearing winds. There are similar relics of extinct civilisation in Beluchistan and Seistan.

Asoka conquered Bengal and Kalinga (the west coast of the Bay of Bengal from the river Mahanadi on the north to the Kistna on the south), the name of which survives in Kalingapatam. Remorse for the infliction of the horrors of war upon this country led to his becoming a Buddhist. After his conversion

Asoka's Edicts.

he published in Prakrit certain edicts and inscriptions on the principles and practice of his new religion, which were engraved on rocks and pillars in various places in a tract of country stretching from Shahbazgarhi, 40 miles N.E. of Peshawar, to Brahmagiri in Mysore. These edicts differ considerably in the dialects used and in the character in which they are written.

Dialects.

The dialects are *Punjabi*, distinguishable by the use of the subjoined R, and by the little distinction made between long and short vowels; *Ujjaini* (edicts of Girnar and Rupnath), which use R as well as L; and *Magadhi*, which has no R, *e.g.* Laja for Raja. Dasalatha for Dasaratha.

Characters.

The characters used are Kharosthi, which is read from right to left. Kharosthi is the alphabet used in N.W. India, and is a variety of the Aramaic character. In this, the Shahbazgarhi and Mansera edicts are written; it is also used for the inscriptions on the coins of the Greek and Scythian princes of Ariana (Herat). The other edicts and inscriptions of Asoka are written in the Brahmi character, which is read from left to right. The

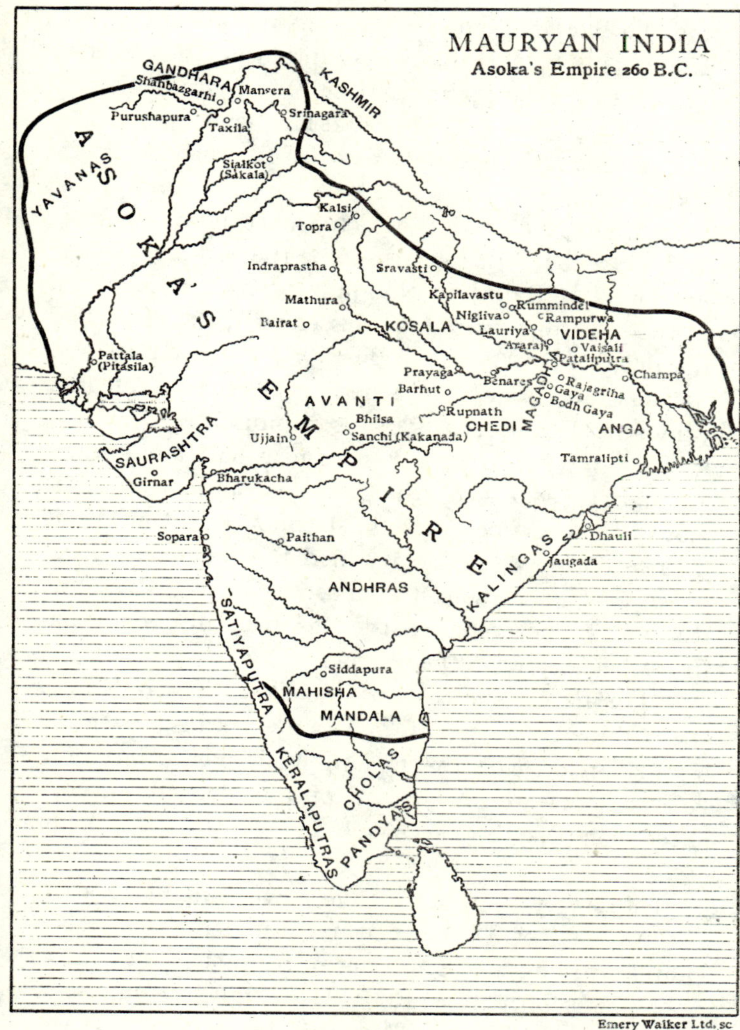

Emery Walker Ltd. sc

Brahmi characters were first read by means of the coins of the Greek princes reigning in Afghanistan and the Panjab from about B.C. 250 to about A.D. 25. These coins have a Greek inscription on the obverse, and on the reverse a translation of the Greek inscription in an Indian character and language.

Classification of the edicts and inscriptions.

The edicts and inscriptions of Asoka may be classified as follows:

Minor Rock Edicts.

1. Minor Rock Edicts, which Senart, F. W. Thomas, and Vincent Smith consider to be the earliest. These are found at Bairat in the Jaipur State, at Rupnath in the Jabalpur district, at Sasseram in the Shahabad district, Bengal, at Brahmagiri, Siddapura, and Jatinga-ramesvara in northern Mysore. In the first Minor Rock Edict, Asoka says of himself:

Fruit of exertion.

"For more than two years and a half I was a lay disciple (upasaka, of the Buddhist order) without, however, exerting myself strenuously. But it is more than a year since I joined the order, and have since exerted myself strenuously. During this time the gods, who were regarded as true all over India, have been shown to be untrue.

"For this is the fruit of exertion. Nor is this to be attained by a great man only, because, even by a small man, who exerts himself, immense heavenly bliss may be won. For this purpose has the precept been composed; Let small and great exert themselves."

The precept is said to have been composed by the "Viyutha" or Traveller, a name under which Asoka alludes to himself on account of his pious tours.

Summary of the Law of Piety.

The second Minor Rock Edict gives a summary of the Law of Piety. Thus saith his Sacred Majesty: "Father and mother must be hearkened to; similarly, respect for living creatures must be firmly established;

truth must be spoken. These are the virtues of the Law of Piety which must be practised. Similarly, the teacher must be reverenced by the pupil, and towards relations fitting courtesy should be shown. This is the ancient nature of piety—this leads to length of days, and according to this men must act."

The Bhabra Edict.

2. The Bhabra Edict is found at Bairat in the Jaipur State. It is addressed to the Buddhist Sangha and names seven passages of the Buddhist scriptures, and the short text, "Thus the Good Law will long endure," as special favourites with Asoka.

The Rock Edicts.

3. The Rock Edicts are fourteen in number. They are generally assigned to the thirteenth and fourteenth years of Asoka's reign, B.C. 257 and 256, dating from his coronation or consecration (*abhiseka*) in B.C. 269. They are found at seven sites, Shahbazgarhi in the Yusufzai country, Mansera in the Hazara district, Kalsi in the Dehra Dun district, U.P., Sopara in the Thana district, Bombay, Girnar in Junagarh State, Kathiawar, Dhauli in the Puri district near Bhubanesvar, and Jaugada in the Gangam district, Madras, 18 miles N.W. of the town of Ganjam.

Date.

Sites.

Sacredness of animal life.

The first Rock Edict inculcates the sacredness of life, and forbids the slaughter of animals for sacrifice, or holiday-feasts.

"Curative arrangements" for man and beast.

The second mentions the "curative arrangements" both for man and beast ordered in Asoka's dominions as well as among his neighbours, the Cholas, Pandyas, the people of Satiyaputra, the people of Keralaputra, "Antiochus the Greek, and likewise the kings near unto that Antiochus." Wells have been dug and trees planted along the roadsides.

Quinquennial circuits to proclaim the Law of Piety.

In the third, Asoka orders his commissioners (*rajjuka*) and his district officers (*pradesika*) to go on quinquennial circuits (*anusamyana*) to proclaim the Law of Piety.

The practice of Piety.

The fourth deals with the practice of piety. Asoka prides himself that " now by reason of the practice of piety by his Sacred and Gracious Majesty the King, instead of the sound of the war-drum, the sound of the drum of piety is heard, whilst heavenly spectacles of processional cars, elephants, illuminations, and the like are displayed to the people."

Censors of the Law of Piety.

By the fifth, censors of the Law of Piety (dhamma-mahamatra) are appointed.

Prompt despatch of business.

Asoka, in the sixth Rock Edict, announces his willingness to hear reports on the people's business in all places and at all hours. " Work I must for the welfare of all and the root of the matter is in effort, and the dispatch of business, for nothing is more efficacious to secure the welfare of all. And for what do I toil ? For no other end than this, that I may discharge my debt to animate beings, and that while I make some happy here, they may in the next world gain heaven."

Imperfect fulfilment of the law.

In the seventh Rock Edict, Asoka desires that " in all places men of every denomination (*pashanda*) may abide, for they all desire mastery over the senses and purity of mind." Even partial fulfilment of the law is better than nothing.

Tours of piety.

In the eighth, tours of piety for visiting ascetics, Brahmans, the country, and the people, and for inculcating and discussing the Law of Piety are substituted by Asoka for hunting.

True ceremonial.

In the ninth, true ceremonial is defined as including

"the proper treatment of slaves and servants, honour to teachers, gentleness towards living creatures, and liberality towards ascetics and Brahmans."

In the tenth, Asoka expresses his opinion that true glory consists in obediently hearkening to the Law of Piety, and in conforming to its precepts. "Whatever exertions his Majesty King Priyadarshin has made, all are made with a view to the life hereafter, so that everyone may be freed from peril, which peril is sin. Difficult, very difficult it is to attain such freedom, whether a man be of high or low degree, save by the utmost exertion and complete self-denial, but specially difficult it is for the man of high degree." True glory.

In the eleventh, Asoka declares "there is no such almsgiving as is the almsgiving of the Law of Piety—friendship in piety, the distribution of piety, kinship in piety." True almsgiving.

In the twelfth Rock Edict, Asoka 'cares not so much for gifts or external reverence, as that there should be a growth of the essence of the matter in all sects. The growth of the essence of the matter assumes various forms, but the root of it is restraint of speech, to wit, a man must not do reverence to his own sect or disparage that of another without reason. Disparagement should be for specific reasons only, because the sects of other people all deserve reverence for one reason or another." Toleration.

The thirteenth Rock Edict declares Asoka's remorse for inflicting the horrors of war upon the Kalingas. He considers that "the chiefest conquest" is the conquest by the Law of Piety. This he has won both in his own dominions, and in all the neighbouring realms as far as six hundred leagues to the country, True conquest.

where the Yona (Greek) king Antiochus II. (surnamed Theos, king of Syria, B.C. 261-46) dwells, and, north of that king, as far as the dwelling-places of the four kings severally named Ptolemy (Philadelphus, king of Egypt, B.C. 285-47), Antigonus (Gonatas of Macedon, B.C. 277-39), Magas (of Cyrene, B.C. 285-258), and Alexander of Epirus, who died between B.C. 262 and B.C. 258.

In the fourteenth Rock Edict, Asoka explains that the form of the edicts has been "sometimes condensed, sometimes written at medium length, and sometimes expanded, for everything is not suitable in every place, for my dominions are extensive, and much has been written and much I shall cause to be written."

The Kalinga Edicts.

4. The two Kaḷinga Edicts are substituted for Rock Edicts XI., XII. and XIII. not published in Kalinga. That found at Jaugada is called "the Borderers' Edict," and addressed to the officers of Samapa, a town probably situated near by. It lays down the duty incumbent on the king's officers to treat the "unsubdued borderers" considerately. That found at Dhauli is called "the Provincials' Edict," and addressed to the officers of Tosali, who are instructed not to imprison or ill-use the king's subjects without due cause. Vincent Smith gives the date of these two edicts as B.C. 256.

The Pillar Edicts. Sites.

5. Pillars inscribed with edicts have been found at Delhi, where one pillar stands on the summit of the Kothila of Firozabad, to which place it was removed by Firoz Shah Tughlak in 1356 from Topra in the Umballa district; another was removed from Meerut by Firoz Shah Tughlak at the same time as

the other Delhi pillar, and erected by the English Government on the Ridge at Delhi in 1867. Another pillar is found at Allahabad, where the column is

Asoka's Pillar, Allahabad.

inscribed with Pillar Edicts I.-VI., the Queen's and the Kausambi Edict, and an inscription by Samudra Gupta. Cunningham conjectures that this pillar was removed from Kausambi, 90 miles S.W. of Allahabad, by Firoz Tughlak. Other sites are

Lauriya Araraj, Lauriya Nandangarh or Mathia, and Rampurwa in the Chumparun district, Bengal, and Sanchi in the Bhopal State, Central India. The pillar at Sanchi stands at the southern entrance of the Stupa.

The Pillars or Lats have, when perfect, an animal sculptured on the top, one of the four Guardians of the Quarters, the elephant guardian of the East, the bull of the West, the lion of the North, and the horse of the South. The abacus or space under the animal sculptured on the top is variously ornamented, sometimes by a row of flying geese, sometimes by designs composed of lotus and honeysuckles. The Sarnath Lat has two lions back to back, and the abacus is ornamented by figures of bulls and of the Wheel of the Law. The capitals are generally the Persepolitan Bell, or the *Amalaka* (lotus fruit).

The complete series of Pillar Edicts is only found on the Allahabad-Topra Pillar. Pillar Edict VII. is not found on the other pillars. Vincent Smith gives the date of the seven Pillar Edicts as 242 B.C.

The principles of government.

The first Pillar Edict deals with the principles of government. In the words of Asoka: "Both this world and the next are hard to secure save by intense love of the Law of Piety, intense self-examination, intense dread, and intense effort. However, owing to my instructions, this yearning and love of the Law of Piety from day to day have grown and will grow."

The king's own example.

In the second Pillar Edict, the king enquires "Wherein consists the Law of Piety?" He answers his own question thus: "In these things, to wit, in abstinence from impiety, in many good deeds, compassion, liberality, truthfulness, and purity. The gift of spiritual insight I have given in manifold ways; on two-footed and four-footed creatures, on birds and the denizens of the waters, I have conferred various favours even unto the boon of life, and many other good deeds have I done."

Self-examination.

The third Pillar Edict inculcates the duty of self-examination.

Powers and duties of the commissioners.

The fourth Pillar Edict describes the powers and duties of the commissioners (*Rajjuka*). "They will ascertain the causes of happiness and sorrow, and, through the (subordinate) officials of the Law of Piety, will exhort the people of the country so that they may gain this world and the next." A respite of three days is to be given to all condemned men lying in prison under sentence of death, that they may devote themselves to deep meditation, or that their relatives may present offerings and undergo fasts to promote the pious meditation of the criminals in the interval.

Regulations restricting the slaughter and mutilation of animals.

The fifth Pillar Edict contains regulations which restrict the slaughter or mutilation of animals.

Object of the edicts.

In the sixth Pillar Edict Asoka says, "after I had been consecrated twelve years, I caused pious edicts (Rock Edicts III. and IV.) to be written for the welfare and happiness of mankind, with the intent that they, giving up their old courses, might attain growth in piety one way and another."

Summary of Asoka's steps taken to spread the Law of Piety.

In the seventh Pillar Edict, Asoka sums up the measures he has taken to spread the knowledge of Dharma. These were the orders to commissioners to give instruction in the Law of Piety, the appointment of censors of the Law of Piety, and the erection of Pillars on which it was inscribed, his endeavour to inculcate it by the force of his own personal example, the planting of trees, the erection of rest houses, and the digging of wells at every half kos along the roads, and the institution of a department to superintend the charities of the king, his queens, and relatives.

Minor Pillar Edicts.

6. The Minor Pillar I. at Sarnath, and the Minor Pillar Edict II., or the Edict to the officers of Kausambi, on the column inscribed with the Third Pillar Edict at Allahabad, order that all monks or nuns, who "break the unity of the Church," are to be deprived of their saffron garments, and to be compelled to put on white clothes, and to dwell in a place not reserved for the clergy. The Minor Pillar Edict III. at Sanchi is also to the same effect.

Minor Pillar Edict IV., or the Queen's Edict, also inscribed on the same column as the third Pillar Edict at Allahabad, orders that all acts of charity done by the Second Queen are to be ascribed to her under the title of "the Karuvạki, mother of Tivara." Vincent Smith gives the date of the Minor Pillar Edicts as B.C. 240.

Commemorative inscriptions.

7. Two commemorative inscriptions of Asoka are found in the Nepal Terai at Rummindei, near the Tilar river, and at Nigliva. Both places were apparently visited by Asoka on one of his "pious tours." At Rummindei, the inscription commemorated the birthplace of Buddha at the Lumbini garden, and at Nigliva the subject of the inscription was the enlargement for the second time by Asoka of the stupa dedicated to Kanakamuni or Konakamana, one of the Buddhas who preceded Gautama. Vincent Smith gives the date of these inscriptions as B.C. 249.

Cave dedications.

8. In the Barabạr caves, near Gaya, are several inscriptions by Asoka commemorating his dedication

of the caves, which he caused to be cut out of the solid granite, to the Ajivikas (a sect resembling the Jains), and founded by Makkhali Gosala. Asoka's dedications, according to Vincent Smith, were made in the years B.C. 257 and 250. A similar dedication on the part of his grandson Dasaratha is found in the Nagarjuni caves near by.

The translations given above are quoted from Mr. Vincent Smith's 'Edicts of Asoka,' and the same author sums up the teaching of the Edicts thus: "The Edicts reveal Asoka as a man who sought to combine the piety of the monk with the wisdom of the king, to make India a kingdom of righteousness as he conceived it, a theocracy without a God; in which the government should act the part of Providence, and guide the people in the right way. Every man, he maintained, must work out his own salvation, and eat the fruit of his deeds." [1]

Teaching of the Edicts summed up.

Asoka in the ninth year of his reign, B.C. 261, joined the Buddhist order as a lay brother, in the eleventh, B.C. 259, he became a member of the order (Minor Rock Edict I.). In the thirteenth, B.C. 257, "he set out for the great wisdom" (sambodhi), *i.e.* he completely adopted Buddhist ideals.

What we learn of Asoka and his empire from the Edicts.

The northern boundary of Asoka's empire was the Hindu Kush mountains. It included Afghanistan, Beluchistan, Sind, and all India down to a line drawn from the mouth of the Palar river near Sadras in the Chingleput district on the east coast, to the river Chandragiri in the Malabar district on the west coast, roughly corresponding with the twelfth parallel

[1] Vincent Smith, 'The Edicts of Asoka,' introduction, p. xiii.

of north latitude. Each pergana or *vishaya* was under the control of a *vishayapati*, the *Pradesika* or District Officers were under the control of the Rajjuka or commissioners, and the *Rajjuka* under the Viceroys. The Kambojas of Kabul (or, according to some authorities, Thibet), the Gandharas and Yavanas of the Kabul valley, the Rashtikas of Maharashtra and Saurashtra (Gujrat), the Bhojas of Vidarbha or Berar, the Petenikas and Pulindas of the Deccan, and the Andhra kingdom between the Godaveri and Kistna rivers were among the protected tribes and states of the empire, under the name of *Aparatanta* (Rock Edicts V. and XIII.).

The Cholas, Pandyas, and the people of Keralaputra (Travancore), and Satiyaputra (Mangalore), and five Greek kingdoms, are spoken of as *Pratyanta* or independent (Rock Edicts II. and XIII.).

Asoka's empire was ruled from Patna, with viceroyalties at Ujjain, Taxila (identified by Cunningham with a site near Kali ki serai station on the North-western Railway between Rawul Pindee and Hassan Abdul); Tosali (for Kalinga) and Suvarnagiri (for the south). The sites of the last two places have not been identified.

Subsequent dynasties at Magadha.

Asoka died in B.C. 232 (or, according to other authorities, B.C. 218), in religious retirement on Suvarnagiri (Songir), one of the hills surrounding Girivraja, a city below Rajgriha. The Maurya dynasty came to an end in B.C. 184, when Pushyamitra, who was the general of Brihadratha, the last Maurya king, slew him and founded the Sunga dynasty, which reigned B.C. 184-72. Pushyamitra is said to have performed the *Asvamedha* or horse sacrifice to advance his claim to supreme power in India. In Pushyamitra's reign Menander, the Greek king of Kabul and the Panjab, who is the king mentioned in the Milindapanha, marched as far as Mathura and Oudh about B.C. 155-153. The kings of the Sunga race founded the Bharhut Stupa in Central India between Allahabad and Jubulpur. They were Brahmans of the Sama Veda school, and therefore familiar with horse sacrifices. They were succeeded by the Kanva dynasty B.C. 72-27. The Kanvas were overthrown by the Andhras.

Empire of the Andhras, 208 B.C. to A.D. 249.

A most important empire was founded by the Andhras, whose capital were Dhanakataka, probably to be identified with the Buddhist Amaravati, on the Kistna, in the Guntur district on the S.E., Pratishthana or Paithan (Greek Plithana) on the upper waters of the Godavery in Aurungabad district on the N.W., and Vaijayanti, modern Banavasi, in the N. Kanara district of the Bombay presidency. The Andhras rose to power about B.C. 180 and continued to exercise sovereignty till 249 A.D. The name of the dynasty was Satavahana or Satakarna, and it was founded by Semuka Satavahana. An inscription in one of the Nasik caves speaks of Queen Gautami, who gave a village to the Buddhist monks in the nineteenth year of her grandson Sri Pulumayu Vasisthiputra Gautami, was the mother of the Satakarna Gautamiputra, sometimes called Vilivayakura II. (the Baleokuros of the Greeks). He established the glory of his dynasty, and is mentioned as the destroyer of the Sakas and Yavanas, who were perhaps Scythian and Indo-Bactrian invaders from Gujrat. The Andhra kings were constantly fighting with the Kshatrapas of

Saurashtra, and were assisted in their wars by the Tamil kings. They had some control over the coasts of Orissa, Bengal, and Arracan ; on this account they styled themselves in inscriptions " lords of the three Kalingas." Gautamiputra or Vilivayakura was a contemporary of the Kshatrapa Nahapana, whom he overthrew A.D. 126. Rudradaman's inscription at Girnar says that he " obtained glory, because he did not destroy the Satakarna Dakshinapati, on account of their relationship, although he had twice conquered him." Their power did not, however, completely

Sri Pulumayu. Reverse : the Ujjain symbol

ANDHRA COINS.

disappear till about 431 A.D. The Andhras are represented in modern times by the Telegus, and the Pergunnah Andhari near the Chilka lake in Orissa marks the modern limit of the power of the Andhras. The Andhra coins are chiefly marked with an elephant which was also the cognisance of the Chera dynasty. Other Andhra coins bear the design of a sailing ship, thus testifying to the prevalence of commerce at the time.

This commerce was chiefly carried on with the coast of Pegu, and with the Talaing kingdom, of which Thatun, called Sadhammanagara by the Hindus, was the capital. The Burmese call the people whom they found in the country Talaing or foreigners, a name which is said to be a corruption of Telegu. Another Hindu settlement in Burma was Thara-khetra near Prome.

Contemporary with the empire of the Andhras was the kingdom founded by the Scythians under Kadphises I., A.D. 45-85, and his son and successor Kadphises II. (Wima or Hima), A.D. 85-120 or 125. The name of the Scythians or Sakas is perpetuated in that of the Persian province of Drangiana or Seistan (Sakastene). Their original home has been discovered by Sir Aurel Stein to have been in the Chinese province of Kansu. Their first appearance is said by some authors to be contemporaneous with the Vikrama era of B.C. 57, by others with the Salivahana era of A.D. 78. They penetrated into the Panjab and destroyed the Greek kingdom of the family of Euthydemus there about B.C. 100. They even progressed as far as Mathura, where the Kharosthi inscription on the pair of red sandstone lions tells us of the existence of a dynasty of Saka satraps. Other sections established themselves in Kathiawar, at Kapisa, capital of Gandhara, and at Taxila. Kadphises united a number of Scythian tribes under the name of Kushan. **The Scythian or Yueh Chi, or Kushan kings.**

Kadphises II. is distinguished among the kings of India as having sent an embassy to congratulate the Roman emperor, Trajan, on his arrival at Rome A.D. 99. The Scythians held the Indus valley and Bactria, and therefore their alliance against the Parthians and Persian Sassanians was useful to the Romans ; so the object of this embassy may have been to negotiate an alliance.

Kanishka, the Kanerkes of the Greek coins, probably **Kanishka.**

succeeded Kadphises II. about the year A.D. 120, and his reign lasted till about the year A.D. 150. His capital was Purushapura (Peshawar), and his empire extended from Kashgar, Yarkand, and Khotan in Central Asia, which he conquered, to the Vindhya mountains in India on the south. It also included Upper Sind. It was owing to the conquest of Khotan that Buddhism was extended to China. Panchao, the Chinese general, defeated the Kushan king of Kabul in Yarkand or Kashgar. After Panchao's death, the Kushan king recovered Khotan between the years A.D. 101 and 123. Hence the extension of the Indian language, script, religion, and art into Chinese Turkestan, and from Chinese Turkestan into China. Kanishka was to northern what Asoka was to southern Buddhism. He, A.D. 143, held a council at Jullundur of the Buddhists of the Northern or Mahayana school, which is distinguished by its worship of Buddha as a divinity and of the Buddhisattvas as subordinate deities. The council was held under the presidency of Nagarjuna or Nagasena, and prepared commentaries on the Pitakas. These commentaries were the Upadesa Sastra on the Sutta Pitaka, the Vinaya Vibhasa Sastra on the Vinaya Pitaka, and the Abhidamma Vibhasa Sastra on the Abhidarma Pitaka. They were composed in Sanscrit, and thus mark the preference of the Mahayana school of Buddhists for that language. The council reconciled as mutually compatible the doctrines of the eighteen schools of Buddhism, which by this time had come into existence. The inscriptions of Kanishka have been found in Afghanistan, in the Panjab mountains, and as far east as Mathura.

Conquest of Khotan.

Kanishka's son and successor was Huvishka, founder of a Buddhist monastery at Mathura, and after him came Vasishka or Vasudeva, whose name shows how rapidly the Kushans had become Hinduised. A pillar has been found at Mathura inscribed with the title "Maharajah Shahi Vashishka." After this king, the power of the Kushans in Northern India appears to have declined, though they held their own for some time afterwards in the Panjab and at Kabul.

Scythian coins.

Coins of Hermæus, the last Greek king, have the name of Kadphises added, showing that Kadphises

Coin of Kadphises.
Reverse: Siva on bull Nandi.

retained the services of Hermæus as a Satrap. The reverse has Siva in the androgynous form of Ardhanarishvara, with his hair dressed in a pointed topknot (jada), a rayed nimbus, and a garland of skulls. Siva is considered as the equivalent of Apollo, if androgynous of Apollo and Artemis. Some coins of Kadphises have the effigy of the Roman emperor Augustus, some an Indian bull on the obverse and a Bactrian camel on the reverse. Kanishka's coins have on the reverse the inscriptions Helios, Mithra or Mithro (the Persian sun), others Nannaia or Nana, the Persian equivalent of Artemis. There is a strange medley of Greek, Persian, and Indian gods on the Scythian coins, including Herakles with his club and Siva with his *trisul*.

The Gupta kings. The period between the downfall of the Andhra and Kushan dynasties about A.D. 220 or 230, and the rise of the Gupta kings, a century later, is one of which we know very little.

1. Samudra Gupta.

2. Obverse: *Asvamedha* Horse. Reverse: Queen Dutta Devi.

COINS OF SAMUDRA GUPTA.

The Gupta kings of Kanauj on the west bank of the Kali Nadi in the Farukhabad district, U.P., absorbed the kingdom of the Andhras into their empire, and reigned from about A.D. 319 to 480. The chronology of this dynasty has been cleared up by Mr. Fleet. According to him the year 1 of the Gupta dynasty is A.D. 319-20. The rise of this dynasty dates from A.D. 308, when Chandra Gupta I., a raja who reigned at or near Pataliputra, married Kumara Devi, a princess of the Lichchavis at Vaisali. He extended his power over Tirhut, Behar and Oudh, and died in the year A.D. 326, leaving the throne to his son Samudra Gupta. Samudra Gupta reigned from A.D. 326-76 and his dominions extended from the Hughli on the east to the Jumna and Chambal on the west, and from the Himalayas on the north to the Narbada on the south, with the kingdoms of Samatata (mouths of the Ganges and Brahmaputra), Davaka (Bogra, Dinajpur and Rajshahi districts), Kamrup (Assam), and Kartripura (Kumaon, Almora, Garhwal and Kangra) in subordinate alliance. The extent of his empire is recorded in an inscription on the Kausambi lat at Allahabad. In token of his supremacy, Samudra Gupta performed the *Asvamedha* or horse sacrifice, which had not been celebrated in India since the time of Pushyamitra, and issued coins with the effigy of a horse upon them in token of having performed the horse sacrifice, thus showing the revival of Brahman influence. During Samudra Gupta's reign, Meghavarma, the Buddhist king of Ceylon, founded the Buddh Gaya temple monastery. Chandra Gupta II. succeeded and reigned A.D. 375-413. Chandra Gupta II. subdued the Arjunayas, Malavas, and Abhiras of Eastern Rajputana, and Malwa, and the peninsula of Saurashtra, or Kathiawar. Chandra Gupta II. is identified by Mr. V. A. Smith with the Vikramaditya of Sanscrit literature, whose court was frequented by the "Nine Gems." The difficulty in accepting this identification lies in the fact that the "Nine Gems" were not contemporary with each other. Inscriptions tell us that the sixteenth and seventeenth caves at Ajanta were excavated by a king of the Vatakatas who married Chandra Gupta's daughter.

Other Gupta kings were Kumara Gupta, 413-55. Kumara Gupta set up the Iron pillar at Delhi in memory of his father, Chandra Gupta II. Skanda Gupta, 455-80, erected the Bhitari Lat, 455 A.D., in the Ghazipur district, to record on his father's *Sradh* pillar his own victory over the Huns. Pura Gupta was king in the Eastern provinces only. Pura Gupta's son, Nara Simha (Baladitya) took part with Yasadharmadeva in defeating the Huns. Of the Gupta age as a whole, A.D. 326 to 500, Vincent Smith speaks thus: "To the same age probably should be assigned the principal Puranas in their present form; the metrical legal treatises of which the so-called Code of Manu is the most familiar example; and, in short, the mass of the classical Sanscrit literature. The patronage of the great Gupta emperors gave, as Professor Bhandarkar observes, 'a general literary impulse,' which extended to every department and gradually raised Sanscrit to the position which it long retained as the sole literary language of Northern India. The golden age of the Guptas, glorious in literary as in political history, comprised a period of a century and a quarter (330 to 455 A.D.), and was covered by three reigns of exceptional length. The death of Kumara Gupta, early in 455, marks the beginning of the decline and fall of the empire." [1]

The Bhitari Lat.

The golden age of the Guptas.

Government of the Guptas.

In the Gupta period, Krishna worship first began to flourish by its union of *karma yoga* with *jnana yoga*. The power of the Gupta kings depended upon the recognition of the principle of self-government based upon the village communities. The

[1] 'Early History of India,' pp. 267-8.

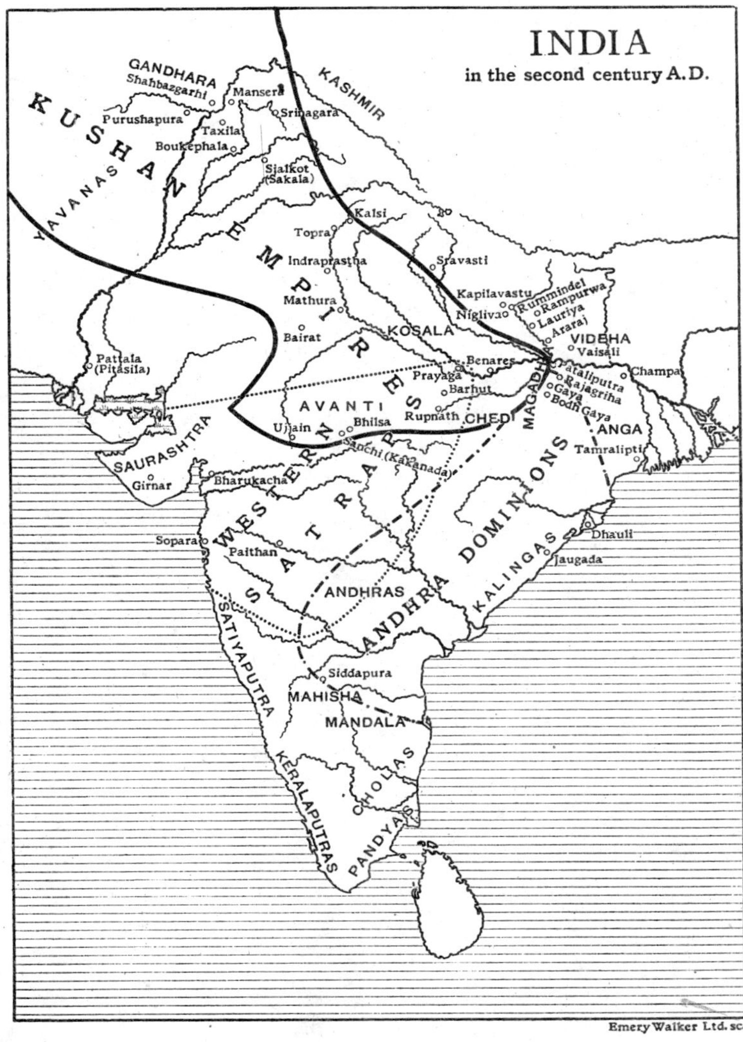

qualifications for membership of these village communities seem to have been somewhat oligarchic. A member had to own more than a quarter of a veli of tax-paying, though if he was a Brahman and learned in one Veda and one of the four Bhasyas, the ownership of one-eighth of a veli would suffice ; he must own a freehold house and live in it ; he must be more than thirty-five and less than seventy-five years of age ; he must know and be qualified to teach the Mantras and Brahmanas.

The Raja presided over a confederation of villages, the Maharaja was the head of a confederation of clans, and the occupant of the throne was the suzerain of the Maharajas as the champion of the Hindu religion. All land belonged to the king, and paid as land tax a certain proportion of the produce graduated according to the means of irrigation used. All the villages also gave customary offerings, which were divided in various proportions between the Rajas, Maharajas and the occupant of the throne.

Kshatrapas of Saurashtra.

Saurashtra or Kathiawar was ruled by the dynasty of the Kshatrapas, who were originally the viceroys of the Kushan kings. The first member of the Kshatrapa dynasty was Nahapana, who set up the inscription in the Nasik caves. He reigned about the beginning of the second century A.D., but his power was overthrown by the Andhra king Vilivayakura II. (or Gautamiputra). Chashtana, another Kshatrapa, conquered Ujjain and Gujrat, but he was reduced to great straits by the Andhra king Pulumayu. Chashtana's grandson Rudradaman rebelled against the Andhra kings, and compelled them to cede Kathiawar, Malwa, Cutch, Sind and the Konkan, about the middle of the second century A.D. The Nasik cave inscriptions relate chiefly to the grant of fields and villages to the Buddhist community by princes of this dynasty. An inscription having reference to Rudradaman is found at Girnar; the Girnar inscription gives his date as equivalent to A.D. 150. The Kshatrapa dynasty was overthrown by Chandra Gupta II. about the year A.D. 388.

Fa Hian, the Chinese pilgrim, visited India about A.D. 406-412. He says that he came to India to search for the Laws and Precepts of the Buddhist religion, "Because he had been distressed in Chang'an (Sian in Shensi, his native province) to observe the Precepts and the theological works on the point of being lost, and already disfigured by lacunæ." He speaks of the record of his travels thus: "The present is a mere summary. Not having been heard by the Masters (the learned body to whom he presented it) hitherto, he (Fa Hian) casts not his eyes retrospectively on details. He crossed the sea and hath returned, after having overcome every manner of fatigue, and has enjoyed the happiness of receiving many high and noble favours. He has been in dangers and has escaped them. And now therefore he puts upon the bamboo what has happened to him, anxious to communicate to the wise what he has seen and heard." After leaving China till he crossed the Indus, six years elapsed. He spent six years in India itself, including two in Tamralipti, where he was employed in copying manuscript, and three years on the voyage from India to China, including two years spent in Ceylon.

Fa Hian's account of India.

He came into India through Udyana (the country round Kabul), Swat, Gandhara, Taxila, Peshawar, and Mathura. He thus describes the Madhyadesa:

Fa Hian's description of Madhyadesa.

"The climate of this country is warm and equable, without frost or snow. The people are well off, without poll tax or official restrictions; only those who till the royal lands return a portion of the profit of the land. If they desire to go they go, if they like to stop they stop. The kings govern without corporal punishment; criminals are fined, according to circumstances, heavily or lightly. Even in cases of repeated rebellion, they only cut off the right hand. The king's personal attendants, who guard him on the right and left, have fixed salaries. Throughout the country the people kill no living thing, nor do they eat garlic or onions, with the exception of Chandalas only. In this country they do not keep swine nor fowls, and do not deal in cattle; they have no shambles, or wine shops in their market places. In selling they use cowrie shells. The Chandalas only hunt and sell flesh. Down from the time of Buddha's Nirvana, the kings of these countries, the chief men and householders have raised Viharas, and provided for their support by bestowing on them fields, houses, and gardens with men and oxen. Engraved title-deeds were prepared and handed down from one reign to another; no one has ventured to withdraw them, so that, till now, there has been no interruption. All the resident priests (in these Viharas) have their beds, mats, food, drink, and clothes provided without stint; in all places this is the case." [1]

Buddhism and Brahmanism existing side by side.

Fa Hian visited Sravasti, Kapilavastu, Kusinagara, Vaisali, and Patna. At Patna he describes the procession in which the images of Buddha and the

[1] Fa Hian (Legge), xvi. p. 43.

Buddhisattvas are carried in company with those of Hindu *devas,* thus showing how tolerant Buddhists and Hindus were of each other's religion. "Every year in the eighth month, they celebrate a procession of images. They make a four-wheeled car, and on it erect a structure of five storeys by means of bamboos tied together. They make figures of devas with gold, silver, and lapis lazuli grandly blended, and having silken streamers and canopies hung out over them. On the four sides are niches with a Buddha seated in each, and a Buddhisattva standing in attendance on him. There may be twenty cars all grand and imposing, but each one different from the others. On the day mentioned, the monks and laity within the borders all come together; they have singers and skilful musicians; they pay their devotions with flowers and incense. The Brahmans come and invite the Buddhas to enter the city. These do so in order, and remain two nights in it. All through the night they keep lamps burning, have skilful music, and present offerings." [1]

From Patna, Fa Hian made a circular tour to Rajgriha, Gaya, Benares, and Kausambi. He thus describes his visit to the hill of Gridhrakuta in old Rajgriha, where Buddha used to meditate: "Fa Hian having purchased in the new town perfumes, flowers, and oil lamps, hired two aged *bhikshus* to conduct him to the grots and to the hill Khi-che. Having made an oblation of the perfumes and flowers, the lamps increased the brilliance. Grief and emotion affected him to tears. He said: 'Formerly in this place was Buddha. Here he taught the Sheou-leng-

Fa Hian's visit to Rajgriha.

[1] Fa Hian (Legge), xxvi. p. 79.

yan.'[1] Fa Hian, unable to behold Buddha in life, has but witnessed the traces of his sojourn. Still it is something to have recited the Sheou-leng-yan before the cave, and to have dwelt there one night." He visited Nalanda and then returned to Patna, where he stayed three years. He next visited Champa, the capital of Anga, or East Behar, near Bhagalpur, and thence he went to Tamralipti (Tumlook). In this country were many Sangharamas or Buddhist monasteries, and he remained there two years copying the sacred books. He tells us the sacred books were very few, as the practice was to hand down the precepts of religion by memory from master to pupil. From Tamralipti, he sailed to Ceylon and remained there two years. He collected in Ceylon copies of the Vinaya Pitaka and other sacred books hitherto unknown in China. Fa Hian returned to China by way of Sumatra about 415 A.D.

[1] Things which are difficult to discriminate from one another.

CHAPTER V.

PURANIC AGE—THE HUNS—YASODHARMADEVA—HARSHAVARDHANA. RAJPUT KINGDOMS—HIOUEN THSANG—I-TSING—U-K'ONG.

The Puranas.

THE fifth and last period of Hindu civilisation from A.D. 500 down to the Mahomedan conquest is called Puranic, because the Puranas assumed their present form in it. The Puranas were written in verse in the form of a dialogue, between an exponent and an enquirer. They were a means of conveying such religious instruction as was requisite for the common people. Interpolations due to sectarian feeling are frequent. They are mutually inconsistent, and were never meant to form one general system of belief. Still, for all that, they are classed on an equality with the Vedas. The Itihasa Puranas in their original forms are very old, as they are mentioned in the Chandogya Upanishad, the Brihadaranyaka and the Satapatha. In the first of these, Narada says to Sanatkumara: "I know the Rig Veda, the Yajur Veda, the Sama Veda, the Atharva Veda, and the fifth, the Itihasa Puranas." [1]

Hinduism, as it at present exists, is based on

[1] Chandogya Upanishad, 7, 1, 2.

the Puranas. In these works honour is given to the Bhakti-sastra (Bhagavat Purana and Bhagavad-gita, relating to Krishna worship, and the Ramayans of Valmiki and Tulsi Das relating to Rama worship) above the Vedas, Brahmanas and Upanishads. Pantheism is " one of their invariable characteristics, and underlies their whole teaching, although the peculiar deity, who is all things, from whom all things proceed, and to whom all things return, is diversified according to their individual sectarian bias. Prayers from them have been copiously introduced into all breviaries; observances of feasts and fasts are regulated by them; temples, towns, mountains, and rivers, to which pilgrimages are made, owe their sanctity to legends, for which the Puranas are the only authorities; and texts quoted from them have authority in civil as well as in religious law." [1]

Signs of a Purana.

Amara Sinha describes a true Purana as " Pancha-lakshana," marked with five signs, these being that it should be a history of:

(1) Primary creation.
(2) Secondary creation (the destruction and renovation of worlds).
(3) The genealogy of gods and patriarchs.
(4) The reigns of Manu or periods called Manwantaras.
(5) The reigns of the kings of the Solar and Lunar races.

The Puranas and the holy places.

No Purana has all the signs, and some depart widely from Amara Sinha's definition.

Each Purana also accounts for the sacredness of some holy place, with which it is specially connected,

[1] H. H. Wilson, Oxford Lectures.

e.g. the Brahma Purana glorifies Orissa, the Padma Purana Pushkara near Ajmere, and the Skanda Purana the Benares Siva temples.

Certain Puranas devoted to the worship of certain gods.

There are eighteen Puranas in all. Those dealing with Vishnu worship are the Vishnu, Bhagavat, Varaha, Padma, Narudiya, and Garuda. Those dealing with Siva worship are the Siva, Skanda, Agni or Vayu, Matsya, and Kurma. Those dealing with Brahma worship are the Brahma, Brahma-vaivarta, Brahmanda, Markandeya, Bhabishya, and the Vaman. The Markandeya Purana is also the chief authority for the worship of the goddess Durga.

Date.

" The principal Puranas seem to have been edited in their present form during the Gupta period, when a great extension and revival of Sanscrit Brahmanical literature took place." [1]

Historical importance of the Puranas.

Historically, the Vishnu Purana is important for the information it gives about Magadha, and the Vishnu, Vayu, and Matsya Puranas for information about the Andhra kings.

The Puranic Trinity.

The characteristic of the Puranic period is that the Supreme Being in his triple form of Brahma the creator, Vishnu the preserver, and Siva the destroyer, is exalted far above all the other deities of the Hindu Pantheon. Each form is anthropomorphised, else he could not be supposed to sympathise with mankind. Their shape is like that of mankind but different. Human art cannot adequately express the form of God, so the gods are sculptured or painted, with some abnormality in the number of their limbs or bodily organs, to differentiate them from mankind.

[1] Vincent Smith, 'Early History of India,' p. 19.

Hence Raban has ten arms, Brahma four faces, Siva three eyes.

Brahma.

Brahma, the only really self-existing entity, without form and unaffected by the three gunas (qualities), assumed the quality of activity (rajas) and became Brahma the Creator. Having created the world, he is assumed to have little more to do with it; he is therefore held in scanty respect.

Vishnu.

Vishnu in the Rig Veda is the wide-striding sun, etymologically, "the active one," who strides over the heavens in three paces, rising, culminating, and setting. Men who are deified for valour, or benevolence, are brought into relation with the Supreme Being by avatars or incarnations, which reconcile monotheism with a desire to multiply objects of worship. As Vishnu, Brahma assumes the quality of sattva (goodness).

Avatars.

Siva.

Siva, who is identified with Rudra, the Vedic deity of the roaring storm, according to Sir Alfred Lyall "represents the earliest and universal impression of Nature upon men, the impression of endless and pitiless change. He is the destroyer and rebuilder of various forms of life; he has charge of the whole circle of animated creation, the incessant round of birth and death in which all nature eternally revolves." [1]

Mr. Havell in his description of the bronze of Siva as Natesvar dancing upon an Asura (spirit of evil) amplifies these ideas.

The first right hand of the figure is raised in the attitude of blessing, the corresponding left is bent down to dispel fear, or to prevent the intrusion of evil spirits. His second right shakes a drum to the

[1] 'Asiatic Studies,' second series, p. 306.

accompaniment of which he is dancing, and his corresponding left hand holds sacrificial fire. An aureole or glory of fire surrounds the image, representing the elemental energy of heat, the first manifestation of the creative power of the Supreme Spirit

Siva as Natesvar dancing.

in Vedic philosophy. When Siva is sculptured as Bhairava as at Elephanta, with a necklace of skulls and a girdle of cobras, he is the personification of the destructive powers of nature only. His cobras symbolise destruction and also reincarnation, as the snake sheds his skin and reappears with a new body.

[1] 'Indian Sculpture and Painting,' p. 70.

Siva teaches men by his example the power of penance, mortification, and suppression of the passions, and the virtue of meditation, leading to union with or absorption in the great spirit. As Siva, Brahma assumes the quality of tamas (indifference).

Antiquity of Siva worship.

Strabo, quoting Megasthenes, tells us that Heracles, who is probably to be identified with Krishna, was worshipped on the plains, and Dionysos, who is probably to be identified with Siva, on the mountains of India.

Saktism.

Closely connected with the worship of Siva is the worship of his wife Durga, Parvati, or Kali, as the Sakti or productive energy of nature. The Tantras (*tantra*, rule or ritual) contain the chief doctrines and ceremonies of the Sakti cult, which is non-Aryan, and seems to have originated from Assam.

Invasion of the Huns.

The power of the Gupta kings was finally broken by the invasion of the White Huns or Epthalites (as Byzantine writers call them) under Toramana and Mihiragula, at the end of the fifth and the beginning of the sixth century A.D., which is spoken of in the inscription on the Stone Boar at Eran (Sagar district, C.P.). The capital of the Huns was at Sakala, which Vincent Smith identifies with Chiniot (Gujranwala) or Shahkot (Jhang district). Another identification proposed is Sialkot.

Yasodharmadeva.

The Huns did not have it all their own way in their conflicts with Indian princes. Yasodharmadeva, king of Malwa, sometimes identified with the Vikramaditya of Sanscrit literature, who patronised the Nine Gems, is said by Alberuni to have gained a great victory over the Huns at Korur, between

Multan and Luni, in 533 A.D. He was called Sakari, enemy of the Sakas, on this account. Yasodharmadeva's victories are recorded in the inscriptions on his two Kirti Stambhas at Mandasor in Malwa. Mihiragula was driven to take refuge in Kashmir, whence he attacked Gandhara, and died, 540 A.D. Yasodharmadeva is supposed to have adopted a local era in use in Malwa, which commenced with the year 57 B.C., and to have given it currency as the Samvat era used by the Hindus up to the present time. This Malwa era may have commemorated the conquest of the country by Chashtana, the first great king of the Kshatrapas. It was known in 473 A.D. as "the reckoning of the Malavas," in 879 as "the Malava time or era," in 738 and 1169 as "the year of the Malava lord or lords." The most famous of the Nine Gems who frequented Yasodharmadeva's court at Ujjain, if he be identical with Vikramaditya, were Kalidas the poet, Varahamihira the astronomer, and Amara Sinha the Sanscrit dictionary writer. It is impossible that the Nine Gems could ever have frequented one king's court, as they did not live at the same time. Kalidas, for instance, lived some time in the fifth century A.D., but most of the other "Gems" were later than this.

Samvat era.

The "Nine Gems."

Yasodharmadeva's son Siladitya or Pratapasila was overthrown by Rajyavardhana, king of Kanauj, 606 A.D. On Rajyavardhana's death, owing to the treachery of Sasanka (Narendra Gupta), king of Karna Suvarna or Western Bengal, his younger brother Harshavardhana succeeded. Harshavardhana, who sometimes goes by the name of Siladitya II., and who reigned from 606 to 648 A.D., was another

Harshavardhana of Thaneswar.

conqueror of the Huns. He brought all Northern India under his sway, but was repelled in his attempt to conquer Southern India by Pulakesin II. of the western branch of the Chalukya Rajputs. Hiouen Thsang, the Chinese traveller in India 629-45, mentions the festivals held at Kanauj and at Prayag (Allahabad) in honour of the Buddhist religion and the Hindu gods, at which learned men were suitably rewarded, and large gifts made to the Brahmins and the poor. Harshavardhana also held a council of the Mahayana or Northern school of Buddhists at Kanauj. On his death, a usurping minister Arjuna or Arunasra succeeded; he insulted a Chinese embassy sent in return for Harshavardhana's embassy to China, and was dethroned by the Chinese with Thibetan aid.

Valabhi.

About the year 509 A.D., a chief named Bhataraka established himself at Valabhi (modern Wala) in the east of Saurashtra (Kathiawar). The earliest Valabhi grant (the Ḳukad grant) is that of his third son Dhruvasena I., dated 526 A.D. The dynasty of Bhataraka lasted till it was overthrown by Arabian invaders from Sind about 770 A.D. Scions of this race subsequently migrated to Rajputana, where they became the ancestors of the Sisodias of Chitor and Udaipur.

Later Guptas.

A later Gupta kingdom was founded by Krishna Gupta, who belonged to a collateral branch of the Gupta royal family. The eighth king of this dynasty, Adityasena by name, declared himself independent in 672 A.D. It was perhaps this dynasty that ruled in Behar and Bengal down to about 840 A.D. This later Gupta kingdom was overthrown by the Pala dynasty.

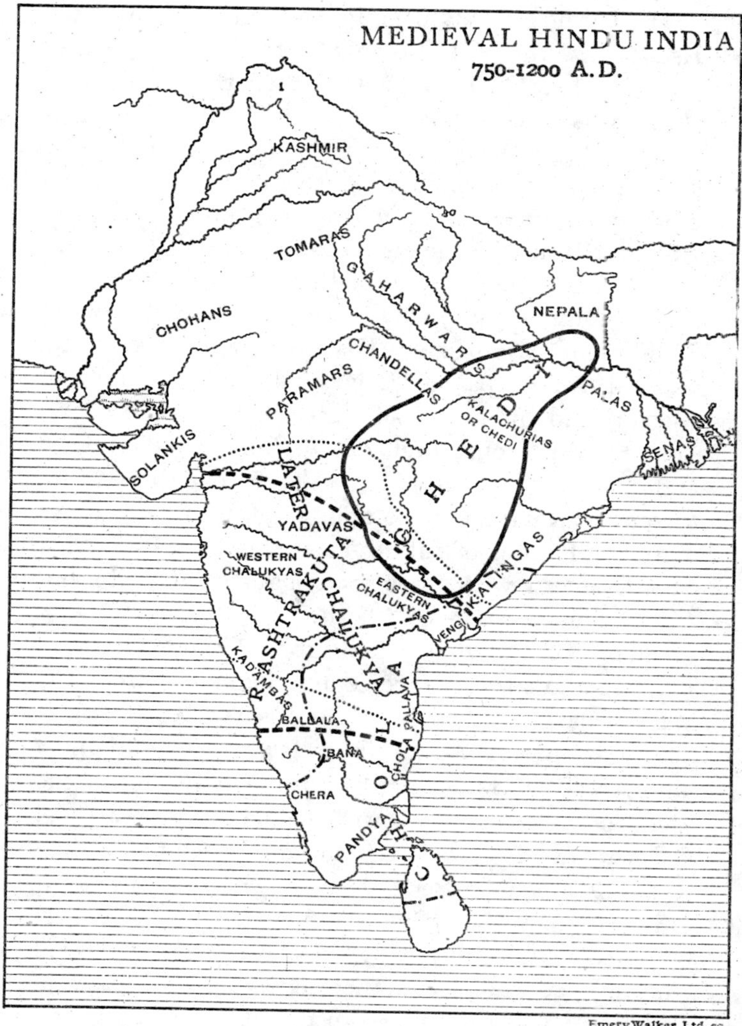

The Rajputs, a race hardly acknowledged as Aryans in the earliest times, now come into prominence.

The legend is that, after Parasurama destroyed the Kshatriyas, the gods brought out of the caldron of fire on Mount Abu the Parihars, the Pawars or Paramaras, the Solankis (of Gujrat), and the Chauhans. About the middle of the ninth century, the

Chandel Rajput Kingdom.

Chandel Rajputs established themselves in Bundelkind, and their king Yasovarman captured the Fort of Kalanjar from the Chedis in the middle of the tenth century. Dhanga, a king of this dynasty, joined the league formed by Jaipal, king of Lahore, against Sabuktagin of Ghazni. His son Ganda, 999-1025, assisted Anangopal of Lahore against Mahmud of Ghazni, and his grandson Vidyadhara attacked and slew Rajyapal of Kanauj 1019, for surrendering to Mahmud. In 1021 or 1022, Ganda had himself to surrender Kalanjar to Mahmud of Ghazni. Paramardi or Parmal of this dynasty, 1165-1203, carried on a long war with Prithviraj Chauhan of Delhi and Ajmere, and he reigned till the fort of Kalanjar was taken by Kutbuddin Aibak in 1203. Trailokyavarma, son of Paramardi, recovered his dominions from the Mahomedans, and the dynasty survived till Sher Shah captured Kalanjar in 1545 A.D. The Chandel kings built the famous temples of Khajuraho in the Chatarpur state in Central India. The Chandel Rajput dynasty is believed to be represented by the Raja of Gidhour in Bengal.

The Gurjara Kingdom.

The Gurjaras, a tribe whose memory is still perpetuated in the Panjab by the names of Gujrat and Gujranwala, established themselves under Vatsaraja at Ujjain, whence they transferred their capital to Kanauj under Bhoja I. about 843. Rajyapal of Kanauj, of this dynasty, was slain as mentioned above by Vidyadhara of Kalanjar in 1019. The Gurjara kingdom of Kanauj never recovered from Mahmud of Ghazni's attack. The Parihar Rajputs are believed to be their modern representatives. The Gaharwar, subsequently called the Rathor Rajputs, afterwards occupied the territory of the Gurjaras.

The Paramara Kingdom of Malwa.

The Paramara or Pawar Rajputs established themselves at Dhara, in Malwa, in the beginning of the ninth century. The most famous king of this dynasty was Bhoj (about 1010-1062). The Rajput kings of Malwa were overthrown by Alaudin Khilji.

The Chedi Kingdom.

The Kalachuri or Chedi era commences from 249 A.D., but nothing certain is known of the kingdom or dynasty till the time of Kokalla, about the year 875 A.D. He was the chief of the Haihaya Rajputs, and his territory included the Central Provinces and Berar. After Kokalla, there is an unbroken line of kings down to the end of the thirteenth century, when the kingdom was subdued by the Khilji sultans of Delhi. The most powerful of the Chedi kings were Sangadeva and Karna, who together reigned for about one hundred years from 1019 A.D.

Prithviraj and Jayachandra.

Towards the close of the twelfth century, Northern India was in the hands of the Chauhan Rajputs at Ajmere, who had brought under their control the territory of the Tomara Rajputs round Delhi, the Gaharwar (subsequently called Rathor) Rajputs at Kanauj, and the Chalukya Rajputs in Gujrat. The Sesodias, who are believed to have migrated from Gujrat in the eighth century A.D., from time immemorial have occupied Mewar, and the Kachwahas have been in possession of Jaipur and Ulwar for many centuries. Thus we see the Mahomedans conquered

India from the Rajputs. Prithviraj was the nephew of Visaladeva, the Chauhan Raja of Ajmere, who brought about the marriage of his nephew's father with the heiress of Delhi. Anangapal, last of the Tomara rajas and builder of the fort of Lal Kot at Delhi, had a daughter who married the father of Prithviraj. Prithviraj succeeded his maternal grandfather, and became Raja of Delhi, besides Ajmere, in 1167. Delhi is strategically important as the key to the narrow strip of habitable country between the Himalayas and the Indian desert, through which every invading army must pass. Prithviraj built the fort of Rai Pithora eleven miles south of Delhi. His accession to the throne of Delhi excited the jealousy of Jaychandra, Raja of Kanauj, who was the son of another daughter of Anangapal. Jaychandra performed the Rajsuya ceremony, but Prithviraj refused to attend. Jaychandra in consequence did not invite Prithviraj to the Swayambhara of his daughter Sanjukta, but placed his clay image as "dwarpal" at the ceremony. Sanjukta cast her garland over the neck of the clay image, and was carried off by her lover who opportunely appeared. The feud which thus arose between Jaychandra and Prithviraj deprived Prithviraj of Jaychandra's support against the Mahomedan invaders.

Mahomed Ghori.

Mahomed Ghori invaded India in 1191, but was defeated by Prithviraj at Trirouri or Thanesvar. Two years afterwards he made a second attempt and was completely successful, Prithviraj being captured and put to death. The conquest of Northern India was completed by the captures of Delhi, Kanauj and Benares, 1193, the defeat of Jaychandra, king of

Kanauj, at the battle of Chandrawar in the Doab, 1194, the surrender of Gwalior, 1196, and the capture of Nahrwala or Anhalwara, capital of Gujrat, 1203. After the defeat of Jaychandra, the Gaharwar Rajputs emigrated to Rajputana, and set up the Jodhpur dynasty under the name of Rahtors.

Hiouen Thsang's account of India.

Hiouen Thsang came to India to study the Yoga philosophy, which was accepted by the Mahayana school of Buddhism. He left China 629 A.D., and passing through Ferghana, Samarcand, Bokhara and Balkh entered India by way of Udyana (the country round Kabul), Nagarahara or Takkha (the capital of the Jellalabad district), and Gandhara (Peshawar district). He next visited Kashmir, Little Thibet, Mathura, Thanesvar, and Hurdwar. Kausambi, Sravasti, Kapilavastu, Kusinagara, Benares, and Vaisali followed, and he describes the decadence of Buddhism in these places. From Vaisali he went to Nepal, and thence he returned to Vaisali.

Nalanda.

Leaving Vaisali he went to Patna and Gaya and visited Nalanda, which he thus describes: "The richly adorned towers were arranged in regular order, the pavilions decorated with coral appeared like pointed hill tops; the soaring domes reached to the clouds, and the pinnacles of the temples seemed to be lost in the mist of the morning. From the windows one could see the movements of the winds and the clouds, and above their lofty roofs the sun and moon could be seen in conjunction. All around pools of translucent water shone with the petals of the blue lotus flowers; here and there the lovely kanaka trees hung between them. In the different courts, the houses of the monks were each four stories in height.

The pavilions had pillars ornamented with dragons, and beams resplendent with all the colours of the rainbow, rafters richly carved—columns ornamented with jade and richly chiselled, and balustrades of carved open work. The lintels of the doors were decorated with elegance, and the roofs covered with glazed tiles of brilliant colours, which multiplied themselves by reflection, and varied the effect at every moment in a thousand manners." [1]

Nalanda was the site of one of the famous Buddhist universities: the others were at Taxila, Benares, and Sridhanya Kataka on the Kistna, and at Vikramasila. They taught mathematics and astronomy as well as metaphysics and religion.

The university of Nalanda.

Hiouen Thsang speaks of the monks of Nalanda as follows: "The countries of India respect them and follow them. The day is not sufficient for asking and answering profound questions. From morning to night they engage in discussion, the old and the young mutually help each other. Those who cannot discuss questions out of the Tripitaka are little esteemed, and obliged to hide themselves for shame. Learned men from different cities, on this account, who desire to acquire quickly a renown in discussion, come here in multitudes to settle their doubts, and then the streams of their wisdom spread far and wide. For this reason, some persons usurp the name of Nalanda students, and in going to and fro receive honour in consequence."

Hiouen Thsang stayed at Nalanda with Bhaskara Varman, Raja of Kamrup (Assam), whose country he visited and of which he has left us a description.

[1] 'Life of Hiouen Thsang' by Stanislaus Julien, pp. 150-151.

While there, the Raja of Kamrup and he were summoned to attend the quinquennial festival celebrated by Harshavardhana at Kanauj. The account he gives of it shows the leaning of Buddhism to the worship of images.[1] It has been said of Nalanda, "What Cluny and Clairvaux were to France in the Middle Ages, Nalanda was to Central India, the depository of all true learning and the foundation from which it spread to all the other lands of the faithful."

He mentions Sarnath, the Deerpark or Mrigadawa, at Isipatna near Benares. This was the site of a monastery with 1500 monks, and the Dhamek Stupa was erected by Asoka there, as well as a Memorial Lat. **Sarnath.**

From Magadha, Hiouen Thsang arrived in Bengal, by way of Hiranya Parvata (Monghyr), and Champa (capital of Anga or East Behar), which corresponds to the modern Bhagalpur. Hiouen Thsang speaks of Bengal as divided into five kingdoms—Pundra or Northern Bengal, Kamarupa or Assam, Samatata or Eastern Bengal, Tamralipti or Southern Bengal, and Karna Suvarna or Western Bengal.

From Bengal Hiouen Thsang went, through Udra or Orissa and Kanyodha (a kingdom on the Chilka lake), into Kalinga, of which he says: "In old days the kingdom of Kalinga had a very dense population; their shoulders rubbed one with the other, and the axles of their chariot wheels locked together, and when they raised their arm-sleeves a perfect tent was formed."[2] From Kalinga, he passed into the Andhra country with its capital at Dhanakataka or **Kalinga.**

[1] Hiouen Thsang, Beale, ii. 170. [2] *Ibid.* ii. 208.

Amraoti,[1] on the Kistna, in the modern district of Guntur. Near Amraoti were the monasteries of Purvasila and Aparasila, which were hollowed out of rock. South of the Andhra country were the Chola kingdom, and the kingdom of Dravida, the capital of which was Kanchi (Conjeveram). This is probably to be identified with the kingdom of the Pallavas.

Still further south, from Dravida, was the kingdom of Malakuta or the delta of the Kaveri river. Here also Buddhism was declining. Speaking of the people of this country he says: "Some follow the true doctrine, others are given to heresy. They do not esteem learning much, but are wholly given to commercial gain. There are ruins of many old convents, but only the walls are preserved, and there are few religious followers. There are many hundred Deva temples, and a multitude of heretics mostly belonging to the Nirgranthas (Jains). To the east of the capital is an old Sangharama (monastery), of which the vestibule and court are covered with wild shrubs; the foundation walls only remain. This was built by Mahendra, younger brother of Asoka raja. To the east of this is a stupa, the lofty walls of which are buried in the earth, and only the crowning part of the cupola remains. This was built by Asoka raja."[2]

Maharashtra.

From Dravida he went through the Konkan into Maharashtra, which was ruled by Pulakesin II. He

[1] Ferguson identifies Dhanakataka with the modern Bezwada. 'Rock Temples of India,' Ferguson and Burgess, p. 95.

[2] Hiouen Thsang, Beale, ii. 231.

speaks of Ajanta as "a *sangharama* constructed in a dark valley. Its lofty *chaityas* with deep *viharas* at their sides stretch through the face of the rock. Story above story, they are backed by the crag and face the valley." The character he gives of the inhabitants of Maharashtra still remains applicable to them. "To their benefactors they are grateful; to their enemies relentless. If they are insulted, they will risk their lives to avenge themselves. If they are asked to help one in distress, they will forget themselves to render assistance. If they are going to seek revenge, they first give their enemy warning, then, each being armed, they attack each other with spears. If a general loses a battle, they do not inflict punishment but present him with woman's clothes, and so he is driven to seek death for himself."[1] From Maharashtra, he visited the country of Bharukachha or Broach, and from Broach he passed into Malwa, the inhabitants of which were only second to those of Magadha in learning. From Malwa, he visited Cutch and Valabhi in Kathiawar, and then left India by way of Multan and the Khotan route through Central Asia, about A.D. 645.

Government of India, and manners and customs of the people.

Hiouen Thsang's account of the government of India, and the manners and customs of the people, is worth quoting: "As the administration of the country is conducted on benign principles, the executive is simple. The private estates of the crown are divided into four principal parts: the first is for carrying on the affairs of State and providing sacrificial offerings; the second is for providing subsidies for the minister and chief officers of State;

[1] Hiouen Thsang, Beale, ii. 256.

the third is for rewarding men of distinguished ability, and the fourth is for charity to religious bodies, whereby the field of merit is cultivated. In this way, the taxes on the people are light, and the personal service required of them is moderate. Each keeps his worldly goods in peace, and all till the ground for their subsistence. Those who cultivate the royal estate pay one-sixth of their produce as tribute. The merchants who engage in commerce come and go carrying out their transactions. The river passages and the road barriers are open on the payment of a small toll. When the Public Works require it, labour is exacted but paid for. The payment is in strict proportion to the work done. The military guard on the frontiers go out to punish the refractory. They also mount guard at night round the palace. The soldiers are levied according to the requirements of the service, they are promised certain payments, and are publicly enrolled. The Governors, Ministers, Magistrates and Officials have each a portion of land consigned to them for their personal support. Although the people are naturally light-minded, yet they are upright and honourable. In money matters they are without craft, and in administering justice they are considerate. They dread the retribution of another state of existence, and make light of the things of the present world. They are not deceitful or treacherous in their conduct, and are faithful to their oaths and promises." [1]

I-tsing.

I-tsing, a third Chinese Buddhist pilgrim, left China for India A.D. 671. He studied at Nalanda, and visited Budh Gaya, Benares, Sravasti,

[1] Hiouen Thsang, Beale, ii. pp. 87, 88.

Kanyakubja, Rajgriha, Vaisali, and Kusinagara, and returned to China *via* Sribhaja (Palembang in Sumatra) A.D. 695. I-tsing is an authority on Buddhistic theology.

U-k'ong. U-k'ong travelled from China *via* Central Asia. He reacned Gandhara 753 and Kashmir 759, where he spent four years. Returning to Gandhara in 764, he set out for Central India, visiting Kapilavastu, Benares, Sravasti, Kusinagara and Nalanda *en route*. At Nalanda he spent three years. About 783 or 784, he set out for China, and arrived there 790, bringing with him the Sanscrit texts of the Dasabhumi and the Dasabala Sutras.

Early history of Bengal. The first we hear of Bengal, in authentic history, is in the pages of Hiouen Thsang, who describes it as divided into five kingdoms—Pundra or North Bengal, Kamarupa or Assam, Samatata or East Bengal, Tamralipti or South Bengal, and Karna Suvarna or West Bengal. Another cursory allusion to Bengal is made when Sasanka (Narendra Gupta), king of Karna Suvarna, Western Bengal, is said to have defeated and killed in battle Rajyavardhana, king of Kanauj, elder brother of Harshavardhana, A.D. 606.

The Pala kings. The first race of kings of Bengal of whom we have any accurate knowledge in history is the Buddhist family of the Palas, who rose to power about the middle of the ninth century. They not only reigned in Magadha with their capital at Odantapuri (Behar in the district of Patna), but also held sway in Northern Bengal and at Vikrampur in Eastern Bengal. Gopal, the founder of the dynasty, reigned from about A.D. 855 to A.D. 875. Devapal is said to have conquered

Kamrup and Orissa. The next king, Dharmapal (about A.D. 880-895) is said to have extended his power as far as the ocean to the east, as far as Delhi in the west, as far as Jullundur in the north, and as far as the Vindhya mountains in the south. Mahipal, ninth king of this dynasty, whose name is associated with the Mahipal Dighi in the Dinajpur district, is known to have been reigning in A.D. 1026. The Senas deprived the Palas of Bengal, but they appear to have lingered on in Behar, till they were finally overthrown by Mahomed, son of Bakhtiyar, in 1197.

The Sena dynasty.

The Senas were, according to some scholars, Karnata Kshatriyas. Adisur, who was perhaps a king of the Sena dynasty, brought five Brahmans and five Kayasthas from Kanauj to Rampal, his capital in Eastern Bengal, to contribute to the restoration of Hinduism. Samanta Sen, a king of this dynasty, had more than a legendary existence. The territory held by the Sena Kings was greatly extended by Samanta Sen's son, Bijay. Bijay's son, Ballal, granted the rank of Kulin (nobility) to all Brahmans possessed of certain virtues. The virtues were *Achar* (obedience to custom), *Vinay* (lowliness), *Vidya* (learning), *Pratistha* (fame), *Tirtha darshan* (pilgrimages), *Nistha* (adherence to rules for religious duty), *Avritti* (marrying sons and daughters into families of equal rank), *Tapa* (penance) and *Dan* (charity). Unfortunately the rank tended to become hereditary, the virtues did not. Kulins were subdivided into Mukhya and Gauna Kulins (those who had strayed from the right path). Other Brahman families which had kept their purity of blood, but had intermarried into families of inferior rank were called Srotriya. Ballal Sen divided Bengal into five divisions :

Barendra, Northern Bengal.

Rarh, Western Bengal.

Banga, Eastern Bengal.

Bagri, corresponding roughly to the Presidency Division.

Mithila, Behar.

Lakhsman Sena was overthrown by Mahomed, son of Bakhtiyar, general of Kutubuddin, in 1198. He fled from Nadia to Vikrampur, near Dacca, in Eastern Bengal. A number of learned Brahmans fled with him to Vikrampur, and made it the stronghold of Brahmanism, and centre of Sanscrit learning in Eastern Bengal. The kingdom of the Senas, which was called Sonargaon, lay between the Brahmaputra on the north, the Lakhiya on the east, the Ishamati on the west, and the Meghna on the south. The last king of the Sena dynasty was Danuj Ray, grandson of Lakhsman Sen.

CHAPTER VI.

SOUTHERN INDIA AND THE DECCAN.

Dravidian civilisation.

FROM the time when Ram Chandra fought with Raban, the Dravidian civilisation of the south was a thing apart. The description in the Ramayan of Rishis settling at places like Panchavati and Chitrakut in the Deccan points to its being gradually brought under Aryan influence, and the Dravidians appear to have accepted Aryan civilisation and Vedic philosophy about the close of the Rationalistic period. Agastya, the sage of the Dandakaranya, one of these Rishis, was the reputed author of the first Tamil grammar. He is described in the Mahabharat as giving to Rama the arrow with which he killed Ravan. The Tamils were divided into the following castes :

Introduction of Aryan civilisation and Vedic philosophy.

Tamil castes.

(1) Ariyar or Sages.
(2) Uluvar or farmers, including vellalar, or lords of the flood.
(3) Aiyar and Vedduvar, shepherds and huntsmen.
(4) Artisan.
(5) Padaiyadchier, soldiers.
(6) Valaiyar, fishermen.
(7) Pulayar, scavengers.

The introduction of the Aryan caste system was difficult, as there were no classes among the Tamils to correspond with the Kshatriyas or Vaisyas. The immigrant Aryans appear to have tried to keep the Vedas to themselves, as the Vedas were long called in Tamil "The four Secret Books," but they were at last translated into Tamil. When non-Aryans were admitted to Brahmanic rank, they were divided into three sub-divisions: Telinga, Dravida, and Karnata.

Dravidian influence on Hinduism.

Hinduism has been profoundly influenced by its blending with the religion and culture of the south. Linga worship is said to have been of Dravidian origin, and the two teachers Sankarcharjya and Ramanuja, to whom the present doctrines of Hinduism are chiefly attributed, were Brahmans from Southern India. Other more material benefits are due to the Dravidians; the Aryans only knew how to build in wood, the Dravidians taught them how to build in stone.

Mention of land of the Tamils in Roman and Greek authors.

Strabo's account of the embassy of Zarmana Chagos from the Pandyan king Poros to the court of Augustus Caesar at Rome, B.C. 26, and the second embassy, B.C. 20, have been referred to. Pliny tells us "In no year does India drain our empire of less than 550 millions of sesterces (£486,979 in modern money), giving back her own wares (perfumes, spices, precious stones, pearls and unguents) in exchange, which are sold at fully one hundred times their prime cost, so dearly do we pay for our luxury and our women."[1] He also speaks of India as "the sole mother of precious stones," and "the great producer of the most costly gems." Petronius Arbiter describes the Roman

[1] 'Natural History,' vi. 23.

Commerce between Egypt, Europe, and Southern India.

ladies dressed in "webs of woven wind" (Indian muslin). The author of the 'Periplus of the Erythraean Sea,' an Egyptian Greek who wrote between 80 and 89 A.D., says that Greek merchants, starting from Egypt in July, brought wine, brass, lead, and glass to the South Indian ports, and purchased in return pepper, betel, ivory, pearls, and fine muslin. Their return voyage commenced in December or January.

The Tamil poets confirm this. "O Mara (a Pandyan prince) whose sword is ever victorious.

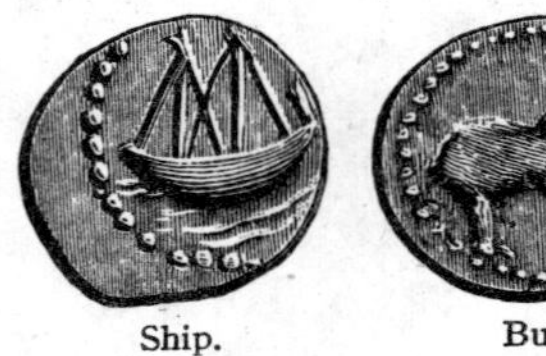

Ship. Bull.

COIN OF THE KADAMBAS.

Spend thou thy days in peace and joy, drinking daily out of golden cups the cool and fragrant wine brought by the Yavanas in their good ships."[1] These Yavanas were Egyptian Greeks, and for the benefit of this trade Ptolemy Philadelphus, B.C. 285-247, built the ports of Berenice and Myos Hormos on the Egyptian coast of the Red Sea. This commerce was greatly assisted by the discovery how to utilise the south-west monsoon on the voyage to India made by an Egyptian Greek named Hippalus in the first century A.D. The coins of the Kadambas, who lived near the modern Goa, bear a ship, from this we infer that the Kadambas must have had considerable use for ships in trade.

[1] Purananuru, 56.

The Periplus Maris Erythrœi, describes the coast of India from the mouth of the Indus up to Masulipatam on the Coromandel coast and Gange Regia at the head of the Bay of Bengal, which is most probably to be identified with Satgaon. Ptolemy, who flourished under Antoninus Pius, wrote a geography about A.D. 150, in which he deals with India, but he describes the coast as a zigzag line from near Bombay to beyond Masulipatam, and thus effaces the Peninsula from existence. Kosmos Indikopleustes also speaks of commerce between Egypt and Europe and Southern India.

Ports in Tamil land.

The ports on the Malabar coast were Muchiris or Muziris (Cranganore) of which the Tamil poet speaks, "Musiri, to which come the well-rigged ships of the Yavanas bringing gold and taking spices in exchange."[1] Tyndis or Tondi, on the Makkali river, corresponding to the modern Palukara, five miles from Quilon. Bakarei, the modern Vaikkarai, near Kottayam. On the Coromandel coast, the ports were Korkai on the Tamraparni river, and Kaveripaddinam or Pukar, at the mouth of the river Kaveri. The trade of Kaveripaddinam is described in the Pattinapalai, a poem in glorification of the Chola king Karikala, thus: "Horses were brought from distant lands beyond the seas; pepper was brought in ships; gold and precious stones came from the northern mountains; sandal and aghil came from the mountains towards the west; pearls from the southern seas, and coral from the eastern seas. The produce of the regions watered by the Ganges; all that is grown on the banks of the Kaveri; articles of food from Ilam

[1] Ahananaru, 149.

(Ceylon), and the manufactures of Kalakam (in Burma) were brought to the markets of Kaveri-paddinam."[1]

Roman coins.

Roman coins are found in Southern India dating from Augustus, B.C. 27, to Zeno, A.D. 491, and they include some copper coins found at Madura of small denomination, which are supposed to have been locally minted for daily use, which would go to show that Roman trade agents resided in India. Mr. Robert Sewell finds that the commercial connection between Rome and India, as shown by the Roman coins found in India, falls into five periods.

1. It was almost non-existent before the time of Augustus.
2. From the commencement of the reign of Augustus down to the death of Nero, pepper, spices, fine muslins (from Masulipatam), perfumes, unguents, pearls and precious stones, especially the beryl, were exported from India to Rome in large quantities from Barugaza (Broach) and the ports of the south-west coast, and the coins are found in greatest abundance where these commodities were produced, notably near the beryl mine of Padiyur in the Coimbatore district. Roman coins are not found in large numbers in Northern India, as the Kushan kings melted down the Roman aurei, issuing their own coins of precisely the same weight.
3 Between the time of Nero and Caracalla, A.D. 217, trade in luxuries was replaced

[1] Pattinapalai, 185-91.

by trade in necessaries, such as cotton fabrics, and the coins are found in the cotton producing districts.

4. From the time of Caracalla, trade almost ceased between Rome and India, but it must have survived down to A.D. 408, as the three thousand pounds of pepper which Alaric included in the ransom of Rome undoubtedly came from India.
5. Trade revived slightly under the Byzantine emperors.

Aureus of Nero found in Southern India.

Tamil literature.

The Tamils had a rich literature, the Augustan age of which is placed in the second century A.D. They had a sort of Licensing system, as before poems could be published, they had to be passed by a Sangam or College of poets as up to a proper standard of literary merit. These Sangams enjoyed royal patronage, and in this connection the Pandya kings Mudattirumaran and Ugra Peruvaludhi, A.D. 128-140, and the Chera king Senguttuvan, are specially mentioned. The Muppal or Kural of Tiruvallur, a poem of 2660 short couplets, dealing with the subjects of virtue, wealth and pleasure, the Naladiyar, and the Tinivasagam of Manikkavasagar are moral and ethical poems, and the epics Sillapadhikaran, or the Anklet by Ilangovodigal, and Manimekali, or the

Jewel-belt by Sittalai Sattanar, belong to the first forty years of the second century A.D. This date depends upon the identification of the Gajabahu mentioned in the Sillapadikaran with the Gajabahu who reigned in Ceylon from A.D. 135, but this is disputed, as the word may be a mere epithet, not a proper name at all.

The Andhra kings were also patrons of literature. The Brihat Katha of Gunadya, which is the source of many of the Tamil *kavyas*, was written in Paisachi Prakrit at the Court of a Satavahana king at Paitan. An Andhra king named Hala, seventeenth in succession out of about thirty kings, wrote the 'Sapta Sataka' or Seven Centuries, an anthology of erotic verse.

Southern India, properly so called, is the country to the south of the Tungabhadra and the Kistna.

Hindu rulers of Southern India.

In the epoch we are at present considering, the history of Southern India may be divided into the following periods:

(1) Early period to the fifth century A.D.
(2) Pallava period, fifth to ninth century A.D.
(3) Chola supremacy, ninth to fourteenth century A.D.

The first historical mention of the Dravidian kingdoms of Southern India is in the thirteenth Rock Edict of Asoka, which speaks of the Chola, Pandya, Kerala, and Satiyaputra countries as Pratyanta or independent. The Chola kingdom lay between the Pennar river on the north, and the Vellar river which flows into the sea south of Point Callimere on the south. Its capital was Tanjore.

Pandya kingdom.

The Pandya territory stretched from the river Vellar to Cape Comorin and from Cape Comorin to the Chera territories on the west coast. It occupied approximately the modern districts of Madura and Tinnevelly, and had Kolkor or Korkai at the mouth of the Tamraparni river, the chief seat of the pearl fishery, Kalyana, near Cape Comorin, and afterwards the city of Madura, as its capital. The pearl fishery was the cause of a widespread foreign commerce, the extent of which is shown by the number of coins of the early Roman Empire found at Madura and Coimbatore. The Pandya kings were said to be descended from the Pandavas of the Mahabharat, and Tamil poets call Madura " Southern Mathura," on account of a supposed connection with Mathura on the Jumna. The Pandya kingdom is referred to by Megasthenes as Pandaia, and the author of the Periplus Maris Erythrœi speaks of Madura and the king thereof as " ho Pandion." The king's cognisance was a fish, Sanscrit Min, and his title was Minavan, the fishy one. Rajendra Chola Kulottunga, 1070-1118, placed his son Gangaikonda on the Pandyan throne under the name of Sundra Pandya. After him, Maravarman Sundarva Pandya, 1216-36, is said to have captured the Chola capital, but to have restored it. Maravarman Kulasekhara, 1268-1308, is mentioned by Mahomedan historians. The king who ruled conjointly with him, Jatavarman Sundara Pandya II., may be perhaps identified with the Sondar Bandi of Marco Polo. Even after the rise of the Naiks, descendants of the Pandya kings maintained themselves in the Tinnevelly hills at Tenkasi and other places.

Chera kingdom.

The Kongani or Ganga dynasty established itself in the Chera territory, which stretched from Calicut south to the Pandya border, and included Coimbatore,

Southern Mysore and Salem. The capital of the Chera kingdom was at Talkad or Dalavampura near Kollegal, just beyond the Coimbatore border, and afterwards at Vanji (Karur), both of which are on the Kaveri. The Chera territory was called Kongudesa, from Kongu, crooked, an allusion to the shape of the country; it included Salem and Coimbatore. The kingdom of Kerala (including Travancore, Cochin, Calicut, and Cananore) was an early offshoot from Kongudesa. Its inhabitants, the Nairs, are of Turanian descent, and are said by tradition to have come with Parasuram from the Himalayas. Kerala and Satiyaputra (the country round Mangalore) are mentioned in one of Asoka's edicts. A king of Kerala, Cheruman Perumal, A.D. 825, became a Mahomedan, and on going on pilgrimage to Mecca he divided his territories among his nobles, and from this the States of Calicut, Travancore and Cochin originated. Calicut is said to be derived from *Kolikodu* (cock crowing), as tradition has it that Cheruman Perumal gave to the ancestor of the Zamorin his sword with all the territory over which the sound of a cock crowing at a certain temple could be heard. The Chera kingdom was conquered by the Yadavas of Deogiri, but the Chera kings went northwards and established themselves in Orissa as the Ganga dynasty.

Pallavas. The Pallavas had originally three principalities at Vengi (Rajamahendri), Palakkala (Pal Ghat in Malabar) and at Kanchi (Conjeeveram). When they were ousted from Vengi, they established themselves at Kanchi. They were the first power to establish themselves in a position of supremacy in Southern India on the decline of the Andhras. They ruled

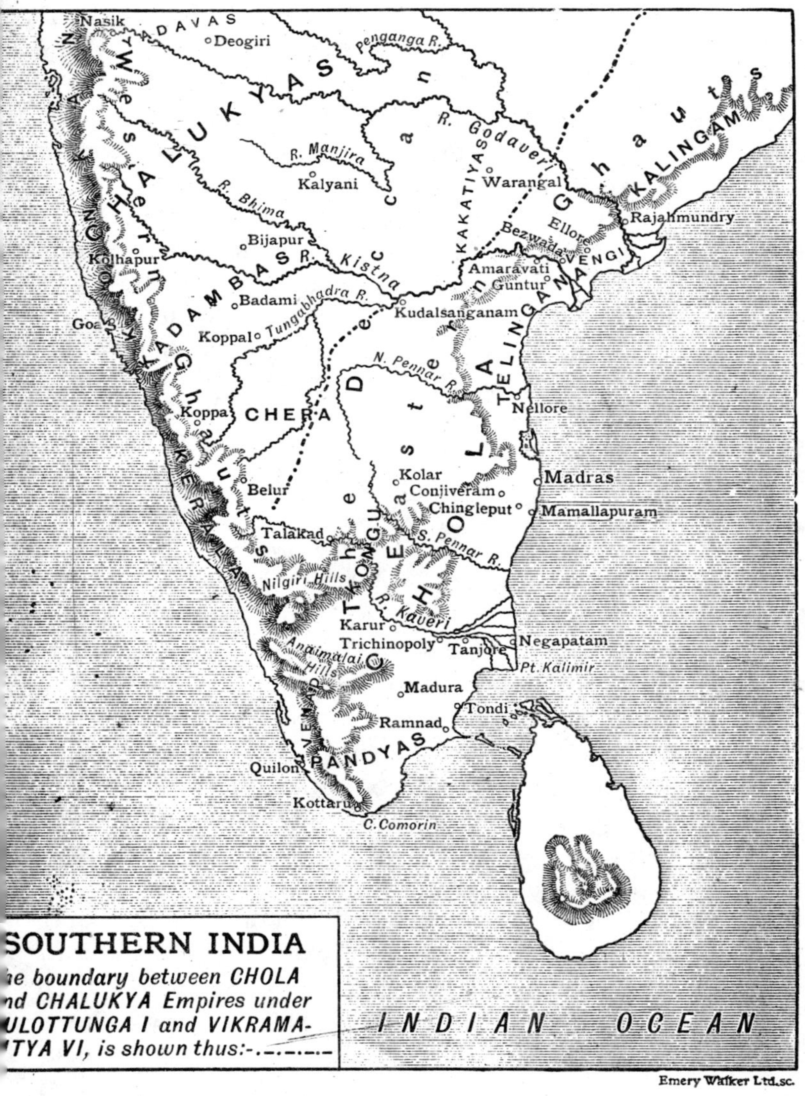

Emery Walker Ltd.sc.

from the Narbada and the southern boundary of Orissa on the north to the Southern Pennar river on the south. A Pallava king, Sivaskanda Varman, is said to have celebrated a horse sacrifice (asvamedha), A.D. 150, which forms a starting point for the dated history of Southern India. Another Pallava king, Mahendra Varman, about A.D. 600 to 625, built the earlier Raths or rock-temples at Mamallapuram, near Chingleput, the name of the place being derived from the word "mamalla," which means the wrestler, a title of Mahendra Varman. A third Pallava king, Narasimha Varman, son of Mahendra Varman, who reigned A.D. 625-45, destroyed the Western Chalukyan capital of Badami about A.D. 640. He also built the later Raths. The Pallava kingdom was eventually overthrown by the Chola king Rajaraja about 1000. The Pallava royal family is represented in modern times by the Raja of Pudukotta.

The Chola kingdom.

The Cholas occupied the east coast from Nellore to Puddukottai, and west to Coorg. The old Chola capital of Uraiyur (Old Trichinopoly) was in the seventh century A.D. transferred to Mailaikurram (the modern Kumbhakonam), and in the tenth or eleventh century A.D. to Gangaikonda-cholapuram in the Trichinopoly district on the Coleroon, and was finally placed at Tanjore, where the Chola king Rajaraja, 980-1013, built the great temple of Siva, with the statue of the Bull Nandi, and the inner temple of Subrahmanya, Shiva's son.

The first great Chola was Parantaka, A.D. 907 to about 947, who ruled over the Chola territory between the Pennar and the Vellar, and also over Tondamandalam or Kurumbabhumi (from Pulicat to Cudalore), and

Kongamandalam (Coimbatore, Salem, and Southern Mysore). The Kurumba state, which was conquered by the Cholas, had its capital at Pural in the Red Hills north of Madras. By this conquest the Chola boundary was advanced to the Eastern Ghats. Rajaditya, Parantaka's son, was slain in battle with the Ganga king Perumanadi Butuga at Takkalam, A.D. 950.

Rajaraja the Great, A.D. 985-1013, gained a naval victory over the Chera fleet in the roads of Kandalur, and conquered Vengi (the Telegu country), Orissa, and Ilam (Ceylon), and all the present Madras Presidency, except Madura and Tinnevelly. His son Rajendra Chola Gangaikonda, A.D. 1013-42, is said to have conquered Bengal and Behar, hence his title. He was called Gangaikonda, either because he reached the Ganges, or because he conquered the Ganga territory in Mysore. In his inscription at Gangaikondacholapuram, he boasts of having defeated the Chalukya king Somesvar, surnamed Adhavamalla (the wrestler in battle), at Kudala Sangam at the junction of the Kistna and Tungabhadra. His inscriptions also describe him as having sent a fleet and army to conquer the king of Kadarim (Prome or Pegu in Burma).

Connection between Southern India and Ceylon.

The descendants of the warriors who conquered Ceylon with Bijay Sinha were devoted to the Buddhist religion and the practice of agriculture, but they were essentially unwarlike. The kings of Ceylon had to look around for mercenaries, especially as cavalry and seamen, to guard the coasts. They found them in the "Malabars" or "Damilos," the name by which the Tamils are known in the Mahavamsa. Tamils first appear in the history of Ceylon, when Sena and

Gottika dethroned Suratissa, B.C. 237, and reigned in his stead. After them, Elala from Mysore conquered all the north and east of the island down to the rivers Mahaveli-ganga and Kaluganga. Elala reigned B.C. 205 to B.C. 161, when he was defeated and slain by Dutthagamini, a king of indigenous race. From this time onward to the end of the eleventh century of the Christian era, the history of Ceylon is a record of almost continuous oppression by the Tamils, who were in their turn ousted by rebellions of the native kings. The principal city of the Tamils was Jaffna (Yalpanam), which was founded about B.C. 100.

Wilagambahu I., in B.C. 104, was driven into the mountainous district of Rahuna around Adam's Peak, but he recovered his throne and expelled the invaders, B.C. 88.

Removal of the capital from Anuradhapura to Pollanarua.

Dhatu Sen, who caused the Mahavamsa to be compiled, succeeded in A.D. 459, after overthrowing the Malabar tyranny, which had lasted since A.D. 434. In the eighth century A.D. the kings of Ceylon moved their capital from Anuradhapura southwards to Pollanarua to escape the Malabars, who dominated more especially Northern Ceylon.

In A.D. 840 the Pandya king of Madura overran the whole of Ceylon, and again in A.D. 990, Rajaraja the Great, the Chola king of Tanjore, assumed the title of conqueror of Ilam, the Tamil name of Ceylon. In 1023 the Chola king carried the king of Ceylon captive to India, and left a Tamil viceroy at Pollanarua for thirty years. After him, Magha, an invader from the Northern Sirkars, established himself at Jaffna as king of the Ceylonese Malabars.

The long continued Tamil occupation of Northern Ceylon accounts for the distribution of its languages. Tamil is spoken north of a line drawn from Chelaw on the west to Batticaloa on the east coast, and Singhalese south of the Dedra-oya and Mahaveli-ganga.

Parakram Bahu, king of Ceylon, conqueror of Southern India.

Parakram Bahu, king of Ceylon, 1153-97, retaliated upon "the Malabars" the troubles they had brought upon Ceylon, by making Tanjore and Madura tributary, and coining money in his own name in Southern India. Parakram Bahu's name occurs as sixty-fifth among the Pandya sovereigns of Madura.

The Cholas annex the Eastern Chalukyan territories.

Gangaikonda's son, Rajadhiraja, 1042-53, was killed in battle with Somesvar Ahavamalla, 1040-69, the Chalukyan king at Koppam, 1053. His brother Rajendra, 1053-62, was crowned on the field of Koppam. Rajendra Chola Kulottunga, 1070-1118, was the son of Ammangadevi, daughter of Rajendra Chola Gangaikonda, who married a king of the Eastern Chalukyan territories. Rajendra Chola Kulottunga succeeded first to the Eastern Chalukyan territories, and afterwards to the Chola empire in 1070. Kulottunga was a contemporary of Ramanuja, whom he expelled from Srirangam and forced to escape into Mysore. He placed his son Gangaikonda on the Pandyan throne under the title of Sundra Pandya. The last Chola king was Rajendra Chola Kulottunga III., who ascended the throne in 1245. An old silver coin of the Cholas shows their cognisance, a tiger, under an imperial umbrella; in front of the tiger are two fish, and behind it a bow. Supremacy is thus claimed for the Cholas over the Pandyas and Cheras.

Final overthrow of the Chola kingdom.

The Chola kingdom was overthrown by Malik Kafur in 1311, and finally destroyed by Malik Khusru in 1319.

Chola administration.

A remarkable feature of the Chola administration was the power of the village communities, composed either of single villages or of groups of villages (kurram), each with its own assembly (mahasabha), which exercised almost sovereign powers in all departments of rural government. Each assembly was divided into certain communities, the "great men of the year," in whom supreme authority was vested, the "great men" for the administration of justice, and the supervision of the wards, fields, tanks, gardens. The village assemblies collected the state revenues; in the event of default, they took over the land and disposed of it at their pleasure, but the defaulter became free of liability. The state took one-sixth of the gross produce of the land as land-tax, but this was supplemented by certain tolls and octroi duties at the gates of the cities. Two detailed land surveys were executed, one in 985 and the other in 1086.

The Cholas were great builders. Karikala, one of the first Chola kings known to history, has his claim to fame based on the construction of the embankments on the Kaveri.

Western Chalukyas.

In A.D. 550 Pulakesin I. established a Chalukya kingdom at Vatapi (modern Badami) in the Bijapur district. This kingdom extended from the Narbada to the Tungabhadra; its eastern boundary was a line drawn northwards from the junction of the Tungabhadra and Kistna to the junction of the Wardha and Godaveri, and thence up the Wardha. The Pallavas were subdued and the Kadambas of Halsi in north-western Mysore also succumbed to the Chalukya kings Kirti Varman and Mangalisa. The greatest king of this dynasty was Pulakesin II. (Satyasraya) (609-642). He made the Chalukyas the paramount power in Southern India, and repulsed Harshavardhana Siladitya, the Lord Paramount of Northern India, in A.D. 620. During his reign the Chinese pilgrim Hiouen Thsang visited his court.

Eastern Chalukyas.

The eastern Chalukya line at Vengi began in A.D. 615, when Pulakesin appointed his brother Kubja Vishnubardhana as viceroy over his eastern territories. The eastern Chalukya kingdom lasted till it was absorbed by Rajendra Chola Kulottunga. In 642 Pulakesin was defeated and slain by the Pallava king Narasimha, who captured and destroyed the Chalukya capital of Badami, and the Chalukya power was in abeyance till 655, when Vikramaditya I. re-established the dynasty. He captured Kanchi, the capital of the Pallavas, and subdued the Cholas and the Pandyas. Throughout the reigns of his successors Vinayaditya (630-696), Vijayaditya (696-733), Vikramaditya II. (733-746), Buddhism was declining, and Puranic Hinduism growing in strength. The last of the line was Kirtivarman II. (746-754). In the latter year, the Chalukya power was overthrown by Dantivarman, the Rastrakuta chief, and did not rise again till A.D. 954. The eastern Chalukya line at Vengi continued to rule over the deltas of the Godaveri and the Kistna. Dantivarman was in his turn dethroned by his uncle Krishna I., who built the Kailasa temple at Ellora about the middle of the eighth century A.D. The Rastrakutas, who had now succeeded to the dominions of the Chalukyas, carried on intermittent wars with the Pallavas and the eastern Chalukyas. Govind III. (790-815), the

Rastrakutas.

greatest king of this dynasty, extended the Rastrakuta power to the Vindhya mountains and Malwa in the north, and to Kanchi in the south. The next king, Amogha Varsha (815-77), transferred the capital from Nasik to Manyakheta (modern Malkhed) in the Nizam's Dominions. Krishna III., about 915, conquered the Cholas, captured Conjeeveram and Tanjore, and made the Kaveri his southern boundary. The Rastrakuta kings, in order to check the power of their enemies, the Gurjaras of Bhimnal, maintained friendly terms with the Arabs who had conquered Sind in the eighth century. In A.D. 973 the last Rastrakuta king, Kakka II., was overthrown by Taila, a Chalukya, who began a new line called the Chalukyas of Kalyan.

Western Chalukyas of Kalyan.

Taila ruled from 973-997, and succeeded in recovering all the ancient territories of his race save Gujrat. In A.D. 1000, during the reign of Satyasarjya, the Chalukya territories were devastated by Rajaraja the Great, the Chola king. The period of the next two kings, Someswar I. (1040-69), and Vikramanka or Vikramaditya VI. (1076-1126), was one in which learning flourished, as the poet Bilhana lived at the court of Vikramaditya, and Vignanesvara, author of the Mitakshara, was one of his retinue. After this, the Chalukyan power declined, and in 1110 the kingdom was swept out of existence by the Yadavas of Deogiri, in the north, and the Hoysalas of Dvarasamudra (modern Halebid) in the south. Mulraj, a scion of the Chalukya royal family, founded a dynasty in Gujrat, which reigned till it was dethroned by the Solankis, A.D. 980.

A new power the Kakatiyas or Ganpatis of Warangal (Ekasilapur), also rose to power at this period by annexing from the Cholas the former Eastern Chalukya territories between the Godaveri and the Kistna. The history of the thirteenth century is a record of the struggle between the Yadavas, the Hoysalas, and the Kakatiya Rajputs of Warangal for supremacy.

The Kakatiya or Ganpati Rajputs.

The first important king of the Yadava dynasty was Bhillama, who established himself at Deogiri (Daulatabad in the Nizam's territory) about 1187. At the end of the thirteenth century, the Yadava Ramchandra, 1271-1310, reigned over all the territories of the Western Chalukyas, as well as the Konkan and part of Mysore. They were always fighting with the Hoysala Rajputs on the south, and the Kakatiya Rajputs on the east. In 1318, Harapala, the last king of his race, rebelled against Mubarak Shah of Delhi and was slain by him.

The Yadava Rajputs.

The Hoysalas were originally feudatories of the Rashtrakuta and the later Western Chalukya kings, and rose to power on the ruin of the latter dynasty. The Hoysala dynasty lasted from the beginning of the tenth to the middle of the fourteenth centuries, and was founded by Bitti Deva or Vishnuvardhana, 1100-41. The capital was fixed at Dwarasamudra (the modern Hallabid in Mysore), and the famous Hoysalesvara and Kedaresvara temples at Hallabid were built by kings of this race. They also built other temples at Somnathpur and Belur. The dynasty reached its zenith under Vira Bellala, grandson of Bitti Deva, and Vira Narasinha, who together reigned for about sixty years, 1188-1249. The whole of the Karnatic was subject to these two monarchs. The provinces of Malabar and Kanara on the west, the

The Hoysala Rajputs.

Dravida country on the south and east, and part of the Telingana country, acknowledged them, if not as immediate masters, yet as exercising supreme authority through their officers, or through the native rajas as vassals and tributaries. Vira Ballala III. surrendered to Malik Kafur in 1310, and the kingdom was finally overthrown by Mahomed Tughlak in 1327.

The Kakatiya or Ganpati Rajputs.

The Kakatiya or Ganpati dynasty founded at Warangal on the Waingunga in the Nizam's Dominions lasted from about 1100 to 1321. Their territory was bounded on the north by Orissa, on the south by the rivers Tungabhadra and Kistna, on the west by the sea, and on the east it stretched as far as Raichur. According to the inscription in the temple of One Thousand Pillars at Hammankondah (Warangal), the first noticeable chief of this race was Prola (about 1150). The last king, Pratap Rudra II., was subdued by Malik Kafur in 1310, and Warangal was finally taken by Juna Khan, afterwards Mahomed Tughlak, in the reign of Ghiasudin Tughlak. The chief architectural remains of this dynasty are the Hammankondah temple, and the four Kirti Stambhas or Torans put up by Pratap Rudra. The chiefs of Bastar in the Central Provinces claim descent from the Kakatiyas of Warangal.

Mahomedans in the south.

Then came the period of the Mahomedan conquest. In 1294 Alauddin Khilji appeared suddenly before Deogiri, and Ramchandra was compelled to cede Ellichpur, and promised to pay an annual tribute to the emperor of Delhi. In 1309 Malik Kafur, sent by Emperor Alauddin, reduced the Hoysala king of Warangal to subjection. In 1310, he completed the conquest of the Hoysalas, and penetrated to the

Malabar coast. He also conquered the Pandya kingdom of Madura. In 1312 the king of Deogiri refused to pay tribute and was defeated and slain. The Yadava dynasty finally came to an end in 1318, and the whole of the Deccan came under Mahomedan rule. But in the country to the south of the Tungabhadra and the Kistna, there arose a new Hindu empire at Vijaynagar, founded by two brothers Harihara and Bukka assisted by their prime minister, the celebrated Madhavacharjya. This power for more than two centuries (1336-1565) kept the Mahomedan advance in check.

CHAPTER VII.

DECLINE OF BUDDHISM AND THE REVIVAL OF HINDUISM.

Hinayana and Mahayana Schools of Buddhism.

BUDDHISM split into two schools, the Southern School of Ceylon, Burma, and Siam, which is called the Sravakayana or Hinayana, the path of Devotees or the Lesser Path, and preserves more of the simplicity of the ancient faith, and the Northern School of Thibet, China, and Japan, which is called the Mahayana or Great Path. Nagarjuna, author of the *Prajnaparimita,* conceived the idea of a deity called Adi-Buddha, who corresponds to the Hindu idea of Ishvara or the Supreme Deity. Adi-Buddha, by union with the primordial female energy, produced from himself by *dhyana,* meditation, other beings called *Dhyani Buddhas,*—whose names are Vairochana, Akshobya, Ratnasambhava, Amitabha, and Amoghasiddha. Each *Dhyani Buddha* had his female counterpart, of whom the most celebrated is Tara, the consort of Amoghasiddha. These *Dhyani Buddhas* are the mystical counterparts in the world of meditation (*rupaloka*) of the human Buddhas,—Krakachanda, Kanakamuni, Kasyapa, Gautama, and Maitreya, the Buddha who is still to come. Each Buddha has produced by emanation from himself a *Dhyani*

Adi-Buddha

Dhyani Buddhas.

Human Buddhas.

Dhyani Buddhisattvas.

Buddhisattva to act as head of the Buddhist community between the death of each Buddha and the advent of his successor. These *Dhyani Buddhisattvas* are Samanta-bhadra, Ratnapani, Manjusri or Visvapani, Padmapani or Avalokiteshvara, and Vajrapani. The latter three form the Buddhist Trimurti. Manjusri corresponds to the Hindu Brahma or Viswakarma. At the supreme Adi-Buddha's command, Manjusri built the mansions of the world, and Padmapani created all animate beings.[1]

Buddhist Trimurti.

The Dalai Lama of Lhasa is supposed to be an incarnation of Avalokiteshvara. There is a female Buddhisattva called Prajnaparimita or the Perfected Wisdom, who corresponds to Saraswati. Other famous authors of the Mahayana school were Asvaghosa, who wrote the Buddha-Charita or life of Buddha, and Aryadeva, a disciple of Nagarjuna, author of a work called Sataka.

Scriptures of Northern Buddhism.

The most important scriptures of the Northern School were Sadharmapundarika or Lotus of the True Law, the Lalita Vistara, and the Jatakas or records of the Buddha in his previous rebirths. The existence of the Northern School permitted a belief in the identity of the Brahmin and Buddhist creeds, Buddha being regarded as an avatar of Vishnu. After the Mahomedan invasion, the Sravak or Hinayana Buddhists left India, and the Mahayana school reigned supreme, but it incorporated a large mixture of aboriginal religious ceremonies in the shape of Tantricism. Assanga, a Buddhist of Peshawar, who lived about 500 A.D., embodied the Tantric creed, which is a mixture of Buddhism, Siva worship, and

Tantricism.

[1] Sir M. Monier Williams' 'Buddhism,' pp. 202, 203.

magic, in the *Yogachara Bhumisastra*. The word Tantra means rule or ritual, and the *Sakti* or productive energy of nature is the chief object of Tantric worship. These Tantric mysteries involved devil worship and indulgence in sensual excess, and most injuriously affected the purity of the Buddhist religion.

Decline of Buddhism.

The morality of Buddhism in its prime was too strict; philanthropy, which gave Buddhism its impulse, was dead, the priests chopped logic on metaphysical topics instead of actively working for the good of the people. It was necessary to convert a cold philosophical creed, based on a pessimistic theory of existence, into a belief that human life was worth living and was controlled by a personal god, who took an active interest in man's welfare. During his lifetime, Buddha was treated with immense respect as a preacher and a moralist, but only as a man. After his death, his relics were honoured, and the virtues, of which he was a type, were held in respect, but images of Buddha either as an ascetic or a divinity are not found. It is only after he had been dead some time that he came to be honoured as a divinity, and the change was indicated by the multiplication of his images. It may thus be said that the purity of the Buddhist faith is in inverse proportion to the number of images of Buddha.

Difference between the Mahayana and Hinayana schools.

In the Mahayana school Stupas, Daghobas or relic shrines were replaced by images of Buddha, and a personal worship of the Buddha, as divine, was undertaken, instead of a worship of the virtues of which Buddha was the type. There was a multiplication of images and of ornaments, as in the later caves of

Ajanta. Buddha was pushed into the background by Buddhisattvas (great saints qualified for Nirvana who have consented to delay their vanishing into nothingness to advise mankind). Other deities, who distract the pious from the worship of Buddha, are the female personifications of Dharma, the goddesses like Prajnaparimita, and the Saktis like Tara, Marmukhi, or Lochana. Even the chouri bearers of Buddha were given the badges of Buddhisattvas.

Influence of Buddhism upon reformed Hinduism.

Buddhism had been atheistic, so Sankarcharjya the Saivite, and Ramanuja and Chaitanya the Vaishnavists, argued strongly in favour of a personal god. The Vaishnavists and Saivites of Southern India adopted the Buddhistic principle of the equality of castes. In the pre-Buddhist period, astronomy, mathematics, law, and philosophical speculation were all intimately connected with the Vedas ; after the revival of Hinduism, the Vedas were comparatively neglected.

Favourite forms of Hinduism.

The Krishna cult, and Saktism were the favourite forms of Hinduism after the decline of Buddhism. They owed their popularity to their greater human element, and their greater congeniality to the tastes of the people.

Buddhism ousted from its position as the State Religion by the revival of Hinduism.

The revival of Hinduism was due to the preaching of three great teachers, Kumarila Bhatta, Sankarcharjya, and Ramanuja, and to the appeal they made to the masses in favour of the worship of a personal god. Kumarila Bhatta was a Brahman of the Deccan, who lived about A.D. 650, and wrote the Tantra Vartika, an explanation of Savaraswami's commentary on Mimansa philosophy. He is said to have travelled through the length and breadth of India, proclaiming the authority of the Vedas, and arguing against all religions opposed to Brahmanism. He was a fierce opponent of the Buddhists and Jains, and upheld the claims of the Brahmans to be the religious guides of the people.

Sankarcharjya, a Namburi Brahman, who was born at Cranganore in Malabar about A.D. 788, and died A.D. 820 at Kedarnath in the Himalayas, wrote the Brahmasutra Bashya, a commentary on Vedanta philosophy. He established Hindu monasteries or *Maths*, each consisting of a Mahant with his Chelas or pupils. He founded an order, that of the *Tridandins*, those who exercise control over their thoughts, words, and actions. He was the champion of the Vedanta school and maintained the philosophic doctrine of pure Monism called *Advaitavada*. Sankarcharjya constructed out of the Upanishads a theological system for the general public, who require concrete images to picture their ideals, instead of abstract truth, and depend upon ceremonial worship without having recourse to meditation. This doctrine was called "*saguna*" or "*apara bidya*" or "*vyâhârika avastha*." He had another system, philosophical, and full of metaphysical truth for those who could understand it; this he called "*nirguna*," or "*paravidya*," or "*paramarthika avastha*." Men of inferior intellect were allowed to believe in a personal God, but final deliverance could only be obtained when men, by "*anubhava*" (absorption into self), recognised that they themselves were identical with the Supreme Self, "*aham Brahma asmi*," and so entered into the state called by Sankarcharjya "*Samradhanam*" (accomplished satisfaction). Men who have attained

Samradhanam view the external world as mere illusion (*maya*), similar to a mirage (*mrigatrishna*) which fades as we approach, and which is not more to be feared than the rope, which seemed to be a snake in the dark. " God alone, and nothing besides him, is real. The universe, as regards its extension in space and bodily consistence, is in truth not real ; it is mere illusion as used to be said, mere appearance as we say now. The appearance is not God as in Pantheism, but the reflection of God, and is an aberration from the Divine Essence. Not as though God were to be sought on the other side of the Universe, for he is not at all in space ; nor as though he were before or after, for he is not at all in time ; nor as though he were the cause of the Universe, for the laws of causation have no application here. Rather to the extent to which the Universe is regarded as real, God is without reality. That he is real, nay the sole reality, we perceive only in so far as we succeed in shaking ourselves free theoretically and practically from this entire world of appearance." [1]

The experimental knowledge which reveals to us a world of plurality where only Brahma exists, and a body, where there is only soul, is a delusion. We are to love our neighbours as ourselves, because, according to the formula " *tat tvam asi*," we and our neighbours are identical ; it is only illusion which makes us believe them different from ourselves.[2]

The Jiv-Atman or individual soul cannot be a part of Brahma, as Ramanuja held (because Brahma is

[1] Deussen, ' Elements of Metaphysics,' p. 330.

[2] Deussen, ' Outlines of Indian Philosophy and the Philosophy of the Vedanta,' 47, 48, 58, 59.

without parts, being timeless and spaceless, and all parts are either successions in time or coordinations in space). It is not a different thing from Brahma, as Madhava held, for Brahma is "*ekam eva advitiyam.*" It is not a metamorphosis of Brahma, as Vallabha held, since Brahma is unchangeable, being not subject to causality. Sankarcharjya therefore concludes that the Jiv-Atman is the Paramatman fully and totally himself. If this is so, then the qualities of all-pervadingness, all-mightiness, eternity, exemption from time, space, causality, belong to man. These qualities are for the present hidden, as the fire is hidden in the wood, and will only appear after the final deliverance.[1]

After Sankarcharjya established the supremacy of the Saivite cult in the eighth century, the Vedic objection to anthropomorphic religious symbolism revived in Upper India, and was maintained from political expediency to avoid persecution at the hands of fanatical Mahomedans.

Ramanuja, 1017-1137 A.D., was also a Brahman of Southern India, born at Perumbur, was the promulgator of Vishnu worship, which he derived from the Brahmasutra and from the Vishnu Purana. He formed into a logical system the doctrines of the Bhagavatas. He wrote *Vedanta saran* (essence of Vedanta), *Vedanta sangraham* (*résumé* of Vedanta), and *Vedanta dipam* (light on Vedanta), which were commentaries on the Brahmasutra and Bhagavadgita. He quarrelled with his Saivite colleagues on a question of discipline, and founded a sect open to all castes, and

[1] Deussen, 'Outlines of Indian Philosophy and the Philosophy of the Vedanta,' 47, 48, 58, 59.

began to preach, not in Sanscrit, but in the vernacular. He promised many blessings to those who practised the virtue of Bhakti or devotion. Unlike the Vedantists, who deny to the deity the attributes of *form* and *quality*, Ramanuja declared that the deity possessed both, and that he was the cause of the universe. The Vedantists teach that the Supreme Spirit and the spirit of man are one and the same, and that the soul gains salvation by losing its individuality after absorption into the deity. Ramanuja opposed this doctrine by maintaining that the true relation between the supreme soul and the individual soul was communion without absorption. God is a personal being, the whole aggregate of the souls of men is, as it were, the mind of God, and the external material world is, as it were, the body of God. This may be described as qualified Monism or *Visishtadwaitavada*. Madhavacharjya held that God, the souls of individual men, and the external world, are all distinct one from the other ; this is the so-called *Dwaita* or Dualistic School of Vedanta philosophy. Ramanuja modified the Vedantic doctrine that the universe is illusion, and that Brahma only exists, by saying that matter, though a manifestation of the universal soul, is yet to be considered as having a separate existence.

Adiyars and Alwars.

During the early middle ages, the doctrines of Saivism were widely promulgated in Southern India by wandering teachers called Adiyars, and the teachings of Saivite philosophy were explained in "Saiva Siddhanta," a Tamil treatise. The tenets of Vaishnavism were at the same time championed by a class of teachers similar to the Adiyars, called Alwars.

Vedagalai and Tengalai, followers of Ramanuja.

Ramanuja's followers split up into the Vedagalai sect, who considered Divine grace to result from co-operation between God and man, and the Tengalai sect, who held it to be the result of the irresistible influence of God upon man.

Ramanuja resided at Belur in Hassan, Mysore, and at the Alagiri rock, twelve miles north-west of Madura, where he composed the Sribhashya, a commentary on the Brahmasutra. He was persecuted by Rajendra Chola Kulottunga, the Chola king of Tanjore, who tried to enforce the repetition of the Sivaite formula, "*Sivât paratarам nasti*" (there is no being greater than Siva). Ramanuja took refuge with Bittideva Vishnu Vardhana, the Hoysala king of Dwarasamudra, who was a Jain, but who was converted by Ramanuja to Vaishnavism. He was eventually allowed to return, and died at the temple of Srirangam on the Kaveri.

Lingayets.

Basava, a Brahman, who was supposed to have been an incarnation of the bull Nandi, the Vahan of Siva, founded the sect of the Lingayets or Vira Sawas in the twelfth century. They are a union of all castes and pay respect to Gurus, Lingam, and Jangam (religious union). They attribute no merit to the Vedic sacrifices. Basava was the minister of Bijjala, a Chedi or Kalachuri Rajput from Central India, who seized Kalyan and held it for twenty years, 1062-82.

CHAPTER VIII.

INDIAN ART.

INDIAN art is essentially symbolic. To begin with the colours, white is the colour of Siva, and is the colour symbol of water, and symbolises purity and bliss. Red is the colour of the sun, and of Brahma the Creator. Blue is the colour of the firmament, and the symbol of Vishnu. Red, white and blue, the colours of the lotus petals, are the emblems of the Hindu Trimurti, the three aspects of the One. Black is the colour symbol of Kali, the mother of the Universe, and the Great Destroyer. Yellow is the special colour of the ascetic's robes.

Colour symbolism.

The open lotus flower, which is so common an ornament on the rails of Bharhut, Sanchi, and Amaravati, was a sun emblem ; the horse-shoe arch, derived from the bent bamboo, suggested the lotus leaf. Buddhist and Hindu domes, which also imitated the curves of a bent bamboo, recall the *amalaka* or bell-shaped lotus fruit. This bell-shaped fruit, which was a symbol of the *Hiranya garbha* or Womb of the Universe, in combination with the water-pot or Kalasha, are the basis of the designs of many of the pillars in Hindu temples. These pillars represent the old wooden posts marking out the sacrificial area,

Lotus symbolism and imitation of parts of the lotus in various parts of the temple.

according to the Vedic rites, to which the animals to be offered in sacrifice were tied. The *amalaka* and *kalasha* are also found as parts of the pinnacles on the domes, even of mosques, and the exterior surface of the domes was ornamented with lotus petals.

Wood the oldest building material.

Wood was the oldest building material in India, and all Indian styles are derived from models constructed in timber or bamboo. Some of the oldest stone buildings are constructed in the same style as they would have been, had they been built of wood. The façade of Lomas Rishi's cave in the Barabar hills near Gaya is a case in point, and is an exact copy of a wooden construction.

The oldest temple.

The oldest temple was the hut of a holy man, and all the additions are but accretions on to this nucleus.

Parts of temple symbolic of certain parts of a village.

The parts of a temple symbolise certain parts of a village. The rail round a Buddhist stupa, which is modified in Mahayana temples to a mere chequer ornament, was a symbolic adaptation to religious purposes of the ordinary timber fence round a village; its three bars had a reference to Brahma, Vishnu, and Siva, or, if Buddhist, to Buddha, Sangha, and Dharma.

The Torans or gateways of Sanchi or Barhut recalled the four gates of an ordinary town or village; they symbolised the four Vedas, or the Nativity, the Enlightenment, the First Serman, and the Parinirvana of Buddha. These gates are called Gopurams in Southern India, and by their name recall the gates through which the cows are driven into the village every evening. The "Halls of a Thousand Pillars" in Southern Indian temples represent the parks or groves which were used as meeting-places in Indian villages. The *mandapam* or hall of worshippers in the temple was modelled on the village assembly hall.

Shrines dedicated to Vishnu are characterised by the *Sikra* or spire, and have an entrance facing the rising sun. Shrines dedicated to Siva are characterised by flat roofs or domes surmounting high pyramidal roofs, and have their entrance facing the setting sun Shrines dedicated to Brahma have four entrances facing the four cardinal points. One temple may have its mandapam, with an entrance in the direction sacred to Siva ; its shrine may have four doors, thus recalling Brahma, whilst the Sikhara which covers the shrine symbolises Vishnu. Different parts of the same temple thus honour the three aspects of the Supreme.

The claim to originality of Indian art.

One view about Indian art denies almost completely its claim to originality, and maintains that the pillars of Asoka were borrowed from Persepolis, the winged animals were adopted from Assyrian models, the lotuses and plant-forms used as ornaments were West-Asian in origin. According to this view, Gandhara art was exclusively the work of Greek settlers in Bactria.

Gandhara art.

The true view is that Indian art is largely original, showing a wonderful power of assimilating whatever it borrowed from foreign sources. The influence of the Greeks upon Indian art was transient and superficial. Sister Nivedita points out that Gandhara art is specially strong in its decorations derived from flowers and plants, and in the attention it paid to the animal world as a whole—elements in which Greek art is deficient. Severity of restraint is characteristic of Greek ; exuberance, of Indian art.

Difference between Greek and Gandhara art.

Some all-pervading influence, possibly the teaching of the universities, seized on the ideas on art which existed in the minds of the various races to be found in India from the eighth to the fourteenth centuries, eliminated what was discordant, and made them national. Thus "Greco-Roman art became gradually Indianised," and combined with Persepolitan traditions into an indigenous Indian art.

Classical ornaments belong to common stock of Asiatic art.

It must not be forgotten that India was open to external influence long before Alexander's expedition, and sculptured ornaments, like acanthus leaves, palmettos, vine leaves, tritons, centaurs, and perhaps the Persepolitan monolithic pillars, may be considered as belonging to the common stock of Asiatic art, rather than specially Greek or Persian in their origin.[1]

The frieze, from the Upper Nathu Vihara Yusufzai, is divided into five compartments, the first ornamented with vine leaves, the second showing a boy plucking grapes, the third a boy playing with a goat, the fourth a goat nibbling vine leaves, and the fifth a boy plucking grapes is an example of the subject of vine leaves treated in a specially Greek manner.

Unmistakable marks of Greek influence.

In some points Gandhara is unmistakably indebted to Greek sources. Doric columns are found in the temple of the Sun at Martand, which belongs to the late Kashmir style, but these are probably copied from Sassanian models. Ionic columns have been found in two temples on the site of Taxila associated in one instance with coins of Azes, the Parthian king, who reigned from B.C. 90 to 40. A niche supported

[1] 'Footfalls of Indian History,' pp. 85-95.

Statue of Athene.

by columns with Ionic capitals has been found on a sculptured fragment at Mathura. A capital with corner volutes of Romano-Ionic form has been found in the Ahinposh stupa near Jalalabad in Afghanistan. Two more Ionic columns have been found at Sarnath

ATLAS (USED TO SUPPORT COLUMN OR CORNICE).

and Patna. Corinthian columns, pilasters, and capitals are fairly abundant in the Panjab, especially at Jamalgarhi. Even the modillions (supports) of the cornices are sometimes made like small Corinthian cornices.

Statues of Greek gods and goddesses, such as Athene in the Lahore museum, the Atlantes from Jamalgarhi in the Peshawar museum, which were used to support columns and cornices, the long garlands carried by Cupids which were used to break up a long frieze into sections, from the Lower Nathu Vihara Yusufzai, mark the influence of the Greek religion and art, but this influence was Greco-Bactrian, not Macedonian, in its origin. Similar cupids carrying garlands are found carved on the Amaravati remains, and they have been called " Indianised adaptations of Alexandrian art," but this theory of the[illegible]igin is not probable. The statue of Hercules and the

GARLAND SUPPORTED BY CUPIDS. (From the Lower Nathu Vihara Yusufzai.)

Nemaean lion found at Mathura, and the effigy of Athene upon the coins of Azes I., are other proofs of the same influence.

On the pediment of the sculptured group in the Peshawar museum, the subject of which is the conversion of the Naga Apalala to Buddhism, is sculptured an orthodox winged Christian an[illegible] dressed in the himation and chiton. No explanati[illegible] is forthcoming of this most unusual feature, but it at least points to some activity of Christianity in Northern India. Statues of Buddha themselves result from Greek influence, as early Buddhist artists scrupulously refrained from introducing Buddha's effigy in any sculptures pourtraying Buddhistic legends. For this reason Havell remarks that

Statues of Buddha attributable to Greek influence.

Gandhara sculptors were "the first iconographers of the person of Buddha." [1]

The statues of Buddha were originally carved on each of the four sides of the Stupa, facing the four points of the compass, but after a time became detached from the Stupa altogether.

Statues are of three kinds—sitting, standing and lying down.

Sitting statues are:

(i) Meditative, hands crossed one above the other.

(ii) Witness attitude, feet turned upwards, left hand on left foot, right hand with second and third fingers pointing to the earth.

(iii) Serpent canopied.

(iv) Argumentative.

Standing statues are:

(i) Preaching; (ii) Blessing; (iii) Mendicant.

Lying down statues are:

(i) In the act of being born.

(ii) At the point of death.

Types of these statues are the figure of Buddha with the bo-tree on the Old Clay Seal from Bodh Gaya, and the statue of Buddha from Mahomed Nari, showing an arrangement of the drapery imitated from the Greek.

Gandhara sculpture.

The Gandhara sculptures are found in the Yusufzai territory (Hashtnagar district) between the Swat and Indus rivers. They have also been discovered in connection with the Manikyala Stupa and the Huta Murta or Body-offering Stupa (called respectively Ventura's and Court's Topes from Ranjit Singh's generals, who excavated them) between Rawal Pindee

[1] 'Indian Sculpture and Painting,' p. 41.

STATUE OF BUDDHA ON THE PADMASANA.

Showing drapery imitated from the Greek, from the village of Mahomed Nari Panjab.

and the Jhelum, the Shah-ji-ki deri Stupa outside Peshawar, and the Vihara of Takt-i-Bahi near Hoti Murdan. Other sites are Udyana (Swat valley), and

Butan (idols), a place in the Palai valley to the south of the Shahkot pass, so called from the multitude of statues it contains, and Kafirkot on the Indus, in the Dera Ismail Khan district.

Among the other well-known groups of statuary belonging to Gandhara art are the visit of Indhra or Sakra to Buddha in the Indrasaila cave from Loriyan Tangai in Swat, which, showing the wild beasts looking out of their dens, herein provides a conventional indication that the scene is laid in a wild and mountainous country. Another group is the statue of Kuvera or Vaisravana, king of the demigods or spirits called Yakshas, and god of wealth, with Hariti, goddess of fertility, in the Peshawar museum. The statue of Garuda and the Nagini from Sanghao Yusufzai, is a curious example of the Indianisation of the classical subject of the Rape of Gannymede by the Attic sculptor of the fourth century B.C., Leochares.

Such was Gandhara art at its best period, which is placed by Mr. Vincent Smith as contemporary with the reigns of the Kushan kings, Kanishka and Huvishka, about the middle of the second century. In its decadence, Mr. Havell's 'Ideals of Indian Art.' speaks of the statues of Buddha as "representing a trim smug-faced Greek Apollo posing in the attitude of an Indian Yogi."

Two notable examples of Gandhara work in metals merit special mention.

Shah-ji-ki deri casket.

In the Shah-ji-ki deri Stupa has recently been discovered a rock crystal receptacle, sealed with Kanishka's seal (an elephant), and containing a portion of the ashes of Buddha. The receptacle was enclosed in a bronze casket with Kharosthi letters giving the name of the Greek maker,—" Agesilaus, Head Engineer in the Vihara of Kanishka in the Sangharama of Mahasena."

The lid, which is slightly curved and incised to represent a full-blown lotus, supports three figures in

SHAH-JI-KI DERI STUPA.
Casket containing Buddha's ashes.

the round; a seated Buddha in the centre, and a Buddhisattva on each side. The edge of the lid is further adorned by a frieze in low relief of flying geese bearing wreaths in their beaks; whilst below on the body of the casket is an elaborate design in high relief of young Erotes bearing a continuous garland, in the undulations of which are seated Buddha figures, and attendant worshippers leaning towards them out of the background. But the chief and central figure is the Emperor Kanishka himself, standing erect with a winged celestial being bearing a wreath on either side.[1]

The Bimaran casket.

Another casket of gold, ornamented with precious stones, was found in the foundation deposit of the

VINDUSAGAR TANK AND TEMPLE, BHUBANESWAR.

second Bimaran stupa, north of the road between Kabul and Jalalabad. Flat pilasters with sunken panels separate niches which enclose four figures—Buddha in the attitude of blessing, a lay follower with hands clasped in the attitude of adoration, a male ascetic with matted hair and a water-pot in his

[1] 'Journal of the Royal Asiatic Society, Bengal, 1909,' pp. 1056-60.

hands, and a female disciple praying. The niches are crowned by arches, circular below and pointed above. The casket agrees with Gandhara sculpture in the arrangement of the figures in compartments separated by pilasters with sunken panels, but differs in the form of the arches, and in the absence of Corinthian capitals.

TEMPLE, BHUBANESWAR.

The gradual decline of Buddhism is shown by the fact that there are few specimens of Buddhist architecture later than the fifth century, and, with the exception of the Ramnagar temple at Ahichatra Bareli district, which is the oldest Hindu temple in India, and dates from the first century B.C. or the first century A.D., there are hardly any Hindu temples standing which date before A.D. 550. Ferguson distinguishes three styles of Indian architecture: Indo-Aryan, Dravidian, and Chalukyan. These may be distinguished by their ground-plans—that of the Indo-Aryan buildings is square with a bulging curvilinear sikra or spire, that of Dravidian buildings is rectangular with *gopurams* or gateways

TIRUVANAMALAI TEMPLE, NEAR TRICHINOPOLY.

built in stories, and that of the Chalukyan buildings is star-shaped with pyramidal towers. In the Chalukyan style, the Vishnu Sikra is crowned by a Siva dome instead of the *amalaka* or lotus fruit. The star-shaped plan is an elaboration of the circular stupa, and a structural application of the symbolism of the eight or sixteen petalled lotus. The Hindu temples in Northern India were destroyed by the iconoclastic zeal of the Mahomedans, but the mediaeval temples of Orissa, Bhubanesvar, Konarak

Porch of Great Tower of the Temple at Bhubaneswar.

and Puri have survived. The Sivaite temples of Bhubaneswar are built of sandstone and were founded by the Kesari kings of Orissa, in the seventh century A.D. According to Ferguson, the Black Pagoda of Konarak dates from the latter half of the ninth century A.D., but Mr. V. Smith considers it the work of Raja Nrisimha, 1238-64, and built between 1240 and 1280. The Black Pagoda is peculiar in being dedicated to the Sun. It is black because built

NAVAGRAHA FRIEZE, KONARAK.

of chlorite, and it is called the Black Pagoda to distinguish it from the White Pagoda of Puri. It is designed to imitate the chariot of the sun, and has eight great wheels, each 9 feet 2 inches across, carved on the plinth, and there are statues of seven colossal horses outside.

The temple of Jagannath at Puri was built by Ananga Bhimadeva of the Ganga dynasty of kings of Orissa in 1174. The Gangavamsa succeeded the

Kesari dynasty in 1132. The Orissa temples are built in sections comprising a Vimana or shrine divided into the *Antarala* or inner chamber, and the *Garbha Griha* or Holy of Holies, and Porch, to which a *Nat Mandir* and a *Bhog Mandir* (dancing and dining-rooms) are sometimes added. The Vimanas of an

TEMPLE OF PURI.

Orissa temple resemble two-thirds of a cucumber stuck in the ground, and the tops are finished off with an ornament called *amalaka* from its resemblance to the fruit of the lotus. The Orissa temples and the modern temples in Bengal are usually of one type, the form of which was probably derived from an ancient tent or hut. Its peculiar curved and bulging form was perhaps at first formed of bent bamboos tied together

at the top, and strengthened by shorter horizontal pieces, and the roof was made of thatch, palm leaves or skins. This original form of temple was afterwards imitated in stone, slabs of sandstone being the material used. Certain temples at Vishnupur district, Bankura, Bengal, do not correspond to the ordinary Indo-Aryan

KISTARAYA'S JOR-BUNGALOW TEMPLE AT VISHNUPUR.

type. They are square in shape, with a curved roof, and one tower in the centre surrounded by four, eight, and even twenty-four small corner-towers. The roof with a convex curvature is intended to form a channel by which heavy rain can drain off. The temple at Kantanagar, Dinagepore, is still more anomalous. The Garuda pillar at Jajpur, the Hindu temples at Khajuraho, Central India, the temple of Bishveshvar at Benares, and the Chitor temple of Vriji, are specimens of Indo-Aryan architecture. In Southern India, the temples of the Dravidian style are built in one large mass (the vimana) tapering gradually towards the summit, and a choultry or pillared hall, surrounded by a rectangular wall with from fourteen to sixteen gateways (gopurams), straight-lined towers divided into stories by horizontal bands, and surmounted by a barrel-roofed ridge or small dome. The most famous temples are those at Madura, Tanjore, Conjeeveram, Srirangam, and Chidambaram ; these are in good repair. The temples of Vithalaswami (Vishnu) at Hampi, the site of Vijaynagar, and at Kalugumalai in the Tinnevelly district are in ruins.

The seven Raths of Mamallipuram or Mahabalipur, eighteen miles from Chingleput, were built in the seventh century A.D. by Mahendra Varman and Narasimha Varman, Pallava kings. These raths are cut out of single blocks of granite and reproduce in stone the model of the Buddhist Viharas, *e.g.* the verandah of Bhima's rath shows where the sleeping cells of the monks were placed ; the structure between the columns and the roof of Sahadeva's rath resembles the horse-shoe front of the cave temple of Bhaja. The raths are important architecturally as marking the transition between Buddhistic and Hindu architecture. The earliest domes were those of the Stupas or relic shrines, which were approximately hemispherical and built of solid brickwork. When images were placed under domed canopies supported by columns, these domes were constructed with ribs

MAMALLIPUR RATHS.

of bamboo bent into the lotus or bulbous shape, as at Mamallipuram and Kalugumalai. The rock carvings, especially Arjun's penance and Durga slaying Mahisha, are of the highest interest.

Chalukyan style.

Ferguson distinguishes a third style of Hindu architecture which he calls the Chalukyan style, and which is best exemplified in the temples at Hallabid

ARJUN'S PENANCE, MAMALLIPUR.

or Dwarasamudra, at Belur, and Somnathpur in Mysore founded by the Hoysala kings, and at Hanmankondah or Warangal in the Nizam's Dominions, founded by the Kakati king, Pratap Rudra.

Jain Art.

The Jains had no heroes who were believed to be incarnations of divine personages, and their saints did not develop into personifications of the powers of nature. Their Tirthankaras could only be represented as absorbed in contemplation, and as assuming the fixed unalterable pose of the ascetic. Hence the poverty of invention shown by the Jain sculptures.

Jain architecture.

The characteristics of Jain architecture are the horizontal arch and the bracket form assumed by the capitals of the pillars. The Aiwalli temple in Dharwar shows that the Jains followed the ground

KALI KILLING MAHISHASURA, MAMALLIPUR.

plan of the Buddhist Chaitya, but made a door through the circular apse at the end of it. In the adjacent temple at Pattadakal, near Badami in Dharwar, the apse has become the base of a tower marking the position of the image. This tower carries a Sikra or spire, which is a marked feature of Jain or Indo-Aryan architecture in Northern India. The nave of the Buddhist Chaitya was altered to form the Jain *Mandapam* or porch.

There are two classes of Jain temples in Southern India: (1) Bettus, (2) Bastis. The Bettus contain images of Gomata Raja, who was a son of the first Tirthankara worshipped. The best known temple of this sort is that at Sravana Belgola, Mysore. Other Jain colossi, erected by Chamuda Raya about A.D. 983, are found at Karkala and Venur in South Kanara. The Bastis are mere ordinary Jain temples. According to Ferguson they show great similarity to Thibetan temples. This is especially true of the Jain temples at Mudbidri, Kanara. A peculiarity of Jain architecture is the massing of a large number of temples in a small space, *e.g.* the Satrunjya hill in the Palitana State, and on the Girnar hill in the Junagadh State, Kathiawar.

The Jains occasionally built Stupas; thus the Stupa on the Kankali mound at Mathura is of Jain origin. The temple railing and many Jain statues from this mound are preserved in the museum at Lucknow. They also sometimes adapted caves to their worship, thus certain caves, which were originally Buddhist, on the Khandagiri hill in Orissa, were converted to Jain use. The Jains also excavated the Indra and Jagannath Sabha caves at Ellora.

The fine arts.

Music or Gandharva Veda was an Upaveda, and the division of the musical scale into seven notes is found in the Vedangas entitled Siksha and Chhandas.

Subjects of Ajanta frescoes.

The frescoes in the Ajanta caves have many subjects, amongst which the following are some of the most remarkable: the Embassy of Khusru Parviz, or Chosroes, to Pulakesin II., king of Maharashtra, in the thirty-sixth year of his reign, A.D. 625-26, from Cave I.; the Great Renunciation, from

Cave I.[1]; the Six-tusked Elephant and Maya, the mother of Buddha, from Cave X.; the Raja's Bestowal of a Sword on his Heir, the Lady's Toilette, and the Royal Love Scene, from Cave XVII.; the Landing of Bijaya in Ceylon, from Cave XVIII.; and the Mother and Child before Buddha, from Cave XIX.

GREAT BULL IN THE TEMPLE, TANJORE.

The Jatakas are the favourite source from which the other subjects are taken. It must be remembered that the Ajanta frescoes are executed on an enormous scale, and that they are intended to be looked at from a distance, accuracy in minute details must not therefore be expected from them. The picture of bulls fighting, from Cave I., is an example of the truth to nature with which the painting is executed, and the two spandrels from the central

Ignorance of the Jatakas is one of the chief causes why the modern observer cannot appreciate the frescoes.

[1] See page 65.

panel of the ceiling of Cave I. are examples of the variety of execution with which a somewhat similar subject can be presented.

The modern critic is handicapped by not possessing the unity in religious sentiment with the painter which would go a long way towards inducing him to

Two Bulls Fighting, from Bracket Capital in Cave I., Ajanta.

sympathise with and understand the painter's work. Other specimens of Indian painting are found at the Jogimara cave, Ramgarh hill, in the native state of Sirguja, and at Bagh in the Gwalior State. In both these places the paintings have suffered sorely from natural decay.

Other Indian frescoes.

Sigiri rock frescoes.

The frescoes on the Sigiri rock in Ceylon were painted by the order of the parricide Kasyapa, king of Ceylon A.D. 479-497, who built a palace on the top of this almost inaccessible rock. The subject of the frescoes is a procession of noble ladies carrying flowers, and attended by female servants, to the Buddhist temple at Pidurangula. Other frescoes are found in Ceylon painted on the roofs and sides of the Dambulla and Aluvihari rock temples. The latter represent a procession of elephants and the torments of hell. The Mahavamsa, a history of the king of

Other Ceylon frescoes.

SPANDREL FROM CENTRAL PANEL OF CEILING OF CAVE I.

Ceylon, composed in the fifth century A.D., speaks of frescoes painted on the walls of the Ruwanweli Daghoba, built by king Duthagamini about B.C. 150. The illuminations and illustrations in ancient manuscripts, and the specimens of painting recovered by Sir Aurel Stein from the sand-covered cities of Chinese Turkestan, show to what perfection the Fine Arts were carried by Indians in the Middle Ages. The Central Asian specimens bridge over the gap in the history of Indian Art between the Ajanta frescoes and the paintings of the time of Akbar.

Instances of portraiture and painting in the epics and dramas.

We have the following mentions of portraiture and painting in the Ramayan and Sanscrit dramas. Raban brings Sita a model of Rama's head to make her believe he is slain ; Indrajit, son of Raban, carries an image of Sita in his chariot in order to make believe

Spandrel from Central Panel of Ceiling of Cave I.

to slay her. A golden image of Sita is made for Rama's Asvamedha. In the Uttara Ramcharita, Bhavabhuti describes the emotion felt by Rama, Sita, and Lakshman, on seeing the events of the Ramayan painted in fresco on the walls of the *Chitrasala*, or picture gallery. The plots of the Ratnavali and the Nagananda turn on portraits. In the Malavikagnimitra, Agnimitra falls in love with Malavika's portrait in the *Chitrasala.* In the Sakuntala, Dushyanta, after his desertion, attempts to console himself with a portrait of Sakuntala.

SRIRANGAM TEMPLE.

Sanscrit philosophy unfavourable to art. Buddhism more productive in art than Hinduism, and the reason for this.

Sanscrit philosophy in general was unfavourable to art. The Vedantic doctrine of Maya, which held all that we see to be illusion, cut away all ground for the artistic presentment of the external world. The mental concentration of the Yoga school led to intellectual sterility. Buddhism was a protest against the tendency of the Brahmanism of the day to induce men to devote themselves to philosophical contemplation, and to cease to interest themselves in the practical realities of life. Its art is therefore more creative than Hinduism. In both cases, however, the intellect of the upper classes was averse to manual labour, and both sculpture, carving, and such painting

SIVA-GANGA TANK AND TEMPLE, CHIDAMBARAM.

as was done were left to craftsmen of low birth, and therefore deficient in lofty conception and creative power.

Difference in the conception of beauty between European and Indian Art.

European art takes as its subject Nature, and the highest development of human beauty. Indian art is always striving to realise something of the Universal, the Eternal, and the Infinite. The highest beauty must be sought in trying to picture something finer and more subtle than ordinary human beauty.

The gods and goddesses are portrayed, not as supremely beautiful men and women, but as possessed of "purified transcendental human bodies formed by the practice of meditation and ascetic restraint." Beauty belongs to mind and not to matter. There is no beauty in men or women, or trees or flowers as such, but beauty is subjective and connected with the thoughts of the mind. All nature is beautiful for us, if we can realise the Divine idea within it.

Reason why the Deities are not represented in ordinary human form.

Indian art is idealistic and transcendental. Its type is not the glorified man, but the Yogi, who is trying to place himself in contact with the Supreme or Universal Soul. It is irreverent and illogical to found artistic ideals of the Divine upon any strictly natural or human prototype. Hindu philosophy recognised the impossibility of human art adequately expressing the form of God. It was not for want of knowledge that anatomical details, such as the muscles, were suppressed, but because it was not considered consistent with the dignity of Divine personages, when represented in human form, for them to be portrayed as in all points resembling men and women. It therefore created in sculpture and painting a humanised but still supernatural form. To differentiate them from mankind, gods are sculptured, like Swa, with four arms and three eyes, or like Raban, ten-headed and twenty-armed. Art becomes creative and imaginative instead of naturalistic. Multiplicity of arms is a conventional means of denoting the universal attributes of divinity, and a "lion-like body" (deep broad shoulders, contracted abdomen, and small waist) is a sign of physical and spiritual strength in gods of heroes. There were thirty-two principal *lakshanas* or marks of divinity, such as short curly hair, long arms, and a golden coloured skin, and the statues of Buddha possess most of them.

Other branches of the fine arts.

The ancient Indians excelled in the weaving and dyeing of the most delicate fabrics, in the working of metals, and in all kinds of jewellers' work. Ktesias of Knidos, who was court physician of Darius II. and Artaxerxes Mnemon, kings of Persia, wrote the earliest Greek book on India under the title of 'Indika,' which was abridged by Photios. In this work the author speaks of the Indian dye prepared from insects (probably lac), and of the value in which swords made of Indian steel were held.

CHAPTER IX.

EDUCATION, LITERATURE, SCIENCE, COMMERCE.

In the first ages of Indian History, all learning centred in religion. Astronomy, Algebra, Geometry originated from the necessity incumbent on Aryans of the offering sacrifices at particular auspicious times, when the planets were in certain relations to each other, and of making their offerings on altars of particular geometrical shapes. Learning was the monopoly of the two higher castes, the Vaisyas only cared for trade, and, to the Sudra, learning was forbidden. If a Brahman explained the sacred texts for gain, he was "a covetous wretch, who displays the flag of virtue, a pretender, and a deluder of the people." The giver of such gifts shared in his punishment, "as one who tries to pass over deep water in a boat of stone, sinks to the bottom, so these two ignorant men, the receiver and the giver, sink to a region of torment."[1] Teaching was chiefly carried out at two classes of schools—*Tols* and *Parishads*. At Tols, there was usually only one renowned *Rishi*, who taught his favourite subject of Vedic learning, whilst his pupils committed his utterances to memory. At *Parishads*,

Education in the early ages.

[1] Manu iv., 191-194.

there were several teachers, and regular courses were given in subjects such as Logic, Law, Grammar. At both *Tols* and *Parishads*, the pupils were supported by their teachers, as teaching was looked upon as a religious duty, and to take fees for teaching was looked upon as sin. If not supported by their teachers, young men receiving education subsisted on charity. Pupils sometimes performed household tasks, such as the collection of fuel, or the pasturing of cattle for their teachers; this was the only return they made for their teaching. "As he who digs with a spade comes on a stream of water, so the student who humbly serves his teacher attains the knowledge which lies deep in the teacher's mind." [1] There were also wandering teachers (*Paribrajaka*).

Use of Sanscrit by the Mahayana School of Buddhist writers.

The Hinayana Buddhists wrote in Magadhi, which was a form of Pali, but their Mahayana opponents adopted Sanscrit as the language in which their religious works were written. This change affected the colloquial language, and caused it to become more Sanscritised, and an early form of Bengali called the Gauriya Bhasha was thus developed. It is on account of this Mahayana use of Sanscrit written in the Brahmi character, and its revival as a literary language, that "the more closely a book or inscription approximates to pure Sanscrit, unalloyed by colloquialisms, by Pali phrases and grammatical forms, the later it is." [2]

Sanscrit literature.

Sanscrit dramas are peculiar in the absence of distinction between tragedy and comedy. Among dramas the most noteworthy are the Mrichchhakatika

[1] Manu ii., 218

[2] Rhys Davids' 'Buddhistic India,' pp. 129-130.

of Sudraka, the Sakuntala, the Vikramorvashi, and the Malavikagnimitra of Kali Das. The drama of court life called the Ratnavali, and the Buddhistic drama Nagananda, are attributed to Harshavardhana of Kanauj. The last great names among Sanscrit dramatists are those of Bhavabhuti and Vishakhadatta. Bhavabhuti composed the dramas Uttara Ramcharita, Mahavir Charita, and Malati Madhava; and Vishakhadatta wrote the Mudra-rakshasa, a play of political intrigue. The name of the curtain *Yavanika* is sometimes cited as a proof of Greek influence on Sanscrit dramas, but it is doubtful whether the Greek theatre had any curtain at all; in any case it did not form the background, as on the Sanscrit stage. The Raghuvansa and Kumarsambhava of Kali Das, and the Kiratarjuniya of Bharavi, are epic poems. Other poems of Kali Das are the Meghaduta and the Ritusanhara. The Gita Govind of Jayadeva, who was a contemporary of Lakhsman Sen, king of Bengal, and lived in the twelfth century, is a most charming poetical work. It treats of the love of Krishna for Radha, and has a metaphorical reference to the relation between the Deity and the human soul. The Katha Sarit Sagara of Somadeva, a Kashmirian poet, is a metrical work composed about A.D. 1070. Specimens of ethical poetry are the Nitishataka, the Vairagyashataka, and the Chanakyashataka. In Sanscrit there are prose works such as the fables of the Panchatantra, the Hitopadesa, and the Vetalapanchavimshati, Bana's panegyric on Harshavardhana, the Kadambari of Banabhatta, and the Dasa Kumar Charita of Dandin.

Geometry.

Geometry was studied in Vedic times in the Sulva Sutras to discover the correct shapes in which sacrificial altars were to be constructed. In the same way, the sixth Vedanga, named *Jyotisha* which gives rules for the determination of the times for the various sacrifices, was the origin of Hindu Astronomy (*Jyotish*). In Vedic times, the solar year was divided into 360 days with an intercalary month every five years, and astronomers were familiar with the phases of the Moon. The planets are mentioned for the first time in the Taittirya Aryanaka. Aryyabhatta, in the fifth century A.D., discovered that the earth is round and rotates upon its own axis, and he found out the true causes of solar and lunar eclipses. Varahamihira, in the sixth century A.D., compiled a work on Astronomy called Panchasidhantika, from five old Hindu works on Astronomy called Sidhanta, one of which was entitled Romaka (Greek), thus showing the influence of the Greeks upon the development of Astronomy in India. He gives the names of planets both in Greek and Sanscrit, and one of his works is called Hora-Shastra, or rules for the calculation of time. Varahamihira also wrote Brihatsamhita, a cyclopaedia of universal science. Other famous Hindu astronomers were Brahmagupta in the seventh, and Bhaskara in the twelfth centuries. Bhaskara was born 1114. He wrote the Sidhanta Siramani, of which the two most famous chapters were the Lilavati on Arithmetic, and the Bijagonita on Algebra. Bhaskara discovered the attraction exercised by the earth, and that it is self-poised in space. The arithmetical figures with which the world reckons and the decimal system were of Indian origin. The Pytha-

Astronomy.

gorean theorem that the square on the hypotenuse is equal to the squares on the sides of a right-angled triangle was well known to the Indians. They understood how to extract the square and cube root, and how to raise numbers to various powers.

Chemistry. The science of Chemistry was known to some extent to Sanscrit writers, who appear to have been acquainted with the acids and alkalies, and the chemical processes of solution, evaporation, calcination, sublimation, and distillation. There were three principal Indian discoveries in applied chemistry :

1. The preparation of permanent dyes, for textile fabrics, by the treatment of natural dyes, such as *manjishta*, with alum and other chemicals.
2. The extraction of indigotin from indigo.
3. The tempering of steel.

Medicine. Medicine was ranked as an Upaveda under the name of Ayurveda. The Hindus had a fair knowledge of the anatomy and physiology of the human body, the action of drugs upon it, and the nature of its diseases, and could perform many difficult operations. There are Sanscrit treatises on medicine by Charaka and Susruta, which were translated into Arabic about the eighth century A.D., and thus their teaching reached Europe. The Khalifa Harun al Raschid is said to have entertained two physicians, Manka and Saleh, who were Hindus. The Mahomedan system of medicine is called Yunani, from some fancied connection with the Greeks who invaded India with Alexander.

Commerce. Ships were early made use of in India. We know this from the fact that ships are mentioned in the Rig

Veda in connection with Varuna,[1] and a Sanscrit compilation by Bhoja Narapati, called *Yukti-kalpa-taru*, classifies the woods used for making ships and the ships themselves. The Hindus made use of a compass in the form of an iron fish (*maccha jantra*), floating in oil, and magnetised so as to point to the north. The Kanhery caves in the island of Salsette, which were excavated by the Andhra kings in the second century A.D., have a sculptured scene depicting a shipwreck at sea.

In the Ramayan,[2] Sugriva tells the monkeys to look for Sita in the land of the Kosakaras (China). Yavana and Suvarna Dvipa and Lohita Sagara are referred to, and are to be identified with Java, Sumatra, and the Red Sea respectively. The mention of these places presupposes the existence of ships by which to reach them.

Baudhayana forbids orthodox Brahmans to make sea voyages, and fixes the duties payable by shipowners to the king.[3]

Manu [4] declares a Brahman who has gone to sea unworthy of entertainment at a *Sraddha*. He also lays down that the rate of interest on money lent on bottomry is to be fixed by men well acquainted with sea voyages or journeys by land. Sailors are to be collectively responsible for damage to the goods of passengers if caused by their default, but not if it proceeds from causes beyond their control. Pearl fishing, which cannot be carried out without boats

[1] See p. 36.

[2] Kishkindya Kandam, 40. 23.

[3] 'Dharma Sutra,' ii. 2. 2.

[4] Manu iii. 158.

and divers, is often mentioned in Sanscrit literature, in which the Gulf of Manaar is spoken of as the " Sea of Gain."

The Buddhist Jatakas make constant mention of commerce. The Supparaka Jataka describes the perils of 700 merchants who sailed from Bharakaccha (Broach) under the guidance of a blind merchant. The Mahajana Jataka describes the voyage of a prince in company with certain traders from Champa on the Ganges to *Suvarna Bhumi*, or the Golden Chersonese (Burma). Another journey is described from Magadha to Sovira on the Gulf of Kach.

Rhys Davids is of opinion that there was considerable trade, as early as the seventh century B.C., between the ports of Kathiawar and Babylon. The Baveru Jatakas mention the export of peacocks to Baveru (Babylon). *Sindhu* (the Indian word for muslin) occurs in an old Babylonian list of clothes. Teak, which probably came from the Malabar coast, has been found in the ruins of Ur of the Chaldees. The ancient Indian astronomy, and the knowledge of iron appear to have been learnt by the early Indians from Babylon. The Egyptians dyed cloth with indigo, and wrapped their mummies in Indian muslin.

Kautilya, the minister of Chandra Gupta, tells us, in the Arthasastra, that a Board of Admiralty was one of the six Boards established by Chandra Gupta for the management of affairs of State. It was presided over by the Superintendent of Ships, who dealt with all maritime and internal navigation, and guarded against any attempt to evade the port dues. He goes on to say, " All foreigners were closely watched by officials, who provided suitable lodgings, escorts, and, in case of need, medical attendance." From this we infer that Magadha was on terms of close intercourse with foreign States.

It is maintained that, when we are told in the Bible (1 Kings ix. 26-28 and x. 11, 12, 22) that Solomon, king of Israel, sent "a navy of Tarshish" (Phoenicia) with the ships of Hiram, king of Tyre, to Ophir, from Elath on the Red Sea, and brought back every three years gold, silver, precious stones, ivory, apes, peacocks, and almug trees or red sandalwood, that the west coast of India, or more particularly Supara, near Bassein, is referred to under the name of Ophir. An argument in favour of this is that the Hebrew words for ape, peacock, ivory and sandalwood are said to be connected with Sanscrit.[1] Some find evidence of a Phoenician commerce with India in the similarity between *cassiteros*, the Phoenician word for tin, and the Sanscrit word *kastira*. In Greek and Roman times there were three famous Indian products: a tree from which the Indians made cotton cloth (Greek *sindon*), a reed from which a sweet juice was expressed (sugar-cane), and a plant yielding a dark blue dye (indigo, Greek *indikon*). As instances of intercourse between Europe and Southern India, the embassy of Poros, a Pandyan king to the court of Augustus Caesar at Rome, has already been mentioned. An embassy from Ceylon

[1] *Kof*, the Hebrew name for ape, is connected with the Sanscrit *kapi*. *Tukhim*, the Hebrew name for peacock, recalls the Sanscrit word *sikhi*. The latter part of the word *Shenabbim*, the Hebrew name for ivory, is connected with the Sanscrit *ibha* (elephant), and *Algum*, the Hebrew name for sandalwood with the Sanscrit *valgu*.

was sent to the emperor Claudius between A.D. 41 and 54, and Pliny obtained from the ambassadors the information about Ceylon which he has embodied in his Natural History.

Secondary evidence of the flourishing state of commerce is derived from the fact that some of the Andhra and Kadamba coins bear the design of a sailing ship.

Roman and Greco-Egyptian commerce with Southern India.

An account has already been given of the Roman and Greco-Egyptian commerce with Southern India.

Internal commerce.

The principal trade routes for internal commerce were from Savathi, the capital of Kosala, to Patan or Anhilwara Patan in Gujrat ; Savathi to Rajgriha, along the Jumna and Ganges ; and across the Bay of Bengal to Burma, then called Suvarna Bhumi, or the Gold Coast. We know from Fa Hian's travels that Tamralipti (Tumlook, called Tamalitta in the Mahavamsa) was a principal port of departure for Further Asia.

Trade Guilds.

The management of internal trade was largely in the hands of Trade Guilds, which generally included all the men who followed the same trade in the same town. Membership of the Trade Guilds was either hereditary or purchased. They were generally under the control of a court of managers, and in every guild there was a special position assigned to the Seths, of whom there were usually two, who held their position by hereditary right.

In Ahmadabad the Nagar Seth was the titular head of all the guilds, and the highest personage in the city. He did not as a rule interfere in the internal management of the guilds, which was left to the Chautama Seth or head of the individual guild.

The guilds fixed the hours of labour and the amount of work to be done in them by by-laws, the infringement of which was punishable by fines.

The influence of the guilds has greatly declined under British rule, which supports the liberty of the individual to practise any trade he pleases, and those handicrafts, the perfection of which greatly depends upon hereditary processes and skill, have considerably suffered in consequence.

Lately there has been a tendency to form all the workmen, who practise one particular trade in a large town, into the shareholders of a Co-operative Bank, to raise capital for loans to individual workers, on the joint and several responsibility of the shareholders. This experiment has been tried with some success in the case of the Benares *kincob* weavers, and may lead to some revival of the collective responsibility for the quality of the goods turned out by individual members of the guild, which was the essence of the guild system.

Traces of Hindu influence in the Far East of Asia.

The most authentic instance of early Hindu colonisation is Java, which was first invaded by Aji Saka, a prince of Gujrat, about A.D. 75. A second invasion was made about A.D. 603. The Hindu immigrants reached the west coast of Java and founded the town of Mendana Kumulan. The sacred language of Java is a dialect of Sanscrit, and there are many inscriptions in the same language. The alien element in the population of Java was increased by fugitives from Bengal and Orissa, who left their country after its conquest by the Thibetans in the eighth century, and also by Buddhist refugees in the ninth century and later times. The Hindu kingdom of Majapahit in Eastern Java was overthrown by

Java.

Mahomedans in 1478, and the persecuted Hindus fled to the island of Bali, where Hindu rites are practised up to the present day.

BÔRÔ BÛDÛR TEMPLE, JAVA.

The temple of Bôrô Bûdûr in the Kedus province of Java has five sculptured galleries or procession paths surrounding the different stories of the shrine ; these

Temple of Bôrô Bûdûr.

sculptures describe one hundred and twenty scenes from the life of Buddha given in the Lalita Vistara, and the same number of scenes from the Divyavadana and the Jatakas. The Kali Bening and Sari temples at Prambanam were begun A.D. 779, and the Chandi Sewa temple in 1098; the Prambanam temples were sacred to Vishnu, and are adorned by sculptures describing scenes from the Ramayan. At Singasari there is an alto-relievo sculpture of Durga slaying the demon Mahishasura. At the temple of Angkor-Vat near Angkor-Thom, capital of the Khmer kings of Cambodia, are sculptures of the churning of the ocean by the Devas and Asuras, and battle scenes from the Mahabharat. Tradition has it that an Indian prince from Indraprastha took part in founding the Indian colony of Cambodia. The main body of colonists came from Kamboja (the country near Taxila in the Panjab). The first recorded Indian ruler of Cambodia was Srutavarman or Kaundinya, who lived in the middle of the fifth century A.D. The Angkor-Vat temple was built by Surya Varman II., one of the last of the Hindu kings of Cambodia in the twelfth century. The Khmers, or ancient inhabitants of Cambodia, seem to have had a fairly close connection with India, if we can judge from the number of figures of Hindu deities found in their temples, such as the Vedic Trimurti, and the four-faced figure of Brahma seated on a seven-headed snake. The religion of the Tchams of Annam is Brahmanism: they worship the Hindu Tri-murti, the Saktis of Siva and Vishnu, the goddesses Uma and Lakhsmi, also the goddess Bhagavati under the name of Po Nagar. The Klings of Singapore are a widespread race of sailors; the name would point to

Temples at Prambanam.

Cambodia.

Tchams of Annam.

Klings of Singapore.

TEMPLE OF ANGKOR VAT, CAMBODIA.

the original source of the race being found in Kalinga (Orissa).

Intercourse with China and Japan.

Sea traders of the Indian Ocean, whose chiefs were Hindus, founded 680 B.C. a colony called Lang-ga (Lanka) in the Gulf of Kiaochau. They retreated before the Chinese, and eventually became merged in the empire of Cambodia about the first century A.D.

The *Milindapanha* tells us that Indians of Sindhu (Debal, the port of Sindh) brought presents by sea to China. There was a constant intercourse of Buddhist priests between Ceylon and China. The Chinese called India Tienchu. I-Tsing, the Chinese pilgrim who visited India in A.D. 673, mentions several halting places for ships sailing between India and China, such as Sribhaja in Sumatra, Kalinga in Java, Mahasin in Borneo, and the island of Bali in the Malay Archipelago. Subhakara visited China and Japan between the years 716 and 735, and left in Kumedeva temple in the province of Yamata (Japan) the Mahavairochanabhi-sambodhi-sutra dealing with Buddhist Tantricism. Bodhisena visited Japan, 736 A.D., and taught Sanscrit to the Japanese priests. The Japanese history, called Nihonkoki, tells us that in A.D. 799 a man was washed ashore from Tenjiku (India), who brought cotton seed to Japan.

The Sungshih, a Chinese historical work, mentions two Chola kings as having sent embassies to China with tribute. These kings may be perhaps identified with Indra Chola, 1033, and Kulottunga Chola, 1077-1118. Marco Polo, on a voyage from China to Persia, touched at Kayal in Southern India. Ibn Batuta was sent by Mahomed Tughlak on an embassy to China.

Mahuam, a Mahomedan Chinaman interpreter to Chengho, a Chinaman who made the voyage to India in the beginning of the fifteenth century, describes the exchange of presents between the kings of Bengal and the emperors of China.

BIBLIOGRAPHY.

Sir Thomas Holdich, 'India' (Mackinder, Regions of the World series).

Sir Bamfylde Fuller, 'The Indian Empire' (All Red series).

Indian Census Reports, 1901 and 1911.

Sir Herbert Risley, 'The People of India.'

Sir Alfred Lyall, 'Asiatic Studies.'

Sir Monier Williams, 'Indian Wisdom.'

Sir Monier Williams, 'Buddhism.'

Deussen, 'The Religion and Philosophy of India.'

Deussen, 'System of the Vedanta.'

Weber, 'Indian Literature.'

Barth, 'Religions of India.'

L. D. Barnett, 'Hinduism.'

E. J. Rapson, 'Ancient India.'

Vedic India (Story of the Nations).

A. Grunwedel, 'Buddhist Art in India.'

Burgess, 'The Ancient Monuments, Temples, and Sculptures of India.'

Griffiths, 'Paintings of the Buddhist Cave Temples of Ajanta.'

Rhys Davids, 'Buddhistic India' (Story of the Nations).

McCrindle, 'Ancient India.'

Vincent Smith, 'The Early History of India.'

Vincent Smith, 'The Edicts of Asoka.'

' Fa Hian,' translated by Legge.

Kanakasabhai Pillai, ' The Tamils 1800 Years Ago.'

Ramaswami Pillai Aiyer, ' Early Indian History.'

Krishnaswami Aiyer, ' Southern India.'

Havell, ' Ideals of Indian Art.'

Havell, ' Ancient and Mediæval Architecture of India.

Vincent Smith, ' History of Indian Fine Art.'

Radhakumud Mukherjee, ' History of Indian Shipping.

BOOK II.

MEDIAEVAL INDIA.

CHAPTER I.

MAHOMED AND THE FIRST MAHOMEDAN INVASIONS OF INDIA. MAHOMEDAN SULTANS OF DELHI.

WE must begin our history of the mediaeval or Mahomedan period of the History of India with some account of Mahomed.

Mahomed and the Mahomedan religion.

Mahomed (the "praised") was born A.D. 570 at Mecca, and was the son of a poor merchant of the Arab tribe of the Koreish. His father died when he was very young, and he gained his living by carrying merchandise in caravans to and from Syria. At the age of twenty-five, he became manager to a rich widow named Khadijah and married her. She bore him a daughter Fatima, who married Mahomed's son-in-law Ali, the fourth Khalif. Mahomed was of a dreamy contemplative disposition, and received his first divine revelation in the solitude of Mount Hira near Mecca, where the archangel Gabriel appeared to him and commanded him to preach the new religion. He opposed the idolatry that was then prevalent at Mecca, and was persecuted in consequence by his fellow-tribesmen, the Koreishites. He fled to Medina on Friday, the 16th July, 622, from which date

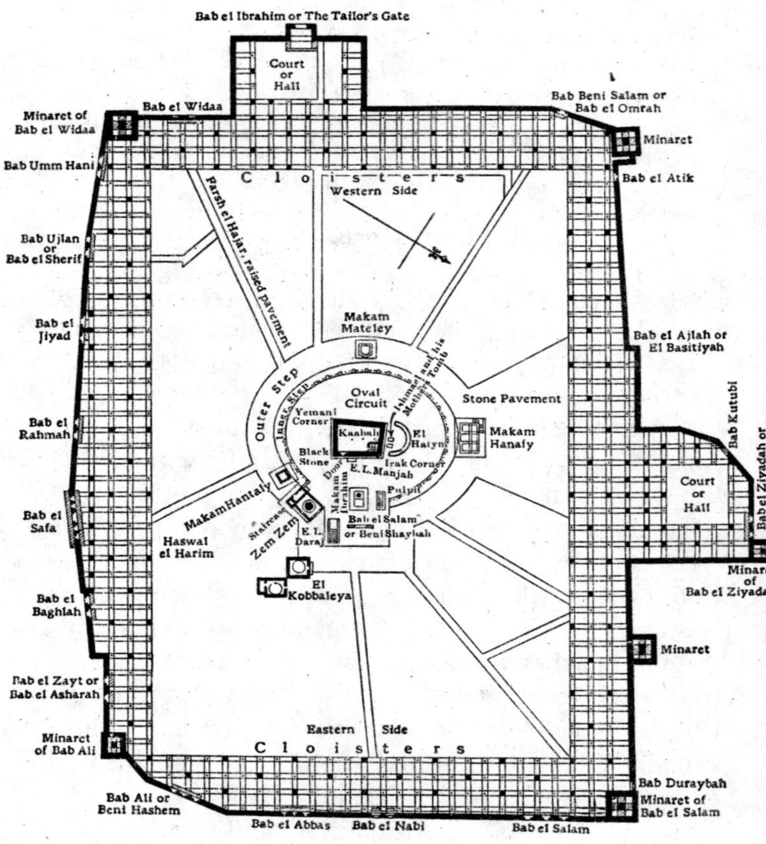

PLAN OF THE PROPHET'S MOSQUE AT MECCA, COMMONLY CALLED BAIT ALLAH OR GOD'S HOUSE.

the Mahomedan era of the Hejirah or "flight" commences. At Medina, he was recognised as a prophet, and there he gradually gathered to himself sufficient adherents to enable him to reconquer Mecca. He died on the 8th June, 632, at Medina, and was buried there.

Before his death, Mahomed had brought the whole of Arabia under subjection. Persia, Syria, Egypt and the whole of Northern Africa fell under the sway of his immediate successors. Spain was conquered early in the eighth century. Thus, within eighty years of the death of Mahomed, the empire of the Saracens extended from the Atlantic to the Indus, under the supremacy of the Khalif or "Successor" of Mahomed, who reigned at Bagdad. Mahomedanism enjoins Islam or submission to the will of God, and Mussulman means one who has so submitted. Its fundamental principle is: "There is no God but God; and Mahomed is God's prophet." The ideas of the unity of God and the hatred of idolatry are all-important. Mahomedanism tolerates Jews and Christians as "people of a Book," who possessed religious Scriptures of their own; they are therefore to be made tributary, but idolaters are to be exterminated. Mahomedanism is an actively proselytising religion. Mahomedan kings made war upon aboriginal tribes, with the cry of "Islam or death." Hindus, on the other hand, preferred to trust to the gradual influence of the assimilating power of their cult. Left to itself, Brahmanism might possibly have evolved "a national church and a unity of political and religious ideas." The irruption of Mahomedan invaders from Central Asia destroyed all chance of this. These invaders were not united among themselves; the Moghals were Sunnis, the founders of the Deccan kingdoms Shiahs.

The Mahomedans could not, therefore, substitute for Hinduism any strong religious organisation of their own.

First Mahomedan invasions of India.

The first Mahomedan invasion of India took place in A.D. 711, when Mahomed bin Kasim, in the time of the Khalif Walid, defeated Dahir, Raja of Sindh, and sacked the cities of Alor and Brahmanabad. Mahomed's invasion was more probably intended to seize the trade route between Western India and Bagdad, which passed through Mekran and Central Persia *via* Tiz to Debal in the Indus Delta, than to punish the Meds and other pirates of Debal and the Indus mouths, who had attacked an embassy from Ceylon bringing presents to the Khalif, as is commonly alleged. The Mahomedans were expelled in A.D. 760 by the Sauviras, a race of Kshatriyas.

Mahmud of Ghazni.

The empire of the Khalifas, which had occupied Kabul, A.D. 870, split up into several independent kingdoms. One of these was founded by Subuktagin at Ghazni in Afghanistan in 976. Mahmud, his son, became Sultan of Ghazni in A.D. 987, at the early age of sixteen years. In 1001 he marched against Jaypal, the Rajput Raja of Lahore, whom his father Subuktagin had defeated in 975. Jaypal was again defeated, and considered himself so disgraced that he burnt himself alive. In 1005-1006, Mahmud attacked Multan. In 1008-1009, Jaypal's son Anangapal, stirred up against Mahmud a great confederacy of the Rajas of Ujjain, Gwalior, Kalanjar, Kanauj, Delhi, and Ajmere, but Mahmud was victorious over the united army of the Hindus on the plain of Peshawar, and captured the temple of Srivajjarishvari Devi at Nagarkot, or Bhimnagar, in the Kangra valley with an immense treasure. In 1011 he plundered the temple of Thanesvar. In 1018-19 Mahmud plundered Mathura, and Rajyapal, the Parihar Raja, surrendered Kanauj. Vidyadhara, son of Ganda, the Chandel Raja of Kalanjar, defeated and slew Rajyapal as a punishment for surrendering Kanauj. Mahmud determined to punish him in consequence, and in 1021-22 he compelled Vidyadhara to surrender the fort of Kalanjar.

The best known of all Mahmud's expeditions was that against the temple of Somnath at Prabhasa in the south of Kathiawar. He started from Ghazni in the middle of December, 1023. His first step was to compel Jaypal, son of Anangapal, to surrender Lahore, which he permanently annexed, and the Panjab became a province of the Ghazni Sultanate, 1030. He appeared before Somnath about the middle of March, 1024. He stormed the temple, broke the image of the god (a Siva linga) in pieces, and placed a fragment on the threshold of the mosque at Ghazni to be trodden under foot. In Gujrat Mahmud overthrew the Solanki dynasty which had replaced the Chalukyas in A.D. 988. He died in 1030. The famous Persian poet Firdusi wrote his Shahnamah in praise of Mahmud's exploits. Alberuni speaks of their results as follows, "Mahmud utterly ruined the prosperity of the country, and performed these wonderful exploits by which the Hindus became like atoms of dust scattered in all directions, and like a tale of old in the mouths of the people. Their scattered remains cherish, of course, the most inveterate aversion towards the Muslims. This is the reason, too, why the Hindu sciences have retired far away from those parts of the country which have been conquered by us, and

Result of Mahmud of Ghazni's conquests.

have fled to places to which our hands cannot yet reach, to Kashmir, to Benares, and to other places." [1]

Mahmud's dynasty reigned for about a century and a half after his death, and was overthrown in 1188 by Ghiasuddin, King of Ghor, and his brother Moizuddin, afterwards known as Sahibuddin Mahomed Ghori.

India at the end of the twelfth century. Prithviraja and Jayachandra.

Towards the close of the twelfth century, Northern India was in the hands of the Chauhan Rajputs at Ajmere, who had brought under their control the territory of the Tomara Rajputs round Delhi, the Gaharwar (subsequently called Rahtor) Rajputs at Kanauj, and the Chalukya Rajputs in Gujrat. Prithviraja was the nephew of Visaladeva, the Chauhan Raja of Ajmere, who had brought about the marriage of his nephew's father with the heiress of Delhi. Anangapal I. refounded Delhi, A.D. 730, and left the Arrangpur Bund near old Delhi as his memorial. Anangapal II., last of the Tuar or Tomara Rajas and builder of the fort of Lal Kot at Delhi, repeopled the city in 1052, as his inscription on the Iron Pillar at Delhi testifies. He had a daughter who married Prithviraja's father. Succeeding his maternal grandfather, Prithviraja united Delhi to his Ajmere territories in 1167. He built the fort of Rai Pithora eleven miles to the south of Delhi. Prithviraja's accession to the throne of Delhi excited the jealousy of Jayachandra, Raja of Kanauj. Jayachandra performed the *Rajsuya* ceremony, but Prithviraja refused to attend. Jayachandra in consequence did not invite Prithviraja to the Swayambhara of his daughter Sanjukta, but placed his clay image as *dwarpal* at the ceremony. Sanjukta cast her garland over the neck of the clay

[1] Alberuni, Trubner, i. 1. 22.

image, and was carried off by her lover, who opportunely appeared. The feud which thus arose between Jayachandra and Prithviraja deprived Prithviraja of Jayachandra's support against the Mahomedan invaders.

Mahomed Ghori invaded India in 1191, but was defeated by Prithviraja at Trirouri or Thanesvar. Two years after he made a second attempt, and was completely successful, Prithviraja being captured and put to death. The conquest of Northern India was completed by the captures of Delhi, Kanauj, and Benares in 1193; the defeat of Jayachandra, Raja of Kanauj, at the battle of Chandrawar in the Doab in 1194; the surrender of Gwalior, 1196, and the capture of Nahrwala, or Anhalwara, capital of Gujrat, 1197; and the surrender of Kalanjar, 1203.

Mahomed Ghori.

Completion of the Mahomedan conquest of Northern India.

After the defeat of Jayachandra, the Gaharwar Rajputs emigrated to Rajputana, and set up the Jodhpur dynasty under the name of Rahtors. Bhika Singh, sixth son of Rao Jodha, founder of the Jodhpur State, founded the State of Bhikanir.

Foundation of the States of Jodhpur and Bhikanir.

Mahomed Ghori, already mentioned, succeeded his brother as King of Ghor in 1202, but was slain by the Gakkars, a wild tribe in the Panjab, in a night attack on his camp in 1206. Mahomed's general, Kutubuddin, shortly afterwards established himself in independent authority at Delhi, and reigned from 1206 till his death in 1210. Kutubuddin's title of Aibak means "Moonlord," and was probably given to him on account of his personal beauty. It has also been taken to mean "maimed," on account of his loss of a finger, but this is most probably owing to the misreading of a passage in the

Tabakat-i-Nasiri. The term Pathan, which is sometimes applied to all the Sultans of Delhi from Kutubuddin to Ibrahim Lodi, is incorrect. Only the Lodi and Sur dynasties were of Pathan, properly so called, that is, Afghan descent. The Slave and Khilji dynasties came from Turkestan. The Tughlak was a mixed race of Turkish and Hindu descent, and the Syed dynasty was of Arab origin.

Slave Dynasty. The first dynasty of Mahomedan Sultans of Delhi was called the Slave Dynasty, because Kutubuddin had been a slave of Mahomed Ghori, and several of the other kings had been slaves in early life.

Altamsh,[1] Kutubuddin's son-in-law, deposed Kutubuddin's son Aram, and ascended the throne in 1211. He conquered Nasiruddin Kubacha, who had made himself independent in Sindh, and reannexed it to the empire of Delhi, 1217. In 1221, the Mongols under Jenghiz Khan migrated from their original home in the north-eastern Gobi desert, and defeated Jeladdin, the last Shah of Khwarizm (Khiva) and drove him into Sindh. Altamsh reduced Bengal to subjection, and conquered the Rajputs of Malwa after capturing the hill-forts of Rinthambor in the Jaipur State, Gwalior, and Mandu, the capital of Malwa. In 1229 Altamsh received a diploma of investiture as Sultan from the Abbaside Khalif Al Mustanzir b'Allah. In 1235 Altamsh erected the Kutub Minar, near Delhi, in memory of the Mussulman saint Kutubuddin Ushi, so called from his birthplace at Ush in Turkestan. Altamsh's tomb in the north-western corner of the Kutub Mosque enclosure is "one of the richest

[1] The name Altamsh is a corruption of Il-tutmish, meaning in Turki, hand-grasper.

examples of Hindu art applied to Mahomedan purposes, that old Delhi affords." Altamsh died in 1236,

THE KUTUB MINAR, DELHI.

and was succeeded by his daughter, Raziah Begum, the only woman who has ever sat on the throne of Delhi. She reigned with great reputation for three years, 1236-39, but was deposed out of jealousy of the favour she showed to an Abyssinian slave Yakut. She married Malik Altunia, the Turki governor of Bhatinda, who in vain espoused her cause, but they were both slain (14th November, 1239).

After the short reigns of Bahram the son, and Masaud the grandson of Altamsh, his youngest son Nasiruddin Mahomed became king in 1246, and appointed as his minister Ghiasuddin Balban. Balban defeated the Mongols in 1243, who had invaded Bengal by way of Thibet. In 1245 Balban compelled the Mongols to raise the siege of Uchh in Sindh on the Indus. Nasiruddin died in 1256, and was succeeded by Ghiasuddin Balban.

The chief event of Balban's reign, 1266-87, was the defeat of the attempt at rebellion by Tughril Khan, governor of Bengal. After the suppression of this revolt Balban's son, Bughra Khan, and his five descendants ruled in Bengal, 1282-1329. In this reign, the Mongols also gave great trouble, and Balban's eldest son Mahomed was killed in battle against them at Dipalpur in Northern India, 1285. Balban died in 1286, and the Slave dynasty came to an end with the assassination of his grandson, Kaikobad, in 1290.

The Khilji Dynasty.

Jelaluddin Khilji, the founder of the Khilji dynasty, 1290-1320, had been the minister of Kaikobad, and was privy to his murder. Jelaluddin had an ambitious nephew, Alauddin, whom he made governor of Oudh and Karra.

In 1294 the Mahomedans made their first invasion of the Deccan, when Alauddin penetrated through the Vindhya mountains, and after attacking Deogiri

(Daulatabad) in the Nizam's dominions, forced the king, who belonged to the Yadava tribe of Rajputs, to pay an immense ransom and cede Ellichpur (Berar).

In 1295 Alauddin murdered his uncle Jelaluddin and ascended the throne of Delhi, and reigned, 1296-1315. Under Alauddin the incursions of the Mongols from 1296 to 1305 were especially frequent, and a general slaughter of the "New Muslims" (Mongols) settled in the country was ordered. In order to improve his army, he fixed the pay of the soldiers, and took measures to keep down the price of their necessaries, and fixed the price of food. The fruit of these measures appeared in his subsequent victories. **Alauddin Khilji.**

In 1297 he captured Anhalwara Patan and added Gujrat to the empire of Delhi. In 1299 Alauddin divided Bengal into the Eastern and Western Governorships, with capitals at Sonargaon and Gaur or Laknauti respectively. In 1303 he captured the Rajput hill-forts of Rinthambor and Chitor. This was the first siege of Chitor, which ended in the Rajputs performing the rite of *johar*. The men sought death in a sortie, and the women, headed by Padmini, wife of Bhimsi, guardian of the minor Raja Lakumsi burnt themselves in the caves under the fortress. In 1307 Malik Kafur, a Hindu converted to Mahomedanism and general of Alauddin, subdued Deogiri. In 1310 he conquered Warangal, and in 1311 Dwarasamudra (the modern Hallabid in Mysore) which was held by the Hoysala Ballal Rajputs. He also plundered Kanchi (Conjeveram) and Madura in 1311. Alauddin died in 1315. He built Siri, a city nine miles south of Delhi, and connected it with the Kutub Minar, the Lal Kot, and the fort of Rai

Pithora about two miles further south, by means of the fortification of Jahan Panah. He also built the Alai Darwaza beside the Kutub Minar. His son, Mubarak, succeeded him, but was dethroned by his favourite, Hassan, by birth a low-caste Hindu, who received the title of Malik Khusru. Malik Khusru, in his turn, was defeated and slain by Ghiasuddin Tughlak, governor of the Panjab, and founder of the Tughlak dynasty, 1320-1414. This dynasty is also called Karauna, the Karaunas being sons of Indian mothers by Tatar fathers. Ghiasuddin Tughlak reigned from 1320 to 1325.

The Tughlak or Karauna Dynasty.

In 1325, on the death of Ghiasuddin, his son, Juna Khan, succeeded to the throne with the title of Mahomed Tughlak. Ibn Batuta thus describes him, "Mahomed, more than all men, loves to bestow gifts and to shed blood." Mr. E. Thomas speaks of him as "learned, merciless, and mad." Another description of him is that he was "one of the most accomplished princes, and one of the most furious tyrants that ever adorned or disgraced human nature." Mahomed built Tughlakabad, a fortress and a tomb of red sandstone and white marble, sixteen miles south-east of Delhi, which is said to have been cursed by Nizamuddin Auliya in the terms, "be it the home of the Gujar or rest it deserted." In 1327 Mahomed Tughlak captured Warangal and put an end to the kingdom of the Kakati Rajputs in Telingana. The mad schemes of this king ruined the Mahomedan kingdom of Delhi. He attempted to make copper coins pass current at a high nominal value, and to regulate the price of all commodities; he sent a large army against China, which perished in the passes of the

Reign of Mahomed Tughlak, 1325-51.

Break-up of the empire of Delhi.

Himalayas, 1337; and he twice attempted to move the people of Delhi 800 miles to Deogiri, which he wished to make his capital. His authority was thus brought into contempt, and many subject countries rebelled. Bengal became independent in 1340 under the Iliyas Shahi dynasty, Bukka Rai founded the kingdom of Vijaynagar in 1343, and Hassan Gangu the Bahmani kingdom of Kulburga in the Deccan, 1347. Insurrections ensued in Gujrat, Malwa, and Sindh, and in the midst of trying to subdue them, Mahomed died at Thattah in Sindh in 1351.

Spread of Mahomedanism

By the conquest of Deogiri, Dwarasamudra and Warangal, Mahomedanism spread all over India. The only refuges of Hinduism were Rajputana and Vijaynagar.

Mahomed's nephew, Firoz Tughlak, succeeded him, and reigned for thirty-seven years, 1351-1388. His long reign was uneventful, and he is chiefly known for constructing Firoz Shah's canal, which connects the Jumna with the Ghagra and the Sutlej by irrigation channels. It has been partly reconstructed by the British Government, and is called the Western Jumna Canal. He also built Firozabad, one of the seven cities of Delhi, between Indrapat or Purana Kila, and New Delhi or Shahjehanabad. He died in 1388, and three kings followed him in four years.

Mahomed, the last of the Tughlak dynasty, came to the throne in 1392. In this reign Gujrat, Khandesh, Malwa, and Jaunpur asserted their independence, and Mahomed's power extended very little beyond the actual limits of Delhi city.

Sack of Delhi by Timur.

In 1398 occurred the Mongol invasion of India and sack of Delhi under Timur. Timur was a descendant in the female line of Jenghiz Khan, the famous leader of the Mongols, about 180 years before. He conquered Samarcand and established a kingdom practically conterminous with Central Asia. When he invaded India, Mahomed fled to Gujrat, and Timur entered Delhi and gave the city up to massacre and plunder for five days. Timur, in his Autobiography, gives the following account of India: "The whole country of India is full of gold and jewels, and, among the plants which grow there, are those fit for making wearing apparel, and aromatic plants, and the sugar-cane, and the whole aspect of the country is pleasant and delightful. Now since the inhabitants are chiefly infidels and idolaters, by the order of God and his Prophet, it is right and fit for us to conquer them." He describes Delhi as consisting of three cities—Siri, Jahanpanah, and old Delhi. "When my mind was no longer occupied with the destruction of the people of Delhi I took a ride round the cities. Siri is a round city. Its buildings are lofty, they are surrounded by fortifications built of stone and brick, and they are very strong. Old Delhi also has a similar fort, but it is larger than that of Siri. From the fort of Siri to that of Old Delhi, which is a considerable distance, there runs a strong wall built of stone and cement. The part called Jahanpanah is situated in the midst of the inhabited city. The fortifications of the three cities have thirty gates. It was ordained by God that the city should be ruined. He therefore inspired the inhabitants with a spirit of resistance so that they brought upon themselves that fate which was inevitable."[1] When Timur returned to Central Asia,

[1] Malfuzat-i-Timur, Elliott's 'History of India,' vol. iii. 447-8.

he carried with him a number of Indian workmen to build a mosque at Samarcand, but Mahomed recovered Delhi and enjoyed nominal power there till his death in 1412.

Syed Dynasty.

After Mahomed's death, Khizr Khan, governor of Multan and Sindh, seized Delhi in 1414, and professed to rule as Timur's Viceroy. He was a descendant of the prophet Mahomed, and his dynasty was therefore called Syed. Alauddin, the last of the Syed dynasty, resigned the throne to Bahlul Lodi, governor of Sirhind, in 1450.

Lodi Dynasty.

Bahlul Lodi, the founder of the Lodi dynasty, reigned from 1450 to 1488. His chief achievement was the conquest of the kingdom of Jaunpur, 1487, which was then held by the Sharqi dynasty founded by the eunuch Khwaja-i-jahan in 1394.

His son, Nizam, succeeded him and assumed the title of Sikundar Shah. He conquered Behar from the kings of Bengal, and removed the capital from Delhi to Agra. He was a bigoted Mahomedan and persecuted the Hindus. He died in 1517, and was succeeded by his eldest son, Ibrahim. Ibrahim's pride and cruelty drove Rana Sangram Sinha of Chitor and Daulat Khan Lodi, governor of the Panjab, into rebellion against him, and the latter invited Baber, Sultan of Kabul, to invade India. Baber, who claimed India in virtue of his descent from Timur, complied; he defeated Ibrahim Lodi at Panipat in 1526, and founded the Moghal Empire in India.

First battle of Panipat, 1526.

The army in the early Mahomedan period.

The army was under the guidance of its local Amirs, and each band owed more loyalty to its own individual Amir, than to the Sultan upon the throne of Delhi. Every man who had sufficient followers called himself an Amir, and the various Amirs subject to the throne of Delhi formed themselves into a body known as the *Amiran-i-Sádá.* The army, in consequence of this constitution, lacked cohesion, patriotism, and the inspiring sense of fighting for a national cause. Tribal jealousies often actuated it instead of the interest of a common country.

CHAPTER II

MAHOMEDAN ARCHITECTURE, PAINTING, LANGUAGE AND LITERATURE. INFLUENCE OF MAHOMEDANISM COUNTERACTED BY HINDU RELIGIOUS REFORMERS.

Effect of the Mahomedan conquest on Indian art.

WHEN the Mahomedans conquered India, they brought with them artistic principles derived from Persia and Central Asia, but these principles soon lost their special peculiarities, and developed into a form of Indo-Mahomedan art, the basis of which was Hindu. Alberuni speaks of the work of Hindu builders, more especially in connection with tanks. "Our people when they see them wonder at them, and are unable to describe them, much less to construct anything like them."[1] What Ferguson calls the Pathan and Ghaznavide styles of architecture were based upon Buddhist Hindu civilisation. The pointed arch was used by Hindus as well as Mahomedans, though the Hindu use was only occasional for connecting massive brick-work pillars, and for constructing in brick the curvilinear roofs derived from the earliest Indian roofs in bamboo, thatch, or wood. The pointed arch derived its reputation in Mahomedan eyes from its

The Pointed Arch.

[1] Alberuni, Trubner, ii. 144.

The *Mihrab* and *Mimbar* form the *Liwan*.

association with the *mihrab* or "prayer niche," or *Kibla*. The *mihrab* and *mimbar* or pulpit are the chief parts of the *Liwan* or sanctuary, and are placed in the wall opposite the chief entrance, which is always towards the rising sun. The *Liwan* always points in the direction of Mecca.

KUWAT-UL-ISLAM MUSJID, NEAR THE KUTUB MINAR, DELHI.

Original form of the Musjids.

The musjids were quadrangles, with their longer walls pointing in the direction of Mecca. The three remaining sides were enclosed with narrow corridors, the corridors and *liwans* were roofed with domes taken from the Hindu *mandapams* or porches. There was often a central dome, flanked by two lower ones of the same horizontal dimensions. A screen of brick sometimes plastered, and sometimes faced with stone, was often built in front of the *Liwan*. The pointed arch replaced the round arch or the horizontal beam

MUSJID AT AJMERE KNOWN AS "ARHAI DIN KA JHOMPRA.

and decorated bracket, because it became a symbol that God is one, and that Mahomed is his prophet. The likeness to the prayer niche was seen everywhere, in the bows of ships and in the doors of tents.

Domes.

Domes were not of exclusively Mahomedan origin. They may be divided :

1. According to method of construction.

(*a*) Those with stone ribs resting upon an octagonal base. These ribs form the structural framework of the dome, and have the interval between them filled up with masonry. Domes with ribs are the earliest kind, as they are developed from primitive or temporary domes built with a framework of wood.

(*b*) Those built of horizontal courses of stone.

There are examples of both kinds in India.

2. According to shape.

The only kind of dome which is exclusively Mahomedan is the "Stilted" dome found on the tombs of the Cairo Mamelukes. The contour of this dome, except for surface ornament in low relief, or on account of ribs or flutings, is unbroken. The springing of the dome from a circular drum or polygonal base is sometimes marked by a plain band. The finial is inconspicuous, and not an integral part of the dome.

The "bulbous" dome is common in Buddhist Stupas and Hindu temples, and was not introduced into India by the Mahomedans. The base of the bulbous dome often springs from a band of lotus petals. This is a marked peculiarity of the Hindu style. The word *kalsa*, the Persian name for the pinnacle of a dome, is derived from the *Kalasha* or *Kumbhu* (waterpot), and the domes of a large number of Mahomedan mosques in India have as finials the *Kalasha*, or *amalaka* or lotus flower, which are Hindu symbols of the creative element or life itself.

RANI SIPRI'S MUSJID, AHMADABAD.

Parts of Dome.

1. The pole or axis fixed in the ground, or on some firm basis, such as an inner roof or dome. Parts of the dome.

2. Ribs, sixteen, two for each petal of the *Maha-padma,* which decorates the body of the dome.

3. Ties by which the ribs are secured to the pole at the springing of the dome, and again directly below the cap.

4. Cap, which secures the ribs at the crown of the dome, decorated by the Mahapadma or eight petalled lotus. Lotus petals are also used as decorations

WINDOW OF SIDI SAID'S MUSJID AT AHMADABAD.
Near view of the arched window, showing the exquisite tracery.

where the ties form a wheel (Buddhist Wheel of the Law, or Hindu symbol of the Universe) by being connected together at the base.

Early Mahomedan Musjids at Delhi.

Early Mahomedan musjids, such as the Kuwat-ul-Islam in connection with the Kutub Minar and the tomb of Altamsh, the Kalan Musjid at Delhi, the mosque at Tughlakabad, and that at Ajmere, called the "*arhai din ka jhompra,*" built in the reign of Altamsh, were often old Jain temples altered by removing the building in the centre, and erecting a wall on the western side provided with "*mihrabs*" or prayer niches. The colonnaded courts of the Jain temples were made use of, and in the case of the oldest Delhi mosques the walls are of Mahomedan and the pillars of Hindu architecture. Perhaps their most characteristic feature is the inward slope of their

WINDOW OF SIDI SAID'S MUSJID AT AHMADABAD.

walls to the top. Kutub-ud-din built the screen of eleven pointed arches, eight smaller, four on each side, and three larger. He used the materials of the Hindu temples erected by Anangopal I. to build the Kuwat-ul-Islam mosque. A similar screen at Ajmere was built by Altamsh of seven arches, the centre arch being 22 feet 2 inches. Altamsh extended the liwan of the Kuwat-ul-Islam and added a quadrangle. Alaud-din built the Alai Darwaza. The upper part of the Kutub Minar is an inferior addition of Firoz Tughlak.

Pathan style of architecture originated in India.

After the reign of Alauddin Khilji, the Pathans adopted a style of their own. It is of this style that Bishop Heber remarks: "The Pathans builded like giants and finished like jewellers. Yet their ornaments, florid though they are in their proper places,

TOMB OF MAHOMED ADIL SHAH AT BIJAPUR, KNOWN AS THE GOL GUMBAZ.

are never thrown away or allowed to interfere with the general solemn and severe character of edifices."[1] This style was not original, and was based on the building traditions which Mahmud of Ghazni and his successors borrowed from India.

Kulburgah Musjid.

The musjid at Kulburgah, the capital of the Bahmani dynasty in the Deccan, was built by

[1] Heber's Journal, vol. i. 536.

Mahomed Shah, second king of the line, in 1367, and is peculiar in having no central court, all the internal

Firoz Shah's Minar at Gaur.

space being roofed over. It has one large dome in the centre of the western end of the roof, four smaller

domes at the corners, and seventy-five still smaller domes on the roof.

Jaunpur Musjids.

The Atala and Jamma Musjids at Jaunpur show the difference between Mahomedan and Hindu architecture in using arches and domes wherever wide openings and large internal spaces were required, but in the cloisters which surround the courts and in the internal galleries, the pillars are short and square, the roofs formed of flat slabs and the pointed arch is not used. The Atala Musjid was completed by Sultan Ibrahim, who reigned 1401-39, in 1408. Its screen is reduced to a single lofty arch, with inwardly sloping buttresses used as minarets on each side. The arch is filled up by a recessed screen in which the pointed arch and the horizontal beam and bracket are combined. The trellis work screens of geometrical pattern, as it is forbidden to reproduce the picture of any living thing, with the panelled ceilings, are the chief features of the interior. The Jamma Musjid was commenced by Husain Shah, who reigned 1452-78.

Sas Bahu or Padmanabha temple of Gwalior

The Sas Bahu or Padmanabha temple at Gwalior resembles these musjids in being built in stories, and in being based upon a plinth of masonry. It is somewhat earlier, as it dates from the eleventh century.

Ahmadabad Musjids.

The Jamma Musjid at Ahmadabad was built by Ahmad Shah, who reigned 1411-33. It has fifteen domes, each supported on eight columns, and built on horizontal courses by the changing of the octagonal into a circular base. The pointed arches of the central screen are reduced to three, one on each side of the central arch, instead of seven ; it has also five smaller beam and bracket arches on the north and south of the *Liwan*, linked together by a bracket after the Hindu fashion. Rani Sipri's Musjid is very small, but ornamented by the most exquisite stone carving.

Sidi Said's Musjid is famous for its lattice windows carved in yellow sandstone so as to represent open

SAS BAHU TEMPLE AT GWALIOR.

lace work. Other famous Ahmadabad Musjids are Rani Rupavati's or the Queen's Musjid, and Mahafiz Khan's Musjid.

Champanir Musjids.

Mahmud Shah Begarah, who reigned 1459-1511, captured Champanir from its Hindu ruler, Jai Singh Patai Rawal, and it remained the political capital of Gujrat till 1536. He built the Champanir Jamma Musjid, the main entrance to which is flanked by

INTERIOR OF SAS BAHU TEMPLE AT GWALIOR.

two minarets, each 100 feet high, with four others, each 50 feet high, at the corners of the *liwan*. There are eleven domes, 20 feet in diameter, four along the front and back, and three along the centre line from north to south, linked by a flat roof and ten smaller domes. The central dome is of the same dimensions as the eleven others, but several feet higher from the springing to the crown.

The chief feature of the Nagina Musjid is the lattice work windows at the base of the minarets.

Type of Gujrat Musjids. The type of the Gujrat Musjids, according to Havell, is the Chaumukh temple built by Kumbho Rana of Mewar, at Ranpur in the Jodpur State.

Mandu buildings. The Mandu Musjids and palaces were built by Hindu masons experimenting for themselves. The arches are irregularly divided, the keystones being the smallest instead of the largest stones of the arch. The *Mihrabs* are adaptations of Hindu shrines, and the domes have pinnacles with Hindu Buddhist emblems, and not Mahomedan finials. The Jamma Musjid Mandu was finished by Sultan Ibrahim, 1454. It has three domes standing on twelve pillars each, the only space left for worshippers being the succession of alleys between the pillars. The Jahaz Mahal (the palace of Baz Bahadur) and the tomb of Hushang Shah are the other principal architectural remains of Mandu.

Gaur buildings. The Gaur buildings are characterised by bent cornices and curvilinear roofs derived from the Buddhist bamboo edifices in Bengal. The pointed arch was in more frequent structural use at Gaur than elsewhere in India, as brick was used instead of stone. Short heavy pillars of stone supporting pointed arches and vaults in brick are also characteristic.

The most important architectural remains in Bengal are found in the old capital of Gaur. The Sona Musjid was commenced by Hossein Shah,

1493-1518, and completed by Nasrat Shah, 1518-32. The Quadam Rasul and Barah Darwaza Musjids and Firoz Shah's Minar at Gaur, and the Adina Musjid at Pandua, built by Sikandar Shah Iliyas, 1358-89, son of Iliyas Shah, are noteworthy.

Traces of Bengali style in Agra and Delhi.

Traces of the Bengali style are seen at Agra and Delhi in the vaulted roof of the upper pavilion of Itimad-ud-daula's tomb, in the curves of the roof of the Golden Pavilion in Agra Fort, and in the bent cornice and cusped arches of the Moti Musjid at Delhi.

Bijapur buildings

Bijapur was a great Mahomedan building centre. The chief architectural remains are the tombs of Ibrahim, 1580-1626, and Mahomed Adil Shah, 1626-56, and the Mehter Mahal. The tomb of Ibrahim, known locally as the Gol Gumbaz, has its dome, which "covers more ground without support than any other dome or vaulted roof in the world," is based upon a square hall, and has at each corner an octagonal tower eight stories high.[1] It has a system of pendentives which counteract the lateral thrust of the great mass of masonry of the dome. The action of the weight of these pendentives is in the opposite direction to the weight of the dome, and it thus acts as a tie, and keeps the whole in equilibrium without interfering with the outline of the dome. These pendentives are placed between the arches which support the dome.

Humayun's tomb.

Humayun's tomb is an Indian imitation of a Persian tomb. It is Persian in style, but differs in the use of white marble as an outer casing round the central dome. The soffits of the arches are not marked with lotus, or their keystones with pipal leaves.

[1] See picture, page 264.

The dome of Humayun's tomb is not "stilted," like the domes on the tombs of the Mamelukes at Cairo; it does not spring directly from the drum on which it is built, but overhangs it. It is like the Arab type of dome in having an unbroken contour from the springing to the crown, and in having a mere spike as its finial.

Sher Shah's Musjid and Tomb.

Sher Shah's Musjid in the Purana Kila at Delhi is Persian in its recessed or semi-domed portal, and in the dwarf minarets round the base of the central dome.[1] The dome is Indian in character, being surmounted by the *Mahapadma* and *Kalasha* finial Sher Shah's tomb in a tank at Sasseram has four minor domes at the angles of the square enclosure, eight smaller cupolas grouped round the central dome, and similar domes on the roof of the corridors which surround the central dome. It stands on a plinth, and the central dome rises from an octagonal sanctuary.[2]

Fatehpur Sikri.

Akbar's architectural memorials are chiefly found at Fatehpur Sikri, the city of his creation—all built in red sandstone. The *Buland Darwaza* or principal gate of the city has a recessed or semi-domed portal, in which the gates are set, and pendentives with intersecting arches in the semi-dome.[3] The mosque of Selim Chishti has the recessed portal also introduced into the facade of the liwan.

Akbar's throne in the Diwan-i-Khas is raised upon a single pillar with a colossal bracketed capital.[4] The Panch Mahal is a pavilion of five stories designed like a Buddhist Vihara.

[1] See picture, page 311.
[2] See picture, page 313.
[3] See picture, page 330.
[4] See picture, page 319.

The use of the Persian semi-recessed portal and pendentives illustrates the way in which, according to Mr. Havell, Akbar's Hindu builders, "welded the Persian and Arabian art tradition on to their own."

Akbar's tomb at Secundra.

Akbar's tomb resembles the Panch Mahal at Fatehpur-Sikri, and is built in five stories, each diminishing in size, adorned with domes at the corners.[1]

The Taj Mahal.

The gem of Mahomedan architecture is the Taj Mahal, but it is not so exclusively Mahomedan as is supposed. The central mausoleum was commenced in 1632 and completed in 1643, and it has two subsidiary musjids in the west and east of the quadrangle. Controversy has raged round the question who was its principal architect. Sleeman has put forward the name of Austin de Bourdeaux, and Father Manrique that of Geronimo Verroneo. Burgess says it was built by Ali Mardan Khan, a Persian refugee. Mahomed Isa Effendi or Ustad Isa has probably the best claim of all the four. He was considered "the best designer of his time," and came from Agra; another account makes him a Persian, who came from Shiraz. The Taj is free from the common defect of Mahomedan buildings, that they only give perfect pleasure to the eye when looked at from the direction of Mecca; whereas from whatever direction the Taj is looked at, it gives the most exquisite delight.[2]

The dome of the Taj.

The Taj has one large dome over the tomb and four smaller over the chapels in the four corners of the building; each of these chapels has a minaret. This arrangement is known as the *panch ratna*, the shrine of the five jewels, symbolising the five elements,

[1] See picture, page 332. [2] See picture, page 343.

earth, water, fire, air, and ether. Mr. Havell compares the arrangement of the domes of the Taj with that followed in the temple of Chandi Seva at Prambanam in Java, built 1078.

The curve of the dome of the Taj is not unbroken, it has three marked divisions which may be thus distinguished:

(1) The incurving at the base, where a band of inlaid decoration marks the springing, and suggests a lotus flower, holding the dome within its unfolded petals.

(2) The main structure or centre of the dome.

(3) The pinnacle, which does not rise abruptly from the crown, but is connected with the centre of the dome by another lotus-like member, which has the petals turned downwards instead of upwards. This is the *Mahapadma* or eight-petalled lotus.[1]

The pinnacle has the Hindu emblems of the *amalaka* or lotus fruit, and the *kalasha* or water pot.

The three divisions of the dome of the Taj correspond to the divisions of the dome of a Dravidian temple vimana, as laid down in Ram Raz's summary of the Silpa-sastras.[2] Mr. Havell considers that the marble trellis work in the corridors which pass round the cenotaph was carved by Bijapur workmen.

Not the least charm of the Taj is its formal Moghal garden laid out in four plots. **Taj garden.**

Professor Lethaby's criticism of Indo-Mahomedan architecture as "elasticity, intricacy and glitter, suggestive of fountain spray and singing birds," is

[1] Havell, 'Indian Architecture,' 23, 24.

[2] *Ibid.* 25.

only true when applied to its later decadent phase, when Persian influence and the power of Nur Jahan were strongest, as, for instance, when the Samman Burj in Agra fort and the tomb of Itimad-ud-daula were built.

Ornaments of sacred places.

Mahomedans were forbidden by the Koran to reproduce the figure of any living creature in their sacred places; they had to confine themselves, for decorative purposes, to Arabic geometrical patterns, floral devices, texts from the Koran written in Tughra or Kufic characters, pierced stone, exquisitely carved lattices, inlaid work, and enamelled or encaustic tiles.

Pierced stone screens or lattices.

Pierced stone screens or lattices are found in Hindu temples of the Chalukyan style. Belur has twenty-eight screens all of different patterns; the work is also used for panels of doors, or for screens and railings round tombs or at the bases of minarets. Mahomedan examples are Sidi Said's musjid at Ahmadabad, and the Nagina musjid at Champanir.

"Pietra Dura."

"Pietra Dura," or inlaid work, composed of slices of precious stones, such as onyx, jasper and cornelian imbedded in sockets prepared in marble, is used with exquisite effect for the adornment of the Taj. The oldest example of the work is the Jain temple, built by Kumbho Rana of Mewar in the Sadri Pass, 1438, in which the interior is ornamented with mosaics of cornelian and agate as mentioned above. The Gol Mandal, a domed pavilion in the Jagmandir palace, Udaipur, prepared for Shah Jehan, when, as Prince Khuram, he took refuge in Rajputana in 1623, has its walls adorned with work like the Taj Mahal. Selim Chishti's musjid at Fatehpur Sikri is inlaid with mother of pearl, and the Shish Mahals at Amber and in Lahore Fort are inlaid with glass. Enamelled or encaustic tiles were a means of colour decoration, in which Mahomedan architects specially delighted. They are used with good effect in Baha-ul-Hakk's tomb at Multan (date between 1264 and 1286), and in his grandson Rukn-ud-din's tomb, 1320.

Enamelled or encaustic tiles.

PALACE OF MAN SINHA, GWALIOR.

The Tantipara and Lotan (Lattan) and Sona Musjids at Gaur, and the palace of Man Sinha, 1486-1518, at Gwalior are remarkable for their enamelled tiles. Man Sinha's palace has a gem in its Baradari, an apartment 45 feet square on twelve columns. The tiles are sometimes combined to form pictures. The work is called Kashi (from *Kas* or *Kanch* glass, or from the Persian town of Kashan), or Chini, from being made by Chinamen. The Lahore fort has on its

Kashi or Chini work.

outer wall, from the Hathi Pol gate to the eastern tower of Jahangir's quadrangle, a distance of 497 yards, a series of tile pictures representing elephant fights, a game at polo, etc. Wazir Khan's musjid at Lahore and the *Chini ka Rauza*, a tomb near Agra, are decorated with panels of this work.

Mahomedan art. Basawan and Daswanth were famous Hindu painters at Akbar's court. Abul Fazl says that Daswanth had "devoted his whole life to the art, and used from love of his profession to draw and paint pictures even on the walls." He praises the skill of Hindu painters. "It passes our conception of things; few indeed in the whole world can compare with them." He goes on to say that "the minuteness in detail, the general finish, the boldness of execution now observed in pictures are incomparable, even inanimate objects look as if they had life." [1]

Under the Moghals down to the time of Aurangzeb, a secular school of painting derived from Persia arose in India. This art spread to Persia from China and Chinese Turkestan, whither it had been originally carried from India by Buddhist missionaries and workmen. Bajna, a painter of Khotan, visited the court of the Emperor Yangti, 605-17, and his son, Wei-chi-isong, remained in China. We know from Abul Fazl that there were a large number of painters at Akbar's court. Akbar insisted on truth to nature, on accurate drawing, and on general finish in the pictures and portraits he approved. He did not share the ordinary Mahomedan prejudice against the representation of forms having life, and generously rewarded artistic merit. His sentiments are thus

[1] Blochmann, 'Ain-i-Akbari,' vol. i. p. 107.

reported: "It appears to me as if a painter had quite peculiar means of recognising God, for a painter

WALL OF LAHORE FORT.

in sketching anything that has life, and in devising the limbs one after the other, must come to feel that he cannot bestow personality upon his work, and is thus forced to thank God, the giver of life, and will thus increase his knowledge." [1] The picture of the sailing boat running before the wind in his Khwabgah, the so-called picture of the Annunciation (two angels bringing a message to a person under a canopy), and the full-length portrait of a lady, in Mariam-uz-zamani's House at Fatehpur Sikri, are examples of Mahomedan painting (wall frescoes) in the time of Akbar. Aurangzeb, unlike Akbar, despised the arts, and painters, sculptors, and musicians were deprived of state patronage, and treated as heretics. The masterpieces of Hindu sculpture and fresco painting were mutilated and defaced, on the ground that they offended against the prohibition of painting the human form.

Scenes from the Akbarnama.

The painter's art was also applied to illustrate incidents in the Akbarnama and in the Razmnamah (the Persian translation of the Mahabharat). There is this peculiarity in these pictures, that one part of the picture was sometimes painted by one painter and another part by another. Most of the pictures mentioned below illustrate Clarke's manuscript of the Akbarnama. The execution of Adham Khan has its outline drawn by Muskina, and the painting is done by Shankar. The Audience Scene (Number $\frac{1}{117}$ of Clarke's manuscript of the Akbarnama) has the outline drawn by Muskina, the painting by Sarwan, the faces (*chitra nami*) by an unknown artist, and the figures (*surat*) by Madho. The picture of elephants executing prisoners has the outline drawn by Muskina, and the painting is done by Banwali the elder. In the

[1] Blochmann, 'Ain-i-Akbari,' vol. i. p. 107.

picture of Akbar's visit to the shrine of Muinuddin Chishti at Ajmere, Basawan is responsible for the outline, Iklas for the painting, and Kanha for the

SONA MUSJID, GAUR. VIEW OF CORRIDOR.

portraits. In the picture of Husain Quli Khan, presenting the Mirzas of Akbar's family, who had rebelled against him, as his prisoners to Akbar dressed in the skins of animals, 1572, Basawan has done the outline and Mansur the painting. In the picture of the *Johar* of the Rajput women at Chitor the artist is not identified.

Ramcharitmanas.

Another manuscript, belonging to the Maharajah of Benares, which is illustrated in the Indo-Persian style, is the Ramcharitmanas of Tulsi Das.

Dara's album.

An Album has come down to us which belonged to Dara Shukoh. It contains amongst others pictures of wild ducks and cranes wonderfully true to nature. Other noteworthy pictures are Reading the Koran, and a portrait of Jehangir as Prince Selim.

History in Mahomedan times.

It is in History that the writers of this period were chiefly superior to their predecessors. Amongst the Mahomedan historians may be noted the Arab

Alberuni.

Alberuni (Abu Raihan), born 973, in the territory of Khwarism (Khiva), who completed his Tahqiq-ul-Hind in 1031. He also wrote "An accurate description of all the categories of Hindu thought, as well those which are admissible, as those which must be neglected." "The world," says Max Müller, "owes to him the first accurate and comprehensive account of Indian literature and religion." Speaking of the Hindu historians, Alberuni says that the Hindus do not pay much attention to the historical order of things, and that they are careless about the chronological order of their kings. He here refers to the fact that, in Hindu lists, contemporary dynasties are often treated as successive. The only Hindu work which enters into comparison, in this branch, is the History of Kashmir, called Rajatārangini, completed by Kalhan in 1149.

Minhaju-s-Siraj.

Minhaju-s-Siraj lived in the early part of the thirteenth century, and was made Kazi of Delhi, and given the title of Sadr-i-Jahan by Ghiasuddin Balban. His work, the Tabakat-i-Nasiri, is a history of the Mahomedan monarchies which existed during the lifetime of the author, and of the Sultans of Delhi, from Kutubuddin Aibak down to the author's own time. It is continued down to the reign of Firoz Tughlak by Ziya-i-Barani.

Abu Abdullah Mahomed Ibn Batuta, 1304-1378, visited Delhi in the time of Mahomed Tughlak. He left Tangiers in 1325 and travelled for twenty-four years in India and the adjacent countries as far as Southern China, and has left an account of his travels and of the history of his time in Persian. He returned to Fez in 1349. Ibn Batuta.

The period saw the birth of Hindi, and the "Prithviraj Rasau," a collection of heroic ballads on the exploits of Prithviraja by Chand Bardai, show the Prakrit passing into the Hindi at the close of the twelfth century. A great impulse was given to the growth of Hindi by the religious prose and poetry of Kabir. The Ramayan in Hindi of Tulsi Das, 1532-1623, dates from 1587 A.D. The blending of the Persian and the Central Asian languages with words of Sanscrit origin, which was afterwards to result in Urdu, is foreshadowed in Kabir's writings, in which we find a large number of words of Persian origin. The Ramayan of Tulsi Das in Hindi.

The first author, who wrote in Urdu, was Amir Khusrau, 1253-1325, who wrote four epic poems dealing with the history of Alauddin and Mubarak Khilji. These are the *Miftah-ul-Futuh*, or Key of Mysteries; the *Kiran-us-Sadain* or Conjunction of two fortunate Planets (which describes the meeting of the Emperor Kaikobad with his father Nasiruddin, Urdu literature.

king of Bengal) ; the *Nuh Sipihr* or Nine Spheres, and the *'Ashika* or *Kidrkhan-u-Duwalrani* (the love story of Khizr Khan, son of Alauddin and the Hindu princess Devala Devi). He also wrote the *Tarikh-i-Alai* or *Khazainu-l-Futuh*, a prose history of the reign of Alauddin Khilji, 1296-1310.

Sanscrit at Vijaynagar.

At this period, Vijaynagar produced two famous Sanscrit scholars in the persons of Madhavacharjya, called Vidyaranya, and his brother Sayana. Madhava was born at Udupi in South Kanara in 1319. He was a great teacher of Mimansa Philosophy, and wrote a compendium of Sanscrit philosophy under the name of Sarbha-Darshan-Sangraha. He was the minister of Bukha Raya of Vijaynagar, 1343-79. Sayana wrote commentaries on the Rigveda, Aitareya Brahmana, and Aranyaka. He was the minister of a royal prince who was viceroy at Udayagiri. Some authors consider Madhava and Sayana one and the same person, who held the office of Mahant of Sankarcharjya's math at Sringeri in Mysore at some date within the fourteenth century.

Hindu reformers.

With the victory of the Moghals, Mahomedanism became the dominant religion in India, but the preaching of the Hindu Sannyasi reformers, Ramananda the Vaishnavite, Kabir the weaver, founder of the "Kabirapanthis," and Chaitanya attracted crowds of followers. Ramananda, 1300-1400, had his headquarters at Benares. Among Ramananda's twelve apostles were a leather worker, a weaver (Kabir), and a barber, a Mahomedan, and a woman.

Vaishnavite revival.

Kabir, 1380-1420, tried to form a religion, which should include Mahomedans and Hindus alike. He rejected caste, image worship, and the doctrine of re-incarnation, denounced the Brahmans, and declared that the chief object of men should be to attain purity of life and perfect faith in God. "He to whom the world belongs, he is the father of the worshippers alike of Allah and of Rama. To Allah and Rama we owe our existence, and should therefore show tenderness to all that live. Of what avail is it to shave your head, prostrate yourself on the ground or immerse your body in the stream? Whilst you shed blood, you call yourselves pure, and boast of virtues which you never display. Of what avail is cleansing your mouth, counting your beads, performing ablutions, and bowing yourself in temples, when, whilst you mutter your prayers or journey to Mecca and Medina, deceitfulness is in your heart? The Hindu fasts every eleventh day, the Musulman during the Ramazan. Who formed the remaining months and days that you should venerate but one? If the Creator dwells in tabernacles, whose residence is the universe? Who has beheld God seated amongst images, or found him at the shrine to which the pilgrim directed his steps? Behold but one in all things; it is the second that leads you astray. Every man and woman that has ever been born is of the same nature with yourself." All the chances and changes of life are the work of *Maya* or Illusion, and what man has to do to obtain salvation, is to recognise the one Divine Spirit under these illusions. "Neither austerities, nor ritual, nor works of any kind are necessary to obtain the highest end; this is only to be obtained by *Bhakti* (fervent devotion) and perpetual meditation on the Supreme —his names of Hari, Ram, Govind being ever on the lips, and in the heart. The highest end is absorption in the Supreme and reunion with Him from whom all proceeded, and who exists in all."

Chaitanya. Chaitanya, sometimes called Sri Gauranga, 1486-1527, was born at Nabadwip in Bengal. He held that liberation of the soul does not mean merely that separate existence comes to an end, but that it should be free from the sins and frailties of the body. He identifies Vishnu with Brahma, and, according to him, Vishnu possesses sensible and real attributes, in opposition to the Vedanta belief in the negative properties of God. "Worship from interested motives (the attainment of happiness or the expiation of sin) was not worship at all, but shop-keeping barter. A man must attain the nature of a tree, which lives solely for the benefit of others, before he can become a true worshipper." He disregarded caste distinctions—"the mercy of God regards neither tribe nor family." He recommended mendicancy and preached the worship of Vishnu, in his incarnation as Krishna, for whom *Bhakti* must be felt. He assigned an important place to woman in his system of religious organisation, and made them the instructors of other women not yet familiar with the tenets of his faith. He founded the Vaishnava sect of Bengal, and among his followers were Nityananda and Adaitya. He also originated the Sankirtan, or Service of Song, and the institution of celibate monks or *gosains*.

Bhakti. *Bhakti* is one of the three paths to salvation, and is open to all men. It bulks largely in the teaching of these religious reformers, and Sir George Grierson summarising Sandibya defines it thus: "*Bhakti* is not knowledge, though it may be the result of knowledge. It is not worship. This is merely an outward act, and *Bhakti* need not necessarily be present in it. It is simply and solely an affection devoted to a person (an affection for the deity as intense as for a human person) and not belief in a system."

Tulsi Das the poet, 1532-1623, was a product of the religious revival originated by Ramananda. His Ramacharitramanasa, or "The Lake of Rama's character," describes sin as hateful, because it is incompatible with the purity of the Supreme Being. Rama in heaven knows by experience man's frailties and temptations, and can sympathise with him.

Krishnaite revival.

Another school of Hindu reformers favoured the worship of Krishna. Mira Bai, wife of Kumbho Rana of Mewar, wrote hymns in honour of Krishna. Tukaram the Mahratta poet, who was contemporary with Sivajee, wrote poems of a similar tendency. Vallabha, a Telegu Brahman, born 1478, preached the "*Pushti Marga*" or Way of Pleasure. He opposed all austerity, and taught that the good things of this world were to be enjoyed by the faithful, and was perhaps the most Epicurean in his ideas of all the religious teachers of India.

Vallabha.

CHAPTER III.

INDEPENDENT KINGDOMS FOUNDED ON THE DECLINE OF THE MONARCHY OF DELHI.

Independent kingdoms founded on the decline of the Monarchy of Delhi.

Bengal.

BENGAL became independent in 1338, under Haji Iliyas, founder of the Iliyas Shahi dynasty, who assassinated Ali Mubarik, the viceroy of Gaur, and assumed the title of Shamsuddin. He united Eastern Bengal, the capital of which was Sonargaon near Dacca, with Western Bengal, the capital of which was Laknauti or Gaur. The independence of Bengal was acknowledged in 1355 by Firoz Tughlak after fruitlessly besieging Shamsuddin in the fort of Ekdala on the Banar river. Its ancient capitals Gaur or Laknauti, Pandua, and Tanda were all in the Malda district. The Iliyas Shahi dynasty was dethroned in 1405 by Raja Kans or Ganesh of Bhaturia in Dinajpur, who reigned from A.D. 1407 to 1414. The district of Rajshahi is supposed to have been called after Raja Kans. His family reigned for forty years, but his son became a Mahomedan and took the name of Jalauddin. After forty years, the Iliyas Shahi dynasty was nominally restored, but anarchy really reigned, as the Habshi or Abyssinian guards set up whom they chose as king, and dethroned him again at pleasure.

In 1493 the Hindu king Subuddhi Rai was dethroned by his general Hossein Khan, who ascended the throne of Bengal under the title of Hossein Shah (1493-1518). Nasrat Shah of this dynasty, 1518-1532, built the Golden Mosque at Gaur. Nasrat Shah summoned the Portuguese to his assistance against Sher Shah, and this was the occasion of their first appearance in Bengal. Hossein Shah's dynasty was deposed by Sher Shah in 1536. On the downfall of Sher Shah's dynasty, Suleiman of the Kararani tribe of Afghans seized the throne of Bengal, and became independent, 1564. His general, Raj Chandra, surnamed Kalapahar, a converted Hindu, conquered Orissa, 1565, by defeating Mukundadev, an inhabitant of Telingana, who had conquered the country.

First appearance of the Portuguese in Bengal.

Louis Vertomannus, of Rome, visited Bengal in 1503, and Caesar Frederick, a Venetian, in 1565.

European accounts of Bengal.

Orissa was conquered by Asoka, but regained its independence under Kharavela. This we know from an inscription in the Hathigumpha cave on Udayagiri, near Cuttack. Orissa was ruled from 474 A.D., when Yayati Kesari expelled the Yavanas, down to 1132, by the Kesari dynasty, which had its capital at Jajpur. The Ganga dynasty (said to be Cheras from Southern India) lasted from 1132 to 1435, and then the Vijaynagar kings attacked the country from the south and founded the Surjya dynasty, 1435-1541. In 1541 the Bhoi dynasty was founded by Govinda Bidyadhara, minister of Pratapa Rudra (1504-32), but it only lasted nineteen years, and then Mukundadeva, Govinda's minister (1551-59), secured the throne. Daud, son of Suleiman Kararani, dethroned him, but was defeated at Mogulmari near Jalesvar in Orissa,

Orissa.

and Bengal was conquered and annexed to the Moghal Empire by Akbar in 1575. The Afghans maintained themselves in independence in Orissa till they were finally defeated under Osman Khan, in the marshes of the Subarnarekha near Rajghat, 1611, by the Moghals under the leadership of Shujat Khan.

Jaunpur.

The kingdom of Jaunpur extended from Bengal to Kanauj. It was founded in 1394 by an eunuch, Khwaja-i-Jahan, who received from Mahomed Tughlak the title of "*Malik-us-Sharq*," and the dynasty founded by Khwaja-i-Jahan's adopted son Mubarak Shah was hence called Sharqi. The kingdom of Jaunpur was re-annexed to the empire of Delhi by Bahlul Lodi.

Malwa.

Dilawar Khan Ghori, a general of Firoz Tughlak, made himself independent in Malwa in 1401, and fixed his capital at Ujjain. His son Alif Khan, better known as Hushang, transferred it to Mandu on the northern slope of the Vindhya mountains. In 1440 Mahmud, an usurper, dethroned the Ghori line; he was defeated by Kumbho Rana of Mewar, who erected the Kirti Stambha at Chitor in honour of his victory over the combined armies of Malwa and Gujrat. Malik Bayazid or Baz Bahadur, son of Sher Shah's governor of Malwa, was the last independent king of Malwa. The story of his love for the Hindu maiden Rupmati is closely connected with Mandu. He was defeated and his country annexed by Akbar's general, Adam Khan Atkah. Malwa was conquered by Bahadur Shah, king of Gujrat, in 1531, and was annexed to the Moghal Empire by Akbar in 1572.

Gujrat.

The independent Mahomedan kingdom of Gujrat was established by Zafar Khan, son of a renegade

Hindu, who took the title of Sultan Muzuffar, about the year 1396. Sultan Ahmad of this dynasty built Ahmadabad in 1411. The most famous kings of this

KIRTI STAMBHA TOWER OF VICTORY, CHITOR.

dynasty were Mahmud Shah Begarah, 1459-1511, and Bahadur Shah, 1526-37. Mahmud Shah Begarah captured Champanir from Jai Sinha Pati Rawel, an Hindu chief, in 1484. Champanir remained the political capital of Gujrat till 1536. Mahmud also waged bitter conflicts with the Portuguese. Bahadur Shah conquered Malwa and attacked Chitor, 1535 Karnavati, Sangram Sinha's widow, summoned Humayun to her aid, by sending him her *raki* or bracelet, but Humayun did not arrive in time, and Bahadur Shah took Chitor in March, 1535. This was the second siege of Chitor. Bahadur Shah was defeated by Humayun at the battle of Mandesor, and slain by the Portuguese in the island of Diu, 1537. Gujrat was conquered by the Moghals in 1572.

COIN OF VIJAYNAGAR. RAMATANKA.
Reverse: Rama and Sita enthroned.

The kingdom of Vijaynagar.

The ruins of Vijaynagar are found at Hampi near Hospett, a station on the Madras and Southern Mahratta Railway, thirty-five miles west of Bellary. Bahauddin, Mahomed Tughlak's nephew, fled to Anegundi, the original part of the city, on the north bank of the Tungabhadra. Mahomed Tughlak captured Anegundi in 1336, and made Harihara Deva, who was said to have been a refugee from Dwarasamudra, king. Harihara founded the first or Yaduva dynasty of Vijaynagar kings. Harihara was succeeded by his brother Bukka, who reigned for thirty-six years, 1343-79.

Harihara Deva II., 1379-87, was the first king of Vijaynagar to assume the title of *Maharajadhiraj*.

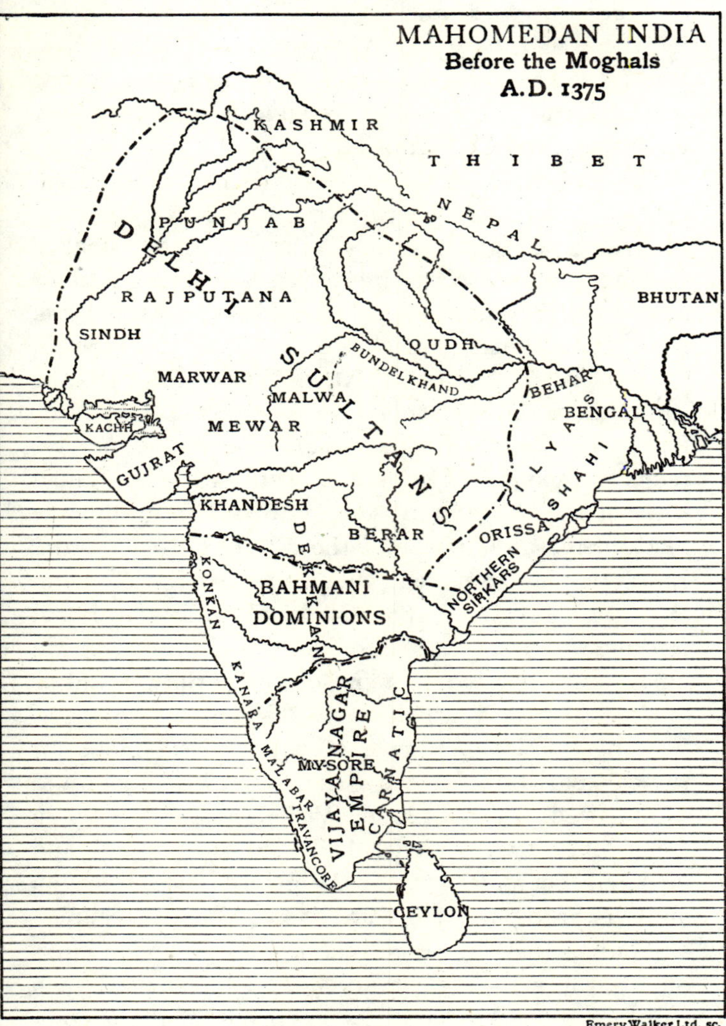

His army was deficient in archers and cavalry. Mahomedans were engaged in these capacities. They were given *jaghirs*, and a place of worship was erected for them in the city of Vijaynagar. Krishna Deva Rai I., 1419-49, was the most powerful king of the first dynasty; his power extended from the river Kistna to Cape Comorin.

The last king of the Yadava dynasty was Virupaksha, who was overthrown by Saluva Narasimharaya, a Telegu, whose inscriptions date back to 1456-57. Saluva Narasimharaya's son and successor was Imadi Narasimharaya, also called Dharmaraya. Both these kings had a Tulu general from South Canara called Narasana Nayak, who usurped the throne from the Saluva or Telegu dynasty about 1501. Krishnadevaraya was Narasana's second son. He reigned 1509-30. He waged war with the Ganga Raja of Ummatur in Mysore, and took from him the fort of Sivasamudram and the city of Seringapatam. In 1513, he captured Udayagiri in Katak from the king of Orissa, and Kondavid from the Bema Reddis, who were descendants of the old Rashtrakuta kings, and who are now represented by the Zemindars of Venkatagiri. Krishna Deva Rai built the temple of Krishnaswami at Vijaynagar, which was famous for the colossal statue of Nara Simha the Man Lion, and commenced the temple of Vithalaswami. Krishna Deva fought with Ismael Adil Shah of Bijapur, and defeated him at Raichur at the junction of the Bhima and Kistna rivers, May 19th, 1520. He also occupied Bijapur and placed a descendant of the Bahmani kings on the throne. The victory of Raichur caused such jealousy of the kingdom of Vijaynagar, that the combination, which was victorious at Talikota, was the result.

Achyuta, 1530-42, son of Krishna Deva Rai, with his successor Sadasiva, 1542-65, were kept in practical captivity by Rama Raja I., 1542-65, who was the son of Saluva Timma, minister of Krishna Deva Rai, and who had probably married Krishna Deva's daughter Tirumalamna. Rama Raja with his brothers Tirumala and Venkatadri monopolised all real power. The battle of Tallikota on the river Don, sixteen miles above its junction with the Kistna, was fought between Rama Raja and the allied Sultans of Bijapur, Ahmednagar, Golkonda, and Bidar, on the 23rd January, 1565. Tirumala fled to Penukonda, eighty-five miles south-west of Bellary in the Anantapur district, murdered Sadasiva, and established the fourth dynasty of kings of Vijaynagar, which was afterwards removed to Chandragiri, where Sriranga Rayan was reigning, when he granted the site of Madras to the English in 1639.

In the fifteenth and sixteenth centuries Vijaynagar was visited by several Europeans. Nicolo de Conti tells us that Vijaynagar was sixty-five miles in circumference, a dimension which Caesar Frederic reduced to seven, and that it contained 90,000 men capable of bearing arms. Another point, typical of de Conti's tendency to exaggeration, is his crediting the Raja with 12,000 wives. In his description of the customs of the people, the prevalence of trial by ordeal seems to have struck him most. Athanasius Nikitin, the Russian, visited Vijaynagar shortly after de Conti.

Domingo Paes wrote his account of Vijaynagar about 1520. In this he tells us that the city seemed to him "as large as Rome, and very beautiful to

MONOLITH STATUE OF NARASIMHA, HAMPI.

the sight; there are many groves of trees within it, and many conduits of water which flow into the midst of it, and in places there are lakes; and the king has

"SASAVIKALU," MUSTARD SEED OR PIGMY (IRONICAL) STATUE OF GANESA, HAMPI.

close to his palace a palm grove and other rich-bearing fruit trees. Below the Moorish quarter is a little river, and on this side are many orchards and gardens with many fruit trees, for the most part mangoes and areca-palms and jack trees, and also many lime and orange trees, growing so closely to one another that it appears like a thick forest ; and there also white grapes." The palace of the king enclosed "a greater space than all the castle of Lisbon,"[1] and Fernando Nunez visited the place about ten years later, and has left us a summary of its previous history. In treating of the condition of the rayats, he tells us, "All the land belongs to the king and from his hand his captains hold it ; they make it over to the husbandmen, who pay nine-tenths to their lord ; and they have no land of their own, for the kingdom belongs entirely to the king."[2]

Abdur Razzak, an ambassador from Persia to Vijaynagar, tells us that at his visit in 1442, "The city is such that the eye has never seen a place like it, and the ear of intelligence has never been informed that there existed anything to equal it in the world."[3]

States which rose to power on the ruins of Vijaynagar.

Tirumala died, leaving three sons, Sriranga Rayan, who ruled at Penukonda, Rama Raja II., who ruled the Kanarese country with headquarters at Seringapatam, and Venkapati Raya, who established himself at Chandragiri. Not long afterwards Sriranga Rayan died childless, and Rama Raja also died, leaving a minor son, Tirumala Raya II. It was by taking advantage of Tirumala's minority that the rulers of Mysore were able to elevate it into an important state. Venkapati Raya ruled over the Nayaks of Gingee, Tanjore, Madura, Madras, Seringapatam, and Penukonda. He died in 1614.

[1] Sewell's 'Forgotten Empire,' pp. 236-290.

[2] *Ibid.* p. 379. [3] *Ibid.* p. 88.

Mysore is a plateau consisting of the Malnad or hilly country occupying the slopes of the Western Ghats from about the 11th to about the 14th parallel of north latitude, and a more level country to the east called the Maidan. Mysore.

The Mysore Rajas are descended from a certain Yadu Raya, a descendant of the Yadava Rajputs of Gujrat, who was in possession of the taluka round the town of Mysore (the buffalo-town) anciently called Puragiri. The title Wodeyar, meaning lord, which the Mysore Rajas always bear, is a term of respect used to a Lingayat priest, and was assumed by Yadu Raya out of gratitude to a Lingayat priest, who helped him in ousting a usurper from Mysore.

The first of the Mysore Rajas to acquire importance was Raja Wodeyar, 1578-1617, who took advantage of the minority of Tirumala Raya of Seringapatam to gain possession of the town. He obtained a confirmation of his title in 1612 from Venkapati Raya, Raja of Penukonda, who was in nominal possession of what remained of the Vijaynagar empire from the Pennar river to Cape Comorin. The viceroy of Madura, however, only nominally acknowledged his supremacy, and really ruled the southern part of this territory. Raja Wodeyar and his grandson and successor, Chama Raja Wodeyar, 1617-37, still nominally acknowledged themselves vassals of Penukonda. The next important holder of power was Raja Wodeyar's nephew, Kantirava Narassa, 1638-59. He was the first Raja of Mysore to make grants and coin money in his own name. He waged successful war with Bijapur, and was succeeded by his cousin, Dodda Deva Raja, 1659-72. Dodda Deva was

Raja Wodeyar.

Seringapatam ceded to Mysore.

Chama Raja Wodeyar.

Kantirava Narassa.

Dodda Deva.

Chikka Deva. followed on the throne by his nephew, Chikka Deva, 1672-1704. Chikka Deva purchased Bangalore

Bangalore purchased by Mysore.

from Ekojee, brother of Sivajee, Raja of Tanjore. Chikka Deva's death, and the succession of his dumb son, Dodda Krishna Rai, with whom the direct line failed in 1731, marks the decline of the power of

Decay of the power of the Rajas of Mysore.

the Rajas, who became mere puppets in the hands of their Dalaways (officers who combined the functions of Prime Minister and Commander-in-chief). Nandi

The Dalaways.

Raja, on whose downfall Hyder Ali climbed to power in 1761, was Dalaway at the time of his overthrow.

Nayaks or local chiefs.

A good part of Southern India, with the exception of the territory belonging to the Nawab of the Carnatic, fell into the hands of local chiefs.

The dynasty of Nayaks of Madura under the suzerainty of Vijaynagar commences with Visvanatha (1559-63). Under Visvanatha, Trichinopoly was obtained from Tanjore in exchange for Vallam, and forti-

Nayaks of Madura.

fied, and Tinnevelly with its chiefs, "the Five Pandavas," subdued. Visvanatha owed his power to his fidelity in expelling his father, Nagama Nayak, who had attempted to make himself independent in Madura. He established a number of feudal estates, the lords of each of which had to maintain a band of feudal retainers to garrison each of the seventy-two bastions of Madura. His general and minister was Ariyanayaka Mudali, who erected the Hall of One Thousand Pillars in the Minakshi temple at Madura.

Visvanatha's son and successor was Kumara Krishnappa, 1563-73, who put down the rebellion of Dumbechi Nayak and conquered northern Ceylon.

Tirumala Nayak, 1623-59, declared himself independent of Vijaynagar. In 1657 war broke out with the Raya of Penukonda. The Mahomedans of Golkonda captured Gingee and Tanjore, and the Mysore Raya, Chama Raja Wodeyar, besieged Madura, which was rescued by the Setupati of Ramnad.

The other two important periods in the history of the Nayaks of Madura were the regency, 1689-1704, of Mangammal, wife of Chokanatha, and grandmother of Vijiaranga Chokkanatha the infant king, who reigned 1724-31, and the regency, 1731-36, of Minakshi. In 1736 Madura fell into the hands of Chanda Sahib the Nawab of the Carnatic. In 1756 Madura and Tinnevelly were assigned in settlement to Mahomed Yusuf. He gave Tinnevelly in farm to a Hindu for eleven lacs of rupees. Mahomed Yusuf was recalled from the south in 1758, but returned in 1759 and himself undertook the farm of the two districts. Mahomed Yusuf ruled till 1763, when he could not or would not pay his tribute, and an army was sent against him by the Nawab, and he was captured and hanged. In 1790 Madura was annexed by the British Government on account of the unpaid debt of the Nawab of the Carnatic.

Mahomed Yusuf.

The Bahmani kingdom.

The Bahmani kingdom originated in the revolt of the Amirs of the Deccan against Mahomed Tughlak. They elected as their first Sultan an Afghan chief called Ismail Fath, who abdicated in favour of Hassan Gangu, entitled Zafar Khan (1347). Hassan Gangu, the viceroy of Daulatabad, had originally been the servant of a Delhi Brahman named Gangu. Hassan Gangu became Sultan under the title of Alauddin Hassan Gangu Bahmani, and assumed the last two names in honour of his master Gangu, whom he made his minister. His capital was

Kulburga, and his territories corresponded to those of the Nizam, and stretched from the Tapti on the north to the Tungabhadra and the Kistna on the south. Hassan's son, Mahomed, succeeded his father, on the latter's death in 1358, and reigned till 1375. Sultan Firoz, who reigned 1397-1422, carried on a successful war with the king of Vijaynagar. His son Ahmad, 1422-1435, built the city of Bidar, 1429, which afterwards became the capital of the Bahmani kingdom. He died in 1435, and a succession of weak kings followed him, whose power was only preserved by the wisdom of the minister Mahomed Gawan, called *Malik ut Tujjar*, or Chief of the Merchants. In 1469 the Konkan was conquered from Vijaynagar, and in 1471 Telingana invaded, Kondapalle and Rajamundry being taken. Jealousy of Mahomed Gawan caused the Deccan nobles to conspire against him, and induce the weak king Mahomed Shah Bahmani III. to put him to death on a false charge, 1481.

The subdivision of the Tarafs of Kulburga into Kulburga and Bijapur, of Daulatabad into Daulatabad and Junair, of Berar into Gawal and Mahur, and of Telingana into Warangal and Rajamahendri, facilitated the declaration of independence of the Tarafdars or local governors. When the guiding hand of Mahomed Gawan was withdrawn, the downfall of the Bahmani kingdom soon followed, after Mahomed Shah's death in 1518. Another cause for the rebellion of the Tarafdars was jealousy of Kasim Barid Shah of Bidar, who used Mahomed Shah Bahmani as his puppet.

Offshoots of the Bahmani kingdom. Bijapur.

Yusuf Adil Shah, a son of Amurad II., Sultan of Turkey, had come to India to escape being put to death by his brother Mahomed II., the conqueror of Constantinople. He took service with Mahomed Gawan, made himself independent, and was crowned at Bijapur, 1489, and formed a kingdom stretching from Sholapur and Kulburga on the north to Goa on the south. Famous kings of this dynasty were Ibrahim Adil Shah, 1534-57. Ali Adil Shah, 1557-80, was the leading spirit in the Mahomedan League which crushed Vijaynagar at Tallikota. His daughter was the famous Chand Bibi, the defender of Ahmadnagar against the Moghals. Mahomed Adil Shah, 1626-56, is buried in the Gol Gumbaz at Bijapur. The dynasty lasted down to 1686, when Bijapur was conquered by Aurangzeb in the reign of the last king, Sikandar Adil Shah.

Ahmadnagar. The first king of the Nizam Shahi dynasty was Hassan Nizam-ul-Mulk Bhavu, a renegade Mahratta Brahmin, who became prime minister of Sultan Mahomed Bahmani III. on Mahomed Gawan's murder. In 1490 he rebelled and seized Bidar. His son Ahmad assumed the title of Shah, 1489. He built Ahmadnagar and took Daulatabad. The dynasty lasted about 110 years, till Ahmadnagar was captured by Akbar's son, Daniyal, in 1600, in spite of the heroic defence of Chand Bibi, aunt of the infant Sultan Bahadur Nizam Shah, who was at last murdered by her own troops. The attempt of Malik Amber and Shahji Bhonsla (father of Sivajee) to maintain the independence of Ahmadnagar was put down by Prince Khuram (Shah Jehan) in 1617. Malik Amber, who died in 1629, is thus spoken of by the Emperor Jehangir in his Memoirs, " Amber, whether as a commander or a strategist, was without an equal in the military art. He kept all the bad characters of that country (Deccan) in perfect order, and to the end of his days lived in honour. There is no record of an Abyssinian slave attaining to such a position as was held by him."[1] Ahmadnagar was finally annexed to the Moghal Empire in 1637, after the capture of Daulatabad and the imprisonment of Hassan II., the last king of the dynasty.

Golkonda. The Qutub Shahi dynasty of Golkonda was founded by a Turk, who was Governor of Telingana and declared himself independent in 1512, and fixed his capital at Golkonda. He is known as Sultan Quli Qutub-ul Mulk, the first of the kings of Golkonda. His territories lay between Bidar and the river Wardha, a tributary of the Godavery. His grandson, Mahomed, founded Hyderabad in 1591. Mahomed's successor, Abdullah Qutub Shah, 1636-1672, employed Mir Jumla as his minister. Mir Jumla rose to great eminence, but, on being disgraced through the jealousy of the nobles, fled to Aurangzeb, who was then Shah Jehan's viceroy in the Deccan. In 1656, Aurangzeb besieged Golkonda, but was induced to desist by orders from Delhi. Peace was made when Abdullah gave his daughter in marriage to Aurangzeb's son Mahomed, with the district of Ramgir. Abdullah was succeeded by his nephew Abul Hassan. In 1687 Aurangzeb took Golkonda, and confined Abul Hassan in prison till his death.

The tombs of the kings near the fort at Golkonda form a splendid series of architectural remains.

Bidar. Kasim Barid, first of the Barid Shahi dynasty of Bidar, used Mahomed Bahmani III. as his puppet,

[1] Elliot, 'Indian History,' vol. vi. pp. 428-9.

and reigned in his name. His son and successor, Amir, 1504-1542, followed the same policy till 1529, when he declared himself independent. Bidar was eventually annexed by Bijapur in 1609.

The kingdom of Berar, with its capital at Ellichpur, belonged to the Imad Shahi dynasty. It became independent in 1484 under Fathullah Imad-ul-Mulk, who was originally a Brahman from Vijaynagar. Berar was conquered by Ahmadnagar in 1572, and annexed to the Moghal Empire in 1595, after Chand Bibi's surrender of the country to Akbar's fourth son, Sultan Murad, whom she had repulsed from Ahmadnagar. **Berar**

CHAPTER IV.

BABER AND HUMAYUN.

The Moghal[1] Emperors of Delhi, Baber.

ZAHIRUDDIN MAHOMED, surnamed Baber, or the tiger, a direct descendant of Mirza Miranshah, third son of Timur, was born in 1483. On the death of his father, Omar Sheikh, in 1494, he inherited the kingdom of Ferghana or Khokand. He twice captured and twice lost the important city of Samarcand, being driven out of it by the Usbegs. In his Memoirs he says, "for the sake of Andejan (capital of Ferghana) I had lost Samarcand, and found that I had lost the one without preserving the other." He captured Kabul in 1504, and subsequently Ghazni and Kandahar. Having defeated Ibrahim Lodi, Baber had next to contend with the Rajput Sangram Sinha of Chitor, whom he defeated at Fatehpur Sikri,[2] March 15th, 1527. Before this battle, Baber broke up his gold and silver drinking goblets, and gave the gold and silver to the poor, and induced his nobles to do the same. In his Memoirs, he thus describes what

Battle of Fatehpur Sikri.

[1] Moghal is the Arabic spelling of Mongol. The term is specially applied to the emperors of India descended from Timur.

[2] The site of this battle is given by some authors as the plain of Kanwaha, near Biana.

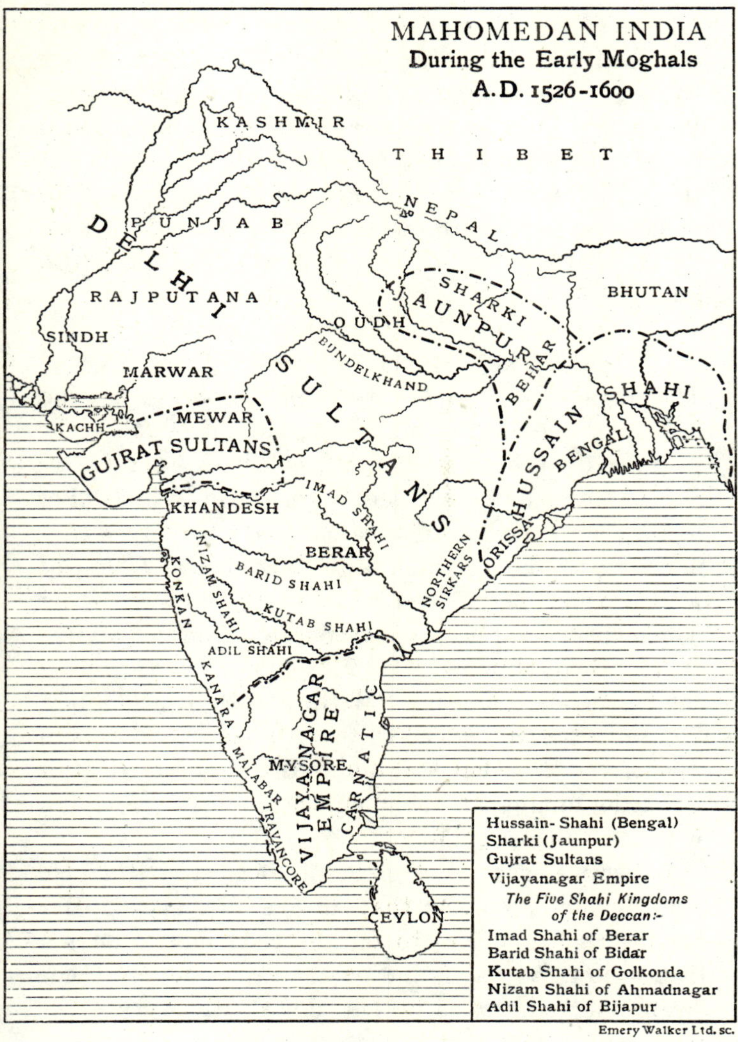

happened. " Having thus knocked with all our might at the door of penitence," he addressed the troops as follows: "Noblemen and soldiers, every man who comes into this world is subject to dissolution. When we are passed away, God only survives unchangeable. Whoever comes to the feast of life must, before it is over, drink from the cup of death. He who arrives at the inn of mortality must, one day, inevitably take his departure from that house of sorrow, the world. How much better is it to die with honour than to live with infamy!

> "With fame, even if I die, I am contented;
> Let fame be mine, as my body is death's."

The most high God has been propitious to us, and has now placed us in such a crisis that, if we fall in the field, we die the death of martyrs; if we survive, we rise victorious, the avengers of the cause of God. Let us then with one accord swear on God's holy word that none of us will even think of turning his face from this warfare, nor desert from the battle and slaughter which ensues, till his soul is separated from his body." Baber then subdued the Rajputs after capturing the forts of Chanderi (Malwa) and Rinthambor. He subsequently expelled the Afghans of the Lodi dynasty from Behar and annexed the province, after a battle fought at the confluence of the Ghaghra with the Ganges, in May, 1529.

Character of Baber.

Baber was a man of great physical strength. He says in his Memoirs that in his old age "after his health had begun to fail, he rode in two days a distance of 160 miles, and on the same journey twice swam the Ganges, as he had done with every other river he had met with."

His Autobiography is full of wise reflections upon India, and contains many touches which reveal his

BABER PRAYING THAT HE MIGHT BEAR AWAY HUMAYUN'S SICKNESS BY INVOKING IT UPON HIMSELF, IN CONSEQUENCE OF WHICH HE HIMSELF DIED.

lovable character. Besides being a consummate general, he was a scholar and a poet and a patron of learning.

He thus describes India: "Hindustan is a country that has few pleasures to recommend it. The people are not handsome. They have no idea of the charms of friendly society, of frankly mixing together, or of familiar intercourse. They have no genius, no comprehension of mind, no politeness of manner, no kindness or fellow feeling, no ingenuity or mechanical invention in planning or executing their handicraft works, no skill or knowledge in design or architecture; they have no good horses, no good flesh, no grapes or musk melons, no good fruits, no ice or cold water, no good food or bread in their bazars, no baths or colleges, no torches, not a candlestick." [1]

BABER.

Humayun. Baber died in 1530, and was succeeded on the throne of Delhi by his son Humayun. His second son, Kamran Mirza, got Afghanistan and the Western Panjab; Askari Mirza, the third son, got a *jaghir* in Sambhal (Rohilkund), and Hindal Mirza, the fourth

[1] Baber's Memoirs, p. 333.

son, one in Mewat (Ulwar). Humayun began his reign by taking Champanir by escalade. Seventy-nine iron spikes were driven into the wall of the fortress, and Humayun mounted, the forty-first of the assailants. He also defeated Bahadur Shah, king of Gujrat, at the battle of Mandesor, and annexed his

SHER SHAH'S MOSQUE AT DELHI.

kingdom, together with Malwa, which he had conquered. Humayun had now to turn his attention to Sher Khan. Sher Khan was an Afghan of the tribe of Sur, and the son of the holder of the pergunnah of Sasseram in Behar as a *Jaghir* under the Sultans of Jaunpur. His original name was Farid Khan. He first submitted to Baber, and in 1529 got possession of the strong fort of Chunar. When Mahomed Lodi, brother of Ibrahim Lodi, with an army of Afghans

Sher Khan.

revolted against Humayun, Sher Khan submitted to him, but afterwards betrayed him to Humayun, by deserting with his troops in time of battle.

Humayun then led his troops against Bahadur Shah, king of Gujrat. In the interval Sher Khan, profiting by the respite foolishly allowed him, sacked Gaur and expelled Mahomed, Sultan of Gaur, from his kingdom. He then subdued Behar, assumed the title of Shah, and fortified the defiles of Teriagarhi and Sikragarhi, between the Rajmehal hills and the Ganges, against the advancing Moghals, 1538. Mahomed of Gaur appealed to Humayun, who advanced into Behar, and after a long siege, captured Chunar. Whilst Humayun was besieging Chunar, Sher Shah was bringing all Bengal under his sway. Humayun then followed up his success by advancing into Bengal and capturing Gaur. Sher Shah then appeared in the rear of Humayun's army, occupied the fort of Rhotasgarh on the Sone, and re-captured Chunar. He then placed himself so as to block Humayun's retreat at Bihiya on the Karumnassa. The two armies remained opposite each other for three months, and then negotiations were entered into ; but while they were going on, Sher Shah unexpectedly attacked the Moghal camp at the Chausa ferry on the Ganges, where the Sone falls into the Ganges (Chupat Ghat), 26th June, 1539, and completely routed their army. Humayun fought one more battle with Sher Shah at Kanauj, but was again defeated and fled to Persia, 1540. Sher Shah reigned as Emperor of Delhi, 1540-45. He was a great road-maker ; one of his roads ran from the Bay of Bengal to Rohtas on the Jhelum, with caravanserais every four miles for travellers, and with wells and fruit trees along its sides. A second road ran from Agra to Burhanpur on the borders of the Deccan ; a third road, starting from Agra, passed through the whole of Rajputana, and a fourth connected Lahore with Multan. Posts were continually passing up and down these roads.

Restoration of Pathan rule under Sher Shah.

SHER SHAH'S TOMB AT SASSERAM.

Sher Shah built the mosque called by his name in the old city of Indrapat (Indraprastha, or the city of the Pandavas), or the Purana Kila at Delhi. He carried on continual war with the Rajputs of Marwar and Mewar ; but after capturing Jodhpur, capital of Marwar, and Chitor, capital of Mewar, he was killed at the siege of Kalanjar, on a spur of the Vindhya mountains, thirty-three miles south of Banda in the

Death of Sher Shah.

United Provinces, 1545. A chronicler speaks thus of Sher Shah : " In a very short time he gained dominion over the country, and provided for the safety of the highways, the administration of the government, and the happiness of the soldiery and people. God is a discerner of righteousness." Sher Shah was succeeded by his son Islam or Selim Shah, who reigned till 1552. Islam's brother Mahomed Adil Shah succeeded, but left all the duties of the sovereign in the hands of Himu, a low-caste Hindu. Certain Afghan chiefs rose in rebellion, and Ibrahim Khan Sur, Mahomed Adil's brother-in-law, declared himself independent in the Panjab, and seized Delhi and Agra, under the title of Sikundar Shah.

Islam Shah.

Mahomed Adil Shah.

Humayun obtained an army from Shah Tahmasp, Shah of Persia, at the price of declaring himself a convert to the Shiah doctrines of Mahomedanism. He invaded the Panjab, and defeated Sikundar Shah at Sirhind. He then re-occupied Delhi and Agra, and died at Delhi, 1556.

CHAPTER V.

AKBAR.

AKBAR, his son, succeeded at the age of thirteen: he was born, during his father's exile, at Amarkot in Sind in 1542. On his accession, he made Bairam Khan, his mother's brother, his tutor and guardian, and under his guidance defeated Himu, general of Mahomed Adil Shah, at the second battle of Panipat, 5th November, 1556.

Accession of Akbar, 1556.

Second Battle of Panipat, 1556.

Bairam Khan ruled in Akbar's name for five years, and then rebelled, when the young emperor tried to take the authority into his own hands. He was conquered and pardoned, and Akbar sent him this message: "Let our well wisher withdraw from all worldly concerns, and taking the pilgrimage to Mecca on which he has been so long intent, spend the rest of his life in prayer far removed from the toils of public life." Bairam went on a pilgrimage to Mecca, but was assassinated on his way there.

Bairam's son, Abdur Rahim, was kindly received by Akbar, and became "Khan Khanam" under Jahangir, and was the real chief of the army of the Deccan in 1615, of which Prince Parviz, son of Jahangir, was the nominal commander.

Akbar and the Rajputs.

Akbar married the daughter of Bihari Mal, Raja

of Jaipur, and his son Selim, afterwards the Emperor Jahangir, married Jodhbai, a granddaughter of Bihari Mal, Raja of Jaipur and daughter of Raja Bhagwan Das. Uday Sinha, Raja of Mewar, refused to acknowledge Akbar's authority or to enter into any alliance, so Akbar laid siege to Chitor. This dynasty of the Gehlote or Sisodhiya Rajputs of Udaipur was founded by Bappa Rao at Chitor, who was born A.D. 713. The Sisodias were descended from the dynasty founded by the Gujar chief Bhataraka, A.D. 509, at Valabhi in the east of Saurashtra. Chitor had stood two previous sieges by Alauddin Khilji and Bahadur Shah of Gujrat. Akbar captured Uday Sinha's capital of Chitor, after a siege which lasted from October, 1567, to February, 1568, in which Akbar shot the Rajput commander, the Rahtor Jaimal, with his own hand, and the garrison performed the rite of *Johar*, according to which the women burnt themselves, and the men made a sortie and died fighting. Akbar erected statues of Jaimal and Patta, the other commanders, before his palace at Delhi, of which Bernier speaks, "These two great elephants, together with the resolute men sitting on them, make an impression of I know not what

Udaipur dynasty.

AKBAR.

greatness and awful terror." The forts of Rinthambor and Kalanjar were also taken from the Rajputs after the capture of Chitor, but Uday Sinha retired to the valley of the Girwoh in the Aravalli hills, where he had dammed the stream to form the Udai Sagar, and where the city of Udaipur grew

Palaces of Bibi Mariam-uz-Zamani and Jodhbai, Fatehpur Sikri.

up around the palace of Nauchoki. His grandson, Pratap, continued his resistance. He was defeated by Man Sinha at Gogunda or Kokandah (also called Haldighat), June 1576. At this battle, according to the story, Pratap's brother, Sakta Sinha, who fought on the Moghal side, supplied him with a horse on which to continue his flight. An attempt was made by the Moghals to hold Mewar by means of detached forts, but it was not successful. Pratap Sinha gained a victory at Deweir, 1580. His son, Amar Sinha, submitted to Jahangir in 1614, but the recognition of supremacy was confined to receiving the imperial firman outside the capital, whenever the throne was vacant.

Akbar's conquests. Malwa. Panjab.

In 1558, Adam Khan, son of Maham or Jiji Anagah, Akbar's foster-mother, was sent on an expedition against Baz Bahadur, the son of Sher Shah's governor of Malwa. He afterwards tried to make himself independent, but was subdued, Gwalior taken, and Malwa reconquered. In 1566 Akbar recovered the Panjab from his brother Mirza Mahomed Hakim, ruler of Kabul.

Gujrat.

Gujrat was conquered in 1572.

Bengal and Orissa.

In 1575 Akbar advanced into Behar, took Hajipur and Patna, and left his generals, Munayim Khan and Todar Malla, to conquer Bengal. This was done between the years 1576 and 1580. The Afghans retired to Orissa, but Qutlu Khan headed a revolt in 1580, and it was not till 1592 that they were subdued by Man Sinha of Jaipur, son of Raja Bhagwan Das. Man Sinha fixed the capital of Bengal at Rajmehal, formerly called Agmehal, when he returned from the conquest of Orissa in 1592. In 1607-09 the capital was transferred to Dacca, and in 1632 retransferred to Rajmehal by Shah Sujah. The final battle in Orissa between the Afghans under Osman Khan, son of Qutlu Khan, and the Moghals under Shujat Khan took place in the marshes of the Subarnnarekha near Rajghat in 1611. Isha Khan, another Mahomedan chief, long maintained himself in East Bengal at the fort of Kalagachhia at confluence of the Lakhiya and Megna. He is mentioned by Ralph Fitch as the king of "Sinnergan" (Sonargaon).

On the death of Akbar's brother, Mirza Mahomed Hakim, 1585, Kabul passed under Akbar's sway.

Kabul. Kashmir. Sind. Kandahar.

DIWAN-I-KHAS (INTERIOR), FATEHPUR SIKRI.

Kashmir was annexed in 1587, Sind in 1592, and Kandahar in 1594.

Conquests in the Deccan.

The Subah of Ahmadnagar, including Ahmadnagar and Khandesh with the fortress of Asirgarh, was constituted by Akbar in 1600, but the local royal family really remained in power till 1637. The Sultan of Bijapur saved his kingdom by giving his daughter in marriage to Akbar's son, Daniyal. S. Lane Poole says: "Nature never intended the same ruler to govern both sides of the Vindya mountains; character and geographical conditions are dissimilar. Nevertheless, to conquer the Deccan has always been the ambition of every great king of Delhi, and the attempt has always brought disaster." Akbar felt this attraction, and began the conquest which Aurungzeb completed.

Akbar's residences.

The emperor lived at Fatehpur Sikri, 1569-84, at Lahore, 1584-98, and at Agra from 1598 till his death.

Death of Akbar.

The greatest of the Great Moghals died in 1605, and was succeeded by his son Selim under the title of Jahangir.

Akbar's administration.

Akbar's empire was divided into fifteen Subahs or provinces, each under a Subahdar. Each Subah was divided into Sirkars, the Sirkars into Dastars, the Dastars into Pergunnahs or Mahals, and the Pergunnahs into Chaklas.

The Subahs were:

Delhi	Ajmere	Behar
Agra	Gujrat	Bengal
Kabul	Malwa	Khandesh
Lahore	Oudh	Berar
Multan	Allahabad	Ahmadnagar

These provinces together produced a revenue of fifteen crores of rupees. Under the Subahdar there was a Dewan for the collection of the revenues, and a Faujdar or military commander. Law was based on the Quran, the traditions (*Hadis*), and the decisions of the Imams or great doctors of the Law. When the great Moghal chose to give a decision it was final. Roe tells us, "Lawes they have none written. The king's judgement byndes."[1] It was too fixed and unchangeable, and too little capable of being modified to suit the changing wants of the times. It was too partial to the true believer at the expense of the non-Mahomedan. Its guardians were the *Ulama* or students of the law, from among whom the Judges were appointed. Justice was administered by Kazis, who conducted trials and declared the law, when the *Mir-i-Adl* pronounced judgment. The Kotwals were the police officers. Below this Mahomedan superstructure, the old indigenous village system remained undisturbed.

The Mahomedan Law.

The emperor was a despot, the land throughout the whole empire was considered his property, he could exalt or degrade a subject at pleasure, and at the death of a man of high rank, all his property reverted to the emperor. Hawkins talks of "the men of Livings or Lordships" (the Mansabdars) who enjoyed their positions for life at the Great Moghal's Court. Albert de Mandeslo, the Holsteiner who was in India, 1638-40, tells us "the Great Moghal was heir general to all the officers in his service." No such thing existed as "inheritance of estates belonging to great persons." Bernier thus describes the position of the great Moghal. "The great Moghal is a foreigner

Character of the Government.

Bernier's estimate of the position of the Great Moghal.

[1] Roe's 'Journal,' Letter to the Archbishop of Canterbury (Hakluyt Society), ii. 215.

in Hindusthan; consequently he finds himself in a hostile country or nearly so, containing hundreds of Gentiles (Hindus) to one Moghal or even one Mahomedan. The court does not now consist, as originally, of real Moghals, but is a medley of Usbegs, Persians, Arabs, or Turks, or descendants from all these peoples. It must not be imagined that the Omrah or Lords of the Moghal's court are members of ancient families, as our nobility in France. They mostly consist of adventurers from different nations, who entice one another to the court, some having been originally slaves. The Moghal raises them to dignity or degrades them to obscurity, according to his own pleasure and caprice."[1]

He thus defends the desertion of Shah Jehan's Omrahs to the party of Aurangzeb: "A few there were who espoused no party; but with this small exception every Omrah declared in favour of Aurangzeb. It may, however, diminish our censure of this ungrateful conduct, if we call to mind that the Omrahs of Hindustan cannot be proprietors of land, or enjoy an independent revenue, like the nobility of France or other Christian States. Their income consists exclusively of pensions, which the king grants or takes away according to his own will and pleasure. When deprived of this pension they sink into utter insignificance, and find it impossible to borrow even the smallest sums."[2]

The Moghal was tied to ceremonies: "As all his subjects are slaves, so he is in a kind of reciprocall bondage, for he is tyed to observe these howres and customes so precisely that, if he were unseene one

[1] Bernier's 'Travels' (Constable & Smith). 209, 211, 212.

[2] *Ibid.* p. 65.

day, and no sufficient reason rendered, the people would mutinie; two days no reason can excuse but that he must consent to open his doores and be seen by some to satisfy others."[1] Chief of these ceremonies was the "Jarruco" (*Jharokha*) or *Darsan*, which Roe explains thus: "He comes every morning to a window called the Jarruco looking into a playne before his gate, and shows himself to the common people."[2] *Sijdah* (prostration) was a special ceremony of prayer, and it excited great odium that Akbar used to receive *sijdah* from the elect of the *Tauhid-i-Illahi* as the representative of God on earth.

The Great Moghal on his birthday used to be weighed against silver and jewels. Sir Thomas Roe has described this ceremony in his 'Journal.' He speaks of the Great Moghal as ruling despotically: "They have no written law. The king by his own word ruleth, and the governors of Provinces by that authority. Once a week he sitteth in judgment patiently, and giveth sentence for crime, capital and civil. He is every man's heir when he dyeth, which maketh him rich and the country so evil builded. The great men about him are not born noble, but favourites raised."[3] The emperor ruled by divine right, and disobedience to his commands was grievous sin. Sir John Shore's Minute of the 10th February, 1790, says: "The Moghal government, in its best times and under the wisest princes, was a *government of discretion*. The safety of the people, the security

Sir Thomas Roe's view.

Sir John Shore's view of the Moghal government.

[1] Foster's 'Embassy of Sir Thomas Roe,' i. 107, 108.

[2] *Ibid.* i. 106.

[3] Letter to Lord Carew, Foster's 'Embassy of Sir Thomas Roe,' i. 110.

of their property and the prosperity of the country depended upon the personal character of the monarch. By this standard his delegates regulated their own demeanour; in proportion as he was wise, just, vigilant, and humane, the provincial viceroys discharged their respective trusts with zeal and fidelity, and as they possessed or wanted the recited qualifications, the inferior agents conducted themselves with more or less diligence and honesty. A weak monarch and a corrupt minister encouraged every kind of disorder, for there was no law paramount to the sovereign's will."

Revenue system.

Akbar discarded the idea that the State was the supreme owner of the soil, and limited his demand to a share of the produce. He caused the cultivated land in all his territories to be surveyed on a uniform standard, and the various soils to be classified according to their productive power, reckoned according to the average out-turn of twenty kinds of crops for the spring, and thirty-two for the autumn harvest. One-third of the net produce was commuted into money, on the basis of the average prices for each crop during a period of nineteen years. This rate of land revenue, nominally fixed at a third part of the net produce, was frequently exceeded owing to the pressure of State necessity, or the rapacity of the farmers of the revenue. This commutation into money was only practised in the case of the more valuable crops, such as cotton and sugar. The State's share of one-third of the net produce was taken in kind in case of the less valuable crops. The settlements of the revenue were to be in force for nineteen years. The option was given of paying the

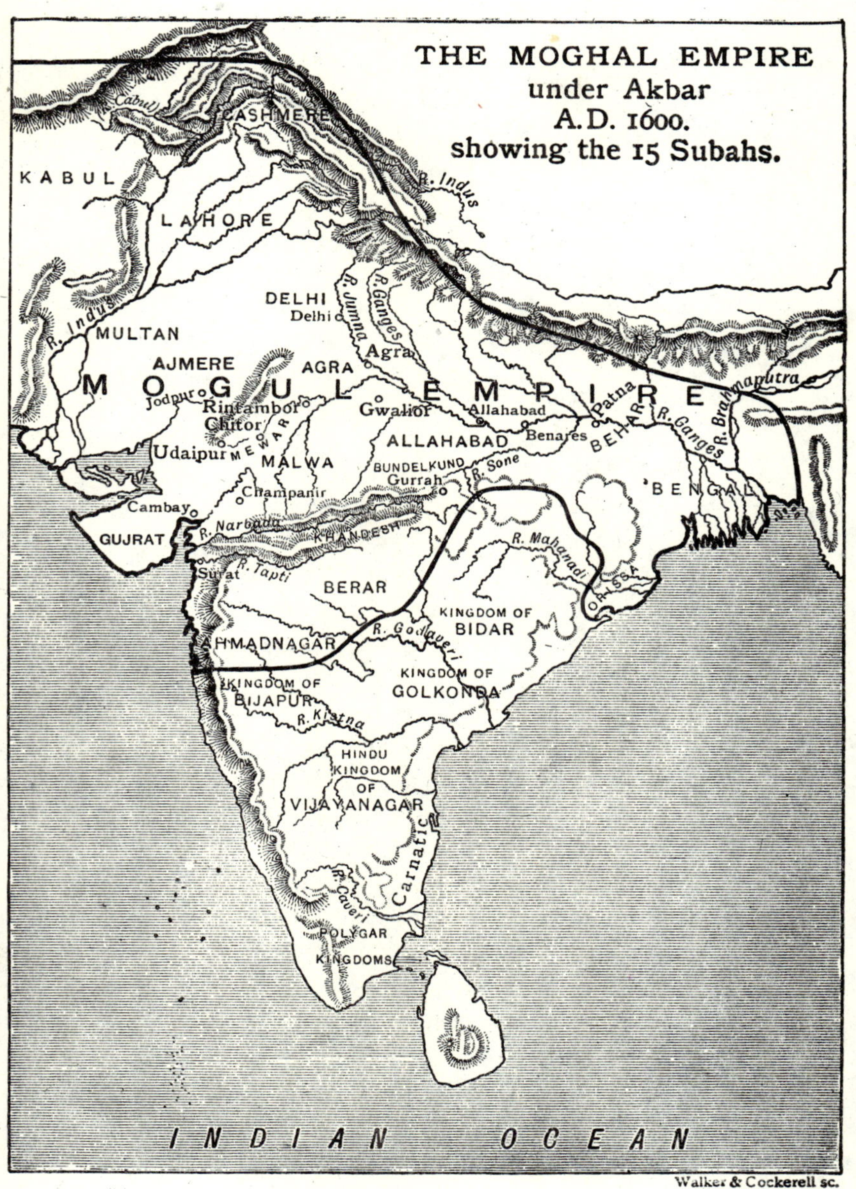

Walker & Cockerell sc.

revenue in money or in kind. The country was divided into portions, each yielding a crore of dams, or Rs. 2,50,000, as 40 dams were equivalent to a rupee. The officer in charge was called a Crori: he dealt direct with the village communities through the headman. Akbar's system left no definite margin between the revenue demanded and the expenses of cultivation, but he made no difference in the payment asked from the Hindu cultivator and the true believer. Injuries done by men from the Imperial camp to the crops of the cultivator were paid for by the Treasury. The 'Ain-i-Akbari' says: "There shall be left for every man who cultivates his land as much as he requires for his own support till the next crop be reaped, and that of his family, and for seed. This much shall be left to him; what remains is land tax and shall go to the public treasury." Thus he seems to have taken an amount as large as the full rack-rent, which might have been exacted by a private landlord.

The 'Ain-i-Akbari' thus lays down the duties of a collector of revenue: "The collector of revenue should be a friend of the agriculturist. Zeal and truthfulness should be his rule of conduct. He should consider himself the representative of the lord paramount, and establish himself where every one may have easy access to him, without the intervention of a mediator." [1]

His principal adviser in financial matters was the Hindu general and statesman, Todar Malla, of whom Abul Fazl writes: "Careful to keep himself from selfish ambition, he devoted himself to the service of

[1] 'Ain-i-Akbari,' part ii., translated by Jarrett, p. 43.

the State, and earned an everlasting fame." Todar Malla executed the settlement of the revenues of the Moghal Empire of 1582. His objects were:

Todar Malla. Ausil Toomar Jumma or Revenue settlement of 1582.

1. To obtain correct measurement of the land.
2. To ascertain the produce of each bigha and the amount it should pay to government.
3. To settle the equivalent in money.

Akbar's fleet.

Akbar had an official called the *Mir Bahri* or Admiral of the Fleet who had to provide ships and men to watch the rivers, and to superintend the imposition, realisation, and remission of duties. The chief centres of shipbuilding were Bengal and Tata on the Indus. The Ausil Toomar Jumma of Todar Malla, 1582, assigned certain perganas for the maintenance of the imperial fleet (*nowwara*), by repair of old ships and the construction of new ships, at an annual cost of Rs. 8.40,000, including the maintenance of 923 Portuguese or Feringhee sailors. The fleet was constructed with timber from Sylhet, and was charged with the defence of the coast, against the Maghs of Arracan and the Portuguese from Mundalghat (at the confluence of the Rupnarayan and Damooda) and Balasore, on one side, to the mouth of the Meghna on the other.

Military reforms.

In the army, cash payments were substituted for *jaghirs* or assignments of land, which was a very economical step. Military officers, who were called Mansabdars, were classified according to the number of men they commanded, the highest class being the commanders of 10,000 men, and the lowest the commanders of ten. Under Akbar, precautions were taken to see that each Mansabdar kept up his required quota of troops, and the horses they rode were branded.

These precautions were neglected by later sovereigns. The best description of Akbar's administration is to be found in the 'Ain-i-Akbari,' which constitutes part of the 'Akbarnamah' or history of Akbar's reign, by Abul Fazl. Abul Fazl was a flatterer of Akbar, so his account of events should be compared with that of Badauni.

'Ain-i-Akbari.'

Akbar's religion.

Akbar was at first a devout Mahomedan. Latterly, after coming in contact with people of many creeds, he formed a religion of his own, the *Tauhid-i-Illahi* or "Divine Faith." This was a mixture of what he conceived to be the best points of all the religions with which he came in contact. He had constant religious discussions in the *Diwan-i-Khas* or Hall of Private Audience, sometimes called the *'Ibadat Khana*, at Fatehpur Sikri, in which the three Jesuit Missionaries at his court may have taken part. One of these, Acquaviva, is specially mentioned by Abul Fazl under the name of "Padre Radalf." Radolpho Aquaviva, Antonio de Montserrato, and Francisco Henriquez, Jesuits, were sent to Akbar's court by the Archbishop of Goa in 1569. They remained till 1583. Similar expeditions were made in 1591 and 1595. Jerome Xavier was sent from Goa to the Moghal court in 1594. He had considerable influence with Jahangir, and wrote *Mir'atu Kadas*, an account in Persian of the facts of Christianity. Francisco Corsi, another Jesuit at the court of Jahangir, was a friend of Sir Thomas Roe. Akbar promulgated a new era, called the "Divine Era," dating from his own accession. He was enabled to do this, after the Maulavis had been induced to declare his authority as a just prince (*imam-i-adil*), higher

Jesuits at the court of Akbar and Jahangir.

than that of the Mujtahids or doctors of the faith, and that, when the Mujtahids differed, his decisions were binding on all the Mahomedans of India. He was thus able to unite in his own person the spiritual as well as the secular headships. He adopted a policy of religious toleration. He remitted the Jiziya, or poll tax, on all non-Mahomedans, and the tax on Hindu pilgrims. When remitting the Jiziya, Akbar expressed his opinion that, "although the tax fell upon a vain religion, yet as all modes of worship were designed for a great Being, it was wrong to throw an obstacle in the way of the devout, and to cut them off from their mode of intercourse with their Maker." Out of 416 Mansabdars, 51 were Hindus (47 Rajputs). He opened high offices of State to the Hindus, and by his own example encouraged intermarriages between them and Mahomedans. He seems to have recognised that the Moghal Empire needed the support of the Hindus, and to have endeavoured to secure that support by religious toleration and admission to high office. His inclination towards Hinduism appeared in his giving up the practice of eating beef and onions, his encouragement of the use of wine and of the shaving of the beard among his

JAHANGIR.

Akbar's religious toleration and the reasons for it.

courtiers, his prohibition of the slaughter of cows, and his wearing a *tilak* on his forehead.

Akbar's court.

The principal members of Akbar's court were Abul Faiz, the author of the 'Tarikh-i-Alfi' or 'History of the Millennium' (Islam had existed a thousand

BULAND DARWAZA AT FATEHPUR SIKRI.

years, a period which was called an *alf*, and was supposed to have done its work). Abul Faiz was the first Mahomedan to study Sanscrit philosophy: he translated into Persian the 'Naldamayanti' and the 'Bijagonita' and 'Lilavati' of Bhaskaracharjya, and the 'Mahabharat,' under the name of the Razmnamah. His brother, Abul Fazl, was the author of the 'Akbarnamah.' He was murdered by Narsing

Deo Raja of Orcha in Central India at the instigation of Prince Selim. Abul Kader Badauni, another historian of Akbar's reign, wrote the '*Muntak habat-ut-Tawarikh.*' Both Baber and his great-grandson Jahangir, and Baber's daughter, the princess Gulbadan, wrote memoirs of their times. Other prominent courtiers were the Raja Todar Malla, a Kshatriya from Oudh, and a devout Hindu; Raja Man Sinha Kachwaha of Jaipur; Gadai Brahmandas, a Brahman of Kalpi, also called Raja Birbal, who was killed in battle with the Yusufzais in 1586; and the poet and musician, Miyan Tansen.

RAJA MAN SINHA.

Akbar's personal appearance.

"He was of middle stature, but inclining to be tall; his complexion was wheaten or nut coloured, rather dark than fair; his eyes and eyebrows dark, and the latter running across into each other; with a handsome person, he had a lion's strength, which was indicated by an extraordinary breadth of chest, and the length of his arms and hands. On the left side of his nose there was a fleshy wart, which in contemporary eyes appeared exceedingly beautiful and was considered auspicious of riches and prosperity. His voice was loud, and his speech elegant and pleasing.

His manners and habits were different from those of other people, and his visage was full of godly dignity." [1]

AKBAR'S TOMB, COMMENCED BY HIMSELF AND FINISHED BY JAHANGIR, AT SECUNDRA, NEAR AGRA.

Akbar's buildings.

Akbar's most famous buildings are the Fort at Agra, the Palace and Mosque of Selim Chishti, at Fatehpur Sikri, the tomb of Humayun near Delhi, and Akbar's own tomb, commenced by himself and finished by Jahangir, at Secundra, near Agra.

[1] Jahangir's Memoirs, p. 45.

CHAPTER VI.

JAHANGIR, SHAH JAHAN, AND AURANGZEB.

MAN SINHA, Raja of Jaipur, is said to have contemplated the enthronement of Khusru, son of Jahangir, on Akbar's death, but Akbar on his deathbed specially designated Jahangir as his successor, so he succeeded without further opposition, 1605. On his accession, he tried to cause Sher Afghan, husband of the beautiful Mihr-un-nissa, of whom he was enamoured, to divorce his wife. Sher Afghan, who had been given a *jaghir* at Burdwan by Akbar, refused, and, in his rage, killed the viceroy of Bengal, who told him of the emperor's proposal. Sher Afghan was in turn put to death, 1607, and two years later Jahangir married Mihr-un-nissa and gave her the title of Nur Jahan. The empress's influence soon became supreme at court; her father, Mirza Ghiasuddin Mahomed, was made prime minister, and her brother, Asaf Khan, enjoyed great power. Mirza Ghiasuddin Mahomed received the title of Itimad-ud-daula, and his tomb is one of the most beautiful architectural

Jahangir, 1605-27.

NUR JAHAN.

Nur Jahan.

remains at Agra. Jahangir said that Nur Jahan was wise enough to conduct the business of state, all he wanted was a bottle of wine and a piece of meat to keep himself merry. The inscription on a gold coin said, "By order of the Emperor Jahangir, gold acquires a hundred times additional value by the name of the Empress Nur Jahan."

The fortunes of the family can be seen by the genealogy on next page.

The family founded by Mirza Ghiasuddin Mahomed.

The family founded by Mirza Ghiasuddin Mahomed proved an exception to the rule that the Omrahs of the Great Moghal's court did not found families. This was because of the exceptional talent of its members, and because the wives of three successive Great Moghals, Jahangir, Shah Jahan, and Aurangzeb belonged to it. Down to quite recent times, there was a succession of titular Naibs Nazim of Dacca, who were descended from this family, and Bishop Heber describes a visit to one of them.

Khusru's Rebellion.

Four months after Jahangir's accession his eldest son Khusru rebelled and seized Lahore. The rebellion was put down, and Jahangir caused his son to be carried on an elephant through lines of his followers who were punished by impalement. Khusru was sent with Khuram to the Deccan, and died there, 1622.

Death of Parviz.

Parviz was Jahangir's favourite son, as he "could drink level with his father." Roe visited him at Burhanpur, and he died there, 28th October, 1626.

In 1608 Captain Hawkins, who commanded the *Hector*, one of the ships sailing to Surat on the East India Company's third voyage to India, visited Agra with a letter from James I. to Jahangir, and in 1615 the same king sent a formal ambassador, Sir Thomas

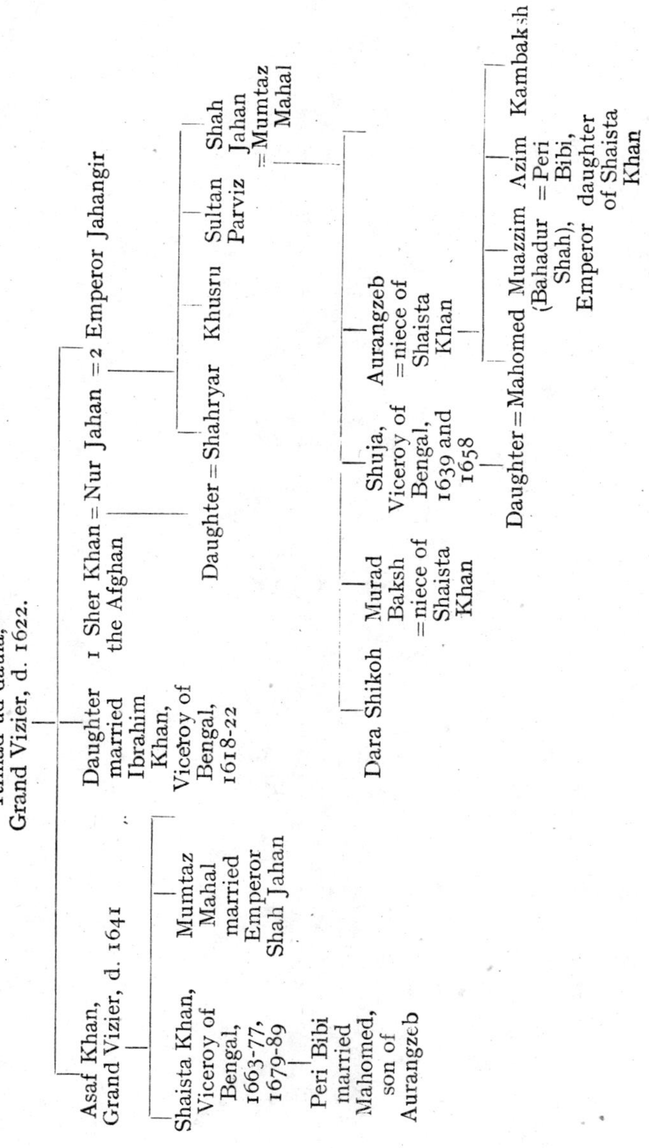
Mirza Ghiasuddin Mahomed,
Itimad ud daula,
Grand Vizier, d. 1622.
Asaf Khan,
Grand Vizier, d. 1641
Daughter
married
Ibrahim
Khan,
Viceroy of
Bengal,
1618-22
1 Sher Khan = Nur Jahan = 2 Emperor Jahangir
the Afghan
Shaista Khan,
Viceroy of
Bengal,
1663-77,
1679-89
Mumtaz
Mahal
married
Emperor
Shah Jahan
Daughter = Shahryar
Khusru
Sultan
Parviz
Shah
Jahan
= Mumtaz
Mahal
Peri Bibi
married
Mahomed,
son of
Aurangzeb
Dara Shikoh
Murad
Baksh
= niece of
Shaista
Khan
Shuja,
Viceroy of
Bengal,
1639 and
1658
Aurangzeb
= niece of
Shaista
Khan
Daughter = Mahomed
Muazzim
(Bahadur
Shah),
Emperor
Azim
= Peri
Bibi,
daughter
of Shaista
Khan
Kambak:h

English visitors to the Court of Jahangir.

Roe. Sir Thomas Roe, who arrived when Jahangir was residing at Ajmere, said of him : " He is of so good a disposition that he suffers all men to govern him, which is worse than governing ill." Very early in his reign Jahangir restored the Mahomedan confession of faith to the place upon the coins, from which it had been left out by Akbar. He was indifferent about religion, and outraged the religious susceptibilities of many by placing his effigy on the coins, with a goblet of wine in his hand. He thus abandoned the tolerant attitude of his father, who saw good in all religions, but did not pin his faith exclusively upon any.

Character of his reign.

Nur Jahan's daughter by Sher Afghan was married to Shahryar, Jahangir's youngest son. Nur Jahan's intrigues to procure the succession for Shahryar drove prince Khuram (afterwards Shah Jahan) into rebellion. Khuram was the son of a Rajput mother. His sympathy with the Rajputs brought about the surrender of Amra Sinha, and, after his rebellion, he took refuge with the Rajputs and lived for some time in a palace on the lake at Udaipur. Mahabat Khan, son of a Kabuli Ghayur Beg, had been a personal attendant of Jahangir as Prince Selim. He put down Prince Khuram's rebellion in 1623, but he excited Nur Jahan's jealousy, and was summoned to answer the charges against himself. In self-defence he made himself master of the emperor's person on the river Beas, 1626, and Nur Jahan joined him in captivity. After a time the empress was able to release both herself and her husband, and Mahabat Khan fled to the Deccan, of which province he was Subahdar when he died in 1634. The chief events of Jahangir's reign were the conquest of Kangra, 1621, the war against

Rebellions of Prince Khuram and Mahabat Khan.

Principal events of Jahangir's reign.

Ahmadnagar in the Deccan, and the submission of Amar Sinha, the Rajput Rana of Udaipur, to the Moghal Empire. In Bengal, the revolt of Pratapaditya, the conqueror of the twelve Hindu chiefs called the Bara Bhuiyas, who occupied territory on the sea-board of the Bay of Bengal, was put down by Man Sinha. The capital of Bengal was transferred from Rajmehal to Dacca by Islam Khan, Subahdar 1608-13, grandson of Shaikh Selim Chishti, the saint of Fatehpur Sikri, in order to contend with the Portuguese pirates under Sebastian Gonzales in the Bay of Bengal. The name Dacca is supposed to be derived from *Dhaka Ishvari*, "the concealed goddess (Durga)" of the Dhakesvari temple, or from the Dhak tree 'Butea frondosa,' which abounds on the site, or from Dhak, a drum, the reference being to the tradition that the original boundaries of the city were fixed by the distance to which Islam Khan's drums beaten on the river bank could be heard. Islam Khan was followed as Subahdar by Kasim Khan, 1613-18, and by Ibrahim Khan, brother-in-law of Nur Jahan, 1618-22. Jahangir died 1627, but Jahan survived him till 1645, and is buried not far from him at Shah Dara, near Lahore.

Foundation of Dacca and origin of the name.

Sebastian Manrique, a Spanish Augustinian monk, travelled in India, 1612-25. He had the unique experience of sailing down the Indus from Lahore to Tatta. He describes the great fertility of Bengal and the splendour of its cotton fabrics. The development of its prosperity was hampered by oppression on the part of the Subahdars. Manrique remarks on *Sati*, self-immolation at Jaggernath and Sagar, and on the reverence shown by the Hindus towards the

Ganges and the Cow. He definitely asserts that the architect of the Taj was a Venetian, Geronimo Verroneo, who drew a large salary from Shah Jahan. In this, he runs contrary to the commonly received

Shah Jahan and Courtier.

idea that the designer of the Taj was a Persian or Turk known as Ustad Isa or Mahomed Isa Effendi.

The Englishman, William Bruton, who, in 1632, made a journey from Masulipatam to Cuttack, is another contemporary authority for Bengal.

Jahangir's buildings.

The finest specimens of architecture built in the reign of Jahangir are the temple of Govind Dev at Brindaban, near Muttra, the tomb of Itimad-ud-daula at Agra, and Jahangir's tomb at Shah Dara, Lahore. The temple of Govind Dev was built by Man Sinha. Its *garbha griha* or inmost shrine, and its *gandhi* or spire, were razed by Aurangzeb's order.

ARGUMAND BANU, OR MUMTAZ MAHAL.

Shah Jahan, 1627-58.

With the assistance of Asaf Khan, brother of Nur Jehan, and father of his wife, Mumtaz Mahal (Elect of the Palace), Shah Jehan put down the intrigue in favour of his brother Shahryar, and ascended the throne in 1627. In the reign of Shah Jehan, the prosperity of the country under the Moghal Emperors was at its zenith. He was three parts a Hindu, as his mother and both his grand-mothers were Rajputnis, yet he was an orthodox Sunni.

Zenith of Moghal prosperity.

Expulsion of the Portuguese from Hughli and its occupation by the English.

In 1631 the Portuguese were expelled from Hughli by the Viceroy Kasim Khan, which was occupied by the English in 1640. The English were allowed to do this owing to the favour they gained on account of the skill with which an English surgeon, Gabriel Broughton, treated Shah Jehan's family. It was for curing Jahanara, Shah Jehan's daughter, from burns that Gabriel Broughton, who had been brought from Surat, asked and obtained, as his reward, permission for the English to trade in Bengal.

A main reason of Shah Jahan's dislike of the Portuguese was that when, as Prince Khuram, he had rebelled against his father, and had asked the Portuguese for artillery, he was refused by the governor of Hughli, Michael Rodriguez. Shah Jahan also caused the Roman Catholic Churches erected by the Jesuits at Lahore and Agra to be demolished.

Conquest of Ahmadnagar.

Under Shah Jahan, the subjugation of Ahmadnagar was completed in 1637, but Kandahar was finally

Loss of Kandahar.

lost to the Moghal Empire. It had been conquered by the Persians under Shah Abbas in Jahangir's reign in 1622. It was betrayed to the Moghals by its governor, Ali Mardan Khan, in 1637, and it was re-

First mention of Aurangzeb.

captured by the Persians in 1648. In 1646 Aurangzeb was Viceroy of Gujrat, and the first mention of him from an European source is in a despatch of the Surat Factory to the East India Company's Directors in London, dated the same year. He is described as "very superstitious," and it is reported that he refused to allow saltpetre to be removed from Ahmadabad, and that he "had been possessed by some of his churchmen that it is not lawful for him to suffer us to export that specie, which peradventure may be employed against the Moores" (Mahomedans). In 1647 Aurangzeb was compelled to retreat from Balkh and Badakshan, and in 1694 and 1652 he unsuccess-

Acquisition of Chittagong.

fully endeavoured to recover Kandahar. In 1638, Mukut Rai, who held Chittagong for the Raja of Arracan, surrendered it to Islam Khan Mashadi, viceroy of Bengal.

Shah Jahan had four sons: Dara Shukoh, meaning "equal to Darius in splendour," who remained with his father; Shuja, who was viceroy of Bengal; **Shah Jahan's family.**

INTERIOR VIEW OF *DIWAN-I-KHAS*, DELHI.

Aurangzeb, viceroy of the Deccan; and Murad, viceroy of Gujrat. He had also two daughters—Jahanara, a close adherent of Dara Shukoh; and Roshanara, a friend of Aurangzeb.

Fratricidal conflict of Shah Jahan's sons.

In 1657 Shah Jahan became ill, and all his sons resolved to fight for the throne. In the event of their father's death, in Bernier's pithy phrase, "not only was the crown to be gained by victory alone, but in the case of defeat, life was certain to be forfeited. There was no choice between a kingdom or death." [1] Death was also almost equally certainly the penalty of inaction. It was either *Takt* or *Takta,* the throne or the bier. As Shah Jahan had exterminated the family of Jahangir, so it was probable that the successful claimant to the throne of Shah Jahan would slay or imprison all who could dispute his right to the succession. Shuja's invading army from Bengal was defeated by Dara's son, Suleiman Shukoh, and Raja Jai Singh of Jaipur near Benares, December, 1657. Aurangzeb pretended to have no designs on the throne and joined forces with Murad. He wrote to Murad: "I have not the slightest wish to take part in the government of this deceitful unstable world, my only desire is that I may make the pilgrimage to the temple of God. But it behoves dutiful sons to rescue their father from the presumption and conceit of that apostate" (Dara). The two brothers defeated Jeswant Singh of Jodhpur at Dharmatpur in the territory of Ujjain (April, 1658), and, advancing on Agra, defeated Dara at Samgarh (7th June, 1658). They then seized the person of Shah Jahan and kept him close prisoner in the fort at Agra, and Aurangzeb, after a vain attempt to conciliate his father, who was deeply attached to his eldest son Dara, proclaimed himself emperor, July, 1658. He formally ascended the throne, 26th May,

Aurangzeb deposes Shah Jahan and proclaims himself Emperor, 1658.

[1] Bernier (Constable's edition), p. 25.

The Taj Mahal from the River Jumna, Agra.

1659. One of his first acts was to abolish the ceremony of the *Darshan* or *Jharokha*, as savouring of idolatry.

Shah Jahan died in prison, 1668, at the age of 74. He excelled as an administrator, and enjoys another claim to fame as the builder of the palace of Delhi, the most notable feature of which is the Diwan-i-Khas, or Hall of Private Audience, and the renowned Taj Mahal, the tomb of his wife, Arjumand Banu, Auliya Begum, Mumtaz Mahal, daughter of Asaf Khan and niece of Nur Jahan at Agra. The Jamma Musjid at Delhi, with its triple domes of the Bijapur type, the city of Shahjahanabad or New Delhi, and the marble pavilions on the Ana Sagar embankment at Ajmere were also his work. Mr. G. W. Forrest remarks, " the monarch who erected the mosque at Ajmere, the Pearl mosque at Agra, and the Taj Mahal, left the world richer than he found it."

Shah Jahan's buildings.

The inscription on the walls of the Moti Musjid is couched in laudatory terms which are not undeserved : " Verily it is an exalted palace of paradise, made of a single resplendent pearl, because, since the beginning of the population of the world, no mosque purely and entirely of marble has appeared as its equal, nor, since the creation of the universe, any place of worship wholly bright and polished has come to rival it."

Whilst in pursuit of Dara, Aurangzeb invited Murad Baksh to dinner, made him drunk, and then sent him a prisoner to the Salimgarh fort at Delhi, on the plea that a drunkard was unfit to reign (July 5th, 1658). He next turned to attack Shuja, and totally defeated him at Khajua in the Allahabad district, 5th January, 1659. Shuja fled to Arracan and met an unknown fate there, 1660. Dara was defeated at Ajmere, fled to Kandahar, was betrayed to Aurangzeb by a Pathan zemindar of Kachh, named Malik Jiwan, and was charged with apostacy from the Mahomedan religion, on account of his sympathy with Sufi mysticism, and executed September the 15th, 1659. His son, Suleiman Shukoh, was surrendered to Aurangzeb by the Raja of Srinagar. Aurangzeb's brother Murad, and his brother Dara's sons, Suleiman and Sipahar Shukoh, were all confined in the fort at Gwalior, and subsequently executed or poisoned by being forced to drink "post," a preparation of opium.

AURANGZEB

In 1681 Aurangzeb left Delhi for the Deccan, and never came back to his capital. Aurangzeb completed the conquest of the Mahomedan kingdom of the Deccan by annexing Bijapur, 1686, and Golkonda, 1687, though it might have been a wiser policy to have left these kingdoms in independence as a counterpoise to the Mahrattas. The fidelity of Abdur Razzak Lari to Abu'l Hassan, the last king of Golkonda, gained for him even the admiration of Aurangzeb. He appears to have conquered Bijapur

Annexation of Bijapur and Golkonda.

and Golkonda not so much to extend the boundaries of his empire, as to convert territories, the inhabitants of which were believers in the Shiah heresy, to the Sunni form of the Mahomedan religion. Tavernier said of him: "Aurangzeb testifies above all things an extraordinary devotion for the sect of the Sunnis; of which he is so zealous an observer that he surpasses all his predecessors in outward profession, which was the cloak under which he usurped the crown." The kingdoms of Bijapur and Golkonda also paid blackmail to the Mahrattas, and Aurangzeb wished to conquer them and so deprive the Mahrattas of the enjoyment of these payments.

Mir Jumla and Shaista Khan, Subahdars of Bengal.

Aurangzeb made Mir Jumla, who had deserted the cause of Golkonda to join the Moghals, Subahdar of Bengal, and Khan-i-Khanam, in 1658. Mir Jumla, who had helped to defeat Shuja at Khajua (January, 1659) and again at Tandah, and forced him to escape into Arracan, succeeded him as Subahdar of Bengal and invaded Kuch Behar and Assam. He penetrated as far as Ghurgaon, the capital of the Ahom kingdom of Assam on the Dihku river to the S.E. of Sibsagar, but had to retreat owing to the approach of the rainy season. He died at Khizarpur in Kuch Behar, on his way back to Dacca, 1663. Aurangzeb remarked to his son: "You have lost a father and I the greatest and most dangerous friend I ever had." Shaista Khan, brother of Mumtaz Mahal, and uncle of Aurangzeb, succeeded Mir Jumla on his death in 1663, and remained Subahdar till 1689, with the exception of two years, 1677-79. The chief events of his government were his expulsion of the Portuguese pirates from the island of Sandip in the estuary of the Megna river, and his quarrel with the English, which caused them temporarily to leave Bengal.

Of Shaista Khan, Streynsham Master says: He is every day more covetous, so that to relate to you the many wayes that are continually invented by his Duan (Dewan), one of the craftiest men in the kingdom, and his governors, to bring money into his coffers, would be as endless as admirable, both for their witt and cruelty."

MIR JUMLA.

Aurangzeb and the Mahrattas.

Aurangzeb devoted the last years of his life to subdue the Mahrattas in the Deccan from his headquarters at Burhanpur on the Tapti. He surprised and took Sambhaji, son of Sivajee, prisoner at Sangameshvar and put him to death, 1689, and repeatedly defeated Ram Raja, Sambhaji's half-brother. He also captured Rajgarh, Jinji, and Satara (1699). Sivajee, the second son of Sambhaji (nicknamed Sahu), had been taken prisoner and brought up at the Moghal court. On his release he assumed the title of king of the Mahrattas, and began to exercise nominal power at Satara, March, 1708, but really left everything in the hands of the Peshwa (or minister)

Separation of the Mahratta power into two kingdoms of Satara and Kolhapur.

Balaji Biswanath. His uncle, Ram Raja, was regent, and on his death in 1700, his uncle's widow, Tara Bai, established another Mahratta kingdom, in the person of Ram Raja's son, Sivajee III., at Kolhapur, 1700. The Mahrattas devastated the country in the rear of the Moghals, and invaded Malwa and Gujrat. Aurangzeb was at last forced to retreat, and died at Ahmadnagar after a fruitless campaign of twenty years, 4th March, 1707. He was buried in a plain tomb, devoid of all ornament, in the village of Khuldabad or Roza near Aurangabad. Dr. John Gemelli Careri visited Aurangzeb at Galgala near the ruins of Bijapur, on the upper waters of the Kistna, 1695. He saw an old white-bearded man, short, slender and bowed with age, with a long nose and an olive skin. He wore plain white muslin and on his head a turban with a large emerald.

Aurangzeb's death-bed letter to his son.

Aurangzeb's death-bed letter to his son Azim is full of unutterable pathos. "I am grown very old and weak. Many were around me when I was born; but now I am going alone. I know not why I am or wherefore I came into the world. I have not done well for the country or its people. God has been in my heart; yet my darkened eyes have not recognised His light. There is no hope for one in the future. The fever is gone, but there is nothing left of me save skin and dried flesh. The army is confounded and without heart or help, even as I am. Nothing brought I into this world, but I carry out of it the burden of my sins. Though my trust is in the mercy and goodness of God, I deplore my sins. Come what will, I have launched my bark upon the waters. Farewell! Farewell! Farewell!"

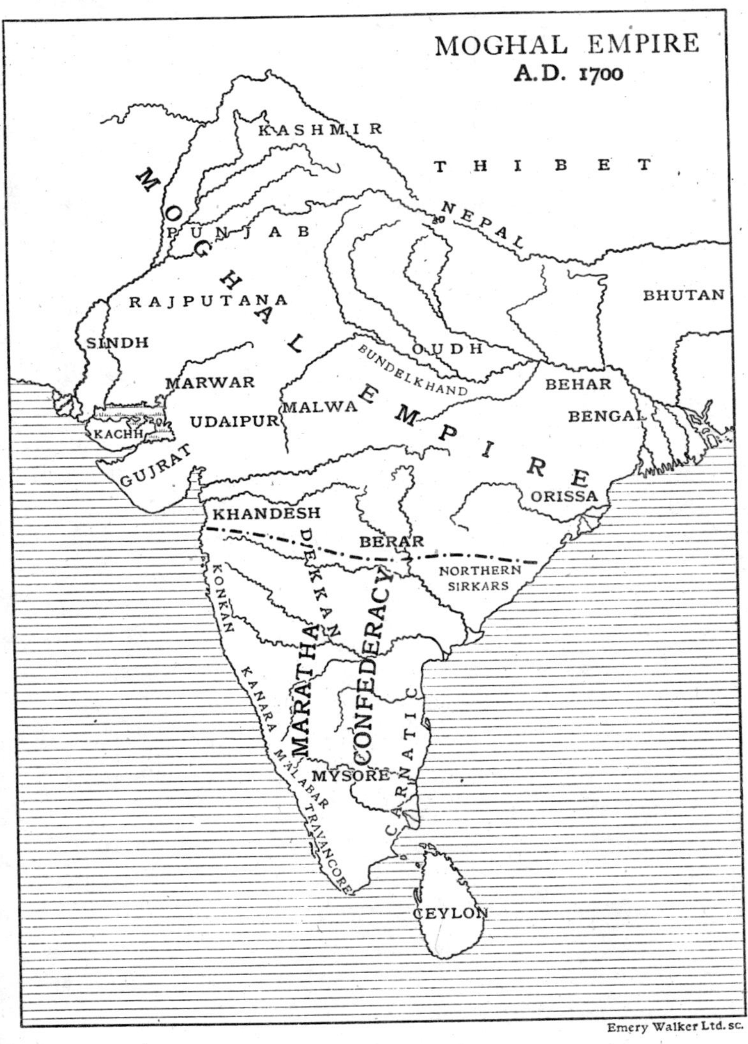

Aurangzeb was a zealous and orthodox Mahomedan of the Sunni type. His religious convictions

Character of Aurangzeb.

governed alike his public policy and his private conduct. His brother Dara characterised him as "namazi" or a man of prayer, and he covered his ambition with this cloak of religion. After attaining the throne he must have known that the only hope for the preservation of the empire lay in compromise and tolerance, but, of his own choice, he became a bigoted champion of the most extravagant claims and doctrines of Islam. He opposed his own brothers partly no doubt for his own security, but also because they were renegades from the true Mahomedan faith and code of manners. Dara was a Sufi mystic, with supposed leanings to Christianity, and Shuja a Shiah. In spite of his zeal for religion, Aurangzeb was treacherous and a hypocrite. In his mind the advancement of the Sunni form of the Mussulman religion, which he set before himself as the end of his policy, seems to have justified the means. He was simple and temperate in his manner of living, and austere. He never drank wine, and had no taste for luxury of any sort. He was appropriately called "the Puritan emperor." As he had treated others, so he expected to be treated himself, and would trust no one, least of all his own sons. He wrote to his son Muazzim: "The art of reigning is so delicate that a king's jealousy should be awakened by his very shadow. Be wise or a fate similar to that of your brother (Mahomed, who married the daughter of Shah Shuja, and was imprisoned for life in Gwalior), awaits you." [1]

Historians of the reign of Aurangzeb.

Mahomed Hashim wrote a history of Aurangzeb's reign. The emperor forbade the writing of history

[1] Bernier's 'Travels,' Constable, p. 84.

in the eleventh year of his reign, so the work was carried on in secret, hence the author is known by the name of Khafi Khan.

Mullah Shafia, or Danishmand Khan, was an official of Persian origin at Shah Jahan's court ; he first patronised Francis Bernier, who afterwards took service with Aurangzeb as a physician, and was in India from 1656 to 1668. He wrote a book entitled 'A History of the Last Revolution of the States of the Great Moghal,' published 1670, which is especially useful as the work of an educated contemporary observer, who had made a special study of political philosophy.

The travels of John Baptist Tavernier, jeweller, who was in India, off and on from 1641-67, are especially useful on the economic side, *e.g.* he has given us a valuable account of the Indian diamond mines in the seventeenth century, and a description of the Peacock Throne as he saw it.

Nicolai Manucci, author of the 'Storia do Mogor,' or 'History of the Moghals,' who was in India from 1656 to his death in 1717, wrote a history of part of Shah Jahan's and all Aurangzeb's reign, with a treatise on the Moghal court, administration and institutions. He was present as an artilleryman in Dara's service at the battle of Samgarh, at which Bernier was present in Aurangzeb's retinue. We have thus two contemporary accounts of the battle from contemporary European witnesses on different sides. Manucci dabbled in medicine, and was employed as a physician in Delhi and at the court of Bahadur Shah when Viceroy of the Deccan ; he was also employed as an envoy from the Portuguese Viceroy of Goa to the Viceroy of the Deccan. He ended his days in 1717 as a sort of Foreign Secretary to the English President of Madras.

Intolerant policy of Aurangzeb.

Aurangzeb made his own personal feelings the measure of the rights of his subjects. In 1669 he revived the Jiziya, or tax on all non-Mahomedans, which had been abolished by Akbar, and declared all Hindus ineligible for government service. Dr. John Fryer, who was in India during the nine years ending 1681, says of this change of policy: "This religious bigot of an emperor, Aurenzeeb, is on a project to bring them all over to his faith, and has already begun by two several taxes or polls, very severe ones, which has made some Rajahs revolt."[1] Jeswant Singh of Jodhpur and Jai Singh of Jaipur were both poisoned at Aurangzeb's bidding. He ill-treated the infant sons of Jeswant Singh, and refused to recognise the claim of Jeswant Singh's son, Ajit Singh, to succeed his father as Raja of Jodhpur.

Alienation of the Rajputs.

Raja Singh, Rana of Udaipur's dignified remonstrance against the imposition of the Jizia.

Raja Singh, Rana of Udaipur, remonstrated against the imposition of the Jizia thus: "If your majesty places any faith in those books by distinction called divine, you will be there instructed that God is the God of all mankind, not the God of the Mahomedans alone. The Pagan and the Musulman are equal in his presence. Distinctions of colour are of his ordination. It is he who gives existence. In your temples, to his name the voice is raised in prayer; in a house of images where the bell is shaken, still he is the object of adoration. To vilify the religion or customs of other men is to set at naught the pleasure of the Almighty." Aurangzeb invaded Mewar, but was ignominiously repulsed. The Rajputs then conceived the idea of dethroning Aurangzeb and

[1] Trubner's 'Roe and Fryer's Travels,' p. 307.

setting up his son Akbar in his stead. Aurangzeb wrote his son a letter, which was dropped by a spy in the tent of the Rajput leader Durga Das, in which he affected to approve of a supposed design of his son Akbar to attack the Rajputs, when engaged with the imperial forces. The Rajputs, nevertheless, escorted Akbar to the Mahratta Sambhaji, whence he escaped in an English ship to Persia. A peace was subsequently patched up without any mention of the Jizia, but with the surrender of the captured districts near Chitor, and the inclusion of Jodhpur in the treaty. The Rajputs, however, remained bitterly hostile to the Moghals, and all Rajputana, except Jaipur, became virtually independent. Aurangzeb prohibited the religious festivals of the Hindus. He was equally severe upon the Shiah sect of the Mahomedans. There were many of Persian race belonging to this sect in Aurangzeb's empire, and they were treated as badly as the Hindus. This intolerant policy caused the eventual break-up of the Moghal Empire, which had been built up by Akbar upon the support of Hindus as well as Mahomedans.

Aurangzeb's buildings.

Aurangzeb demolished the Hindu temples at Mathura, and built the Mosque at Benares above Panchgangaghat and another near the Golden Temple out of the ruins of the temple of Bishveshvar. He built the Badshahi Mosque at Lahore out of the confiscated funds of his brother Dara. The tomb of Rubia-ud-Daurani, wife or daughter of Aurangzeb, at Aurungabad, belongs to the same period. The want of the assistance of Hindu builders, which was rejected by Aurangzeb's bigotry, produced a notable decadence of Mahomedan architecture during his reign.

CHAPTER VII.

THE MAHRATTAS AND THE SIKHS.

SIVAJEE, the founder of Mahratta independence, was born in 1627; his grandfather was Madhoji Bhonsla, commander of 5000 horse, and the governor of the district of Chakan and the fort of Shivner in the service of Ahmadnagar. His father, Shahji Bhonsla, married Jijabai, the daughter of the Deshmukh of Sindkheir, and helped Malik Amber in the maintenance of the independence of Ahmednagar.

Sivajee. Sivajee comes first into notice by seizing the hill forts of Tornea, Singgarh, Supa, and Purandhar, and building a new fort at Rajgarh, 1646-47. These forts lay mostly in the Western Ghats, and in the Konkan, the tract between the Western Ghats and the Indian Ocean. Most of the country in which they were situated belonged to the kingdom of Bijapur. The king of Bijapur seized Shahji Bhonsla, and threatened him with death, unless Sivajee surrendered. Sivajee then appealed to Shah Jehan, and was appointed commander of 5000 horse, and received an order for his father's release.

By 1659, Sivajee had conquered all the country south of Poona, as far as the Kistna river. He also gained a treacherous victory over the Bijapur army under Afzal Khan, whom he murdered at an interview at Pratabgarh near Mahabaleshvar. In 1663, Aurangzeb sent Shaista Khan against Sivajee. Shaista Khan was surprised by Sivajee in Puna, and barely escaped with his life to the hill-fort of Pratabgarh. Jeswant Singh of Jodhpur, and Aurangzeb's son

SIVAJEE'S FORT, PURANDHAR.

Muazzim, were next sent, but they could effect nothing.

In 1663 Sivajee besieged Surat, but was repulsed by the English under Sir George Oxenden, the President of the East India Company's factory there. Oxenden sent him a message desiring "Siva Gi, the grand rebel of the Deccan, to spare the labour of his servants running to and fro, and to come himself with his army." In 1663 Sivajee also took the title of

Raja, and began to coin money. Aurangzeb then despatched against him Jai Singh of Jaipur and Delir Khan ; these generals forced Sivajee to conclude the Treaty of Purandhar by which (1) Sivajee was to surrender twenty of his forts, and retain twelve as a *Jaghir*, (2) Sivajee's son, Sambhaji, was to be made a commander of 5000 horse in the Moghal army, (3) Sivajee was to be allowed to levy chauth (a fourth of the revenues), and Sirdesmukhi (a further ten per cent.) in certain districts of Bijapur. This was the beginning of the Mahratta claim to levy chauth throughout the Moghal Empire.

In 1666 Sivajee went to Delhi, but was badly treated by Aurangzeb, and escaped. He was ever afterwards an irreconcilable foe of the Moghals. Jeswant Singh, Prince Muazzim and Mahabat Khan took the field against him, but without success. In 1670, he again plundered Surat. In 1671, he levied chauth in Khandesh, thus establishing a precedent for the exaction.

In 1674 Sivajee crowned himself as an independent king, and had extended his dominions as far as the Tungabhadra river. In 1676 he was powerful enough to invade the Carnatic as far south as the Coleroon. At the time of the death, in 1680, his kingdom embraced an area 400 miles long and 120 broad. It stretched from the Satpura hills on the north to a line drawn eastward from Goa on the south, and from the Indian Ocean on the west to the Waingunga river on the east.

Sivajee's system of Government.

The villages of Sivajee's country were all under Patels, who supervised the cultivation and collected the revenue. A certain number of Patels were placed under hereditary officers called *Deshadhikaris* or *Deshpandias*. The State took as land revenue two-fifths of the harvest converted into money. The revenue was collected directly by officers of government, and there were no lands given as jaghirs for military service.

Sivajee's army.

The Mawallees of the Konkan formed the *Pagah* infantry regiments of the Mahratta army. The cavalry were chiefly enlisted from the plain country overrun by the Mahrattas, and were of two sorts, Bargis, whose horses were supplied by the State, and Zilladars, who rode their own horses. In hardiness and speed of movement these horsemen were not to be surpassed. Their method of warfare has been thus described. "They would disperse in all directions in the presence of a superior army, and observe it from a neighbouring hill or wood, ready to cut off solitary horsemen or surprise small parties in ambush. If the pursuers gave up the useless chase, in a moment they were upon them, hanging on to their flanks and despatching stragglers. To fight such a people was to do battle with the air or strike blows upon water." The luxurious Moghals were utterly unable to cope with these hardy and mobile horsemen.

Sivajee's fleet.

Sivajee had a powerful fleet under Kanojee Angria, with the title of *Darya Saranga*. This fleet was based upon the ports of Kolaba, Ratnagiri, Vijayadurga, Anjanvela, and Malvan. Kanojee Angria founded a dynasty of pirate princes whose strongholds at Gheriah and Saverndroog had to be stormed by Clive and Watson in 1756.

Sivajee's policy.

Sivajee was able to rely upon strong religious and racial feeling in his subjects. His policy was "to unite all who are Mahrattas together and to propagate the Dharma of Maharashtra." The Dharma of Maharashtra consisted in the protection of Brahmans and cows. He united all classes in his army, and was a great respecter of the local gods and the Brahmans. The Brahmans in return enthusiastically supported his plans.

Sivajee's character.

Elphinstone thus described the Mahrattas, and Sivajee was probably a typical Mahratta: "They are small, sturdy men, well made though not handsome. They are all active, laborious, hardy, and persevering. If they have none of the pride and dignity of the Rajput, they have none of their indolence or want of worldly wisdom. A Rajput warrior, so long as he does not dishonour his race, seems almost indifferent to the result of any contest that he is engaged in. A Mahratta thinks of nothing but the result, and cares little for the means if he can obtain his object. For this purpose he will strain his wits, renounce his pleasures and hazard his person; but he has not a conception of sacrificing his life or even his interest for a point of honour."[1] Sivajee was a skilful general and a consummate statesman. No one but a born leader of men could have attained the same power and influence, with the inadequate means with which he started, but the splendour of his success must not blind us to the treachery and unscrupulousness with which he gained it. Sivajee's actions in this respect must be judged by the morality of his time. The murder of Afzal Khan under a pretence of surrender, and the murder of Chandrarao More of Javli, which Sivajee's officers

[1] Elphinstone, 'History of India,' Book xi. Chapter i. p. 540.

Ragho Ballal and Sambhaji Kavji contrived, when his suspicions were lulled by the proposal of a marriage between Sivajee and his daughter, were examples of a policy in which the employment of any means was justifiable as long as success was achieved.

Separation of the Mahratta power into the two kingdoms of Satara and Kolhapur.

We have seen that Aurangzeb took Sambhaji, son of Sivajee, prisoner and put him to death in 1689. Sivajee, nicknamed Sahu, the second son of Sambhaji, was also in the hands of the Moghals. Aurangzeb released him, and he assumed the title of King of the Mahrattas and exercised nominal power at Satara, but he really left everything in the hands of his Peshwa (or minister), Balaji Biswanath. His uncle, Ram Raja, half-brother of Sambhaji, was regent, and, on his uncle's death in 1700, Ram Raja's widow, Tara Bai, established another Mahratta kingdom in favour of Ram Raja's son, Sivajee III., at Kolhapur in 1700.

Progress of the Mahrattas. The Peshwas.

The chief power of the Mahratta State was in the hands of the Peshwa or chief minister, the chief or Mukhya-Pradhan of the Mahratta Council of eight Pradhans or ministers, who ruled nominally in the name of the Raja of Satara, but who gradually acquired a hereditary kingdom, with Poona as its capital. These Pradhans included the Mazumdar or Auditor of Accounts and Superintendent of Finance, the Niadesh or Chief Judge, and the commanders of the infantry and cavalry.

The first Peshwa was Balaji Biswanath, a Konkan Brahman, who exercised his office 1714-20, and made it hereditary in his own family. Balaji obtained a treaty from Farukh Siyar by which he was given

(1) the right to levy chauth, a fourth of the revenue, and Sirdesmukhi, a further 10 per cent., in the Six Sirkars of the Deccan, *i.e.* Khandesh, Aurungabad, Berar, Bidar, Bijapur and Hyderabad; and (2) the Swaraj or independent sovereignty over Poona and fifteen other districts. The Sirdesmukhi and 34 per cent. of the chauth were to be made over to the Raja; the Mokasa, or remaining 66 per cent., of the chauth was assigned to the chiefs on condition of maintaining a fixed quota of cavalry each.

Balaji was succeeded by his son Baji Rao, 1720-40. In 1735 Baji Rao crossed the Chambal and levied chauth from Delhi. In 1738 Baji Rao conquered Malwa and the territories between the Narbada and the Chambal from the Moghals—these territories were ceded to him by the Convention of Seronje, which was signed in 1738 between him and the Nizam-ul-Mulk, after the latter had been hemmed in under the walls of Bhopal. Mahomed Shah confirmed the grant of Malwa, as a reward for the assistance granted by the Peshwa Balaji Rao against Raghuji Bhonsla of Nagpur, who had invaded Bengal. Baji Rao also acquired Bassein from the Portuguese.

Gwalior and Indore dynasties.

He established in Malwa his generals Ranaji Sindhia and Mulhar Rao Holkar, and from this time dates the establishment of the Gwalior and Indore dynasties in north-eastern and southern Malwa, respectively.

Other Mahratta principalities, 1755.

His son was Balaji Baji Rao, 1740-61. While he was Peshwa, the other Mahratta principalities were founded by Pilajee Gaekwar at Baroda, to whom the chauth of Gujrat was made over for collection by Baji Rao in 1738, and by Raghuji Bhonsla in Berar and the Central Provinces, who was the ancestor of the Bhonsla rajas of Nagpur. In 1749, Sahu Raja of Satara on his death-bed gave Balaji Baji Rao and his heirs the right to govern the whole Mahratta empire. A small Jaghir round Satara and a fixed revenue were given to the Rajas of Satara, and the Peshwa henceforward became the legal sovereign of the Mahrattas, and removed to Poona. Balaji waged successful war with the Nizam Salabat Jang. In 1760, Sivadas Rao, the Peshwa's cousin, defeated the Nizam's forces at Udayagiri, and forced him to surrender Asirgarh, Daulatabad, Aurangabad, Ahmednagar and Bijapur to the Mahrattas.

In the Carnatic, Sivajee's brother Venkajee or Ekojee, who was in charge of the Bijapur conquests in the Carnatic, ejected Sengamaladas of the dynasty of Naiks of Tanjore, and placed himself on the throne, 1674-75, and in 1741 the Mahrattas captured Trichinopoly, which was placed under Morari Rao Ghorepuray. In 1752 Raghuji Bhonsla conquered Orissa from Aliverdi Khan, and forced him to pay twelve lacs of rupees as chauth of Bengal.

Third Battle of Panipat, 1761.

Raghunath Rao, brother of the Peshwa, invaded the Panjab in 1758. This was the zenith of Mahratta pre-eminence, as "the Deccan horses quenched their thirst in the waters of the Indus," but it brought upon them the nemesis of Panipat. As the Panjab was part of the dominions of Ahmad Shah Abdali, Ahmad Shah made his fourth invasion of India to punish the insult. He was joined by the Rohillas under Najib-ud-daula and Shuja-ud-daula, the Nawab Wazir of Oudh. The Mahrattas were led by Viswas Rao, son of the Peshwa, and Sivadas Rao, his cousin. Ahmad Shah cut off the Mahratta provisions, and at last forced them to fight, and gained a complete victory at Panipat, 6th January, 1761. A report was made to the Peshwa that "two pearls" were lost in the battle, these were his son and his cousin.

Aurangzeb's intolerance was also shown towards the Sikhs, the *Sishyas* or disciples of a religion founded by Nanak. Nanak was born in 1469 at Talvandi on the Ravi, near Lahore, and lived to 1539. The Adi Granth, or Bible of the Sikhs, is the work of Nanak, Kabir, and Ramananda. That part of the Adi Granth which is attributed to Nanak is called the Japji, and places salvation in good works. He wrote the Granth in Gurmukhi, an antiquated dialect of Panjabi, the name of which means "from the mouth of the Guru." Repentance must be timely. "If not until the day of reckoning, the sinner abaseth himself, punishment shall overtake him." Asceticism was unnecessary, and all castes were equal. "Think not of race, abase thyself and attain to salvation. God will not ask a man of his birth: he will ask him what he has done." Nanak preached the existence of one God, and attempted to unite both Hindus and Mahomedans in worshipping one God. He would not wear the sacred thread. He told his followers "make mercy thy cotton, contentment its thread, continence its knot, and truth its twist." To the Mahomedan he said, "make kindness thy mosque, sincerity thy prayer-carpet, the will of God thy rosary." He took especial care to prevent his followers from forming a sect; it was on this account he rejected his son, Sri Chund, the founder of the sect of the Udasis, as his successor, and adopted his disciple Lehna, whose name he changed to Angud

Rise of the Sikhs.

(Ang i khud, or "own body"). Mr. Macauliffe thus sums up the moral and political merits of Sikhism: "It prohibits idolatry, hypocrisy, caste exclusiveness, the cremation of widows, the immurement of women, the use of wine and other intoxicants, tobacco-smoking, infanticide, slander, and pilgrimages to the sacred rivers and tanks of the Hindus, and it inculcates loyalty, gratitude for all favours received, philanthropy, justice, impartiality, truth, honesty, and all the moral and domestic virtues known to the holiest citizens of the country." Among the nine Gurus of the Sikhs, the following are noteworthy. Ram Das, the third Guru, founded the sacred city of Amritsar, the original name of which was Ramdaspur. Arjun, son of Ram Das, fourth Guru, 1581-1606, first compiled the Granth, made the guruship hereditary, converted the customary offerings of his followers into a regular tax, and first gave the Sikhs a written rule of conduct and a civil organisation. He also founded the Har Mandir or Durbar Sahib (the Golden Temple) at Amritsar. Hur Govind, 1606-45, fifth Guru, was the first to have guards and mounted followers. Under him we find the first traces of the warlike spirit of the Sikhs. He was imprisoned by Jahangir in Gwalior on a charge of assisting Prince Khusru in rebellion. Hur Rai, sixth Guru, 1645-62, was an adherent of Dara.

Govind Singh, ninth Guru, 1676-1708, carried on war with the Moghals to avenge the death of his father, Tegh Bahadur, the eighth Guru, who was put to death by Aurangzeb in 1675. He first gave the Sikhs a distinct political existence, and established the *Khalisa* or Sikh people in arms, and the *Guru mata* or federal council of chiefs which used to assemble at Amritsar. The word *Khalisa* means the peculiar property (of God), and Govind Singh's doctrine was that the people and the army alike belong to God. Caste was to be neglected; all were to accept *Pahul* (literally "the gate" or means of entrance to Sikhism) from the Guru, the sign of which was drinking water stirred by a two-edged dagger; all social distinctions were to be abolished; and in adherence to the Sikh religion there was to be *Kritnash, Kulnash, Dharmnash, Karmnash, i.e.* all previous deeds and all distinctions of race, religion, and virtue were to be annulled. The worship of steel was combined with that of the "book," and instead of combining with the Mahomedans in one brotherhood, the Sikhs were to swear undying hatred against them. The necessity of wearing the *kesh* (long unshaven hair), and of using the *kach* or *kara* (iron bangles), the *khanda* (two-edged steel knife), and the *kanga* (comb) was impressed on all Sikhs.

Persecution of the Sikhs.

Bahadur Shah persecuted the Sikhs under their leader Banda, drove them out of Sirhind, where they had settled, and forced them to take refuge in the sub-Himalayan state of Nahan. Govind Singh, ninth Guru, declared that the Granth Sahib was to be looked upon as the Guru of the Sikh nation, so after him there were no more personal Gurus, and Banda was only the secular leader. After Govind Singh's death on the banks of the Godaveri, 1708, the Sikhs were divided into:

1. Sahijdharis, including Nanakpotras or Nanakpanthis and Udasis, who were more or less heterodox.

Golden Temple of Amritsar.

2. Govindi Singhs or Kesdharis, who wore their hair long, accepted "Pahul," and carried the Sikh equipment.

Both sections alike disregarded the Vedas, reverenced the Granth, and were strict monotheists. The persecution of the Sikhs under Bahadur Shah completely changed their character, and made them enthusiasts for war with the Mahomedans.

Torture and death of Banda, 1716.

Banda was defeated by Abdus Samad Khan, Viceroy of Lahore, and was besieged in the fort of Gurdaspur, between the Beas and the Ravee. He was taken prisoner, tortured, and put to death under Farukh Siyar, 1716. The Akalis or "Immortals," guardians of the Golden Temple at Amritsar, where the Guru mata, or Council of Chiefs, was held, then exercised the chief control over the Sikhs. In 1762 the Sikhs defeated Ahmad Shah Abdali's governor of Sirhind, and occupied all the country between the Jhelum and the Jumna. The control of the Afghans over the Panjab gradually weakened, and by 1785 the Sikhs had got into their hands the control of the whole country between the Sutlej and the Jhelum.

Towards the end of the century Zeman Shah seized Lahore and temporarily re-established Afghan power, and Ranjit Singh began his career by submitting to him. The Sikh rule in the Panjab was useful for the consolidation of British power, as it defended the north-western frontier till Mysore and the Mahrattas were brought under subjection.

CHAPTER VIII.

THE PORTUGUESE IN INDIA.

The first European to arrive in India by sea. THE first European to arrive in India by sea was the Venetian Marco Polo, who left Venice on his travels in 1271. He came to India with the embassy from Kublai Khan, the Mongol emperor of China, which was charged to convey a bride chosen among the Mongols to Tabreez in Persia, to marry a Persian Khan who was related to Kublai Khan. The embassy put in at the port of Kayal in Malabar in Southern India in 1292. Marco refers to a certain Sondar Bandi as the ruler of Southern India, who may perhaps be identified with Jatavarman Sundara Pandya II., the Pandya king.

Other Europeans who visited India in the fifteenth and early part of the sixteenth century were Nicolo de Conti, a Venetian, who travelled in India and Eastern Asia, 1419-44. Nicolo was compelled to embrace Mahomedanism in Egypt to save his life. Pope Eugenius IV. imposed on him the penalty of recounting his experiences to the Papal Secretary Poggio Bracciolini, who has given a Latin version of them in his book 'De Varietate Fortunæ.' Athanasius Nikitin, a Russian, was in India, 1468-74. Ludovico di Varthema, a native of Bologna, who travelled 1502-07. His travels are especially useful for Gujrat, where Mahmud Shah Begara, 1459-1511, was reigning. Duarte Barboso, whose travels were written either by the reputed author or his cousin the explorer Magellan, describes his visit to Vijaynagar which took place between 1504 and 1514. Joao Peres de Covilham was despatched by Joao II., king of Portugal, in 1487, to seek out the Christian Priest-king, Prester John, who was believed to reign somewhere in Central Africa, and to enquire into the source of the Venetian trade in drugs and spices. De Covilham went by Egypt and the Red Sea to Cananore, Goa, Ormuz, Zeila on the coast of Abyssinia, to Aden and Cairo, and thence back to Ormuz, Aden and Zeila. He died after a thirty-three years' stay at the court of the King of Abyssinia, who was believed to be Prester John.

Articles of trade between India and Europe.

The chief articles of trade between India and Europe were spices, indigo, cotton, muslin, silk, and opium, and India took from Europe, in return, woollen cloth, silver, copper, quicksilver, iron and steel goods. The silver was exported because the Indian trade would not take enough woollen goods to pay for the Indian calicoes. The balance had to be paid in silver. This export of the precious metals was much disliked owing to the Mercantile Fallacy, which considered that a country's wealth consisted only in the gold and silver it possessed. Mun's book, 'England's Treasure by Foreign Trade,' published 1664, contests this. After gunpowder was invented, saltpetre, one of its essential elements, was largely exported from India to Europe, especially from the Bengal districts of Patna and Purnea. Sir

George Birdwood, in his supplement to the Report on the old Records of the India Office, says: "The history of Modern Europe, and emphatically of England, is the history of the quest of the aromatic gum, resins and balsams, and condiments and spices of India, further India, and the Indian Archipelago."[1] The chief traders from India were Arab merchants, and the chief trade routes lay through Syria and Asia Minor and Trebizond, by way of Busrah and the Persian Gulf, which was the favourite route from India whilst its commerce was in the hands of the Arabs, or up the Red Sea and across Egypt, a favourite route in the time of the Romans, and reopened by the Venetians, or across Central Asia by camels from the Indus to the Oxus, and thence to the Caspian and the Black Seas. The Romans attached much importance to the maintenance of the Red Sea route for commerce from India. They destroyed Palmyra, because its merchants endeavoured to divert the trade to a route up the Persian Gulf and across Syria.

Trade routes.

In 1456 the Turks took Constantinople; and soon afterwards Sultan Selim, 1516-17, conquered Egypt, and became masters of Western Asia. The trade routes between India and Europe were thus closed, and it became essential to discover a sea-route to India. This was done by the Portuguese Vasco da Gama, who started from Lisbon 8th July, 1497, and arrived at Calicut in August, 1498. He doubled the Cape of Good Hope, and discovered the coast of Natal on Christmas Day, 1497. He sailed up the west coast of Africa and arrived at Mozambique, March, 1498,

Arrival of the Portuguese, 1498.

[1] 'The Modern Quest and Invention of the Indies,' edition 1891, p. 101.

and at Quiloa (the modern Kilwa), April, 1498. At the end of April he was at Melinde, 200 miles north of Zanzibar. He left Melinde, 6th August, and in twenty days sighted Mount Dely near Cannanore, and arrived at Calicut towards the end of August. He entered into trading relations with the Hindu Raja of Calicut, who was called the Zamorin,[1] and was a sort of suzerain of most of the petty Hindu Rajas on the Coromandel coast, and the quarrel between the ports of Calicut and Cochin gave the Portuguese their first footing on the Malabar coast. Cochin was aggrandised at the expense of Calicut by the Portuguese influence. The Zamorin wrote to the king of Portugal: "In my country there is abundance of cinnamon, cloves, ginger, pepper, and precious stones. What I seek from thy country is gold, silver, coral, and scarlet."

Vasco da Gama's return voyage.

On his return voyage from India, Vasco da Gama arrived at Lisbon on the 18th of September, 1499. He brought back a cargo sixty-fold as valuable as the expenses of his outfit.

Vasco da Gama's voyage the culmination of a series of geographical discoveries.

Vasco da Gama's successful voyage to India was the culmination of a series of geographical discoveries set on foot by Prince Henry the Navigator, son of John I., king of Portugal, which prospered under the enlightened patronage of Kings John II. and Manuel. The Portuguese were slowly creeping down the west coast of Africa. In 1433 the Azores islands were discovered; in 1434 Gil Eannes doubled Cape Bojador. In 1455 and 1456 Luigi Cadamosto discovered the Cape de Verde islands, and visited the

[1] The title is believed to be the Malayalam word Tamatiri or Tamuri, a corruption of *Samudra*, the Sanskrit word for sea.

Senegal, Gambia and Rio Grande rivers. In 1461-62 Pedro de Cintra explored the coast for some distance south of Sierra Leone. In 1471 the Equator was passed. In 1484 Diego Cão, or Cam, discovered the River Congo. In 1487 Bartholomew Diaz and Joao Infante doubled the Cape of Good Hope and arrived in Algoa Bay. Diaz and Infante gave the

VASCO DA GAMA AND THE ZAMORIN.

name of the Cape of Storms to the southern promontory of Africa, but John II., for the sake of the omen, altered its name to its present title.

The Genoese Christopher Columbus resided at Lisbon 1470-84, and proposed to King John II. to arrive at India by sailing west across the Atlantic. The king consulted the wise men of his kingdom, but they decided to reject the plan as too visionary. Ferdinand of Arragon and Isabella accepted it, and

Columbus set sail from Palos in Andalusia on the 3rd August, 1492.

Bull of Alexander VI.

This discovery of America rendered it necessary to demarcate the Spanish discoveries in the New World from the Portuguese acquisitions in Africa and in the East of Asia. The Bull of Pope Alexander VI., 1493, granted to Spain all territories west of a line drawn north and south 100 leagues west of the Azores and Cape de Verde Islands, and to Portugal all territories to the east of this line.

Treaty of Tordesillas.

This agreement was modified by the Treaty of Tordesillas between Spain and Portugal, 1494, by which the line laid down by Alexander VI. was extended to 370 leagues west of the Cape de Verde Islands.

Treaty of Saragossa.

It was still further modified by the Treaty of Saragossa, 1529, by which Spain sold to Portugal her rights to the Molucca Islands for 350,000 ducats of gold, and the line of demarcation was fixed at 297½ leagues east of the Moluccas, corresponding to the seventeenth parallel of latitude.

Commerce on the Coromandel coast at the time of the arrival of Vasco da Gama.

At the time of the arrival of Vasco da Gama in India, the commerce of the Coromandel coast was in the hands of the Moplah merchants, who were the descendants of Arabs by native women. These Moplahs were from the first jealous of the interference of the Portuguese with their trade, and began to intrigue against them from the time that they formed their first trading posts at Calicut and Cochin. The Moplahs compelled the Portuguese to abandon the attitude of peaceful traders, and compelled them to protect their commerce by building fortresses and the acquisition of territory.

Cabral's voyage.

Pedro Alvares Cabral was in command of the next

Portuguese fleet sent to India. He started on 9th March, 1500, and returned to Lisbon on the 21st July, 1501, with a return cargo loaded at Cochin and Cannanore. This cargo included opium, then for the first time imported into Europe. Cabral's voyage is remarkable, in that he was carried out of the proper course to India by contrary winds and currents, so far to the west that he discovered Brazil by accident.

Discovery of Brazil.

Vasco da Gama started on his second voyage to India in February, 1502, and returned on the 1st September, 1503. The chief events of his voyage were the bombardment of Calicut, in revenge for the murder of the Portuguese factor, Ayres Correa, who was killed in a riot got up by the Moplahs, and the defeat of the Calicut fleet in a naval battle, 1502. In 1503-04, Alphonso de Albuquerque made his first voyage to India, Cochin was fortified, and a famous defence of the fortress against the Zamorin's fleet and army was conducted by Duarte Pacheco, 1504.

Vasco da Gama's second voyage.

In 1502, Manuel, king of Portugal, assumed the title of *Lord of the Conquest, Navigation, and Commerce of Ethiopia, Arabia, Persia, and India.* He conceived the policy of ruining the Mahomedan trade between India and Europe by seizing Aden, Ormuz, and Malacca. These were the ports by which the Eastern trade reached Europe via Alexandria, and Beyrout in Syria respectively. Malacca was the place where the Mahomedan, especially Arab, traders exchanged goods with China. In 1505, he appointed Francis da Almeida governor of Cochin, Cannanore and Quilon, and First Viceroy of Portuguese India, who arrived at Cannanore, 12th September, 1505,

Additional title assumed by the King of Portugal.

Policy of King Manuel.

with orders to erect forts at Anjediva (an island off the coast of North Kanara, 51 miles S.E. of Goa), Cannanore, Cochin, and Quilon. On his voyage out, Almeida built a fortress at Quiloa (Kilwa), and made Mombassa tributary to Portugal. Almeida seems to have differed from King Manuel and his successor Albuquerque as to this policy of fortress building. He wrote to the king: "With respect to the fortress of Quilon, the greater the number of fortresses you hold, the weaker will be your power. *Let all our forces be on the sea.*"

As it was the object of the Portuguese to divert the trade between India and Europe to the route round the Cape of Good Hope, and to close the trade route passing by the Red Sea, Cairo, and Alexandria, the Mahomedan Moplah merchants of India easily stirred up the Mameluke Sultan of Egypt against them. An Egyptian fleet under the Emir Hussein arrived on the Gujrat coast in 1508, and the Sultan of Gujrat, Mahomed Shah Begara, and the Nawab of Diu, Malik Ayaz, entered into an alliance with the Egyptians, which had for its object the expulsion of the Portuguese from India. Lorenzo da Almeida, son of the Viceroy, was defeated and slain in a naval battle off Chaul by these allies in 1508, but the allies were conquered and dispersed in a subsequent sea-fight off Diu by the Viceroy on the 2nd February, 1509. Other victories followed off Bandra in 1528, and off Diu in 1546. In the latter the Guzrat fleet under Coje Zofar, a Turk admiral, was decisively defeated.

Indian alliance with the Sultan of Egypt against the Portuguese.

Alphonso da Albuquerque left Portugal in 1506 with instructions that he was to succeed Almeida as

Viceroy, when the latter had had three years of office. On his outward voyage he erected a fortress at Socotra, 1507, with the object of closing the Red Sea trading route. Socotra was not held for long, but was abandoned in 1512. He also caused a fortress to be built at Ormuz, to shut the Persian Gulf to commerce, 1507, but this fortress did not come completely under the Portuguese till 1515. On arrival in India, Albuquerque was imprisoned by Almeida at Cannanore, and was not released till the arrival from Portugal of Ferdinand Coutinho, his nephew.

Socotra and Ormuz fortified.

Alphonso de Albuquerque assumed office as Governor on the 5th November, 1509. Albuquerque's first important action as Governor, under the advice of Timoja or Timmaya, a pirate who had assisted Vasco da Gama, was to seize upon the city and island of Goa, which belonged to Yusuf Adil Shah, Sultan of Bijapur, in the early part of 1510. He was compelled to retire from Goa before Yusuf Adil Shah's army, May, 1510. His fleet could not pass the bar of the harbour of Goa, and had to lie there three months under fire of the castle of Panjim. Albuquerque made a second and more successful attack upon Goa on the 25th November, 1510. Yusuf Adil Shah died in November, 1510. His son and successor, an infant, agreed to surrender Goa in 1511, but Albuquerque had to relieve the city, which was again besieged by the Bijapur army in 1512.

Albuquerque's governorship.

Capture of Goa.

The next important success of the Portuguese was the capture of Malacca, which surrendered to Albuquerque in 1511. The Portuguese were thus ensured the full command of the spice trade, and the control of all commerce with China and Japan.

Capture of Malacca.

They also struck a heavy blow at Mahomedan trade, as Malacca was the chief place where Arab traders used to exchange the goods of the West for the silks of China and Japan.

Failure to capture Aden.

In 1513 Albuquerque was repulsed in an assault at Aden, but he spent most of the year in exploring the Red Sea. He conceived a scheme to divert the Nile from Egypt by digging a channel from the Red Sea to the river. In this year a factory was founded at Diu, an island off the south point of Kathiawar.

Factory at Diu.

Complete control of Ormuz.

In 1515, Albuquerque got the fortress of Ormuz completely under his control, and endeavoured to form an alliance with the "Sophy" (Sufi) Sheikh Ismail against the Mameluke Sultan of Egypt. Albuquerque died at Goa in December, 1515.

Policy of Albuquerque.

The policy of Albuquerque is explained in his letters to King Manuel. In 1513, he wrote, with reference to the retention of Goa: "If your Highness thinks it possible to secure your dominions in these parts by means of the fortresses at Cochin and Cannanore, it is impossible; for if once Portugal should suffer a reverse at sea, your Indian possessions have not power to hold out a day longer than the kings of the land choose to suffer it. And I hold it to be free from doubt, that if fortresses be built in Diu and Calicut, when once they have been well fortified, if a thousand of the Soldan's ships were to make their way to India, not one of these places could be brought again under his dominion. Your Highness cannot be lord over so extensive a territory by placing all your power and strength in your marine only; for this, and not to build fortresses is the very thing which the Moors (Mahomedans, of these lands wish you to do, for they know well that a dominion founded on a navy cannot last, and they desire to live on their own estates and property, and to carry the spices to the ancient and customary markets which they maintain, but they are unwilling to be subjects of your Highness, neither will they trade nor be on friendly terms with you." [1]

Again, 6th December, 1515, just before his death, he sums up the events of his Viceroyalty: "Events in India will speak for themselves as well as for me. I leave the chief place in India in your Majesty's power, the only thing left to be done being the closing of the gates of the Straits" (of Bab-el-mandeb).[2]

There are four chief points of his policy:

1. Conquest and direct rule of certain points important for trade.

2. Colonisation of certain districts by the encouragement of mixed marriages between Portuguese and the women of the country. Hindus were to be induced to settle on Portuguese territory, especially the island of Goa, by the levy of moderate taxes, and a large share of self-government. Yusuf Adil Shah had doubled the rate of taxes formerly levied under Vijaynagar rule. Albuquerque reduced them to the former rate. The native system of government was maintained upon the island of Goa under Timoja and Mulhar Rao. The taxes were collected by Portuguese acting conjointly with Hindus. A gold and silver coinage was established, with tin and pewter coins for the smaller denominations. This was a step extremely beneficial to the development of trade.

[1] Danvers, 'Portuguese in India,' vol. i. pp. 260-261.
[2] *Ibid.* p. 327.

3. Where conquest or colonisation was impossible, fortresses were to be built.

4. Native princes were to be induced to become tributaries of Portugal. This was the status of the Sultan of Ormuz, the Zamorin of Calicut, and the Raja of Cochin.

The Hindu Rajas of Southern India, except the Zamorin, were opposed to the monopoly of commerce by the Moplah merchants, so Albuquerque wished to pose as the ally of the Hindus, particularly of Vijaynagar, the paramount Hindu power, against the Mahomedans.

Albuquerque was succeeded as Governor by Lope Suares de Albergaria, 1515-18. In 1516 Suares refused the surrender of Aden, thinking he would be able to receive it at a more favourable opportunity, which never came.

In 1517, the Portuguese had to face a more formidable foe in Egypt than the Mameluke dynasty of Sultans, as Selim the Turkish Sultan of Constantinople conquered Egypt, but adopted the same hostile attitude towards Portuguese trade as that taken up by the Mameluke Sultans. In 1518 the Portuguese established themselves at Colombo, and Fernao Peres reached Canton. In 1521 King Manuel died, and was succeeded by John III., a bigoted Catholic.

Portuguese occupy Colombo, and appear at Canton.

In 1523 Vasco da Gama returned to India a third time as Viceroy, but died in 1524 at Cochin. The next important governor was Nuna da Cunha, 1529-1538. Under him the Portuguese first appeared in Bengal, as allies of the Mahomedan Sultan of Gaur against Sher Shah. Aden became tributary, 1530. In this year also the Portuguese occupied Daman.

Portuguese appear in Bengal.

In 1531 a fortress was erected at Chaul. Bahadur Shah, Sultan of Gujrat, being hardly pressed by Humayun, allowed the Portuguese to occupy the island of Bassein, and to fortify Diu. This concession was made in December, 1534, and ratified October, 1535, but it led to war.

Cession of Bassein and fortification of Diu.

In 1538 a Turkish fleet under Suleiman Pacha, sent by the Sultan Selim, blockaded Diu by sea, and Mahomed III., son and successor of Bahadur Shah, besieged it by land. The allies abandoned the siege in November, 1538. John de Castro was Governor, 1545-48, and Viceroy during the last year of his tenure of office. He relieved Diu, and defeated Mahomed III. of Gujrat in a great naval battle, and died at Goa in the arms of St. Francis Xavier.

Occupation of Macao and Jaffnapatam.

In 1557 the Portuguese occupied Macao, an island in the Canton river in China, and in 1560, Jaffnapatam in Ceylon.

Establishment of the Inquisition.

In 1560 the Inquisition, a tribunal to inquire into and punish offences against the Roman Catholic religion, was established. The significance of this step will appear when we come to discuss the causes of the downfall of Portuguese power in India.

Division of Portuguese territories in the East into three governments.

In 1571 the Portuguese possessions in the East were divided into three governments:

1. Monomotapa, comprising the possessions in Africa—the forts of Sofala and Mombassa, and the city and territories of Mozambique.

2. India—comprising the possessions between Cape Guardafui and Ceylon, including Muscat, Ormuz, Diu, Daman, Bassein, Thana, and Goa; on the Malabar coast, the forts of Mangalore, Cannanore,

Cranganore, Calicut,. Cochin, and Quilon; on the Coromandel coast, Negapatam, St. Thomé, Mylapore, Masulipatam; in Ceylon, the forts of Colombo, Manaar, Jaffnapatam and Galle; in Bengal, the trading factories of Hughli and Chittagong.

3. Malacca, comprising all trading factories in Japan and China.

Portuguese in the Spice Islands.

In 1532 the Portuguese occupied the islands of Sunda, Ternate and Banda, and in 1564, the Molucca Islands, which had been in dispute with Spain. They thus acquired the control of the clove and nutmeg trade.

Portuguese in Bengal.

We have seen that the Portuguese first appeared in Bengal as allies of the Mahomedan Sultan of Gaur against Sher Shah. The Emperor Akbar allowed the Portuguese to settle at Hughli and Chittagong on condition of keeping the Bay of Bengal clear of pirates. They also had another trading station at Betor on the Hughli opposite Kidderpur. At this time the principal place of trade in Lower Bengal was Satgaon on the Saraswati branch of the Hughli (the Gange Regia of Pliny and Ptolemy, and the Porto Pigueno of the Portuguese).

Portuguese piracy in the Bay of Bengal.

Portuguese piracy seems to have been rife in the Bay of Bengal in the beginning of the seventeenth century, and it was to control them that the Subahdars transferred the capital from Rajmehal to Dacca.

Sebastian Gonzales at Sandip.

Taking advantage of the wars between the kings of Arracan and Pegu, the Portuguese pirate, Sebastian Gonzales seized the island of Sandip and maintained himself there, 1609-16, till he was expelled by the king of Arracan. The Portuguese after allied themselves with the king of Arracan against the Moghals, but

Settlement of the Portuguese at Feringhi Bazaar, Cacca.

were induced to desert them by Shaista Khan, who gave them lands on the Ishamati at Feringhi Bazaar.

Sebastian, the last king of Portugal, was killed at the battle of Alcacer Kibir in Morocco, in 1578, and in 1581 Philip II. of Spain was proclaimed King of Portugal also. This brought upon the Portuguese in India the hostility of the Dutch, who, in 1580, threw off their allegiance to Philip II. of Spain, and elected William of Orange Stadtholder, and of the English who were fighting the Spanish in defence of Protestantism, and also to gain access to America.

Extinction of the Portuguese monarchy.

Philip II. of Spain becomes king of Portugal.

In 1585 Philip II. closed the ports of the Peninsula, and ordered all Dutch and English ships in Spanish waters to be seized. He wished thereby to bar their way to any share in the Indian trade. The Portuguese and Spaniards held that "the East and West Indies are our house privately possessed by us for more than a hundred years; and no one has a right to enter without our permission." The Dutch reply was to make their way to India by force. The first Dutch fleet sailed to India in 1595, and was absent two and a half years. They gained so firm a control over the spice trade that they were able to raise the price of pepper to the English in 1599 from 3s. to 6s. and 8s. a pound. This brought about the formation of the English East India Company, 1599. The Dutch Company was formed in 1602. From the date of the formation of these two Companies may be also dated the downfall of the Portuguese power in India, and their history becomes little more than a record of disasters.

In 1603 and 1609 the Dutch blockaded Goa, in 1640 they took Malacca, in 1656 Colombo and Cannanore,

Downfall of the Portuguese power in India.

in 1658 Jaffnapatam, and with it they obtained control over all the plain country of Ceylon. In the same year the Dutch captured Negapatam. In 1662 Cranganore and Cochin, in 1663 Cannanore, and in 1669 St. Thomé and Macassar fell into their hands.

In 1611 Sir Hugh Middleton won a sea-fight over the Portuguese off Cambay, and Captain Best and Captain Downton were victorious in similar combats at Swally, the port of Surat, in 1612 and 1615 respectively.

English factory at Gombroon (Bander Abbas).

In 1622 the English, in conjunction with Shah Abbas, the Shah of Persia, turned the Portuguese out of Ormuz, and, in recompense, were permitted to open a trading factory of their own at Gombroon (Bander Abbas). This was in spite of the fact that peace had been concluded between England, Spain, and Portugal in 1622.

Cession of Bombay.

In 1662 the Portuguese ceded the island of Bombay to the English as part of the dowry of Catharine of Braganza, wife of Charles II., but possession was not given till February, 1665. The local Portuguese were bitterly opposed to the transfer. The Viceroy of Goa wrote to the King of Portugal, 28th December, 1662: "I see the best port which your Majesty possesses in India, with which Lisbon is not to be compared, treated as of little value by the Portuguese themselves." [1] He wished the king to buy back Bombay for a money payment.

Remonstrances of the local Portuguese against the cession of Bombay.

Again, in January, 1665, he wrote: "I confess at the feet of your Majesty, that only the obedience I owe to your Majesty as a vassal, could have forced

[1] Danvers, 'Portuguese in India,' vol. ii. p. 337.

me to this deed (the cession of the island), because I foresee the great troubles that, from this neighbourhood, will result to the Portuguese, and that India will be lost the same day in which the English nation is settled in Bombay."

Plundering of Diu.

In 1670, Arabs from Muscat plundered Diu.

Capture of Bassein.

Cession of Chaul.

In 1739, the Mahrattas captured and plundered Bassein, and were only prevailed upon to leave the Portuguese in peaceable possession of Goa by the cession of Chaul, 1740.

Causes of the decay of the Portuguese power in India.

1. The Abbé Raynal thus sums up the causes of the decline of the Portuguese power in India. "No Portuguese pursued any other object than the advancement of his own interest; there was no zeal, no union for the common good. Their possessions in India were divided into three governments which gave no assistance to each other and even clashed in their projects and interests. Neither discipline, subordination, nor the love of glory animated either the soldiers or their officers. Men of war no longer ventured out of the ports; or, wherever they appeared, were badly equipped. Manners became more and more depraved. Not one of the commanders had power enough to restrain the torrent of vice; and the majority of these commanders were themselves corrupted. The Portuguese at length lost all their former greatness, when a free and enlightened nation, actuated with a proper spirit of toleration, appeared in India, and contended with them for the empire of that country." [1]

[1] Abbé Raynal, 'A Philosophical and Political History of the Settlement and Trade of Europeans in the East and West Indies.'

Moral deterioration of the people.

It appears to be an undoubted fact that the luxury and vicious surroundings of the East had deteriorated the moral fibre of the Portuguese, and they had become effeminate and cowardly.

Subjection to Spain.

2. The subjection of Portugal to authority of Philip of Spain injured the Portuguese in two ways. They incurred the hostility of the Dutch and English. Secondly, the revenues of Portuguese India, instead of being spent on its defence, were expended in the attempt to put down the Dutch revolt, and on the support of an excessive number of priests and monks both in Europe and India.

Religious intolerance.

3. The Portuguese were bound by the Bull of Alexander VI., and by other Bulls of succeeding popes confirming their authority. There is no doubt, however, that their intolerance and attempts to forcibly convert the natives to Christianity were most prejudicial to the success of their rule. St. Francis Xavier, in 1542, obtained control of the College of St. Paul at Goa for the Jesuits. His letters show that he advised the king of Portugal to order all government officials to use their influence for the conversion of the natives to Christianity. We find governors protesting against the claim of the Inquisition to punish natives, who had never been Christians, and to fill the prisons with criminals, whose only crime was that they refused to embrace Christianity, but nothing was ever done to restrain its authority.

Attitude taken up by Robert de Nobili and the Jesuit missionaries towards the caste system, and other Indian customs, in the case of persons converted to Christianity.

A curious movement was started by Robert de Nobili at Madura in 1605. He sought to commend Christianity to the Hindus as the highest philosophy. He declared he was a prince in his own land, which was true, as he was a nephew of Cardinal Bellarmine and nearly related to Pope Marcellus II. He assumed the yellow robe of a *Sannyasi*, and consented to the perpetuation of caste among his converts. Separate churches were built for the higher and lower castes, the pariah or low-caste Christians could not approach their fellow-believers of a higher caste, and at their death the sacrament was administered to them at the end of a staff, lest the officiating priest should be contaminated. He was familiar with Hindu learning, claimed to be the bringer of a fifth Veda, and called himself *Tatwabodha*. He was suspended from his ministry by an order of the Pope in 1611, on a charge of following unchristian methods in allowing his converts to retain their old customs and manners. He was the author of the *Jnanopadesa*, an instruction in Tamil on the attributes of God, the *Mantramalai*, a translation into Tamil of the principal parts of the Roman Catholic liturgy, and the so-called fifth Veda composed with materials taken from the Bible. He died in 1656. After his death his methods were largely adopted by his successors, who divided themselves into *Sannyasins* who preached to Brahmins and adopted their dress, manners and customs, and *Pandaram* missionaries who addressed themselves to the lower castes.

Tolerance of the English towards the religions of the Indians a ground of their success.

The English carried their policy of religious tolerance to a somewhat excessive length, but they reaped their reward in the crowding of the natives into their settlements. There was an altogether excessive number of priests and monks in Portuguese India.

Excessive number and influence of the priests and religious orders.

In 1631 the Viceroy complained that they would not obey his orders. The Jesuits kept up an armed force at their own expense, they seized Tuticorin, and kept Travancore and the pearl fisheries under their control. In 1635 it was estimated that the priests and monks exceeded the soldiers and citizens of Goa in number. Their power and influence was excessive. In 1635 they were forbidden to receive legacies or purchase land without permission, because "when the religious orders are rich, the vassals are poor."

Drain of men to the East.

4. A heavy strain was constantly acting on Portugal, which, in the sixteenth century, had a population of not much more than a million, by the constant drain of men to the East. This strain was increased by the necessity of finding men for Brazil also.

Heavy Customs Duties.

5. The heavy Customs Duties, which were imposed to make the ports self-supporting, were very prejudicial to trade, and caused constant smuggling.

Loss of profitable market by fall of Vijaynagar.

6. The loss of their most profitable market, by the fall of Vijaynagar in 1565, was a blow to Portuguese trade. The commerce intended for Vijaynagar passed through the port of Bhatkal on the coast of Malabar, and there are constant references in Portuguese treaties to the trade in horses passing through this port.

CHAPTER IX.

DECLINE OF THE MOGHAL EMPIRE.

WHEN Aurangzeb died, Muazzim or Shah Alam was Governor of Kabul, Azim Shah Subahdar of Gujrat, and Kam Baksh Governor of Bijapur. Azim Shah was defeated and slain with his son Bedarbakt in the battle of Gajao near Agra, June, 1707, and Kam Baksh was mortally wounded in battle near Hyderabad, February, 1709. The way was thus opened for Muazzim to ascend the throne as Bahadur Shah. Bahadur Shah, 1707.

Bahadur Shah died in 1712, and was succeeded by his son, Muizuddin, under the title of Jahandar Shah, 1712-13. Jahandar Shah, after reigning six months, was dethroned by Syed Abdullah, governor of Allahabad, and Syed Hossein Ali, governor of Bihar. He was succeeded by Farukh Siyar, grandson of Bahadur Shah, who merely reigned, whilst the Syed brothers governed. When Farukh Siyar tried to throw off the rule of the Syeds, they caused him to be put to death, 1719. Farukh Siyar, 1712-19.

Rafi-ud-darajat and Rafi-ud-daula, grandsons of Bahadur Shah, occupied the throne for two and three months, respectively, and were followed by Mahomed Shah. Mahomed Shah, son of one of the brothers of Jahandar Shah, who owed his throne to the Syeds Mahomed Shah, 1719-48.

and came to the throne in 1719, soon began to conspire against them. Syed Hossein Khan was assassinated, and Syed Abdullah defeated and slain in battle at Shahpur, 3rd November, 1720.

Invasion of India by Nadir Shah.

Tahmasp Quli Khan, called Nadir Shah, king of Persia, invaded India in 1738; he defeated Saadat Khan and Chin Kilich Khan (Nizam-ul-Mulk) at Karnal. He entered Delhi unopposed, but when his army was attacked he ordered a wholesale massacre, 1740. Nadir coined money in Delhi bearing the inscription: "King over the kings of the world is Nadir, king of kings and lord of the period." He carried off to Persia on his return the famous jewel, the Kohinur and Jahangir's Peacock Throne. Kabul, Sindh, and Multan were at the same time ceded to Persia by treaty.

NADIR SHAH.

First invasion of Ahmad Shah Abdali, 1748.

After Nadir Shah was assassinated at Meshed, 1747, his treasurer, Ahmad Shah Abdali, an Afghan of the Durrani tribe, seized the kingdom of Kandahar. Ahmad Shah invaded India in 1748, but was defeated by Mahomed Shah's son, Ahmad, and his Wazir, Kamaruddin, a cousin of the Nizam's, at the battle of Sirhind.

Ahmad Shah, 1748-54.

Mahomed Shah died in 1748, and was succeeded by his son, Ahmad Shah. Ahmad Shah Abdali again invaded India in 1751, and captured Multan and Lahore, but was bought off by the surrender of the Panjab. At this period occurred the rise of the Jats at Bhartpur under Suraj Mal. In 1754 Ahmad Shah was deposed by his Wazir, Mir Sahibuddin or Ghaziuddin II., son of Ghaziuddin and grandson of Chin Kilich Khan Asaf Jah, who had been made Wazir and Subahdar of the Deccan under Mahomed Shah, 1723. Ahmad Shah's eyes were put out, and a son of Jahandar Shah placed on the throne, by the name of Alamgir the Second. Ghaziuddin II. then treacherously attacked Lahore, and thus incurred a third invasion from Ahmad Shah Abdali, 1757. On Ahmad Shah's departure, Ghaziuddin II. summoned the Mahrattas to Delhi to enable him to contend against Najib-ud-daula, the Rohilla leader, and nominee of Ahmad Shah Abdali to the wazirate, and put Alamgir the Second to death, 1759. The fourth invasion of Ahmad Shah resulted in the third battle of Panipat, and the total defeat of the Mahrattas, 1761.

Second invasion of Ahmad Shah Abdali, 1751.

Jats of Bhartpur.

Alamgir the Second, 1754 59.

Third invasion of Ahmad Shah Abdali, 1757.

Fourth invasion of Ahmad Shah Abdali, 1761.

The decay of the Moghal Empire.

The chief reason for the decay of the Moghal Empire was that it was a despotism, a personal rule, which depended for its prolonged existence upon the physical and mental qualities of the reigning prince. After Aurangzeb, there were no more "great Moghals," and the nominal emperors were but the puppets of opposing factions. They were weak, vacillating, and vicious, the products of seraglio education, but destitute of those qualities of mind which enabled their predecessors to escape its baneful effects. The education of the time was singularly defective, as is shown by the reproach of

Aurangzeb to his old tutor.[1] There was no private property in land, and hence no nobility independent of the sovereign, and no middle class. Such great men as there were kept their position by time serving. The officials of government were a law unto themselves in haste to recoup themselves for the bribes which purchased their offices, and to get rich quickly. The condition of the peasantry is thus described by Tavernier: "You may see in India whole provinces like deserts, from which the peasants have fled on account of the oppression of the governors. Under cover of the fact that they are themselves Mahomedans they persecute the poor idolater to the utmost, and if any of the latter become Mahomedans, it is not to work any more; they become soldiers or Fakirs."[2] Mandeslo corroborates this: "The only way to keep anything being to appear to have nothing." The evidence of Nicolai Manucci is to the same effect: "In no part of Aurangzeb's empire was there any justice, no one thought of anything but how to plunder, the revenue was collected by violence and no remissions were allowed for loss of crops. In these days every one's thought is to steal, and whatever happens it rarely reaches the ears of the king, the orders coming from whom his officers do not obey. Those who are most distant from the court suffer most." Arbitrary enhancements of revenue and illegal cesses were constantly levied. Under such a condition of things it is not to be wondered that the peasantry welcomed any change.

[1] Bernier (Constable's edition), pp. 158-161.

[2] Tavernier (Ball's translation), vol. i. p. 391.

Toleration and compromise were necessary to unite all classes in India in support of the foreign empire of the Moghals. In spite of this, intolerance alienated the Hindus, and caused the destruction of the Shiah kingdoms of the Deccan, which might have been a counterpoise to the power of the Mahrattas.

Luxury and an enervating climate destroyed the military qualities of the army, which was no longer recruited from men of the temperate climates of Central Asia. As Sir William Hunter puts it: "The ancestors of Aurangzeb were ruddy men in boots. The courtiers among whom Aurangzeb grew up were pale persons in petticoats." The soldiers of Aurangzeb's time could not move without huge camps and commissariats, and hordes of camp followers: they were consequently never able to bring the Mahrattas to battle, for the Mahrattas lived on the country, and carried their necessary supplies on their horses. Corruption was also rife. Omrahs received a large yearly payment on condition of keeping up a fixed number of troops, but they only maintained many less than their proper quota, and pocketed the difference in the pay. All these causes combined brought about the decay of the Moghal Empire.

CHAPTER X.

INDEPENDENT PRINCIPALITIES FOUNDED UPON THE RUINS OF THE MOGHAL EMPIRE.

Independent principalities founded.

The Nizam.

CHIN KILICH KHAN, Asaf Jah, born 1644, was the rival of Zulfikar Khan, viceroy of the Deccan, to whom Bahadur and Jahandar Shah owed their thrones. He was Subahdar of the Deccan, and was removed from that post to make room for Syed Hussain, and was only given the small government of Moradabad. He thus became an enemy of the Syeds, and was privy to a plot of Farukh Siyar to murder Syed Abdullah, and was bribed by the promise of succession to the Wazirship. Farukh Siyar, however, broke his word, and promised the Wazirship to a personal favourite. Chin Kilich was thus alienated, and was won over to the cause of the Syeds by the gift of the Subahdarship of Malwa. The Syeds were thus free to revenge themselves on Farukh Siyar, who was murdered. Chin Kilich became Wazir of the empire with the title of Nizam-ul-mulk, or Deputy of the Empire, in 1721, but he retired to the Deccan in 1723, and made himself independent there. He was still enjoying the Subahdarship of Malwa when he defeated Mubariz Khan, Subahdar of Hyderabad, at Shakarkhelda in the Buldana district of Berar in October, 1724, and the Subahdarship of Hyderabad has been an independent possession of his family ever since. He died 1748.

Nawab of Oudh.

Saadat Ali Khan, originally a Khorasan merchant, established himself in Oudh, the Nawabs of which were recognised as kings by the British in 1816. He was originally governor of Biana, and entered into a conspiracy to overthrow the Syeds. The power of his family commenced from the time when Mahomed Shah made Saadat Ali Khan, "the infamous son of a still more infamous Persian pedlar," Subahdar of Allahabad and Oudh. Saadat Khan occupied this position, 1723-47. He was succeeded in his viceroyalty by his nephew, Safdar Jang, a Shia and head of the Persian faction, who was the principal opponent of the Nizam's grandson, Mir Sahibuddin or Ghaziuddin II., who was a Sunni, and the head of the Turkoman faction. Safdar Jang died in 1754, leaving his power to his son and successor, Shuja-ud-daula.

Nawab of Bengal.

In Bengal, Aliverdi Khan set aside Sarfaraz Khan, the son of Shuja-ud-din, the last Subahdar nominated by the Emperor, and was perforce recognised by Mahomed Shah. Aliverdi was the first Subahdar who discontinued sending revenue to Delhi.

Mahratta States.

The foundation of the States of the Peshwas at Poona, Gwalior, Indore, Baroda, and Nagpur has been described in the chapter on the Mahrattas.

BIBLIOGRAPHY.

Sir H. M. Elliott, 'History of India as given in her own Historians.'

E. B. Havell, 'Indian Architecture.'

E. B. Havell, 'Indian Sculpture and Painting.'

E. B. Havell, 'Ideals of Indian Art.'

V. A. Smith, 'A History of Fine Art in India and Ceylon.'

R. Sewell, 'Forgotten Empire.'

Baber, 'Memoirs.'

'Akbar' (Rulers of India).

'Ain-i-Akbari,' translated by Blochman and Jarrett

Foster, 'Embassy of Sir Thomas Roe.'

Tavernier, 'Travels.'

Bernier, 'Travels.' V. A. Smith & Constable.

'Manucci Storia do Mogar,' translated by Irvine.

'Aurangzeb' (Rulers of India).

Grant Duff, 'History of the Mahrattas.'

Danvers, 'Portuguese in India.'

'Albuquerque' (Rulers of India).

BOOK III.

MODERN INDIA.

CHAPTER I.

ESTABLISHMENT OF THE ENGLISH, DUTCH AND FRENCH IN INDIA.

Importance of sea power.

FROM the first appearance of the Portuguese in India, sea power has been of importance. Even before their arrival, it was by their nautical skill that the Arab or Moplah traders gained their monopoly of Indian commerce. Europeans in any number have always arrived in India by sea, and, at first, they only settled near the sea in places where their ships and sailors could protect their trade. It was by predominance at sea that the Dutch ousted the Portuguese, and the English the Dutch and French. On one or two occasions the French have been superior at sea, and gained marked successes over the English. In the War of the Austrian Succession the English fleet left the coast, and the French seized Madras. In the War of American Independence, when the Bailli de Suffren and Admiral Hughes were fighting their battles in Indian waters, it was considered that only the opportune conclusion of the Peace of Versailles saved the English in India from great disaster.

North-East and North-West Passages to India.

In 1553 Sir Hugh Willoughby and his pilot Richard Chancellor endeavoured to find a passage to India by sailing north-east along the coast of Siberia. The only practical result of this voyage was that Chancellor discovered the White Sea and opened up trading relations with Russia, which led to the Muscovy Company being founded. In 1497 John Cabot, a Venetian settled at Bristol, in seeking a North-West passage to India round the northern coast of North America, discovered Labrador. Martin Frobisher in 1576, sailing west with the same object, discovered the Straits called by his name at the entrance to Hudson's Bay.

The first Englishmen to appear in India.

The first Englishman actually to arrive in India was Thomas Stevens, who became Rector of the Jesuit College at Salsette in 1579.

In 1585 John Newberry, Ralph Fitch and William Leedes penetrated over land to Ormuz, and thence by sea to Goa, and from Goa they travelled *via* Bijapur, Golkonda, Burhanpur, and Agra to Fatehpur Sikri. They brought a letter from Queen Elizabeth to Akbar. Newberry became a Roman Catholic and remained at Goa Fitch was travelling in Bengal, Burma, Malacca, Macao from 1583 to 1591; he speaks of Bengal in 1586 as "abounding in rice, cotton, and silk goods." He also visited Cooch Behar where he notes "the people have ears which be marvelous great, of a span long, which they draw out in length by devices, while they be young." This custom is still prevalent among the Garos. He returned to England by sea from Bengal, and took part in founding the East India Company. Leedes remained to cut gems for Akbar. In 1587 Sir Francis

Drake captured the Portuguese carrack *St. Philip* on its voyage from Goa to Portugal. This capture was important to the English owing to the additional information it gave them as to the value of the Indian trade. The Dutchman John Huyghen van Linschoten published his 'Voyages into the East and West Indies' in 1586, and the charts which it contains materially increased the knowledge possessed by the Dutch and English of the Far East. Tom Coryat, author of 'Coryat's Crudities,' not long afterwards made his appearance in India, having walked all the way from England overland. He died in India, December, 1617, and was buried in Surat. He speaks of himself as "the Odcombian leg-stretcher" (from Odcombe, a village in Somerset, which was his birthplace).

The Dutch, after being debarred from the ports of the Peninsula by Philip II. of Spain in 1585, made their first voyage to India ten years later. They soon gained such a firm control over the spice trade that they were able to raise the price of pepper from 3s. to 6s. and 8s. per pound to the English, who then determined to undertake the trade for themselves. The East India Company was formed in 1599, its first charter was dated December 31, 1600, being postponed for eighteen months at the advice of Elizabeth's Privy Council, who were frightened of offending Spain, with which country England was trying to make peace. English merchants had asked licence to trade with the East as far back as 1589 on the plea that "such a trade would by degrees add to the shipping, seamen and naval strength of the kingdom, in the same manner as it has increased the Portuguese fleets." In 1599 Queen Elizabeth

Formation of the East India Company.

sent John Mildenhall as her ambassador to Akbar to ask for favourable conditions of trade. Captain Lancaster sailed on the 13th February, 1601, from London with five ships to Achin and Bantam, and returned on the 11th September, 1603, with a cargo consisting chiefly of spices.

France endeavours to secure a share of the Indian trade.

The French merchants of St. Malo, Laval and Vitré soon afterwards made their first attempt to gain a share of Indian commerce and the spice trade, and fitted out the expedition which was absent from France for ten years, 1601-11, and of which an account has been left us by Francis Pyrard de Laval.

Spice trade.

The English at first aimed at the trade with the Spice Islands of the Eastern Archipelago, rather than with the mainland of India. With this object they established their first trading factories at Bantam in Java and at Acheen in Sumatra. The Bantam factory was ruined by the Dutch in 1621, but was re-established in 1635. The profits of the spice trade were so large that the Dutch strove to monopolise them. Bruce's 'Annals of the East India Company' speaks of an English ship's voyage to the Clove Islands, which paid a profit of 234 per cent. on the original outlay.

Financial arrangements of the early East India Company.

On account of the remoteness of the Indian trade, the East India Company was established on the principle of "a joint and united stock,"[1] but the accounts of each voyage were kept distinct, and, up to 1662, the dividends included not only a share of the profits, but also the return of the capital advanced to meet the expenses of the voyage. This

[1] Stevens' 'Dawn of Trade,' p. 8.

method had the following results. The Company could follow no continuous line of policy, it could accumulate no reserves, and there was always a danger of a sudden lack of funds, from inability to raise new capital after paying off the old. On the other hand, by allowing the general public to subscribe at stated intervals to their funds, the English East India Company made a large number of persons interested in its prosperity, and obviated the principal objection to its monopoly of trade.

The Dutch East India Company.

The Dutch East India Company was established in 1602 with the exclusive privilege of trading east of the Cape of Good Hope, and west of the Straits of Magellan, with a great capital subscribed by all the States of Holland, and with full power to make peace or war in the name of the United Provinces. The Dutch, in the early part of the century, before the two nations quarrelled over the Spice Trade, were friendly to the English and proposed a united joint stock company, but James the First refused, as he leaned towards a Spanish alliance. The company owed a great deal of its success to having the States of the United Provinces, as, in Sir Alfred Lyall's words, " a sleeping partner " in its business. It was a joint stock enterprise from the first, and enjoyed more than double the capital of the English East India Company. Like the English Company, its object was to procure spices from the East after being shut out from the trade with the Spanish ports, but also it strove to overthrow the Spanish predominance in Eastern Asia, and to deprive the Spanish Government of the financial benefit of its trade. The Dutch Company suffered from too great independence of action, its Directors had much latitude in following their own selfish ends, as they were responsible to no one, except to the States General. They had no Court of Proprietors to upset their action, like the English East India Company.

Policy of Chartered Companies.

Chartered companies were a device for extending trade and securing it by the acquisition of territory, without directly pledging the government to be responsible for the acts of its subjects in distant lands.

The Dutch founded Batavia, their capital city in the East, in 1619, and after the massacre of Amboyna, 1623, they ousted the English from the spice trade, and became the most powerful European nation in Eastern Asia. They blockaded Goa, and deprived the Portuguese of Malacca, Cochin. Cranganore, Negapatam, Jaffnapatam, Colombo and Macassar. In later times they occupied Chinsurah in Bengal, and Sadras and Pulicat on the Coromandel coast. They held Chinsurah till 1828, when they exchanged it for the English settlement of Fort Marlborough, or Bencoolen, in Sumatra.

Deprived of a share of the trade with the Spice Islands of the Malay Archipelago, the English turned their attention to trade with India, the Coromandel and Malabar coasts of which were the chief seats of the pepper trade.

William Hawkins, captain of the *Hector*, one of the ships sent by the East India Company to Surat in 1606, was sent with a letter from James the First to Jahangir, asking for leave for the English to trade with India, and to build a factory at Surat. He remained with Jahangir from 1608 to 1611, in spite of the jealousy of the "Portugals," who, as he says. "became as mad dogs." The first English factory in India was founded by a trader named Thomas Aldworth at Surat in 1612, with a subordinate factory at Karwar on the Malabar coast. Surat commanded the trade with the Red Sea and the Persian Gulf. It was a collecting centre for the fabrics of Broach and Baroda, the indigo of Sarkhej near Ahmadabad, and Biana, and of pepper from Malabar. It was followed by a factory at Cochin in 1660. The Portuguese vehemently opposed the English acquisition of any share of the Indian trade, and sea fights were constantly happening. Middleton, in 1611, off Cambay, and Best, in 1612, off Swally, the port of Surat, showed the prowess of the English at sea, and in 1615 Downton defeated the fleet of the Portuguese Viceroy off Swally. As a recognition of the valour of the English at sea, they were granted a *tankha*, or assignment on the revenues of Surat, in return for protecting the pilgrim ships to Mecca.

First English factory at Surat.

English victories by sea.

William Hawkins was followed by Sir Thomas Roe, as James the First's "true and undoubted attorney, procurator, legate, and ambassador to that high and mighty monarch, the Great Mogoar (Jahangir) king of the oriental Indyes, of Condahy, of Chismer and of Corason" (Kandahar, Kashmir and Khorasan). The object of Roe's embassy is thus described in Stowe's 'Annals.' "Towards the end of this present year, 1614, viz. in the beginning of January, his Majesty, at the request of the East India Company, sent Sir Thomas Roe ambassador to the Great Maghore, whome some corruptly call Mogall, unto whom this ambassador had commission, to make and contract a league between his Majesty and his subjects for commerce and traffique in his dominions,

Sir Thomas Roe at Jahangir's court. Warning against the Dutch.

Kandahar, Kashmir and Khorasan.

and to procure and establish a factory for our nation in sundry parts of his dominions, as well seaports as inland towns, with other instructions yet undiscovered. He is the first that ever was employed in this hie (high) nature to any of those farre remote eastern princes." [1] How Roe prospered in his mission he tells us himself. "Neither will this overgrown elephant (the Great Moghal) descend to article or bind himself reciprocally to any prince upon terms of equality, but only, by way of favour, admit our stay as long as it either likes him, or those that govern him." [2]

Roe sailed early in 1615, and arrived at Swally road, Surat, in September. His chaplain was the Rev. Edward Terry, on whose picture are inscribed the lines:

> "In Europe, Africk, Asia have I gonne,
> One journey more and then my travel's done."

Terry has also left behind him a journal of his life in India. The presents he brought were but mean —a pair of virginalls (an old English musical instrument) with an English player, an English coach and an English coachman, and some scarlet cloth. He was a man of clean hands. He tells us: "I never gave a knife for my own ends, or used the least baseness of begging, my riches are accordingly." He was determined, "as well of necessity, as judgement to break this custom of daily bribing." He would ask nothing for himself, "if the emperor

[1] Stowe's 'Annals' continued by Edmund Howes (London, 1615), p. 359.

[2] Letter to the English Ambassador at Constantinople, August 21, 1617. Introduction Foster's 'Embassy of Sir Thomas Roe,' xxviii, xxix.

knew not better to give than he to ask, he must have nothing from him." [1]

He is severe on the Dutch. "They traduce King James' name and royal authority, they rob in English colours to scandal his subjects, and use us worse than any brave enemy would, or any other but unthankful drunkards, that we have relieved from cheese and cabbage, or rather from a chain with bread and water. You must speedily look to this maggot; or else we talk of the Portugal, but these will eat a worm in your sides." [2]

He describes Jahangir's drinking bouts in the *Ghosul Khana*, when he had to grope his way out of the room in the dark, because the emperor had fallen asleep "after drinking of our Alegant (Alicant wine), and the candles were popped out." [3]

Though every one about the court knew how the emperor had spent his night, woe betide any one who alluded to it even by the most distant hint on the morrow.[4] Roe reported, "I think three or four handsome cases of that red wine will be more welcome than the richest jewel in Cheapside." [5]

He stoutly maintained his dignity, as an Englishman and an ambassador at Jahangir's court. He absolutely refused to be searched by the Surat Customs officers. He had a long drawn-out quarrel with Zulfikar Khan, governor of Surat, on account of his exactions. He

[1] Foster, i. 256, 257; note quoting Terry, 397.

[2] Letter to the East India Company, 14th February, 1617[18]. Foster, ii. 481.

[3] Foster, i. 214, 216.

[4] *Ibid.* ii. 303.

[5] Letter to the East India Company, 25th January, 1615[16]. Foster, i. 219.

refused to place his forehead on the earth, or to prostrate himself before the Great Moghal, or to indianise his dress. Roe was badly handicapped by knowing no native language. He briefly sums up the situation as he found it: "Religions infinite, laws none." Roe advised his countrymen "to seek their profit at sea and in quiet trade, and not to effect garrison and land wars in India. The Portuguese, notwithstanding their many rich residences, are beggared by the keeping of soldiers; and yet their garrisons are but mean. They never made advantage of the Indies since they defended them. Observe this well. It has also been the error of the Dutch, who seek plantations here by the sword. They turn a wonderful stock; they prole (prowl) in all places; they possess some of the best; yet their dead pays (unremunerative expenses, such as factory buildings) consume all the gain."[1] Surat was the fittest place for their trade. "The roade of Swally, and the port of Surat are fittest for you in all the Mogolles territory. A port to secure your ships, and a fitt place to unlade will not be found together."[2] He also recommended the Directors to increase their factors' salaries, and then to prohibit them from engaging in private trade. He remained in India 1615-18, and left Surat on the 17th February, 1619, arriving at Plymouth the end of August, and at the Downs a fortnight later. By his efforts the English were allowed to establish factories in Moghal territories at Broach, Surat, Goga, Cambay and Ahmedabad, Burhanpur, Ajmere, Agra and

Roe's advice to the English East India Company.

Negotiations carried out by Sir Thomas Roe.

[1] Letter to East India Company, 24th November, 1616. Foster's 'Embassy of Sir Thomas Roe,' ii. 344.

[2] Roe to the East India Company, Foster, ii. 345.

Lahore on a payment of an export duty of 3½ per cent. on all shipments.

Factory at Gombroon (Bander Abbas).

In 1622 the English, in conjunction with Shah Abbas, Shah of Persia, expelled the Portuguese from Ormuz, and were allowed to establish a factory at Gombroon (Bander Abbas).

Masulipatam, Pipli and Balasore.

In 1628 they established factories at Masulipatam, and shortly afterwards at Armagaon, forty miles north of Pulicat, and in 1633 at Pipli, near Puri, on the Subarnarekha, about sixteen miles from its mouth, and in 1642 at Balasore.

Hughli.

Other Bengal factories.

Riches of Dacca.

In 1629 Shah Jahan expelled the Portuguese from Hughli, which was occupied by the English in 1640, when branch factories were established at Patna (for saltpetre), Dacca (for muslins), Kasimbazar (for silks) and Murshidabad. In 1658 the Bengal factories were made subordinate to Madras instead of to Bantam. Dacca carried on a great trade in cloth through Surat, and, though purchasing chanks and tortoise-shell, Dacca sold a greater value of goods than it bought; so Arcot rupees had to be imported to pay for the balance. Tavernier in 1668 found "cossas, muslin, silk and cotton stuffs imported to France and Italy." Dacca had a great trade in coral, amber and tortoise-shell with Bhutan, Assam and Siam; in cloth with Nepal; and in otter-skins and shell bracelets with the Coromandel coast. Rice was abundant; it was commonly sold at Dacca in the seventeenth century at over 300 seers to the rupee.

The Dacca climate from its dampness was favourable to weaving muslin, such as *ab-i-rawan*, *shab-nam*, *jamdani* flowered muslin, and *malmal-i-khas*, the muslin reserved for the use of the Great Moghal. The work was so fine and trying to the eyes that the weavers could only work at it from 16 to 30 years of age. Dacca muslins were introduced into England between 1660 and 1670. In 1770 the value of the whole commerce of Dacca was estimated at a crore of rupees, and the value of the muslins sent to Europe at thirty lacs.

Madras.

In 1639, the English purchased the village of Chennakuppum, the original site of Madras, from Damarta Venkatadri Nayudu, Zemindar of Kalahasti, and obtained a sanad from the Raja of Chandragiri confirming the grant. The settlement extended five miles along the sea-shore, but only one inland, and stretched but a little towards St. Thomé on the south and Trivatore on the north.

It was to be called Chennapattanam in memory of the Zemindar's father Chennappa Nayudu. The name Madras is supposed to be derived from Madre Dios (mother of God) or St. Mary, to whom the old Armenian church in Blacktown is dedicated. In 1652 the settlement at Madras was raised to the rank of a Presidency, and Aaron Baker from Bantam became the first President. In 1691 they acquired Fort St. David, at Tegnapatam, near Cuddalore, from Ram Raja, the Mahratta who held Gingee.

Dangers of the infant settlement.

In 1687 Aurangzeb was besieging Golkonda, and it was feared that he would attack Madras, but the crisis passed off safely. Subsequently, when Zulfikar Khan was besieging Ram Raja and the Mahrattas in Gingee, which he took in 1698, he obtained his military stores from Madras, and in return he confirmed the English in their trading privileges. When Daud

Khan, the Viceroy's deputy in the Carnatic, was at Arcot in 1701, Manucci was sent to him at the head of an embassy from Madras. Daud Khan approached as near as St. Thomé at the head of 10,000 men, and blockaded the Fort, giving as his reason that the English had failed to perform their contract to protect the Moghal subjects against piracy. Thomas Pitt, the Governor 1698-1709, then landed sailors from the ships in the roads, embodied the militia, and showed fight to such purpose that Daud Khan, after receiving a payment of Rs. 18,000, from the English, ordered that they might continue to trade according to custom. Though the Directors called Pitt "a roughling and immoral man," he evidently believed in making Madras as strongly defensible as his means allowed. He replaced the previous mud wall round Black Town with a brick cased rampart provided with flanking works, and built redoubts to protect the suburbs, which were growing up round the original city. Fort St. George was in better repair than Fort William, but its western face at this time was only an old wall kept from falling down by the houses built up against it. He increased the garrison from the 160 Europeans, who were entertained on regular pay in the time of Streynsham Master, who was governor 1677-81, to 360 at Fort St. George, and the same number at Fort St. David, but these numbers included topasses, or half caste Portuguese, whose fighting qualities were rather dubious.

Improvement of the fortifications of Madras.

Increase of the garrison.

Madras was expected to pay its way. Sir Josiah Child, Chairman of the Directors, wrote to the President and Council at Madras: "Our meaning

Madras expected to pay its way.

as to the revenue of the town is that one way and another, by Dutch, Portuguese, or Indian methods, it should be brought to defray at least the whole constant charge, which is essential to all governments in the world. People protected ought in all parts of the universe to defray the charges of their protection and preservation from wrong and violence. The manner of raising which revenue we shall leave to your discretion as may be most agreeable to the humour of that people." [1] The original rent for Madras and Triplicane was 1200 pagodas per annum.

Expansion of the original limits.

The first expansion outside the Fort, and Blacktown, the native city immediately outside it, took place on the 23rd August, 1682, when Cowle (lease or grant in writing) was obtained to rent St. Thomé. In 1692 it was noted in the Proceedings of the President and Council: "Cowle obtained from the Grand Vizier, Assid Khan, and from the Nabob, Zulfikar Khan, for the out-towns of Egmore, Pursewaukum, and Tandore." In 1709 Trivatore, Perambore and Nungumbaukum were granted by Daud Khan. Surman's embassy to Delhi, 1715-17, obtained the confirmation by the Great Moghal of the Company's right to occupy the villages of Trivatore, Sutangodu, Catawaucha, Vizallawarrow, and Lingambauca.

Acquisition of the fort of Devikottah.

In 1749 the English gained their first increase of territory outside the limits of Madras itself, in the shape of the fort of Devikottah on the Coleroon, which was granted to them by Sayaji, Raja of Tanjore,

[1] Directors East India Company to President and Council at Madras, 20th September, 1682.

in return for their assistance in the deposition of his illegitimate brother Pratap Sinha.

The revenue and its sources.

The revenue amounted to between 60,000 and 70,000 pagodas, or £24,000 and £28,000. Customs duties, revenue from the mint and liquor shops, taxes on the sale of houses and slaves, and payments for the monopoly of the sale of betel, bhang, and tobacco were the chief sources of revenue.

Courts of Law.

A Mayor's Court of a mayor and nine aldermen was constituted by Royal Charter in 1726 for Madras, Bombay, and Calcutta, and was the chief tribunal for civil cases, with an appeal to the Governor and Council. This court superseded another set up by the Company in 1687 of a mayor and twelve aldermen including three Englishmen (Company's servants), three Portuguese, the other six being Hindus or Mahomedans. The senior members of Council constituted a Court of Quarter Sessions competent to try and punish all offenders except those guilty of high treason. Similar Courts existed in Calcutta, but as the Courts of Quarter Sessions only punished offenders by deportation to England, they were not very efficacious in preventing crime. The Choultry Court dispensed justice in which natives only were concerned. It corresponded to the Zemindar's Kacheri in Calcutta.

Bombay.

On the 27th March, 1668, the island of Bombay, which was part of the dowry of Catharine of Braganza, queen of Charles II., was made over to the East India Company in return for a yearly rent of £10. It became the headquarters of the East India Company in India from 2nd May, 1687, after the suppression of Keigwin's military mutiny in 1684. The first

President or Governor of Bombay was Gerald Aungier, who succeeded Sir George Oxenden as President of Surat, 1669. Oxenden had been President of Surat, 1662-69, and had been made Governor and Commander-in-chief of Bombay in 1669, the year of his death. It was on account of the grant of Bombay and the charter of 1661, which authorised the East India Company to make peace or war with any prince or people, not being Christian, and to administer justice for themselves and their dependents, that Sir William Hunter wrote that "Charles II. found the Company a trading body; he left it a nascent territorial power." In spite of his frivolities, Charles II. took a very real share in the development of commerce, as is shown by his establishment of the Committee of Trade and Plantations, the prototype of the Board of Trade. His policy towards the East India Company was another instance of the intelligent interest he took in the subject. Aungier died 30th June, 1677, and the next Governor of any note was Sir John Child, brother of Sir Josiah Child, Chairman of the East India Company, 1682-88. Child interfered with the pilgrim ships to Mecca, and had to be dismissed on Aurangzeb's demand, supported by the Sidee Nawab Yakut Khan of Jinjira, who seized Bombay island, and shut the English up in the Castle, 1689.

The Company a nascent territorial power.

Governorship of Sir John Child, and its result.

Nine months later Aurangzeb issued a Firman which may be compared with that issued to Ibrahim Khan, Subahdar of Bengal, for the restoration of the English on that side of India. "All the English having made a most humble submissive petition that the crimes they have done may be pardoned, and

Aurangzeb's edict for the restoration of the English to Bombay.

having requested another Phirmaund to make their being forgiven manifest, and having sent their vakils to the most heavenly palace, the most illustrious in the world, to get the royal favour; and Ettimaund Khan, the governor of Surat's petition to the famous court equal to the sky being arrived, that they would present the great king with a fine of 150,000 rupees to his most noble treasury resembling the sun, and would restore the merchants' goods they had taken away to the owners of them, and would walk by the ancient customs of the port, and behave themselves no more in such a shameful manner; therefore his Majesty, according to his favour due to all people of the world, hath pardoned their faults, mercifully forgiven them, and out of his princely condescension, agrees that the present being put into the treasury of the port, the merchants' goods should be restored, the town flourish, and they follow their trade as in former time, and Mr. Child who did the disgrace, be turned out and expelled. This order is irreversible."[1] About the year 1680, the English were not well thought of in India. Fry records "the language we have daily cast in our teeth. Why vaunts your nation? What has your sword done? Who ever felt your power? What do you possess? We see the Dutch outdo you; the Portugals have behaved like men; everyone runs you down; you can scarce keep Bombain, which you have got, (as we know,) not by your valour, but by compact, and you will pretend to be men of war, or to cope with our princes. It's fitter for you to live by merchandise and to submit to us." Sir Edward

English held in small reputation.

[1] Anderson, 'The English in Western India,' p. 248.

Winter, governor of Fort St. George (Madras), 1665-68, remonstrated with the Naik of Poonamallee on account of the blackmail he levied on the Company's goods coming into Madras, and he replied when the English horns and teeth grew, then he would free them from these imposts.

Bengal independent of Madras.

On the 14th November, 1681, William Hedges was appointed Agent and Governor in the Bay of Bengal, independent of Madras, with Job Charnock as Second in Council.

There was a proposal about this time to fortify Saugor Island, at the mouth of the Ganges, but President Gifford was refused permission to do this by Shaista Khan in 1685.

When Shaista Khan gave up the Subahdarship of Bengal in 1689, rice was selling at Dacca at 320 seers to the rupee. The Subahdar walled up the western gate of Dacca at his departure, and gave orders that it was not to be opened till rice was again selling at an equally cheap price. This happened forty-seven years afterwards when Serferaz Khan was Naib Nazim at Dacca.

Calcutta.

In 1687, after a fight with the Moghal authorities, the English abandoned Hughli and retired from the country on account of their quarrels with Shaista Khan, Subahdar of Bengal. About this time the Company attempted to wage war with the whole Moghal Empire. Child attacked the pilgrim ships, and Nicholson and Heath, with a squadron of ships, made a disastrous attempt against Chittagong, which it was intended to seize and hold. The English, on their retreat from Hughli, tried to maintain themselves at Hijli, at the mouth of the Hughli, and were besieged there by the Moghal troops. In 1690 Job Charnock, who was then the Company's Agent in Bengal, and his factors, were allowed to return to Bengal, and occupied the village of Sutanuti, which was situated on the northern portion of the present site of Calcutta. The text of the Firman of Aurangzeb, dated 23rd April, 1690, to Ibrahim Khan, who

CALCUTTA UNDER THE ENGLISH, OLD STYLE—OLD FORT WILLIAM.

succeeded Shaista Khan as Subahdar of Bengal, is as follows: "You must understand that it has been the good fortune of the English to repent of their irregular past proceedings; and they, not being in their former greatness, have, by their vakils, petitioned for their lives and pardon for their faults, which out of my extraordinary favour towards them I have accordingly granted. Therefore upon receipt here of my Phirmaund, you must not create them any further trouble, but let them trade freely in your government as formerly And this order I expect you to see strictly obeyed." After the rebellion of Sobha Sinha, Zemindar of Chitla, who, in union with an Afghan chief, Rahim Khan, rose against Raja Krishna Ram of Burdwan, who tried to plunder him, they were permitted to build a fort in 1696. In

Old Fort Ghat, Calcutta.

1698 the English were allowed to occupy the villages of Sutanuti, Govindpur and Kalikatta (an area of one and a half square miles), in perpetuity on payment of an annual rental of Rs. 1,200. This was the commencement of the modern town of Calcutta. "Dihee Calcutta" lay between Babu Ghat (Eden Gardens) and a point about 100 yards north of Clive Street. North of this came Sutanuti, or the cotton market, which stretched from Jorabagan Ghat or

Nimtollah Ghat on the south, to Chitpore on the north, and included Hatkola between the Mint and Sobha Bazar. Govindpur stretched from Babu Ghat to Surman's Ghat, or Tolly's nullah.

Captain Alexander Hamilton, an "eighteenth century Sindbad," who travelled in the East Indies, 1688-1723, thus writes of Calcutta: "Mr. Job

CALCUTTA UNDER THE ENGLISH, OLD STYLE—CHITPORE ROAD, 1787.

Charnock then being the Company's Agent in Bengal, he had authority to settle an emporium in any part on the river's side below Hughli, and for the sake of a large tree (the Peepul tree in Baitakhana, Bow Bazar), chose that place (Calcutta), though he could not have chosen a more unhealthy place on the river, for three miles to the north-eastward is a salt lake that overflows in September and October, and then prodigious numbers of fish resort there, but in November and December, when the floods are dissipated, those fishes are left dry, and with their putrefaction affect the air with thick stinking vapours, which the north-east winds bring with them to Fort William, so that they cause a yearly mortality."[1] Charnock was spoken of by his masters, the Directors of the East India Company, as "our honest Mr. Charnock, no prowler for himself beyond what was just and modest." In a despatch dated a year after his death they allude to him as "always a faithful man to the Company."

Calcutta was built haphazard to suit the temporary exigencies of the moment. There was no fixed plan for building the city, and little regard was paid to drainage or sanitary arrangements.

Early history of the English in Bengal. Oppression of local officials.

In 1650, the Subahdar Sultan Shuja granted freedom of trade on condition of receiving Rs. 3,000 a year from the Company. The firmans of the Great Moghal met with little respect from the Subahdars and other local Moghal authorities. In spite of the firman referred to above, Shaista Khan imprisoned the Company's factor at Dacca, and demanded a payment of 3½ per cent. on the value of all the Company's goods.

The English in Bengal were more inland, and therefore more in the power of the local authorities than elsewhere in India, where they could be protected by their ships. Dacca, Patna, Kasimbazar and Hughli were all connected by river channels, and so the traffic was liable at any point to be held up by greedy native officials. The muslins of Dacca, the

[1] Alexander Hamilton's 'New Account of the East Indies,' vol. ii. p. 7.

saltpetre of Patna, the silks of Kasimbazar could only be collected at Hughli with the goodwill of the Subahdar and his officials, and could only be shipped down the river at Hughli with the consent of the Governor, and in every case permission had to be paid for. The saltpetre boats from Patna were stopped by the Subahdar's order in 1708 and 1709, and he would not allow them to proceed without payments of Rs. 14,000 and Rs. 45,000. The local authorities could also forbid the merchants to supply the Company with goods for their investments, and in this case also the withdrawal of the order had to be paid for.

When Fort William was once built, it was added to and strengthened under various pretences, thus bastions were built in the corners of the factory under the pretence that they were closets. The opportunity of the death of Aurangzeb was seized upon to strengthen the two landward bastions, as "an interregnum offers the properest opportunity" for new works. The Directors wished to be able to defy the Subahdar, but grudged the expense requisite thereto. The President and Council sought and obtained an imperial grant of the thirty-eight towns nearest Calcutta as the result of Surman's embassy to Farukh Siyar, 1715-17. This embassy was sent from Calcutta in the time of Governor Hedges. It consisted of two Company's servants, John Surman and Edward Stephenson, an Armenian Cojee Serhaud, and Surgeon William Hamilton. As in the case of Gabriel Broughton and Jahanara, the success of the mission was due to the medical skill of Hamilton, who cured Farukh Siyar of a tumour in his back.

Fort William.

The mission left Calcutta in April, 1715, and reached Delhi on the 7th July.

Subahdars of Bengal during the first half of the eighteenth century.

Murshid Quli Khan, who was Subahdar of Bengal at the time, delayed the execution of the Firman during his lifetime. He died in 1726, having been in high office in Bengal as Dewan or Subahdar since his appointment as Dewan in 1701. He was succeeded as Subahdar by his son-in-law, Shujauddin Khan. On his death, his son Sarfaraz Khan and Aliverdi Khan governor of Behar fought for the post. The latter succeeded, and held the Subahdarship, 1741-56.

The Directors demurred to the territorial extension sought by the President and Council of Calcutta, on the plea that the additional revenues would allow an increase of the garrison to be paid for. They considered that if the towns ceded were prosperous, the Moors (Mahomedans) would wish to get them back, and "it is not politic for us to be encumbered with much territory." The keynote of their policy was the saving of expense.

Fort William allowed to fall into disrepair and to become defenceless.

In 1725 it was discovered that the timbers in the Fort William bastions were rotten and had to be propped up. In 1729 it was brought to the notice of the Directors that the south curtain of the Fort was defenceless, on account of the outhouses which masked the flanking fire of the bastions. The old Church of St. Andrew's, in the present Old Court House Street, was allowed to be built in such a position as to completely block the fire of the Fort guns, and to allow the Fort to be fired into by an enemy taking cover in it. The embrasures were not fit to hold the guns, and the gun carriages were too rotten to allow the guns to be fired.

Obstacles to the development of the East India Company.

The chief obstacles to the successful development of the East India Company were:

1. Interlopers disputed the validity of the Company's trade monopoly.
2. Private trade.
3. Piracy.

Interlopers and disputes about the East India Company's monopoly of trade.

1. Interlopers were persons not being members of the East India Company, or licensed by it, who claimed to trade with India at their pleasure. The King was the greatest supporter of such persons, for motives of private gain. In 1604 James I. licensed Sir Edward Michelborne and his associates "to discover the countries of Cathaia, China, Japan, Corea, and Cambaia, and the islands and countries thereto adjoining, and to trade with the people there, notwithstanding any grant or charter to the contrary."

In 1617 the same king allowed the Scotch East India Company under Sir James Cunningham to be set on foot, and they had to be bought out.

Assada merchants.

In 1637 Charles I. granted a license to Sir William Courten and others to trade to Goa, Malabar, and China. The association was called the Assada Merchants, and formed a colony at St. Augustine's Bay at Madagascar. In 1650-51, at the recommendation of the Council of State, the East India Company, the Assada Merchants, and the Merchant Adventurers trading to the Indies were united. In 1654 the Assada Merchants and the Merchant Adventurers petitioned for free trade, which was granted, but the East India trade was so disorganised by unlimited competition, that Cromwell had to restore the East India Company's charter.

In 1694 the House of Commons voted that it is the right of all Englishmen to trade with the East Indies, unless forbidden by Parliament. This resolution led to the formation of the New or English Company for trading to India, the chief officer of which in India was Sir Nicholas Waite. This Company entered into the most bitter rivalry with the Old or London Company, which was presided over in India by Sir John Gayer. Sir William Norris came to India in 1701, as ambassador from the King of England, at the expense of the English Company. This mission was unsuccessful, and Norris died on his voyage home in 1702. Both Companies intrigued with the natives, and the Governor of Surat imprisoned Gayer at the instigation of Waite. At last this cut-throat competition was given up, and both Companies were amalgamated in 1708 as the United Company of Merchants trading to the East Indies, under Lord Godolphin's scheme. Gayer was made President of Bombay, and Waite of Surat.

Rival Companies formed.

Rival Companies amalgamated as the United Company of Merchants trading to the East Indies, 1708.

2. Private trade.

The Dutch East India Company claimed the monopoly of both the trade to Europe and the trade from port to port in Asia. The East India Company claimed the former, but were content to allow their factors to take part in the trade from port to port, up to the time of the reforms of Clive and Cornwallis, which ensured the Company's servants adequate salaries. In early times, the rate of salary paid by the East India Company to its servants was not as inadequate as is generally supposed. That portion of the salary which was paid in India was only for the purpose of buying clothes. The factors lived at a common table kept up for them at the

Question of the adequacy of the salaries paid by the Company to its servants in India.

Company's expense. The balance of their pay was kept in the Company's hands as a security for good conduct, and invested in the Company's stock.

Kanojee Angria, a Mahratta, founded a pirate 3.
state at Gheriah, on the Konkan coast. Pirate fleets

CALCUTTA UNDER THE ENGLISH, NEW STYLE—SHIPPING ON THE HUGHLI.

starting from this point preyed on European and native commerce alike, till Clive and Admiral Watson captured the fort and dispersed the pirates in 1756. Piracy was not confined to natives. In 1635, Endymion Porter and Thomas Kynaston carried on piracy in the Indian seas, and did such damage that the Governor of Surat imprisoned Methwold, the English

President there, for not controlling them. Captain Kidd, an Englishman, who was eventually hung in chains at Deptford, was appointed to wage war on the pirates, but in 1697 he turned pirate himself, and haunted St. Augustine's Bay in Madagascar, and the neighbouring island of St. Mary.

Change of policy. Trade no longer chief object, but revenue.

In 1687 the East India Company, under the chairmanship of the masterful Sir Josiah Child, passed a resolution which involved a notable change of policy. "The increase of our revenue is the object of our care as much as our trade; 'tis that must maintain our force when twenty accidents may interrupt our trade; 'tis that must make us a nation in India; without that we are but a great number of interlopers united by his Majesty's royal charter, fit only to trade where nobody of power thinks it their interest to prevent us; and upon this account it is that the wise Dutch, in all their general advices that we have seen, write ten paragraphs concerning their Government, their Civil and Military policy, warfare, and the increase of their revenue for one paragraph they write concerning trade."

Their purpose was "to establish such a politie of civil and military power, and to create and secure such a large revenue as may lay the foundation of a large, well grounded, sure English dominion in India for all time to come." [1]

Commercial Potentialities of the Company.

The commercial potentialities of the East India Company were recognised early. We have seen how Mun's 'England's Treasure in Foreign Trade, 1664'

[1] Letter to Fort St. George, 12th December, 1687, quoted in Sir C. P. Ilbert's 'Government of India,' p. 25, from Bruce's 'Annals.'

defended their export of silver bullion against the champions of the Mercantile Fallacy. Sir Charles Davenant's 'Essay on the East India Trade' thus describes the great importance of the East Indian trade: "Whatever country can be in full possession of it (the East Indian trade) will give the law to the

CALCUTTA UNDER THE ENGLISH, NEW STYLE—HOWRAH BRIDGE.

commercial world. By losing trade, we should lose the dominion of the sea, for only foreign trade can maintain a great fleet."

The French were the last great European power to establish themselves in India. French companies for trading with India were formed in 1604, 1611, 1615, and 1642 (the last by Cardinal Richelieu). The French Company of the Indies was formed by John

The French in India.

Law in 1719, and lasted till 1796. In 1668 Francis Caran appeared at Surat in connection with the French East India Company formed by Colbert in 1664. In 1672 the English and French were allied against the Dutch, and the French under De la Haye occupied Trincomalee and St. Thomé. In 1674 they purchased Pondicherry from the sultan of Bijapur, but it was in the occupation of the Dutch, 1693-97. In 1688 Aurangzeb allowed them to settle at Chandernagore on the Hughli. Towards the end of the seventeenth century, the German philosopher Leibnitz in his 'Consilium Ægyptiacum,' tried to induce Louis XIV. of France to occupy Egypt, alleging that "the weakness of Orientals is no longer a secret." In 1715 the French occupied Mauritius, which had been abandoned by the Dutch. In 1725 they acquired Mahé on the Coromandel coast, and in 1739 they were given Karikal as a reward for lending troops to the Raja of Tanjore. The French East India Company suffered from too much Government interference. From 1723 its Directors were appointed by the King, and the Company borrowed large sums on the security of its privileges and revenue farms. It was dissolved in 1770. Between 1725 and 1769 it lost capital to the amount of 169 millions of francs, and the French Government had made it advances to the amount of 376 millions of francs.

The Danes in India.

The first Danish company for trading with India was formed in 1612, the second in 1670. The Danes settled at Tranquebar in the Tanjore district in 1620, and at Serampore in 1616.

Tranquebar is chiefly famous for its Christian missionaries, Ziegenbalg 1706-19, Fabricius 1739-91, and Schwartz, the friend of Hyder Ali, 1750-98. This was some years before missionaries were allowed to preach Christianity in British territory.

Other European companies trading to India.

Other European companies trading to India, were the short-lived Ostend Company, 1714-27, founded by Charles VI., Emperor of Germany, which had a factory at Bankipur on the Hughli, and which was suppressed in 1727, on account of the remonstrances of England, France and Holland. The Swedish Company was established 1731.

CHAPTER II.

WARS OF THE FRENCH AND ENGLISH IN INDIA. ENGLISH ADMINISTRATION OF BENGAL DOWN TO 1771.

Nawabs of the Karnatic.

SAADATULLAH KHAN, 1705-32, was the first of the semi-independent Nawabs of the Karnatic. He was succeeded by his adopted son, Dost Ali, in 1732. Dost Ali was killed in battle 1740, and his son-in-law, Chanda Sahib, contested the succession with Anwar-ud-din.

DUPLEIX.

The Karnatic Wars.

The first Karnatic War, 1744-48, between England and France in India was the result of the War of the Austrian Succession in Europe. In 1744 Barnett, the Admiral of the English fleet, was prevented by Nicholas Morse, Governor of Madras, 1744-48, from destroying Pondicherry, to please Anwar-ud-din, Nawab of the Karnatic. His successor, Peyton, deserted Madras, so that Labourdonnais, whom Joseph Francis Dupleix, Director-General of the French possessions in India and governor of Pondicherry, had placed in command of the French forces, was able to capture it, 1746. The Nawab of the Karnatic besieged Madras, in which the French had placed a garrison, but the place was relieved, and the Nawab's army was utterly defeated by the French under Paradis at St. Thomé. Of this battle, Malleson says that it "first proved the absolute and overwhelming superiority of the disciplined European soldier to his Asiatic rival." Pondicherry was afterwards besieged by a combined English and Dutch fleet, and Paradis was killed in a sortie, 1747. The war was brought to an end by the peace concluded at Aix-la-Chapelle in 1748, by which the French surrendered Madras that they might recover Cape Le Breton in North America.

Dupleix had been previously in charge of French affairs at Chandernagore. He had the advantage of a wife born in the country and familiar with its intrigues.

Dupleix originated the policy of taking advantage of disputed successions to interfere as much as possible with the native powers, and, in order to interfere with effect, he raised a body of native troops armed and disciplined after the European fashion.

Disputed succession to the position of Nizam and of Nawab of the Karnatic.

The second Karnatic War, 1749-1754, was caused by the death of the first independent Nizam, Chin Kilich Khan, who died in 1748. His second son, Nazir Jang became Nizam, but the succession was disputed by his grandson, Muzaffar Jang, who was supported by the French. There was also at the same time a contest for the subordinate position of Nawab of the Karnatic between Chand Saheb, the French nominee, son-in-law of Dost Ali, killed in battle by the Mahrattas at Damalcheruvu, May, 1740, and Anwar-ud-din, and afterwards his son, Mahomed Ali, who relied on English aid.

After a time, Nazir Jang was murdered at Gingee, and Muzaffar Jang became Nizam. He appointed Dupleix governor of his dominions south of the river Kistna, and Chand Saheb Nawab of the Karnatic in subordination to Dupleix.

ROBERT CLIVE.

In 1751 Chand Saheb and the French besieged Mahomed Ali in Trichinopoly. To relieve the siege, by creating a diversion, the English under Clive attacked and took Arcot, the capital of Chand Saheb, in September, and defended it for seven weeks against Chand Saheb's army under his son, Raza Saheb. When the besiegers retired, Clive pursued them, and won the battle of Arni against them. In 1752 Clive defeated the French at Kaveripak, and forced them to surrender at the Srirangam Pagoda in the Kaveri river (13th June, 1752). In 1753 Major Stringer Lawrence was again besieged in Trichinopoly by the French under Astruc. On the 1st October Lawrence managed to defeat the French and drive them into the Kaveri.

The recall of Dupleix was rendered necessary by the financial position of the French East India Company, which was on the verge of bankruptcy, and which was dissolved in 1770.

FORT AND TEMPLE AT TRICHINOPOLY.

Peace was made after Dupleix had been superseded by Godeheu, by which Mahomed Ali was recognized as Nawab of the Karnatic and Salabat Jang, another son of Chin Kilich Khan, whom the French had placed upon the throne, as Nizam of the Deccan, after Muzaffar Jang had been assassinated in 1751. This Salabat Jang was in his turn dethroned by his fourth brother, Nizam Ali, in 1761.

Outbreak of the Seven Years' War in India. Third Karnatic War, 1756-1763.

War again broke out in 1756 with the outbreak of the Seven Years' War in Europe. The French under Thomas Arthur Lally, an exiled Irishman, unsuccessfully besieged Madras from December, 1758 to the middle of February, 1759, and Lally made the fatal mistake of recalling the French general Bussy from the court of the Nizam. In 1759 Colonel Forde expelled the French from the Northern Sirkars (the districts of Ganjam, Kistna, Vizagapatam and Godaveri), and they have remained a British possession ever since. In 1760 Colonel Eyre Coote defeated the French at Wandewash and captured their General Bussy. He followed up this victory by the capture of Pondicherry on the 16th January, 1761. Pondicherry and Chandernagore in Bengal, which had been also taken by the English, were restored to the French by the Peace of Paris, 1763. By this Peace it was agreed that both the French and the English should recognize Salabat Jang as Nizam, and Mahomed Ali as Nawab of the Karnatic.

Battle of Wandewash.

Events in the Karnatic and Bengal were closely linked together. Had it not been for the ambition of Dupleix, the war between France and England on the continent of Europe need not have spread to India, and had it not been for the increased military forces necessitated by the Karnatic wars with the French, Clive would never have had men enough to have recovered Calcutta.

Conquest of Bengal by the English. Accession of Suraj-ud-daula.

In 1756, on the death of Aliverdi Khan, Nawab of Bengal, his daughter's son, Mirza Mahomed, became Nawab, with the title of Suraj-ud-daula. Immediately on his accession he quarrelled with the English because they sheltered Krishna Das, son of Rajballabh, and because they would not demolish the fortifications of Calcutta as he wished. Rajballabh was the Naib or Dewan of Nowarish Mahomed Khan, the Nawab's uncle, who had been Naib Nazim of Dacca and had died in December, 1755, and Suraj-ud-daula wished to secure an account of his uncle's property. He wished to force the English to give up the trading privileges they had obtained under Farukh Siyar. The most important of them were:

SURAJ-UD-DAULA.

(1) That a *Dastak*, or trading pass, signed by the English President in Calcutta should exempt all goods from being stopped or searched by the native Customs officers.

(2) All persons, European or Native, indebted to the English should be given up to the President in Calcutta.

(3) The English were to be allowed to purchase thirty-eight towns and villages near Calcuttta to the south, and thus obtained complete command of the Hughli.

(4) The English should be allowed to use the Mint at Murshidabad, without paying taxes on the bullion carried thither.

Suraj-ud-daula, having previously made himself master of the English factory at Kasimbazaar, attacked Fort William at Calcutta on the 18th June,

Surrender of Calcutta, 1756.

1756, and on the 20th it surrendered. One hundred and forty-six English prisoners were confined in a small room in Fort William, and one hundred and twenty-three died. This was called the "Massacre of the Black Hole," but Manik Chand, governor of Hughli, to whose care the English prisoners had been committed, was more responsible for this than the Nawab. The refugees from Calcutta betook themselves to Fulta, where they were joined by other refugees from Dacca, as Jusserat Khan, Naib Nazim at Dacca, had expelled all the English and seized their property.

Massacre of the Black Hole.

Recovery of Calcutta, 1757.

Colonel Clive and Admiral Watson, shortly before this, had destroyed the pirate Angria's forts of Gheriah and Saverndroog on the Konkan coast (1756). They were now despatched in command of an expedition from Madras. After capturing the fort at Budge Budge, and after a skirmish with the Nawab's forces there, 30th December, 1756, they recovered Calcutta, 2nd January, 1757, and captured Hughli on the 10th January. A battle was subsequently fought in the neighbourhood of Calcutta with the Nawab's forces on the 5th February, in which the English were victorious; Suraj-ud-daula then made peace, 9th February, allowing the English freedom from all inland transit duties for their merchandise and compensation for their losses. They were also permitted to fortify Calcutta as they pleased, and to erect a Mint there. In March, 1757, Clive and Watson attacked the French at Chandernagore, and the French Governor Renaud surrendered after a siege of nine days, 23rd March. A bitter contest was going on all this time between Watts and Law, the representatives of the English and French, at the Nawab's

Durbar, and their respective parties at Murshidabad. When England attacked Chandernagore, Law strongly advised his countrymen to make common cause with the Nawab against the English, to bring Bussy from Hyderabad, and so to expel the English from Bengal. De Leyrit, the Governor of Pondicherry, forbade this course being taken, and the Nawab was too afraid of the English to oppose their attack on Chandernagore. Suraj-ud-daula now began to intrigue with the French at Pondicherry and Hyderabad, so a conspiracy between Seth Mahtab Rai and Seth Swarup Chand, bankers at Murshidabad, and Watts the English representative, was formed to depose him in favour of Mir Jafar, paymaster of the army, who had married the sister of Aliverdi Khan. This plot was concealed from Omichand (Aminchand), who had wished that Yar Lateef Khan should be Nawab, so the false treaty between Mir Jafar and the English, in which a stipulation for a payment of twenty lacs of rupees to him was inserted, was shown to him. This treatment of Suraj-ud-daula was justified by his intrigues with the French in the Northern Sirkars under Bussy, and with Law, who was at the head of some French refugees from Chandernagore, who were kept in Suraj-ud-daula's pay at Patna. Suraj-ud-daula's army, led by Mir Madan Khan, was defeated at Plassey in the Nadia district on the 23rd June, 1757. Suraj-ud-daula fled towards Rajmehal, where he all but met with Law and the French troops, but was brought back and put to death at Murshidabad by Miran, son of Mir Jafar, 2nd July, 1757, who in his turn was struck dead by lightning in camp near Patna, 2nd July, 1760.

Conspiracy at Murshidabad

Battle of Plassey, 23rd of June, 1757.

Cession of Calcutta and the Twenty-four Pergunnahs.

When Mir Jafar became Nawab, he ceded to the East India Company all the land of Calcutta within the "Mahratta Ditch" and 600 yards beyond it, with the zemindari rights over the district to the south of Calcutta between the Salt Lakes and the Hughli, as far as Culpee. The building of the new Fort William was commenced with part of the one crore and seventy lacs of rupees paid as compensation for the damage done to Calcutta by Suraj-ud-daula's siege by the Nawab Mir Jafar.

Defeat of the Dutch at Biderra.

In 1759 Mir Jafar attempted to intrigue with the Dutch, but the British fleet captured seven of their ships full of troops on the way up the Hughli to Chinsurah from Java, and Colonel Forde defeated the Dutch at Biderra, midway between Chandernagore and Chinsurah, 25th November, 1759.

Invasion of Behar by Ali Gauhar.

In 1759 Prince Ali Gauhar, afterwards Shah Alam II., invaded Behar in alliance with the Nawab Wazir Shuja-ud-daula of Oude and besieged Patna, but the allies retreated at the news of Clive's approach. In 1760-61 Ali Gauhar was defeated and driven out of the English territories by Colonel Caillaud and Major Carnac.

Mir Kasim, Nawab of Bengal.

In 1760 the English "persuaded Mir Jafar to resign," and made his son-in-law, Mir Kasim, Nawab instead. Clive's successors discovered that "a revolution in Bengal was a mine more easily worked and more productive than the mines of Potosi and Mexico," and they made Mir Kasim pay a bribe of twenty lacs of rupees. Mir Kasim ceded to the English the districts of Burdwan, Midnapur, and Chittagong, 1761. He wished to make himself independent of the English, and, with this object,

Cession of Burdwan, Midnapur, and Chittagong.

looked carefully into his revenues, raised his assessments by over seventy-four lacs of rupees, and removed his capital from Murshidabad to Monghyr. He caused his troops to be disciplined in the English fashion, and placed them in charge of an Armenian, Gurghin (or Gregory) Khan.

Question of the exemption from taxation of English trade.

The English had obtained freedom from all transit dues for the East India Company's trade on payment of a *Peshcush* of Rs.3,000 a year. The English officers claimed this freedom also for their private trade, and the custom had grown up that any native gomasta who possessed an English *Dastak*, or pass, could claim exemption from all inland taxation. The Nawab's revenue suffered great loss, and he naturally resented this abuse. When the English refused redress, the Nawab abolished transit dues altogether, thus placing English and Native traders on an equality, to the great disadvantage of the former.

War between Mir Kasim and the English.

In May, 1765, Mir Kasim detained a boat at Monghyr, which was carrying arms and goods for the English factory at Patna. Mr. Ellis, chief of the English factory, then attacked and took possession of the city. Patna was soon recovered by the Nawab's troops, and all the English there made prisoners. The Kasimbazar factory was also attacked, and Mr. Amyatt, the president of the factory, on his way to Calcutta, was arrested and murdered by the Nawab's troops.

War followed: the English troops under Major Adams entered Murshidabad and gained two victories at Gheriah near Suti (Murshidabad district) on the 2nd August, and Udaynala, six miles from Rajmehal, in October. Mir Kasim then fled to Oudh, and on his way ordered the massacre of the English prisoners

Massacre of Patna.

at Patna, 5th October, 1763. Patna was retaken by the English on the 6th November.

Mir Kasim allied himself with the Emperor Shah Alam the Second, and with Shuja-ud-daula, son of Safdar Jang, Nawab of Oudh, but the English under Sir Hector Munro gained a complete victory over the allies at Buxar, 23rd October, 1764.

Battle of Buxar.

Mir Jafar had been replaced on the *Gadi* as Nawab of Bengal, when the war with Mir Kasim broke out. He undertook to reimpose all the old transit duties, and restore the Company's servants to all their former immunities from taxation. On his death in 1765, he was succeeded by his illegitimate son, Najam-ud-daula. Najam-ud-daula died next year, 1766. His brother, Saif-ud-daula, succeeded and held the title till 1770, when a third brother, Mubarak-ud-daula, became Nawab until his death in 1793. Jafar's widow, Mani Begum, was appointed guardian of the infant Nawab, though his real mother, Buboo Begum, was alive. Mahomed Reza Khan, a scion of Aliverdi's family, as Naib Subah or Deputy of the Nawab in charge of his person and household, and Gurudas, son of Raja Nand Kumar, as Dewan, enjoyed all real power.

The English obtained the Dewani of Bengal, Behar and Orissa, 12th August, 1765.

Clive returned to India a second time in 1765. He found "a presidency divided, a government without nerves, a treasury without money, a service without subordination, discipline or public spirit." His first act was to restore Shuja-ud-daula to his position as Nawab of Oudh, and to give Korah and Allahabad to the Emperor Shah Alam, son of Alamgir II., for the support of his dignity. The English also promised to pay twenty-six lacs of rupees per annum to the Emperor. In return for this Shah Alam, by the Treaty of Allahabad, gave the English the Dewani, or right of collecting the revenue in Bengal, Behar, and Orissa, and made over the Northern Sirkars (Guntur, Kistna, Ganjam, Vizagapatam, and Godaveri) to the English. It is to be observed that Orissa, properly so called, was in the hands of the Mahrattas, and that the

SHAH ALAM GRANTS THE DEWANI TO CLIVE.

territory transferred under this name comprised little more than the district of Midnapur. Clive deprecated any acquisition of territory by the English beyond the Karamnasa, the river which is the northern boundary of Bengal, though he knew, to use his own words, that "it is scarcely hyperbole to say that to-morrow the whole Moghal empire is in our power." Six years before this he had written to Pitt suggesting the acquisition of Bengal by the British nation in full sovereignty and promising a net revenue of two millions sterling. The English assumed the obligation of the military defence of the country, and extended their sway over all Bengal. They gave the Nawab fifty-six lacs of rupees to carry on the civil government and the administration of justice. The Nawab had two deputies, Mahomed Reza Khan at Murshidabad for Bengal, and Raja Shitab Rai at Patna for Behar. This was Clive's system of "Double Government," the Company being Dewan and the Nawab Nazim.

Clive's plea for the "Double Government System."

He gives his reason for his policy to the Select Committee (the governing body of the East India Company) in a letter under date, 10th January, 1767. "Under the sanction of a subah (Subahdar), every encroachment that might be attempted by foreign powers can be crushed without any apparent interposition of our own authority, and all real grievances complained of by them can be, through the same channel, examined into and redressed. Nor can it be supposed that the French, Dutch, or Danes would readily acknowledge the Company's Subahship, and pay into the hands of their servants the duties on trade, or the quit rent of those districts which they may long have been possessed of by virtue of the royal Phirmaunds or grants from former Nawabs." Mir Gholam Husain, author of the Seir Mutaqherin, thus describes the system of "Double Government": "The new rulers paid no attention to the concerns of the people of Hindustan, and suffered them to be mercilessly plundered by rulers of their own appointing." The English were only concerned with getting the revenue: they did not care how much oppression was exercised in the levying of it, and they did not interfere in the internal government of the country.

Wish for restriction of territory.

In 1767 the Directors of the East India Company wrote to their President at Calcutta: "The Dewanni of Bengal, Behar, and Orissa are the utmost limits of our view on that side of India. On the coast the protection of the Carnatic and the possession of the Sirkars, and on the Bombay side the dependencies thereon, with Salsette, Bassein, and the Castle of Surat. If we pass these bounds we shall be led from one acquisition to another, till we find no security but in the subjection of the whole, which, by dividing our force, would lose us the whole, and end in our extirpation from Hindusthan." The English in India were not so moderate. As far back as 1762, before the victory of Buxar, the council at Calcutta sent home a plan for restoring Shah Alam by force of arms to the throne of Delhi, and for extending English political influence throughout northern India.

This wish not shared by Englishmen in India.

Clive's reforms.

Clive obtained from all civil servants a written contract not to accept presents from natives, and not to engage in private trade. As a compensation he put aside the proceeds of the Salt Revenue as a means of increasing the pay of the civil servants. The Directors disallowed this expedient, but they were forced to increase the salaries of their servants to free them from the temptation to private trade. In 1769, three European officers of the East India Company's service—Vansittart, an ex-President at Calcutta, Colonel Francis Forde, and Luke Scrafton—were appointed with a general power of superintendence over native officers of government, and called "Supervisors." These officers were drowned at sea on

Supervisors.

the voyage to India, and no further appointments of the same sort were made. The army officers were forced to give up their extra allowances which they had obtained from the Nawabs under the name of "Double Bhata." This change caused considerable discontent, and the officers, headed by Sir Robert Fletcher, attempted to force the hands of Government by simultaneously resigning their commissions, but Clive accepted the resignations and filled up the vacant places.

Abolition of "Double Bhata."

In 1759 the English captured the fort of Masulipatam from the French, and the district adjoining it was conferred on them by the Nizam-ul-Mulk. In order to obtain possession of the Northern Sirkars, which lay in the Nizam's territories, the English entered into an offensive and defensive alliance with Nizam Ali, the Nizam who had dethroned and succeeded Salabat Jang in 1761. This involved them in war with Hyder Ali, 1722-1782, a soldier of fortune, who had been originally in the service of Nandi Raj, minister of Krishna Rai, a descendant of the old Yadav family, who was Raja of Mysore. Hyder Ali, whose first important appointment had been that of Faujdar of Dindigul, became Commander-in-Chief, and in 1761 deposed the Raja and usurped the throne of Mysore. In 1766 he overran Malabar. Nizam Ali, Nizam of the Deccan, was afterwards in alliance with Hyder against the English. The cause of this war in 1766 was the Northern Sirkars. These districts had been ceded to the English by the treaty of Allahabad, and a treaty was concluded with Nizam Ali, by which a tribute of five lacs was to be paid for the Northern Sirkars, and an additional four lacs

First Mysore War with Hyder Ali, 1767-69.

for Guntur on the death of the Nizam's brother, Basalat Jang. The Nizam resented the fact that the English treated the district of Guntur as if it already belonged to them. The English under Colonel Smith defeated Nizam Ali and Hyder at the battles of Changama and Trinomalli, and Colonel Peach landed in the Northern Sirkars, captured Khammamet and Warangal and threatened Hyderabad. This campaign was badly managed by the Madras council, who sent some of their members into the field to superintend the movements of the army. Nizam Ali was then glad to make peace, 1768, but Hyder, suddenly appearing with an army before the walls of Madras, forced the English to enter into an offensive and defensive alliance with him, 1769.

Field deputies of the Madras council with the army.

Hyder Ali.

Offensive and defensive alliance between the English and Hyder. Terms of the alliance not kept

In 1772 the Mahrattas attacked Hyder Ali, who, relying on the alliance of 1769, unsuccessfully appealed to the English for aid. The English refused, on the ground that Hyder had withheld Chauth from the Mahrattas, to which they had a legitimate claim. Hyder never forgave this desertion, as, in spite of the strength of his forts of Bangalore, Dharwar and Nandidrug, and the difficulty of penetrating the mountain defiles leading into

Mysore, the Mahrattas under Trimbak Rao defeated him at Chercolee, 5th March, 1771, and he had to cede to them Goorumconda, Ooscota, and Sera on his northern frontier, but recovered them, 1773-74. Shortly afterwards Hyder profited by the Mahratta dissensions. To purchase his support for Raghunath Rao he was promised the cession of all the Mahratta territories between the Tungabhadra and Kistna, and this grant was confirmed by "the *Matsaddis*" or Ministerial party at Poona, headed by Nana Farnavis, to induce Hyder to join the coalition against the English of the First Mahratta War.

Beginning of the Madras Presidency.

In 1765 the Nawab of the Karnatic granted to the English the district of Chingleput immediately round Madras, but the Madras Council farmed the district on lease to the Nawab, and did not enter on the direct management of it till fifteen years after.

Attempt of the English ministry to interfere in India without reference to the East India Company.

In 1767 Sir John Lindsay, the officer commanding the British navy in Indian waters, was given a commission as envoy of the British Government to treat with the native states independently of the East India Company. Sir John Lindsay refused to allow the Madras Government to assist Hyder under the terms of the alliance of 1769. Sir Robert Harland succeeded him in this position. This novel policy, which was not continued, was the result of the secret despatch to England of Mr. John Macpherson by Mahomed Ali, Nawab of the Karnatic, and his access to the Duke of Grafton, Prime Minister, 1768-70.

Bengal famine.

One of the worst famines recorded in Indian history happened in Bengal, 1769-70.

CHAPTER III.

WARREN HASTINGS IN BENGAL.

In 1769 Clive left India for good, and, with two unimportant holders of office (Messrs. Verelst and Cartier) between, was succeeded by Warren Hastings, who became President of Bengal on the 13th April, 1772. Almost his first act, in pursuance of orders from England, was to depose from power and bring to trial Mahomed Reza Khan, who was the Deputy of the Nawab of Bengal at Murshidabad, and Rajah Shitab Rai, who occupied a similar position in Behar at Patna, but they were both acquitted. The office of Naib Subah was conferred on Mani Begum, and Raja Gurudas, son of Nand Kumar, was given the superintendence of the Nawab's household. The Nawab was Mubarak-ud-daula, son of Mir Jafar by Buboo

Warren Hastings, President of Bengal, 13th April, 1772.

Warren Hastings.

Begum, who succeeded in 1770. Hastings persuaded the Directors of the East India Company that they could no longer shelter themselves under any phantom of superior authority, "You must establish your power, or you must hold it dependent on a superior, which I deem to be impossible." The Directors agreed in their despatch of the 28th August, 1771, "to stand forth as Dewan and to take upon themselves by the agency of their own servants, the entire care and administration of the revenues." In pursuance of this policy the Khalsa or Treasury, and with it the capital, was transferred from Murshidabad to Calcutta, and the office of Naib Dewan, which was held by a native, who represented the Company in the administration of the revenue, was abolished.

New Policy. Assumption of new responsibility.

Transference of capital to Calcutta.

Reforms: Provincial Revenue Councils.

In 1773 Provincial Revenue Councils were set up at Calcutta, Murshidabad, Burdwan, Dinajpur, Dacca and Patna. These Councils were to hear appeals in civil suits, inquire into and supervise the methods of land tenure, and the collection of the land revenue. The Provincial Revenue Councils reported that the Nawabs exacted what they could from the zemindars, by way of *abwabs* or cesses, over and above the rate at which they had agreed to farm the revenue, and that the zemindars, in their turn, could oppress the people as they chose, with impunity. In 1776 amins were appointed to make a "*hustabood,*" or measurement of lands held by revenue contractor. The country was divided into districts, with an English Collector of Revenue in each, with criminal and civil courts under the Collector to exercise the powers of the former Faujdars and Dewans. In the criminal courts the Collector had the benefit of the advice of Hindu and Mahomedan assessors, and in revenue matters his proceedings were supervised by a Committee of Revenue, sitting daily in Calcutta. This committee was established in 1781, and was intended to supersede the Provincial Councils in revenue matters. The jurisdiction of the English Collectors over criminal matters was found unsatisfactory, and the native Faujdari courts, which had been temporarily abolished, were restored in 1775. This change only lasted till 1781, when it was settled that the judges of the Dewani courts should arrest criminals and send them to be tried by the Daroga of the nearest Faujdari. Dakaity was to be put down with a strong hand, by the enlistment of "*goendas*," or informers, every convicted Dakait being hanged in his native village. His family were to "become the slaves of the State, and be disposed of for the general benefit and convenience of the people, according to the discretion of Government."

Committee of Revenue.

Measures against Dakaity.

Two courts of Appeal, the Sadr Diwani Adalat for civil cases, with the President and two Members of Council as judges, and the Sadr Nizamat Adalat for criminal cases, with native judges, were constituted. In April, 1780, six grand provincial divisions of the Sadr Diwani Adalat, distinct from the Revenue Councils, were constituted in Bengal, and the number was soon increased to eighteen. In November, 1780, these courts were placed under the superintendence of Sir Elijah Impey, Chief Justice of the Supreme Court, with a considerable addition to his salary. The Regulations which he drew up for their guidance, and which were the first attempt at a code of English

Judicial system.

Law for India, were published in July, 1781. For accepting this additional salary and for his conduct in the Nand Kumar, Patna and Cossijurah cases, and for his attempt to extend the jurisdiction of the Supreme Court, Impey's impeachment was moved in 1787 by Sir Gilbert Elliot. Digests of Hindu and Mahomedan Law to be observed in these courts were also drawn up by Sir William Jones, Judge of the Supreme Court, Calcutta, 1783-94. This measure was rendered necessary by the conflict of jurisdiction which had arisen between the Supreme Court and the District Courts. The Supreme Court claimed jurisdiction over natives to the extent of making them argue that they were not liable to its jurisdiction, if a writ was served on them. This claim was repelled by armed force in the Cossijurah case (1779), in which it was sought to arrest the zemindar for acts done by him as a revenue officer. The Patna case, 1777-79, in which certain Mahomedan law officers were heavily fined by the Supreme Court for exercising their legal functions, was another instance of the extravagant exercise of power. This state of things was remedied by the Amending Act of 1781, by which all revenue cases were declared to be outside the jurisdiction of the Supreme Court. The authority of the Supreme Court was limited to natives of Calcutta, and British subjects elsewhere. If Hindus or Mahomedans were parties to a suit, their own law was to be followed. The Company's civil and criminal courts were recognized as legal, and no official of the Company could be arrested or tried in the Supreme Court for any act done in the course of his duty.

Amending Act, 1781.

Revenue system.

After a committee, headed at first by Hastings himself, had visited every district in the province, the powers of the zemindars to punish crime and preserve order within the areas entrusted to them were abolished. This committee was intended to furnish accurate statistics of the value of land drawn up on a uniform plan. Hastings entered into settlements with the zemindars for periods of five years, agreements being entered into with the highest bidders. Between 1779, the end of this period of five years, and 1786, the date of the Decennial Settlement of Bengal, the settlements of revenue were made for a period of one year. No European and no native in Government employ was allowed to enter into a contract for farming the revenue, or to stand security for a farmer. Every zemindar who was in arrears with his payments was deprived of his position. Zemindars were given preference in tendering for collection, and the powers retained over the lands in their possession were held to be sufficient security for the performance of their contracts.

Hastings and Bhutan. Negotiations with Thibet.

In 1772 Hastings had to send troops to repel the aggression of Bhutan upon the little state of Kuch and Bihar in the north-east of Bengal. The Kuch Bihar State dates from 1515, when it was founded by Bisva Singh, 1515-40. Under a king, Nar Narayan, 1534-84, it was the most powerful monarchy in Assam, and brought even the Ahoms under its sway. Its kings lost their power after its territories were divided. The eastern or Kuch Hajo branch were represented by the Rajas of Darrang, who were vassals of the Ahom king, whilst the kings of Kuch Bihar acknowledged the supremacy of the Great Moghal. When the Teshu

Lama of Thibet asked that the Deb Raja of Bhutan should be mercifully treated, Hastings sent the first English embassy into Thibet under George Bogle and Dr. Hamilton. Another mission was subsequently despatched under Captain Turner in 1783.

Measures for the improvement of trade.

Local taxes were removed, and a uniform customs duty imposed at the low rate of $2\frac{1}{2}$ per cent. The weavers were no longer forced to work off their debts by forced labour, but were allowed to make their own bargains. Salt was to be a monopoly of Government, and to be manufactured for the Company, and sold at moderate fixed rates, which were to be settled at the beginning of every year, or bought by the Company's agents at a fixed price and sold at a fixed, but higher, price to the wholesale dealers. The privilege of selling opium was let out to the highest bidder under contract for four years. The contractor was to manufacture the crude opium which he bought from the cultivators at a fixed price, and to supply the Government with as much opium as was required at a fixed price.

Salt and opium revenue.

Hastings in difficulty about raising money on account of the wars with the Mahrattas and Mysore.

Hastings was often in great difficulty about raising money to meet the expenses of Government, on account of the wars with the Mahrattas and Mysore. He reduced the payment to the Nawab of Bengal, as arranged by the Dewani Grant, from 56 to 16 lacs of rupees, and took advantage of Shah Alam's being in the hands of Mahdaji Scindia to discontinue the annual payment of 26 lacs promised to him by Clive, and to sell Korah and Allahabad to the Nawab of Oudh for 50 lacs by the treaty of Benares, 1773.

The Second War with Mysore arose from Hyder

Ali's annoyance at the refusal of the English to assist him against the Mahrattas according to the alliance of 1769. On the outbreak of the War of American Independence, in India, 1778, the English captured Pondicherry in October, 1778, and attacked the French settlement of Mahé, March, 1789. Hyder then declared war on the ground that the English, in attacking the French, had invaded his territories. The Nizam had been alienated from the English by their attempt to march troops through his territories to his brother Basalat Jang's *Jaghir* of Adwani in the Guntur district, and was inclined to join Hyder against the English. Hastings dissuaded him from doing this by renouncing the English claim to Guntur. Colonel Baillie's detachment was crushed at Perambakam near Pollilor, 10th September, 1780, when attempting to join Sir Hector Munro at Conjeeveram. The battle of Porto Novo, south of Cuddalore, was fought on the 1st July, 1781, and, in August, Coote was joined by Colonel Pearse, who had marched overland from Bengal. The battle of Pollilor was fought on 27th August, and that of Sholinghur on the 29th September. In November, 1781, Negapatam was taken from the Dutch. In 1782 Coote relieved Vellore and won the battle of Arnee, but on the other side, Tipu, son of Hyder, inflicted a crushing defeat upon Colonel Braithwaite at Tanjore. The French captured Cuddalore, and their fleet under the Bailli de Suffren took Trincomalee in Ceylon. Many naval battles were fought in Indian waters between the French fleet under Suffren and the English under Sir Edward Hughes. English fortunes in Southern India looked very gloomy, and

Second War with Mysore, 1780-84.

the cessation of arms produced by the negotiations for the Treaty of Versailles was very opportune.

Hyder died December, 1782, and his son, Tipu, after forcing General Mathews to capitulate at Bednore, and Colonel Campbell to surrender Mangalore, concluded the Treaty of Mangalore, 1784, which restored the position of affairs before the war. This peace was hurriedly concluded by the Government of Madras, in spite of the insults offered by Tipu to the English envoys, and regardless of the fact that the English under Colonel Fullarton had entered Mysore and were marching on the capital, and that therefore more favourable terms might have been demanded.

Treaty of Mangalore, 1784.

First Armed Neutrality.

The War of American Independence, 1775-83, in which France, Spain and Holland were fighting England, and which was nearly contemporaneous with the Second Mysore and First Mahratta wars, was accompanied by a declaration of Armed Neutrality on the part of certain of the continental powers, which was almost as prejudicial to English trade as the hostility of the open enemies of the country. In 1780 Catharine, Empress of Russia, Frederic the Great, king of Prussia, with Sweden and Denmark, joined in this declaration, the object of which was to insist on the principle of free ships free goods, and that enemies' goods are not liable to capture by a belligerent on neutral ships. Great Britain had always previously claimed the right to capture such goods.

The Peshwa, Balaji Baji Rao, died of grief at the defeat of Panipat, and was succeeded by his son, Madhu Rao, 1761-72.

A powerful Mahratta army entered Delhi in the winter of 1770. It was intended to chastise the Rohilla Najib-ud-daula, who held the position of Amir-ul-amara, and Shuja-ud-daula, the Nawab Wazir of Oudh. Shah Alam was induced to return from Allahabad to Delhi, and from 1771 fell completely into the hands of Mahdaji Scindia, who induced him to make the Peshwa his Bakshee or commander-in-chief, and to give up Korah and Allahabad. Shah Alam was blinded and imprisoned by the Rohilla Gholam Kadir, son of Zabita Khan and grandson of Najib-ud-daula. He was rescued from him by Mahdaji Scindia in 1788, and was induced to issue two patents, one appointing the Peshwa Vice-Regent of the Empire and the other appointing Scindia to command the army as the Peshwa's Deputy. Shah Alam remained under the control of the Mahrattas from 1788 till 1803, when he fell into the hands of Lord Lake after the capture of Delhi, and was re-established in nominal power.

History of the events leading up to the First Mahratta War.

In 1772 Rohilkand was invaded and devastated by the Mahrattas under Visajee Kishen. Madhu Rao died suddenly in 1772, and was succeeded by Narayan Rao, his younger brother. Narayan Rao was assassinated the 30th of August, 1773, at the instigation of Ananda Bai, wife of Raghunath Rao. The succession was now disputed between Raghunath Rao or Raghoba, and a posthumous son of Narayan Rao called Madhu Rao Narayan, 1774-95. Madhu Rao Narayan's cause was taken up by the chief minister at the Peshwa's court, Balaji Janardan, called in virtue of his office Nana Farnavis (a corruption of the Persian *fard navis*, keeper of the records).

First Mahratta War. Treaty of Surat.

The English supported Raghunath Rao's claim to be Peshwa as, by the Treaty of Surat, he agreed to cede to them Salsette and Bassein, and the Mahratta share in the revenues of Broach and other places in the district of Surat. The Treaty of Surat was negotiated by the Government of Bombay, but the Supreme Government at Calcutta disapproved of it, sent Colonel Upton as their special envoy to Poona, and entered into the Treaty of Purandhar, 1776, with "the Matsaddis," as the Ministerial party at Poona was called, by which they bound themselves to give up Salsette for a district near Broach, and an indemnity of twelve lacs, and not to assist Raghoba. A sort of hollow truce followed till a quarrel occurred at Poona between Nana Farnavis and his cousin Moraba. Jealous of his cousin's power, Moraba invited the Bombay Government again to assist Raghoba. The Bombay Government responded with alacrity, and the Supreme Government, which was very suspicious of the intrigues of a French adventurer, the Chevalier de St. Lubin, with the Mahrattas, and of the reported intention of the Poona Government to surrender the port of Choul to France, reluctantly joined in the war. In 1778 Hastings empowered the Bombay Government to evade the execution of the conditions of the Treaty of Purandhar, and to enter into an alliance with Raghunath Rao and Sakhuram Bapu of the Poona Regency, against Nana Farnavis and the French. By this treaty, Raghunath Rao was only to be Regent till Madhu Rao Narayan attained his majority. Hastings maintained that the policy of the Bombay Government was not unjust, as Sir Philip Francis asserted it to be, "since the

Treaty of Purandhar.

principal party (Sakhuram Bapu) with whom the treaty (of Purandhar) was formed, now applied for the interference of the Company."

Hastings' Mahratta policy.

After the extinction of the royal house of Satara, Hastings entertained the design of elevating Maduji

GWALIOR FORT, EAST SIDE.

Bhonsla, Raja of Nagpur, to the headship of the Mahrattas, and of sweeping away the authority of the Peshwa. Alexander Elliot, who died among the swamps of Katak, was on his way to Nagpur as Hastings' secret envoy. Hastings was forestalled in this policy by the sudden activity of the Bombay Government in favour of Raghunath Rao, but he remained on terms of friendship with Maduji Bhonsla, and Benaram Pandit, the Nagpur vakil, was constantly present wherever Hastings happened to be. In 1785, Jawan Bakt, son of Shah Alam, asked for English assistance against the Mahrattas, a policy which Hastings took into serious consideration, but rejected.

Convention of Wargaon.

The chief events of the war were the defeat and surrender of the English army from Bombay to the Mahrattas at Wargaon, 15th January, 1779; Colonel Goddard's march across India from Bengal, and capture of Bassein and Ahmadabad; Captain Popham's successful attack upon the hill-fort of Gwalior, on a high rock of sandstone capped with basalt, one and a half miles long, 3rd August, 1780; and the surprise and rout of Scindia himself by Colonel Camac on the 24th of March, 1781.

Treaty of Salbai, 1782.

The war was brought to an end by the Treaty of Salbai, by which Raghunath Rao was pensioned and Madhu Rao recognised as Peshwa. The English restored Bassein and Gujrat, which they had conquered, but retained the islands of Salsette and Elephanta. No Europeans other than the English were to be received at Poona, and only the English and the Portuguese were to trade in Mahratta country. Fateh Sing was to be recognised as Gaekwar of Baroda. The district of Broach was given up to Scindia, and Gwalior to the Rana of Gohud. Scindia subsequently picked a quarrel with the Rana and seized Gwalior. This treaty did not result in the annexation of much territory, but it was the first recognition of England *as a peacemaker* by the principal Indian states, except Mysore.

This was the period of the height of the power of Mahdaji Scindia, who had been summoned to Delhi by Afrasiab Khan, son of Shah Alam's minister, Najaf Khan. His troops, disciplined by the Frenchman de Boigne, carried everything before them, and chiefly contributed to the victory of Kurdla, on the 11th March, 1795, won over the Nizam by the confederate Mahratta princes. Scindia rescued Shah Alam from the Rohilla Gholam Kadir, and obtained the post of commander-in-chief of the imperial army. He was also appointed Amir-ul-amara and Subahdar of Agra and Delhi, and enjoyed supreme power in Northern India as the Deputy of the Peshwa till his death in 1794. Grant Duff says of Mahdaji: "He was a man of great political sagacity, and of considerable genius; of deep artifice, of restless ambition, and of implacable revenge." He aspired to occupy the position of his great rival, Nana Farnavis, and to curtail the overgrown power of the Brahmans. He wished to maintain a coalition among the Mahrattas "such as would unite the chieftains of the empire against all foreign enemies." He was succeeded by his grandnephew, Daulat Rao Scindia, grandson of his brother Tukaji.

Power of Mahdaji Scindia in Upper India.

In 1772 the Mahrattas invaded Rohilkand; the Rohillas promised, by an agreement attested by Sir Robert Barker, to pay forty lacs of rupees to the Nawab of Oudh for his protection against the Mahrattas. When the Mahrattas retreated before a combined movement of troops from Oudh and Bengal, the Rohillas refused to pay, and so the Nawab of Oudh conquered them, in 1774, with the help of British troops, for which he paid forty lacs of rupees.

The Rohilla War.

Hastings defended his step by alleging the necessity of securing for the English ally, the Nawab of Oudh, and indirectly for the British territories, the protection of the frontier of the Ganges by the conquest of Rohilkand. Faizulla Khan, a Rohilla chief, was permitted to retain the territory of Rampur, and 18,000 Rohillas were allowed to migrate across the Ganges to join Zabita Khan, son of Najib-ud-daula, who was in occupation of the country round Meerut.

Lord North's Regulating Act, 1773.

The employment of a large amount of capital in the heavy loans made by the Company to the English Government, the system of Investments begun in 1767, by which surplus revenue in India was invested in buying raw produce and manufactures for exportation to Europe, the requirement since 1766 of a payment of £400,000 a year to the English revenues, the heavy Customs and Tea Duties imposed, and the abuses consequent on the system of Double Government, had forced the Company to incur heavy debts. Before the English Ministry would allow the Company to borrow further funds in England, two Parliamentary Select Committees enquired into "the state, nature and condition of the Company and of British affairs in the East Indies," and the Company was forced to consent to the Regulating Act, 1773. This Act vested the Government of Bengal, Behar, and Orissa, in a Governor-General (Hastings) and four Councillors (General Clavering, Colonel Monson, Philip Francis, and Barwell, a civilian). Bombay and Madras were made subordinate to the Governor-General, and a Supreme Court, consisting of a Chief Justice (Sir Elijah Impey) and three other judges, was established in Calcutta. The worst point of the new arrangement was that Clavering, Monson, and Francis were in constant opposition to Hastings, and, being in a majority, could thwart all his measures. Other weak points were the want of a definite connection between the three Presidencies, and the vagueness of the relation between the English Ministry and the Government of the Indian settlements.

Weak points of the new arrangement.

The Act affected the Board of East India Company Directors in London. Up to 1773, all the twenty-four Directors were elected annually, and the whole Board could be changed and a new policy inaugurated every year. After 1773, more continuity of policy was established, as it was arranged that the Directors should be elected for four years, six going out annually in rotation.

Change in the election of the Directors of the East India Company. Six to go out annually in rotation.

In 1774 the new Councillors called on Hastings to produce the letters which had passed between him and Middleton, his agent at Lucknow. Hastings refused, but he was forced to recall Middleton, and replace him by Bristow, a nominee of the majority. Champion was ordered to withdraw his troops from Rohilkand, and to enforce the payment of all the money due from the Nawab of Oudh by a threat of withdrawing the British troops, even from Oudh.

Hastings and his Council.

In 1776, on the death of Monson, Hastings regained his power by means of his casting vote. In 1779 Hastings and Francis came to an agreement, but when Barwell sailed for Europe, Francis went back upon his word, and he and Hastings fought a duel on the 17th August, 1780. Hastings' successor, Lord

Duel between Hastings and Francis.

Cornwallis, before he would undertake the Governor-Generalship, insisted on being allowed to overrule his Council, if necessary.

Dispute about Hastings' resignation.

On the 19th June, 1777, the news arrived at Calcutta that Hastings' resignation, which he had empowered Macleane, his agent in England, under certain circumstances, to offer to the Court of Directors, had been accepted, and that Clavering had been appointed Governor-General. Clavering summoned a Council next morning in his own name, took the oaths as Governor-General, demanded from Hastings the keys of Fort William and the Treasuries, and ordered the troops to obey no orders but his own. Hastings declared that his agent Macleane had exceeded his powers in tendering his resignation, the troops refused to obey Clavering's orders, and the judges of the Supreme Court declared Clavering's action illegal.

Hanging of Nand Kumar, 1775.

In March, 1775, Nand Kumar accused Hastings before the Council of having been bribed to acquit Mahomed Reza Khan, the Naib Subah of Bengal, and to appoint Mani Begum, guardian of the young Nawab, Najam-ud-daula, son of Mir Jafar, instead of his own mother, Buboo Begum, who was alive. Hastings refused to sit in Council whilst this accusation was going on, and retired with Barwell, but the hostile majority voted the accusation proved. In 1775 Nand Kumar was arrested on the suit of a native merchant, Mohun Pershad, for a forgery committed five years before. He was tried before Sir Elijah Impey, and Justices Chambers, Hyde and Le Maistre and an English jury, as he was a native of Calcutta, and so subject to the jurisdiction of the High Court.

On conviction, he was hanged on the 5th August, 1775. Later investigations go to show that Hastings' opponents on the Council deliberately withheld from him Nand Kumar's appeal for suspension of his execution till the King of England's pleasure was known, in order to be able to use his execution as a weapon against Hastings.

Case of Chait Singh, Raja of Benares.

Hastings demanded an annual subsidy of five lacs of rupees from Chait Singh, Raja of Benares, as a contribution to the cost of the Mahratta and Mysore Wars, as the revenue rights over the Benares zemindari had been transferred to the East India Company by treaty with Asaf-ud-daula, Nawab of Oudh, 1775. Chait Singh paid it for two years, and excused himself, on the ground of poverty, the third. In 1781, he offered twenty lacs as a peace offering. Hastings demanded fifty lacs, and went to Benares to levy them, and arrested the Raja, but the people rose in rebellion and Hastings had to fly. The Raja was subsequently deposed, and his dominions were made over to his nephew, Mehip Narayan.

Case of the Begums of Oudh.

The subsidy which the Nawab of Oudh had agreed to pay was five crores of rupees in arrears, and Asaf-ud-daula declared he could not pay the sum due, unless the personal and landed property of his grandmother and mother was placed in his hands. The widow of Shuja-ud-daula, the late Nawab, had been allowed to claim for her private use the money in the treasury, to the amount of some two millions sterling. Hastings allowed the extortion of property worth seventy-six lacs of rupees from the Begums.

Impeachment of Warren Hastings.

The treatment of Nand Kumar, the cases of Chait Singh and the Begums of Oudh, formed the principal charges against Warren Hastings at his impeachment, which was voted by the House of Commons on the 10th May, 1787. Burke opened the impeachment, and Sheridan made the most famous speech at the trial on the case of the Begums of Oudh. The trial commenced 13th February, 1788, and the House of Lords pronounced the final verdict of acquittal on the 23rd April, 1795. The speeches of Hastings' opponents are thus characterised by Sir Fitzjames Stephen: "Instead of being short, pointed, and precise, they are like bulky pamphlets sprinkled over with imitations of legal phraseology. They are full of invective, oratorical matter, needless recitals, arguments, statements of evidence, everything in fact which can make an accusation difficult to understand and to meet. They are, moreover, extremely tricky, being full of insinuations, and covering, by their profusion of irrelevant matter, the total designed absence of averments essential to the conclusion they are meant to support." [1]

Hastings thus summed up his administration in speeches at his impeachment: "The valour of others acquired, I enlarged and gave shape and consistency, to the dominion which you hold there; I preserved it, I sent forth its armies with an effectual but economical hand, through unknown and hostile regions, to the support of your other possessions; to the retrieval of one from degradation and dishonour (Bombay); and of the other from utter loss and subjection (Madras). I won one member of the

[1] Nuncomar and Impey, Vol. ii., p 8.

great Indian confederacy from it by an act of reasonable restitution (the district of Guntur to the Nizam); with another, I maintained a secret intercourse and converted him into a friend (Mudaji Bhonsla, Raja of Nagpur); a third, I drew off by diversion and negotiation and employed him as the instrument of peace (Mahdaji Scindia). When you cried out for peace and your cries were heard by those who were the object of them, I resisted this and every other species of counteraction by rising in my demands, and accomplished a peace, and I hope an everlasting one, with one great State (the Mahrattas); and I at least afforded the efficient means by which a peace, if not durable, more seasonable at least, was accomplished with another (Tipu Sultan). I gave you all, and you have rewarded me with confiscation, disgrace and a life of impeachment."

"Every division of official business which now exists in Bengal, with only such exceptions as have been occasioned by the changes of authority enacted from home, are of my formation. The establishment formed for the administration of the revenue, the institution of the courts of civil and criminal justice in the province of Bengal and its immediate dependencies; the form of government established for the province of Benares, with all its dependent branches of revenue, commerce, judicature, and military defence; the arrangements created for the subsidy and defence of the province of Oudh, and every other political connection and alliance of the government of Bengal were created by me." [1]

[1] Speech read to the Lords, 1791.

The financial results of the government of Hastings may be shortly stated thus :

1772.	Receipts - -	£2,373,750
	Expenditure -	1,705,379
	Surplus - - -	£668,371
1785.	Receipts - -	£5,315,197
	Expenditure - -	4,312,519
	Surplus - - -	£1,002,678

Hastings added 12½ million pounds to the total debt of the East India Company, the interest of which at 5 per cent. more than equalled the increase in the revenue.

Hastings urged that all his oppressive acts were justified by State necessity, the urgency of obtaining money to meet the expenses of the government. He denied that loans could be obtained. "I could not borrow to the utmost extent of my wants, during the late war, and tax posterity to pay the interest of my loans."

Sir Alfred Lyall speaks of the Impeachment thus : "When the storm had blown over in India, and he had piloted his vessel into calm water, he was sacrificed with little or no hesitation to political exigencies in England ; the Ministry would have recalled him ; they left him to be baited by the Opposition, and to be ruined by the law's delay, and the incredible procrastination, and the obsolete formalities of a seven years' trial." [1]

[1] 'British Dominion in India,' p. 205.

CHAPTER IV.

CORNWALLIS AND WELLESLEY.

HASTINGS left India, 16th February, 1785, and Sir John Macpherson, senior member of Council, managed affairs for twenty months till Lord Cornwallis arrived in 1786. One of Lord Cornwallis' first acts was to enforce the promise of the Nizam to surrender to the English the district of Guntur south of the Kistna river.

Lord Cornwallis, second Governor General, 1786-93.

Acquisition of Guntur.

Indian affairs were arousing increased interest in Parliament. In 1780, Lord North carried a motion in the Commons to give the East India Company the three years' statutory notice of an intention to annul their charter.

Fox's India Bill, 1783.

Fox's India Bill, 1783, provided that India should be ruled by seven commissioners nominated by Parliament. This bill was based on the reports of the Select and Secret Committees of the House of Commons on Indian affairs. It passed the Commons, but was thrown out in the Lords by the production of the King's letter to Earl Temple, that he would regard any peer who voted for the Bill as his personal enemy.

Pitt's India Bill, 1784.

Pitt's India Bill vested the supreme power over the civil, military and revenue affairs of the East

India Company's Indian territories in a Board of six Privy Councillors nominated by the King, one of whom was to be a Secretary of State, acting as President. The powers of the Directors of the East India Company were transferred to the Secret Committee of their body, which was not to exceed three in number. Pitt himself declared that the object of his bill was "to prevent the Government of Bengal from being too ambitious." The Governor-General in Council could not declare war, or enter into any offensive or defensive treaty which might involve the Company in war, without the previous permission of the Directors acting through the Secret Committee.

LORD CORNWALLIS.

Parliamentary disclaimer of conquest and extension of English dominion in India.

Parliament declared, 1793, that "to pursue schemes of conquest and extension of dominion in India is repugnant to the wish, the honour, and policy of this nation." Marshman says, "The dread of territorial expansion was in fact the prevailing bugbear of the day." The real fact was, as Vansittart, President in Bengal, 1760-64, wrote to the Directors: "Our connections in this country are at present on a point where they cannot stand; they are either too great or too little." Retreat was impossible, therefore advance was necessary. Pitt's India Bill also provided for the reduction of the number of Councillors in the Governor-General's Council from four to three.

Governor-General allowed to override the decision of his Council.

In 1786 a law was passed by the British Parliament to free the Governor-General from dependence on the majority of his Council, and to enable him to override their decision. It also permitted that one man should combine the offices of Governor-General and Commander-in-Chief.

Obligation to declare amount of property on return from India abolished.

Another law repealed the provision of Pitt's India Bill, which made it necessary for any person employed under the Government of Bengal to declare the amount of property in his possession on his return from India.

The Permanent Settlement, 1793.

Sir Philip Francis appears to have been the first to suggest that the settlement of the Bengal land-tax should be perpetual, and Sir John Shore, afterwards Lord Teignmouth, supported the proposal. Under the rule of the Moghal Emperors the zemindars paid to the government nine-tenths of what they received and retained the remaining tenth for themselves, they possessed the power of levying local cesses, they could transfer the title to their office by gift or sale, and at death their right to collect the revenue passed to their heirs on payment of a fine or present to the Emperor. The English took the mistaken view that they were hereditary lords of the soil. Sir Fitz-james Stephen considered three points determined with reference to the Permanent Settlement :

"(1) That the zemindars were the most conspicuous of the numerous persons interested in the land.

"(2) That intricate and imperfectly understood relations existed between them and the rayats.

"(3) That the right of the Government to exact a share in the produce of the land ascertained by no fixed rule, and varying from time to time in proportion to the increased yield of the land, was practically inconsistent with the rights of private property, and reduced the value of such rights where they existed to a shadow. The great object of the Permanent Settlement was to put an end to this uncertain, indefinite, and fluctuating state of things, and to substitute a system of permanent property in which the zemindars were to be landlords according to the English model, and the rayats tenants, also on the English model, and in which the land revenue was to form a permanent rent charge of fixed amount to be paid to Government by the zemindar."

Orders of the British Parliament on the collection of the Revenue and the administration of justice in Bengal.

In 1784 an Act of Parliament directed the East India Company "to enquire into the alleged grievances of the landholders, and, if founded in truth, to afford them redress, and to establish permanent rules for the settlement and collection of the revenue and for the administration of justice founded on the ancient laws and local usages of the country."

Terms of the Permanent Settlement.

Hastings had been in favour of long leases of the revenue, but had been forced by the Court of Directors to make his settlements yearly. The Permanent Settlement allowed the zemindars to lease their lands for ever from Government on payment of a fixed revenue, which was never to be increased. Uncultivated land when brought into cultivation was to become subject to a charge to be fixed when it was brought into cultivation. If any zemindari were sold or forfeited for non-payment of revenue, the Government were not to be bound by any previously existing arrangement. If it escheated by failure of issue of the zemindar, the Government was to hold the land on the same terms as the last possessor. On the other hand, no plea would be accepted for non-payment, but the estates of the zemindars could be sold by auction after sunset of the day on which payment was due, in case of default.

Sunset Law.

The text of the Resolution is as follows: "The Governor-General in Council trusts that the proprietors of land, sensible of the benefits conferred on them by the public assessment being fixed for ever, will exert themselves in the cultivation of their lands, under the certainty that they will enjoy exclusively the fruits of their own good management and industry, and that no demand will ever be made upon them or their heirs, or successors, by the present, or any future Government, for any augmentation of the public assessment, in consequence of the improvement of their estates." The loss to Government from giving up the right to increase the Land Tax was deliberately faced, in order to create a class of landed proprietors loyal to the British Government. The amount of this loss can be estimated from the fact that at present the zemindars pay a revenue of only three and a quarter millions sterling, but their annual rental amounts to upwards of thirteen millions sterling. The net rental, only ten per cent. of the gross rental, left to the zemindars at the time of the Permanent Settlement, was about forty lacs of rupees. This was insufficient for their needs and, in 1796, one-tenth of the land in Bengal was for sale. When the zemindaries were large, *e.g.* Burdwan, Birbhum and Kharakpur, which were each of them

Text of Resolution on the Permanent Settlement, 1793.

nearly 4,000 square miles, or 2,500,000 acres, a sufficient income was provided, but in most instances it was not so. In a despatch of the 12th April, 1786, the Directors expressed their disapproval of frequent changes in the revenue system and of heavy arrears being left outstanding. "A moderate jumma or assessment regularly and punctually collected unites the consideration of our interest with the happiness of the natives and the security of the landholders better than any imperfect collection of an exaggerated jumma to be enforced with severity and vexation." Since then, by the industry of the rayats, the peaceful development of the country, and the expenditure of the State, this amount has become an immense "unearned increment" in the coffers of the zemindars. The objects of Government were never realized. It was hoped that the restriction of the Government demand upon the land would be followed by a proportionate improvement of the estates of the landholders; that capital would accumulate, expenditure would increase, and the people be placed in circumstances favourable to an augmented consumption of articles both of necessity and luxury; that a system of indirect taxation like that which is the main source of revenue in Europe, might be introduced into India; and that, in the end, the revenue of Government would augment with the augmented affluence and prosperity of the country.

Cornwallis withdrew from the zemindars the right of levying *Saer* or internal excise duties and taxes on commerce at their *Gunjes* or *Chokies*, and transferred it to Government, with the avowed object that "the Company may, through the medium of duties upon an increased consumption of the necessaries and luxuries of life, participate in the wealth and advantages which, I trust, will be the consequences of a permanent revenue settlement to the inhabitants of this country." (Cornwallis to Court of Directors, Fort William, 2nd August, 1789.)

Omissions in the Permanent Settlement.

The great omission of the Permanent Settlement was the failure to safeguard the rights of the rayats. It was originally intended to record all rights. The Minute of the Governor-General in Council, dated the 18th September, 1789, says: "Many regulations will certainly be hereafter necessary for the security of the rayats in particular, and even of those talukdars, who, to my concern, must still remain in some degree of dependence on the zemindars." The words of the Permanent Settlement are: "The Governor-General in Council will, whenever he may deem it proper, enact such regulations as he may consider necessary for the protection of the dependent talukdars, rayats and other cultivators of the soil." Sir Edward Colebrooke, in a Minute, 12th July, 1820, said of the Permanent Settlement: "The errors were two-fold; they consisted firstly of what may be denominated the neglect of the interests of the Yeomanry, by merging all village rights, whether of property or occupancy, in the all-devouring recognition of the zemindar's paramount property in the soil; and secondly, in sacrificing the peasantry by one sweeping enactment, which left the zemindar to make his settlement with them on such terms as he might choose to require." The Kanungoes and Patwaris were to register all holdings, all transfers, all rent, rates and all receipts and payments; and every five years there was to be filed in the public offices a complete register of all land tenures. The Executive, however, soon ceased to concern themselves with the protection of the subordinate tenants. The Kanungoes were abolished, the Patwaris became the servants of the zemindars, and no record of rights of the rayats and inferior tenants was ever made. Though Lord Cornwallis specially reserved to the State the right to legislate in the interests of the rayats, yet Regulation VII. of 1799 ("*Haftam*"), and Regulation V. of 1812 ("*Pancham*"), and Regulation XI. of 1832 all extended the powers of the zemindars, especially in the way of allowing them to distrain for arrears of rent. This has been amended by the Rent Law of 1859, which forbade any arbitrary increase of the rent of a tenant who could claim occupancy rights by having occupied his holding for twelve successive years, but the burden of proof of occupancy rights was placed upon the rayat. The zemindar had to prove that produce had increased in value in proportion to the increase of rent which he asked. The Bengal Tenancy Act of 1885 prevents the zemindars from increasing the rent of occupancy tenants whose tenure has been in existence for twelve successive years, except for certain well-defined causes. The rights of the rayats have been still further protected by the Record of Rights provided by the Cadastral Survey.

Amount of the Permanent Settlement.

A Decennial Settlement had been made for Bengal in 1786, and the assessment of 1789-91 was declared perpetual in 1793. The revenue of Bengal and Behar was fixed at Rs. 2,68,00,989, or £3,108,915, and that of Benares at Rs. 34,53,574, or £400,615. This may be compared with other previous settlements.

REVENUE OF BENGAL AT VARIOUS PERIODS.

Revenue of Bengal at various periods.

Ausil Toomar Jumma of Todar Malla, 1582 - - - - - - - Rs.1,06,93,152
Sultan Shuja - - - - - - Rs.1,31,15,907
Jafar Khan or Murshid Kuli Khan, 1722 - - - - - - - Rs.1,42,88,186
Shujauddin Khan, 1722 - - - - Rs.1,42,45,561
Kasim Ali, 1763 - - - - - Rs.2,58,65,689
of which Kasim Ali alone added Rs.74,81,340.

In addition to the Ausil Toomar Jumma, there were a number of Abwabs or extra payments imposed by the Nawabs. The exactions of Kasim Ali alone under this head amounted to over nineteen lacs of rupees.

Judicial reforms.

Collectors were deprived of their judicial powers, and became concerned only with the revenue. The system of payment of Collectors was altered. They were no longer paid by salaries and a percentage of their receipts, but by largely increased though fixed salaries. Lord Cornwallis, in a despatch of the 14th August, 1787, mentioned a collector, with a salary of Rs. 1000 a month, whose income amounted to at least £40,000 a year, from his percentage. Civil and Sessions Judges were appointed in most of the British districts, with criminal and civil powers, and Magistrates with superintendence over the police. Criminals were to be arrested by the magistrates, but their trial and punishment was left to Mahomedan law officers, with the reservation of a right to British officers to interfere to prevent cruel and unusual punishments. Provincial Courts of Appeal were established at Calcutta, Patna, Dacca, and Murshidabad, to hear Criminal Appeals, and an appeal lay from them to the Sadr Faujdari (criminal cases) and Nizamat or Diwani Adalat (civil cases), in which the Governor-General and the members of his Council sat as Judges. The District Judges had Pandits or Hindu assessors up to 1821, and Kazis or Mahomedan assessors up to the introduction of the Code of Criminal Procedure in 1860.

In 1790 the office of Naib Nazim was abolished and the Company assumed the criminal as well as civil jurisdiction. The Criminal Law followed was the Mahomedan, but it was modified, so as to bring it into accordance with European ideas, in the following ways:

1. In cases of homicide, the intention of the criminal as far as it could be ascertained, and not the instrument used to commit the murder, was to be the test of criminality.
2. The heirs of the murdered person were not to be allowed to prevent the punishment of the murderer. Their refusal to prosecute was to be no bar to his punishment.
3. Mutilation was abolished as a punishment of crime.
4. Forgery, perjury, and the subornation of perjury were to be punished by branding on the forehead.
5. No one was to be disqualified from giving evidence on religious grounds. A "*Zimmi*," or heretic, who does not profess Mahomedanism, was formerly debarred from giving evidence in a court where Mahomedan law was followed; this disqualification was abolished.

Tipu Sultan attacked Cranganore and Jaikotah in Travancore, the Raja of which was an ally of the English. The Travancore Raja had purchased these places from the Dutch. Tipu claimed that the Dutch held them by grant of the Raja of Cochin, who was his feudatory. The English argued that the Dutch title to these places arose by right of conquest from the Portuguese. The Madras Government hampered Cornwallis considerably by neglecting to make adequate military preparations. John Holland, the Governor of Madras, was chiefly to blame for this. On this, Lord Cornwallis declared war, and assumed command, 12th December, 1790. The Mahrattas and the Nizam were the allies of the English. In 1791 he captured Bangalore, defeated Tipu at Arikera, and formed, but had to abandon, the siege of Seringapatam. In 1792 he marched upon Seringapatam and forced Tipu to come to terms, which were that he should surrender the Baramahal (now called Salem), Dindigul (now called Madura), and Malabar, and pay to the English three crores of rupees.

Third Mysore War, 1791-92.

TIPU SULTAN.

Lord Cornwallis left India in October, 1793. Sir John Shore (Lord Teignmouth) succeeded him, and

Lord Cornwallis succeeded as Governor-General by Sir John Shore, 1793-98.

held power till 1798. In 1795, the zemindari of Benares, including the districts of Benares, Ghazipur, and Mirzapur, which had been previously ruled by Chait Singh's nephew, Mehip Narayan, was annexed to the territories of the East India Company. In 1797, on the death of Asaf-ud-daula, his brother Saadat Ali was placed upon the throne of Oudh, on condition of ceding Allahabad and of paying seventy-four lacs of rupees a year for a British contingent. This was after Asaf-ud-daula's son, Wazir Ali, had been adjudged illegitimate. Wazir Ali's intrigues caused an outbreak at Benares, in which George Cherry, the British Resident, was murdered in 1799.

Acquisition of Benares.

Cession of Allahabad.

Renewal of the Company's Charter.

In 1793, Parliament renewed the East India Company's charter. The Governors of Madras and Bombay were allowed to override their Councils, if they judged it necessary. These Councils were to make laws and regulations for each Presidency, but the supreme authority of the Governor-General in Council over the whole of British India was recognised.

War with France.

War with France broke out in 1793. Chandernagore was taken, and Pondicherry besieged and capitulated, 23rd August, 1793.

Disaffection among the officers of the East India Company's army.

The officers of the East India Company's army were very discontented, and with reason. Under the rules as they then stood, no officer could go to Europe, even on short furlough, without resigning his commission. There were no appointments as general officers, and only fifty-two as field officers (above the rank of lieutenant) in an authorised establishment of 1000 infantry officers. There was at the same time great jealousy of the officers of the king's army. The Company's officers made the following claims :

1. That all promotions should go by seniority.
2. That no generals of the king's army were to be eligible for staff appointments.
3. That no general officer was to be selected for command, but all such appointments were to go by seniority.

The situation was considered so dangerous, that it was at one time contemplated that Lord Cornwallis should have again gone out to India in 1797, to settle it. He recommended the amalgamation of the Company's and king's armies, which was eventually carried out after the Indian Mutiny. For the time a compromise was arrived at, and the prospects and leave rules of the officers were slightly improved.

Lord Wellesley, 1798-1805.

In 1798 Lord Mornington (afterwards Marquis Wellesley) succeeded Sir John Shore as Governor-General. He abandoned his predecessor's Non-Intervention Policy. His first act was the disbandment of the Nizam's French-drilled troops under de Boigne and Raymond. Scindia's troops drilled by Perron were disbanded in 1803.

Subsidiary system.

The Nizam agreed to the English Subsidiary System, by which he recognised the English as the paramount power, and bound himself not to enter into any treaties or make peace or war without their consent. He also agreed to pay for a British Subsidiary force. In return for his submission in these respects the British guaranteed him protection. Soon after agreeing to this treaty, the Nizam ceded to the English the territory between the Tungabhadra and Mysore, or the districts of Bellary and Cuddapah, which had been assigned to him on the division of Tipu's territories, to meet the expenses of the contingent he agreed to keep up. Similar subsidiary

Subsidiary treaties.

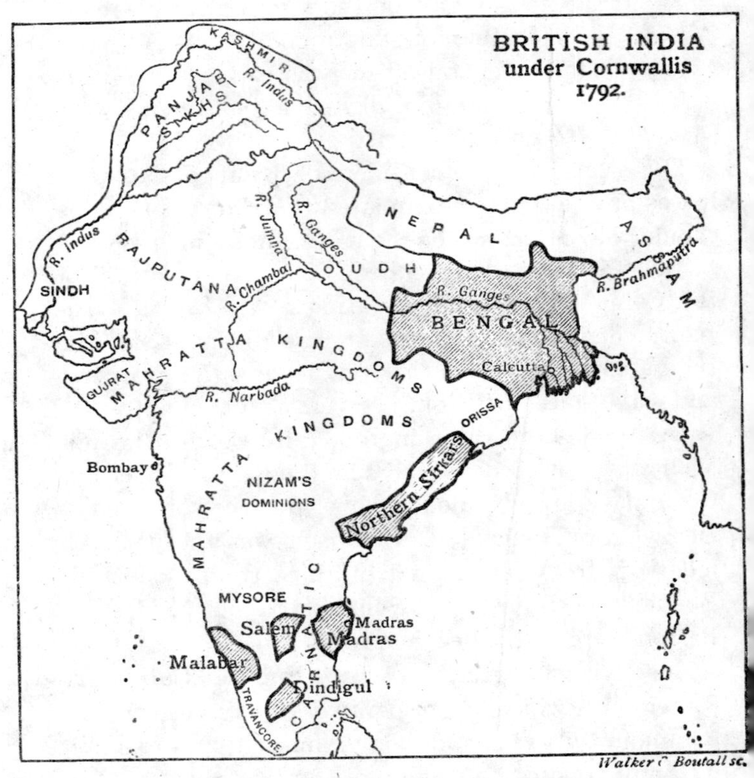

BRITISH INDIA UNDER CORNWALLIS, 1792.

treaties were executed by Lord Wellesley's government with the Peshwa, Scindia, the Bhonsla Raja of Nagpur, the Nawab of Oudh, and the Regency government of Mysore.

Fourth Mysore War, 1799.

Tipu refused to agree to the Subsidiary System,

and was believed to be intriguing with the Revolutionary government of France which had sent him an embassy with letters addressed to "Citizen Tipu"; so war followed. Tipu was defeated by General

RICHARD COLLEY WELLESLEY, MARQUIS WELLESLEY.

Stuart at Sedasir, and by General Harris at Mallavelli. The latter General successfully stormed Seringapatam, and Tipu was killed in the assault, 1799.

Second Mahratta War.

The Peshwa, Madhu Rao Narayan, committed suicide in 1795, and was succeeded by Baji Rao, the second son of Raghoba. He was attacked by

Jeswant Rao Holkar, son of Tukaji Holkar, the adopted son of Ahalya Bai, widow of Mulhar Rao, the founder of the Holkar dynasty, who died in 1765. Scindia came to his assistance, but Holkar defeated the allies in the outskirts of Poona (1802). The Peshwa was thus compelled to seek the aid of the English, who forced him to sign the Treaty of Bassein, December, 1802, in accordance with the Subsidiary System introduced by Lord Wellesley. By this treaty he was bound :

Treaty of Bassein.

1. To maintain a subsidiary force under English discipline at a cost of twenty-six lacs of rupees a year.
2. To admit no enemy of the English into his territories.
3. To abandon all claims to Surat.
4. To allow the English to mediate between him, the Nizam, and the Gaekwar.
5. To remain an ally of the English.

The Second Mahratta War.

Scindia and the Bhonsla Raja took offence at this treaty, and advanced their armies to the Narbada. Besides the jealousy of the Treaty of Bassein felt by Scindia and Holkar, the position of the Frenchman Perron, the commander of Scindia's troops, who were disciplined according to European methods at Agra, Delhi, and Alighur, was viewed with great dislike by the English. The Second Mahratta War was the combined result of these causes. Sir Arthur Wellesley defeated the army of Scindia at Assaye and that of the Bhonsla Raja at Argaum, 1803, and captured the city of Burhanpur, and the forts of Asirgarh and Gawalgarh, and Lord Lake received the submission of Scindia. General Perron captured Aligarh and

Battles of Assaye and Argaum.

defeated another army of Scindia under the French general Bourquin at Patpargunj near Delhi, 11th September, 1803. Lord Lake also captured Delhi and Agra, and gained a further victory over Scindia's troops under the command of Dudrenec, another Frenchman, at Laswaree, adjoining the Mewati hills, 20 miles east of Ulwar.

Battle of Delhi.

Battle of Laswaree.

In consequence of this war Scindia was compelled by the Treaty of Sirjee Anjengaon to cede Delhi and all his territories as far as the Chambal. The English thus acquired the territory between the Ganges and the Jumna, comprising the districts of Etawa, Mynpuri, Alighur, Bulandshahr, Meerut, Muzaffarnagar and Saharanpur, the districts of Agra and Mathura on the right bank of the Jumna, and the Delhi districts west of the Jumna, comprising Gurgaon, Delhi, Rohtak, Hansi, Sirsa, Panipat, and Banda, which were called the Conquered Districts, with Ahmednagar (Deccan) and Broach (Gujrat). Scindia gave up Gwalior to the Rana of Gohud, but regained it in 1805. The Bhonsla Raja, by the Treaty of Deogaon, agreed to give up Orissa and Khandesh, 1803. The cession of Orissa was important to the English, as it connected their territories in Bengal with the Northern Sirkars and Madras. In 1803 the Gaekwar of Baroda came under Lord Wellesley's Subsidiary System. War subsequently broke out with Holkar, and Colonel Monson had to make his disastrous retreat from Malwa to Agra (August, 1804). In February, 1805, Lake was repulsed from before Bhartpur, but Holkar was defeated at the battle of Dig, 1804, and peace made with him in 1805.

Treaties of Sirjee Anjengaon and Deogaon, 1803.

Second Armed Neutrality.

The Armed Neutrality of 1801 was stirred up against England by Paul I., the half-mad Czar of Russia. Sweden and Denmark were also parties to the agreement, the object of which was to contest the English claim to search neutral vessels for French goods. England has acknowledged the principle that "free ships make free goods" by the Treaty of Paris, 1856.

The Battle of the Nile, or the Battle of Aboukir Lay, 1798.

The Battle of the Nile, or the Battle of Aboukir Bay, 1798, in which Nelson destroyed the French fleet off the coast of Egypt, was the death blow to Napoleon Buonaparte's hope of using Egypt as a stepping-stone to conquer India.

Annexations.

The English retained Canara, Coimbatore, the Wynaad and Nilgiri Hills, from Tipu's territories, but restored Mysore to Krishnaraja, a descendant of the old Yadav Hindu Rajas, who was a child of five years of age. Krishnaraja's rule was fairly successful during the lifetime of the regent Purniah, who died in 1812. Afterwards it proceeded from bad to worse, till Lord William Bentinck had to take Mysore again under British administration, and it continued to be so administered till 1881. Tulsaji, Raja of Tanjore, was deposed by the British in 1773, but restored by the Court of Directors in 1776. Sharabhaji, Raja of Tanjore, resigned his territories to the British by treaty, 25th October, 1799. The Nawab of Surat also resigned his territories in 1799. In 1781 the territories of the Nawab of the Karnatic were temporarily taken under English management during the Mysore War, but a sixth of the revenue was assigned to the Nawab.

Restoration of Hindu Rajas of Mysore.

After the fall of Seringapatam in 1799 it was

discovered that Mahomed Ali, Nawab of the Carnatic, had been in correspondence with Tipu Sultan; his territories were therefore annexed in 1801. The English thus acquired the districts of Nellore on the north, North and South Arcot in the centre, and Madura and Tinnevelly in the south of the present Presidency of Madras. The English thus brought under their control all the territory from the Northern Sirkars to Cape Comorin except Pondicherry, Karikal, Mahé, Tranquebar, Cochin and Travancore. In the same year, Saadat Ali, Nawab of Oudh, who was in danger of invasion by Zeman Shah, was compelled to cede the Doab, or country between the Ganges and the Jumna, and Rohilkand, to meet the expenses of the Subsidiary force he was bound to keep up. The districts of Fatehpur, Cawnpore (Lower Gangetic Doab), Gorakhpur, Azimgarh (north of the Ganges), Bareilly, Moradabad, Bijnour, Budaon, and Shahjehanpur (Rohilkand) were thus acquired by the British, and, with Allahabad, were long called the Ceded Districts. He was guaranteed British protection in the enjoyment of his other territories, provided that in his administration he established "such a system of administration to be carried into effect by his own officers as should be conducive to the prosperity of his subjects and calculated to secure the lives and property of the inhabitants." The Nawab of Farrakkabad also gave up his territories to the English and received a pension.

Madras constituted a regular province.

Madras was constituted as a regular province divided into districts, each of which was provided with a collector and a judge. Four provincial Courts of Appeal with Sadr Diwani and Faujdari Adalats were established. The Madras Supreme Court dates from 1800.

College of Fort William.

This College was founded by Lord Wellesley to train the East India Company's servants in their duties. The young men, according to the Governor-General, on landing in the country, lapsed into "sloth, indolence, low debauchery, and vulgarity, and laid the foundations of their life and manners among coarse vices and indulgences." This state of things he wished to remedy by providing instruction in the native languages, and in other subjects of study useful to young servants of the Company at the outset of their careers.

The cost of Lord Wellesley's administration.

The cost of Lord Wellesley's administration may be arrived at by comparing the financial position in 1794 and 1805 respectively. At the former date, the revenue was £8,276,770, and the total charges, including interest on debt, £6,663,951, so that there was a surplus of £1,612,819. In 1805 the revenue was £15,403,409, and the charges, including interest, £17,762,017, so that there was a deficit of £2,258,608. The debt of British India had risen from £16,962,743 in 1793 to £31,638,827 in 1805.

Lord Wellesley's own summing up of the results of his administration.

"A general bond of connection is now established between the British Government and the principal states in India, on principles which render it the interest of every state to maintain its alliance with the British Government."[1]

Sir George Barlow, 1805-07. Treaty of Mustafapur, 28th November, 1805, with Scindia.

Lord Cornwallis was sent out a second time in 1805, to reverse Lord Wellesley's annexation policy, and to put into practice a system of Non-Intervention instead. He died in the same year, and Sir George

[1] Despatch to the Directors, July, 1804.

Barlow acted as Governor-General. The only events of importance during his tenure of power were the treaty with Scindia, by which the fortresses of Gwalior

British India under Wellesley, 1799.

and Gohud were restored to him, and the British Government agreed to make no treaties with the Rajas of Udaipur, Jodhpur, Kota, or any of Scindia's tributaries in Malwa or Rajputana, and not to interfere with Scindia's arrangements with reference to them.

The Subsidiary Treaty with Scindia, planned by Lord Wellesley, was given up. The English Government was not to concern itself with anything Holkar or Scindia might do in the territories north of the Taptee or south of the Chambal. Of this treaty, it was said to Lord Lake by the envoy of Jaipur that "This is the first time, since the British Government was established in India, that it has been known to make its faith subservient to its convenience."

Mutiny at Vellore.

Another important event which happened during Sir George Barlow's tenure of power was the Sepoy Mutiny at Vellore in the Madras Presidency, 1806. The mutiny was believed to have been instigated by the descendants of Tipu, who had been allowed to reside at Vellore. It must be allowed that there was some cause for it, from the sepoys' point of view, as they were ordered to shave, to wear a hat-shaped turban, and to appear on parade without their caste marks. All these changes were supposed to prepare the way for the forcible conversion of the native troops to Christianity.

CHAPTER V.

BRITISH INDIA, 1807-48.

Lord Minto,
1807-13.
Capture of
Mauritius and
Java.

Lord Minto landed in Calcutta, July, 1807, and held the Governor-Generalship till 1813. During his tenure of power the island of Mauritius was taken from the French, and the island of Java from the Dutch by military expeditions sent from India. Lord Minto pursued a non-interference policy towards the Native States in spite of its disastrous effects, such as the internecine war between the Rajas of Jaipur and Jodhpur for the hand of Krishnakumari, daughter of Bhim Singh, the Rana of Udaipur, who eventually took poison in 1810 to put an end to the strife. Raja Man Sinha of Jodhpur claimed Krishnakumari as betrothed to his predecessor, but he was a ruffian, and Jaggat Sinha of Jaipur was a profligate.

Ranjit Singh.

Effect of the policy of Non-Interference.

The Mahrattas by themselves could ruin any state, but in "the scavengers of the Mahrattas"—the Pindarees—they had allies who could outdo their worst extravagances of evil. Rajputana was the chief field for their exactions; disputed successions and contentions for power between rival factions provided the chief occasions for their interference. Mahdaji Scindia was induced by a bribe of a crore of rupees from a pretender named Ratna Sinha to attack Arsi Rana of Udaipur, 1762-72. He besieged Udaipur, but was bought off by a promise of sixty lacs, part in cash and part in territories mortgaged as security for payment. These territories were never redeemed, and were permanently incorporated with Gwalior territories. Arsi was succeeded as Rana of Udaipur by his son Hamir, 1772-75, and Hamir by his brother Bhim Sinha, 1775-1825. From their first invasion in 1735, when Udaipur agreed to pay a yearly tribute of sixteen lacs of rupees to Scindia and Holkar, to the death of Hamir in 1775, a period of forty years, the Mahrattas robbed Udaipur of over seven crores of rupees. A similar disputed succession in Jaipur between Essuri Sinha and Madhu Sinha, sons of Maharaja Jai Singh, provided Holkar with an excuse for invading Jaipur.

An internecine conflict between the Chondawats, who held Chitor, and the Suktawats, induced the Rana Bhim Sinha to summon Mahdaji Scindia to help him to expel the Chondawats. Mahdaji came, and left Ambaji as his deputy at Udaipur, and after him Lakwa Dada. These two chiefs plundered the country of all they could, and after Mahdaji's death, fought out their rivalry on Udaipur territory.

The Mahrattas did not have it all their own way. Mahdaji Scindia was defeated at Lalsot, near Jaipur, in 1787 by a combination of the Udaipur, Jodhpur and Jaipur states, and in 1790 at Patan, between Gwalior and Ujjain, it was only after desperate fighting that Scindia's disciplined troops under Benoit de Boigne, a Savoyard soldier of fortune, were victorious over Ismail Beg, a Persian leader of cavalry, in alliance with the armies of Jaipur and Jodhpur.

In the period immediately preceding the subjugation of the Pindarees, Jeswant Rao Holkar was mad, and Amir Khan, the Pindaree chief, ravaged from Nagpur to Jodhpur in the name of Holkar's illegitimate son by the daughter of a potter, whom Tulsi Bai, Holkar's mistress, and her party had proclaimed heir to Indore. Whilst these horrors were being perpetrated, the English looked on impassively, and made no sign till Lord Moira took up the campaign in earnest against the Pindarees.

After the subjugation of the Pindarees a Treaty of Alliance was entered into between the British Government and the Rana of Udaipur, 1817, and Colonel Todd, author of 'Todd's Rajasthan,' was installed as British Resident at Udaipur. The other Rajput states were taken under British protection, and the Raja of Bandi was rewarded for the assistance he had given to the British during Monson's retreat by the restoration of all the territories the Mahrattas had taken from him.

Desolation caused by the Mahrattas.

The population of Udaipur city was reduced during the Mahratta inroads from 50,000 to 3,000; the roads were so unsafe and plundering so general that goods had to pay 8 per cent. of their value for insurance between Udaipur and Nathwara, a short distance within the state; after British influence was established, this rate was soon reduced to ¼ per cent. from frontier to frontier.

The condition of Udaipur when exposed to the Mahrattas' inroads has been thus described: "In the space of 140 miles all was desolate; even the traces of the footsteps of men were effaced. The babul and gigantic reed, which harboured the boar and the tiger, grew upon the highways; and every rising ground displayed a mass of ruins. Bhilwara, the commercial entrepot of Rajputana, which, ten years before, contained 6,000 families, showed not a vestige of existence. All was silent in her streets—no living thing was to be seen except a solitary dog, that fled, in dismay, from his lurking-place in the temple, scared at the unaccustomed sight of man."

Foreign policy. The Peace of Tilsit, 1811, by which Russia gave France a free hand in Europe in return for a similar privilege in Asia, is generally taken as the starting of the anti-Russian policy of the Government of India, and it is marked by the despatch of Sir John Malcolm to Persia and of Mountstuart Elphinstone to Afghanistan to check Russian intrigues.

Ranjit Singh. The famous Ranjit Singh, son of Maha Singh, was at this time rising to power. He was born in 1780, and in 1798 was appointed Governor of Lahore by Zeman Shah, grandson of Ahmed Shah Abdali. This prince invaded the Panjab and temporarily re-established the Afghan power, to the great alarm of the English in 1797. Zeman Shah was deposed and blinded by his half-brother, Mahomed Shah, 1801. In

1803 he was released by Shah Shuja, his brother of the whole blood, who dethroned Mahomed Shah. These Amirs were all Sadozais; they were constantly quarrelling with the Barakzais, their principal opponents,

Gateway to Palace, Amber (Old Capital of Jaipur).

who were descended from Ahmad Shah's minister. Ranjit Singh acquired Amritsar, 1802. He gradually made his "misl," or confederacy, that of the Sookerchukeas, supreme among the Sikhs, and acquired the dominion of the Panjab. At this time there were

Manjha and Malwa Sikhs.

two sections of the Sikhs, the *Manjha,* living in the Bari Doab between the Beas and the Ravi, and the *Malwa,* including those living east of the Sutlej. Ranjit Singh owed much to his alliance with the powerful " misl " of the Kuneias, through his mother-in-law, Sada Kour, and his wife, Mehtab Kour. He was a man of no literary attainments and little education, and, as such, he bears a strong analogy to Hyder Ali. He had a powerful army drilled by European officers, among whom Avard, Court, Ventura and Avitable may be mentioned. In 1809 he wished to attack the States of Jhind, Patiala, and Nabha, east of the Sutlej, but was persuaded by Sir Charles Metcalfe, the envoy sent him by Lord Minto, to agree to the Treaty of Amritsar, by which he bound himself to abstain from interfering with them. His wishes to conquer Sind, and march on Kabul, were also checked by the British. He subsequently extended his sway over Kangra, Ladak, Hazara, Jammu, and Kashmir in 1819, Multan in 1819, and Peshawar in 1834. He had a meeting with Lord William Bentinck at Rupur, on the Sutlej, to discuss the opening of the Indus to commerce, October, 1831.

Treaty of Amritsar.

East India Company's monopoly of the trade to India discontinued.

In 1813 the East India Company's Charter came up for renewal by the British Parliament, and it was decided that the Company's monopoly of trade should be discontinued, except in the case of the China trade. A great expansion of trade followed; the price of cotton fell one half, pepper one quarter, whilst the rates of freight fell from £25 to less than £1 the ton. Christian missionaries were also to be allowed to enter India for the first time. This was the recommendation of the Parliamentary Committee on Indian affairs, which sat 1808-1812, and which published its famous Fifth Report in 1812.

Marquis of Hastings, 1813-23.

Lord Moira, afterwards Marquis of Hastings, succeeded Lord Minto in 1813.

Foundation of the Hindu College.

The Governor-Generalship of Lord Hastings was the era of the commencement of an effort for the education of the people. The Hindu College which developed into the Presidency College, was founded, 1817, by the efforts of the Chief Justice (Sir Edward Hyde East), Mr. David Hare, Ram Mohan Roy and Baidyanath Mukherjee.

LORD HASTINGS.

First vernacular newspaper.

The first vernacular newspaper was issued in 1822 from the Serampore Press, founded by the missionaries Carey, Ward, and Marshman, under the name of "Samachar Darpan." The same missionaries also started a college for native students at Serampur.

Committee of Public Instruction.

The Committee of Public Instruction was formed in 1823.

War with Nepal.

The war with Nepal was caused by the Goorkha aggressions upon territories ceded to the English by the Nawab of Oudh, 1813. The Goorkhas, who are believed to be originally Rajputs, established themselves in supremacy over a subject population called Newars, under Prithvi Narayan, in 1769, and conquered as far as the Sutlej on the west and Sikhim on the east. A loan of two millions sterling to meet the expenses was borrowed from Ghaziuddin Hyder, Nawab of Oudh, who was permitted in return to assume the title of king, 1816. General Gillespie penetrated into Dehra Dun, but was killed in the assault upon the fort of Kalunga. General Ochterlony drove Amar Sinha, the Goorkha general, from Ramgarh and forced him to capitulate at Maloun, 1815. In 1816, the cousins William and Edward Gardner occupied Kumaun, and cut off the Ghoorkha supplies which were drawn from Almore. Ochterlony marched towards Khatmandu and forced the Goorkhas to conclude the Treaty of Segowlie, 1816, by which they surrendered Garhwal and Kumaun.

Assumption of the title of King by the Nawab of Oudh.

Treaty of Segowlie.

The Pindaree War.

The Pindarees were bands of robbers of mixed descent in Central India. Mr. Thornton thus describes them: "Active and enterprising almost beyond belief, and wicked to the full measure which the most ardent lover of horror can desire, their adventures and their crimes were undignified by any of the nobler characteristics of our nature, which have shed a deceptive glory over actions of great atrocity, and averted from their perpetrators the penalty of unmitigated disgust. Even animal courage, often the sole ennobling virtue of their profession, they possessed not." Armies advanced against them from Gujrat, the Deccan, and Bengal. The Treaty of Gwalior was entered into on the 5th November, 1817, with Scindia for joint operations against the Pindarees, and for the cession of Ajmere. By another clause of this treaty the British Government was released

Treaty of Gwalior, 1817.

from its obligation not to enter into alliances with Scindia's tributaries in Malwa and Rajputana. An army in the centre, under Lord Hastings, was to bar Hindustan against the Pindarees, whilst a Bombay

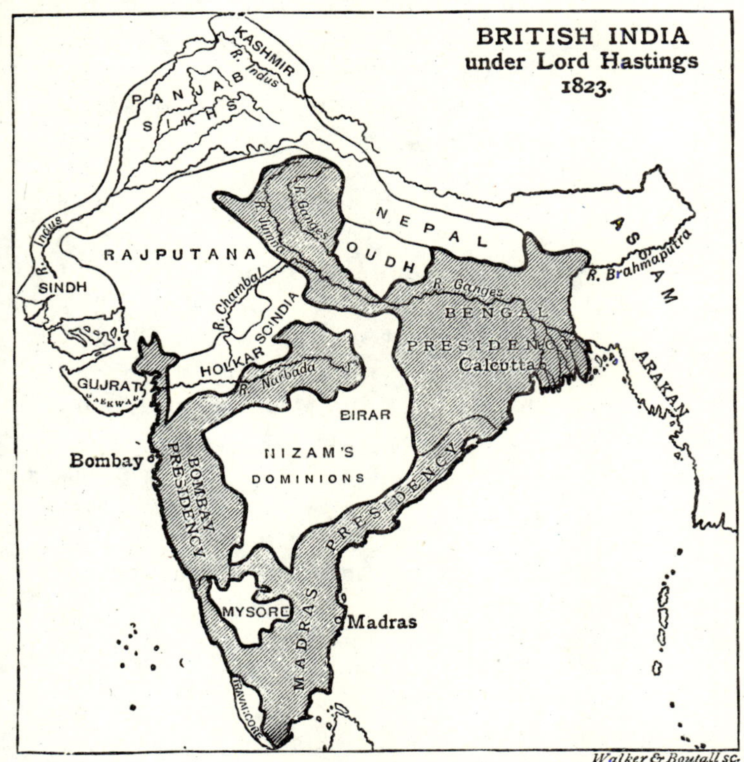

British India under Lord Hastings, 1823.

army held Gujrat, and a Madras army advanced into Central India. The Pindarees were hemmed in and forced to surrender, and their Chief, Amir Khan, was given the principality of Tonk in Rajputana, which

Pindaree chief made Nawab of Tonk.

he was to hold as Nawab, and Karim Khan, another leader, was given an estate in Basti in the United Provinces.

The Third Mahratta War, 1817.

The Third Mahratta War was the fruit of the timid policy of non-intervention pursued by the English from 1805 onwards, and was forced on Lord Hastings' Government by the lawlessness of Central India. Relations were strained between the British Government and the Peshwa, because of the murder of the Gaekwar's minister, Gangadhar Shastri, who had gone to Poona under a British safe conduct. The Peshwa's minister, Trimbakji, was believed to have had a hand in this murder, and the British Government forced the Peshwa to surrender him. Trimbakji's escape from imprisonment at Thana near Bombay was the signal for the Peshwa to draw the sword against the English. In 1817 Mountstuart Elphinstone, whilst British Resident at Poona, seeing that Baji Rao was intriguing against the English, compelled him to sign the Treaty of Poona, 1817, by which he was deprived of the power of making treaties with other Native States without the consent of the English, and forced to surrender Ahmadnagar. He treacherously attacked the Residency at Poona and fought the battles of Kirkee and Koregaum. He was defeated and his dominions annexed to the Bombay Presidency, and he himself was given a pension and allowed to live at Bithoor. The State of Satara was revived out of the Peshwa's dominions and given to a descendant of Sivajee. The Peshwa's ally, Appa Sahib, regent for an imbecile brother, at Nagpur also attacked the British, but was defeated at Sitabaldi. An infant of the Bhonsla family was allowed

Annexation of the Peshwa's territories, 1818.

to retain the kingdom of Nagpur, except a large tract near the source of the Narbada, which was taken under the direct control of the Governor-General in Council with the title of the "Saugor and Narbada Territories," and ultimately became the nucleus of the Central Provinces. The rest of the Nagpur kingdom was eventually annexed by Lord Dalhousie in 1853 on the failure of male heirs.

Holkar's troops murdered the Regent Tulsi Bai in consequence of the Peshwa's intrigues for a common rising of the Mahrattas against the English, and they opposed the English when they entered Indore territory in pursuit of the Pindaree chief Chitu, and were defeated by Sir John Hislop at Mehidpur, 1817.

Lord Amherst, 1823-28.

Lord Amherst succeeded Lord Hastings, and was Governor-General, 1823-28. The great event of his tenure of power was the First War with Burma, 1823-25, which was provoked by the aggression of the Burmese kings of the dynasty of Alompra (founded 1750), upon Kachar and the Chittagong frontier, and their claim to Eastern Bengal, including Dacca, Chittagong and Murshidabad. as having originally belonged to their empire.

First Burmese War, 1823-25.

Treaty of Yandabu, 1825.

The English under Sir Archibald Campbell captured Rangoon and Martaban, and conquered Assam. The war was concluded by the Treaty of Yandabu, by which the Burmese paid an indemnity of a crore of rupees to the English, and ceded Assam, Arracan, and Tenasserim, and promised not to interfere in Kachar, Jaintia, and Manipur.

Assam.

The word Assam is said to have been derived from the Ahoms, a tribe of Shans who invaded Assam from Maulung in the north of Burma early in the thirteenth century, and established the most powerful monarchy in Assam with its capital at Garhgaon on the Dikhu river, and subsequently at Rangpur, a town near by, but to the north-west of Garhgaon. Assam is mentioned by Hiouen Thsang as the kingdom of Kamrup, in which a king named Bhaskara Varman was reigning. Its capital was Gauhati, anciently called Pragjyotishpur. This monarchy lasted down to the beginning of the nineteenth century, when, having been weakened by a rising of the Moamarias, who were Vaishnavite sectaries who rebelled against Brahman persecution, it was overthrown by a Burmese invasion.

One of the causes of the First Burmese war was the Burmese claim that Chandrakant, an Ahom king, who had escaped into British territory, should be given up. Another was the Burmese interference with Kachar, which was under British protection.

Kachar. The Kacharis are the aborigines of the Brahmaputra valley, and are sometimes called Mech in Goalpara and North Bengal. They had a kingdom which embraced the Dhansiri valley and the district of Kachar, with its capital first at Dimapur on the Dhansiri, and after Dimapur was destroyed by the Ahoms, at Maibong. Gobind Chandra, the last Kachari king, was dethroned by the Burmese. He was restored in 1826, but died without an heir in 1832, when his country was annexed by the British, except a tract called "Tularam Senapati's country," roughly corresponding to the subdivision of North Kachar, which was not annexed till Tularam's death in 1854.

Jaintia. Jaintia was a small tract, partly in that part of the Khassia hills, which is inhabited by the Synteng tribe, and partly consisting of the level country of Sylhet between the Khassia hills and the Barak river.

WILLIAM PITT, EARL AMHERST OF ARRACAN.

It was annexed by the British in 1835 on account of the prevalence of human sacrifices at the famous shrine of Durga.

The independence of Manipur, a country between Assam and Burma, was recognised by the Treaty of Yandabo, 24th February, 1826. **Manipur.**

Storming of Bhartpur, 1826.

A dispute in the succession to Bhartpur necessitated the storming of the city—from which Lord Lake had been repulsed in 1805—by the British troops under Lord Combermere.

Lord William Bentinck, 1828-35.

In 1828 Lord Amherst was succeeded by Lord William Bentinck, a former Governor of Madras, who was Governor-General of India, 1828-35.

Renewal of the East India Company's Charter, 1833.

When the Charter of the East India Company came up for renewal before the British Parliament, on the expiration of twenty years since 1813, it was decided to abolish the Company's monopoly of the trade to China, and to allow all Europeans to settle freely in India and hold property. A Legal Member appointed in England was added to the Council of the Governor-General, and this body was empowered to make laws for the whole of India, instead of for Bengal only. The Governor-General was empowered to appoint the Indian Law Commission, of which Macaulay was the most prominent member, and whose labours resulted in the Indian Penal Code. It was also enacted that "no natives of the said territories belonging to the Company or any natural-born subject of His Majesty resident therein, shall, by reason only of his religion, place of birth, descent, colour, or any of these, be disabled from holding any place, office, or employment under the Company." The North-West Territories were formed into a separate province under a Lieutenant-Governor.

Indian Law Commission.

Religion, place of birth, descent, or colour, to be no bar to office.

North-West Provinces formed.

Settlement of Land Revenue.

The system of settling Land Revenue with the individual cultivators (Rayatwari) was inaugurated by Sir Thomas Munro in Madras, 1827, and by Goldsmid and Wingate in Bombay, 1836. Mr. Martyns Bird in 1833 commenced the North-West

System of making agreements for the payment of revenue with each village as a whole, but the settlement was not completed till 1849. The weak point in the settlement of the North-West Provinces was the neglect of the rights of the Talukdars or hereditary revenue contractors, who were not allowed to settle for any land to which they could not show an exact legal title. The enquiry into Rent-free Tenures was also excessively severe, and made British rule very unpopular. After the annexation of Oudh, the same policy was pursued towards the Talukdars of that province, and had disastrous results in embittering their opposition to British rule.

Lord William Bentinck is chiefly known for his efforts for the diffusion of Western Civilisation in India. An annual grant of a lac of rupees for Education had been made since 1813, but it was chiefly spent in the support of Arabic and Sanscrit literature. The Governor-General diverted this grant to the spread of European learning in India through the medium of the English language. In this new departure he followed the advice of Thomas Macaulay, who had come out to India as the first Legal Member of Council.

Government money spent for the first time in giving an English education to people.

The Calcutta Medical College and the Elphinstone Institution in Bombay were established by Lord William Bentinck in 1834.

Establishment of the Calcutta Medical College and the Elphinstone Institution, Bombay.

Persian was discontinued as the language in use in the Courts of Law in favour of the vernaculars. This change was very prejudicial to Mahomedans.

Persian discontinued as the language of the Courts of Law.

Lord William Bentinck passed a law exempting all converts from Hinduism to Christianity from the forfeiture of property, which, by Hindu law, followed conversion. He also forbade the custom of Sati, by

Interference with Native religious customs.

which Hindu widows used to burn themselves on the funeral pyres of their dead husbands. In this reform the Governor-General had the support of Ram Mohan Roy, who founded the Brahmo Samaj, on the 28th August, 1828. The representative of the British Government also persuaded the Khands of Ganjam and Orissa to discontinue the human sacrifices which they used to offer every year to promote the fertility of their crops. Bentinck set on foot an elaborate machinery for the suppression of Thuggee, a system of highway robbery which was carried on in honour of the goddess Kali, in which Sir William Sleeman took the prominent part. The widespread prevalence of this crime is seen by the fact that between the years 1826 and 1834, 1,562 Thugs were tried and 1,404 hanged or transported for life.

LORD WILLIAM BENTINCK.

Judicial reforms.

Lord William Bentinck improved the pay of native Civil Judges, Munsifs and Sudder Amins, and placed the administration of civil justice almost entirely in their hands. He also appointed native Deputy Collectors to assist in the revenue administration. He abolished the Provincial Courts established by Cornwallis, and gave magisterial powers to District

Judges, who were to hold monthly gaol-deliveries. An additional High Court and a Board of Revenue were established for the North-West Provinces at Allahabad. Up to 1836, British subjects were under the jurisdiction of the Supreme Courts alone. The so-called "Black Act," passed in 1836, made British subjects amenable to the civil courts of the Company in the same way as natives.

"Black Act," 1836.

Annexations.

Coorg and Kachar were annexed, and Mysore placed temporarily under British administration, on account of the misgovernment of their native rulers. Mysore was restored to the rule of the ancient family of its native Rajas by Lord Ripon in 1881. Between the years 1836 and 1843, the Cis-Sutlej States, comprising the districts of Thanesvar, Umballa, Ludhiana and Firozpur, were annexed by the British. In 1841, the Nawab of Karnul, in the north of the Madras Presidency, was discovered to be plotting against the British, and his territory was confiscated as a punishment.

Character of Bentinck's rule.

The general opinion of Bentinck's rule is inscribed on his statue in Calcutta. "Who never forgot that the end of Government is the happiness of the governed; who abolished cruel rites; who effaced humiliating distinctions; who gave liberty to the expression of public opinion; whose constant study it was to elevate the intellectual and moral character of the natives committed to his charge."

Liberty of the Press under Sir Charles Metcalfe, 1835-36.

Lord William Bentinck left India in 1835, and Sir Charles Metcalfe, senior member of Council, acted as Governor-General for a year. He abolished the special Press regulations, leaving newspaper editors subject only to the laws against sedition and libel.

In 1809 Lord Minto had made a treaty with Shah Shuja, the chief of the Sadozai tribe and ruler of Afghanistan, the grandson of Ahmad Shah Abdali and younger brother of Zeman Shah.

During the Governor-Generalship of Lord William Bentinck, Shah Shuja was driven out of Afghanistan by his brother Mahomed, who in his turn was murdered by Dost Mahomed, chief of the Barakzai tribe, who was descended from Ahmad Shah's minister. Dost Mahomed wished to obtain the restoration of Peshawar from Ranjit Singh by English assistance, but Lord Auckland refused to interfere, and Dost Mahomed began to intrigue with the Russians. It was determined, therefore, to restore by force of arms the Durani house in the person of Shah Shuja, who had taken refuge in India, and an alliance with Ranjit

First Afghan War.

Singh was formed for the purpose. An English army captured Kandahar, Ghazni, Kabul, placed garrisons in Kandahar under General Nott, and in Jelalabad under General Sale, and restored Shah Shuja, 1839.

Persian Siege of Herat.

About this time, 1838, the Persians unsuccessfully besieged the Afghan city of Herat, which was defended against them by Eldred Pottinger. This action of Persia was believed to have been inspired by Russian intrigue, and our interference with Afghanistan was the English answer to it. In 1840, Dost Mahomed yielded himself a prisoner, but in 1841 the Afghans rebelled under his son, Akbar Khan. The English envoy, Sir William Macnaghten, and the Agent, Sir Alexander Burnes, were murdered, and the English army under General Elphinstone was destroyed in its retreat to Jelalabad, January, 1842, with the exception of a single survivor, Dr. Brydon, who escaped.

Lord Auckland, 1836-42. Occupation of Aden.

Lord Auckland's Governor-Generalship is remarkable, not only for the Afghan War but for the occupation by England of Aden, "the Gibraltar of the Red Sea," 1839.

Lord Ellenborough, 1842-44.

Lord Auckland was recalled after the retreat from Kabul, and succeeded by Lord Ellenborough, 1842-44. A British army under General Pollock fought its way through the Khyber Pass, relieved Jelalabad, and marched on Kabul. Another army under General Keane relieved Kandahar, where General Nott had maintained his defence, and captured Ghazni. General Nott then joined Pollock at Kabul, the city was taken and the Great Bazar (Bala Hissar) blown up, as a retaliation for the treacherous attack on the British troops. As Shah Shuja had been killed by Akbar Khan's soldiers, Dost Mahomed was released from India and recognised as Amir of Afghanistan.

LORD AUCKLAND.

Conquest of Sind, 1844.

The Amirs of Sind had been guilty of intrigues against the English, and they subsequently made an attack upon an English official, Sir James Outram, Political Agent in Upper Sindh and Khelat, in the Residency at Hyderabad. Sir Charles Napier defeated the Amirs at Meanee and Hyderabad, 1844, and their country was annexed.

War with Scindia, 1843.

The war with Scindia arose from the fact that Jankaji Scindia died childless in 1843, his widow adopted Jyaji, but a dispute about the guardianship of the minor followed. The Gwalior army attacked British territory, but was defeated by Sir Hugh Gough at Maharajpur and Punniar, 1843. After the peace the Gwalior army was reduced from 40,000 to 9,000 men.

Sir Henry Hardinge, 1844-48.

Lord Ellenborough was recalled in 1844, and was succeeded by Sir Henry (afterwards Lord) Hardinge, 1844-48.

Since the death of Ranjit Singh, 1839, anarchy had reigned in the Panjab. His son, Kharak Singh, died in 1840, and his grandson, Nao Nahal Singh, met his death by an accident. Eventually, after the murder of Sher Singh, reputed second son of Ranjit, it was settled that Dhulip Singh, another reputed son of Ranjit Singh, should be the ruler of the Panjab, and his mother the Rani Jindam, the regent. The Sikh soldiers refused to obey orders, and the real power lay with the army Panchayets. It was agreed between the Rani and her lover Lal Singh, that to get rid of the turbulent Sikh army from Lahore, it should be sent to invade British territory. Accordingly, in December, 1845, the Sikh army crossed the Sutlej and attacked Firozpur.

First Panjab War, 1845-46.

The Sikhs were defeated at Mudki and Firozshah, December, 1845; at Aliwal, January, 1846; and at Sobraon, February, 1846. The British army then crossed the Sutlej and advanced to Mian Mir, near Lahore. Peace was then concluded by the Treaty of Lahore, 1846, the Jullundur Doab (between the Sutlej and the Beas) was annexed by the British;

RANJIT SINGH'S TOMB, LAHORE.

a British Resident, Sir Henry Lawrence, was stationed at Lahore, and the Sikh army reduced to 20,000 men. Lord Hardinge demanded the expenses of the war from the Sikhs, to the amount of a crore and a half rupees. There was half a crore in the Sikh treasury, so Gulab Singh, who was Governor of Kashmir and Jammu, offered to pay the rest of the indemnity, equivalent to a crore of rupees, or one million pounds, if he was recognised as independent ruler of the province. Lord Hardinge accepted the offer, and Kashmir and Jammu have belonged to Gulab Singh's family ever since.

Kashmir. Hiouen Thsang spent two years, 631-633, in Kashmir, which he calls Kia-chi-me-lo. It was ruled by Hindu kings down to 1294, of whom Laladitya, 724-760, built the Temple of the Sun at Martand. In 1294, Udiana Deva, the last Hindu king, was dethroned by his Wazir Amir Shah, who became Sultan under the name of Shamsuddin. He founded a Mahomedan dynasty which lasted down to the Moghal conquest in 1588. A king of this dynasty, who is prominent as a persecutor of Hinduism, under the title of *But-Shikast* = Idol breaker, submitted to Timur at the end of the fourteenth century.

Kashmir was conquered by Ahmed Shah Durani in his third invasion of India, 1756, and was taken by Ranjit Singh from the Afghans in 1819.

CHAPTER VI.

LORD DALHOUSIE.

Lord Dalhousie, 1848-5 .

SIR HENRY HARDINGE was succeeded by Lord Dalhousie, 1848-56.

Second Panjab War, 1848-49.

The signal for the Second Panjab War was given by the revolt of Mulraj, Governor of Multan, against the central government of the Panjab, and the murder of two English officers, Messrs. Agnew and Anderson, at Multan. Mulraj was beaten at Kineyree by Herbert Edwards and General Cortlandt, who eventually laid siege to Multan. The Nawab of Bahawalpur also came to their assistance. Multan was eventually stormed by a British army under General Whish, 2nd January, 1849. Lord Gough, in command of the English, fought an indecisive battle with the Sikhs at Chilianwala, 13th January, 1849, but completely defeated them at Gujrat, 22nd February, 1849.

LORD DALHOUSIE.

The surrender of 16,000 of the flower of the Khalsa army followed at Rawal Pindi, March, 1849.

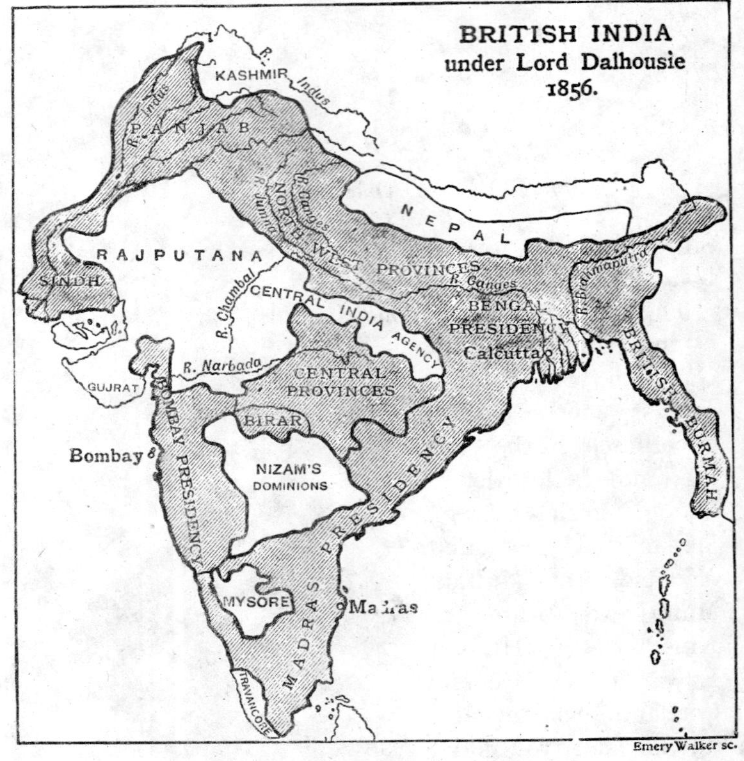

British India under Lord Dalhousie, 1856.

Annexation of the Panjab, 1849.

The Panjab was annexed 29th March, 1849, and placed under the administration of a Board of three members, Henry and John Lawrence and Mr. Mansel.

Annexation of Darjiling.

The hill-station of Darjiling was annexed in 1850, as a punishment inflicted on the Raja of Sikkim for imprisoning the British Agent, Dr. Campbell, and Dr. Hooker.

The Second Burmese War resulted from the oppression of British merchants, the refusal of redress to a British envoy, and the firing by the Burmese upon

Second Burmese War, 1852.

SHWAY DAGON PAGODA, RANGOON.

a British warship. Rangoon, Martaban, Bassein, Prome, and the province of Pegu were in consequence annexed to British territory.

Doctrine of lapse.

Holding that the British rule was a blessing to the people of India, Lord Dalhousie strove to extend it by all the means in his power, and when any of the native princes died childless, he refused to recognise the right of an heir adopted by the prince himself before his death, or his widow, unless the consent of the Supreme Government had been previously granted. Satara, 1848, Jhansi, 1853, were annexed because the consent of the paramount power had not been asked previous to the adoption. Nagpur was annexed in 1853, because there was no heir at all. Berar was handed over to be administered by the British, because the Nizam's payment for his subsidiary force was in arrears. The annexation of Kerowli, in which an heir had been adopted without the permission of the Supreme Government, was not sanctioned by the Directors, as Kerowli was an old Rajput state which did not owe its foundation to the British power.

Annexations of Satara, Jhansi, Nagpur, and Berar.

Annexation of Oudh.

Oudh was annexed 4th February, 1856, on account of continual misgovernment, and its king, Wajid Ali, was deported to Calcutta and given a pension of twelve lacs of rupees. This was after he had refused to sign a treaty surrendering the administration of Oudh to the East India Company, but securing to the king and his heirs his title, full jurisdiction in his palace and park in Lucknow, and a pension of twelve lacs of rupees, whilst the Company took upon itself the support of all the collateral members of the royal family.

Misgovernment.

The misgovernment chiefly consisted in the king's total abdication of all the necessary functions of government, which were entrusted either to "worthless favourites of the court," or "to violent and corrupt men, unfit for their duties and unworthy of trust." Lord Dalhousie puts it thus: "Secure of the safety of his person, secure of the stability of his throne, each successive ruler has passed his lifetime careful for nothing but the gratification of his individual

GATEWAY OF THE SHWAY DAGON PAGODA.

passions. Were it not for the support which the Government of India is known to be bound to afford the king against all domestic as well as foreign enemies, were it not for the constant presence of British troops in Lucknow, the people of Oudh would speedily work their own deliverance, and would impose upon their ruler the effectual check of general revolt by which Eastern rulers are best controlled. If our troops were withdrawn from Oudh, the landholders would in one month march over it all and pillage the capital of Lucknow." [1]

The Amils or Revenue Collectors, to whom the revenue was farmed out, and to whom permission was given to extort the utmost they could from the landholders without regard to assessments, engagements, or rights of any kind, were most oppressive. If the landholders offered armed resistance to the Amils, and were victorious in the struggle, they were left alone; if not, their estates were confiscated, and they were driven into their jungles with their retainers to increase the number of those who lived by pillage of the people. The landholders naturally strengthened their position as far as possible against the Amils, and the country became studded with forts which had to be taken by British troops, after the Mutiny, before the country was pacified. The number of these forts is given in the Secretary of State's despatch of 13th October, 1858, as amounting in September, 1856, to 623, of which 351 were in good repair. The tenants of the landholders were overtaxed to pay for these forts and for the armed retainers necessary to garrison them. Colonel Sleeman in 1849, and General Sir James Outram, the Resident in Lucknow, reported on this misrule.

Warnings of previous Governor Generals.

Lord William Bentinck, in 1831, threatened the King of Oudh that the British Government would assume the direct control of Oudh, if the government did not improve; but when his advice was asked how the country should be ruled, in pursuance of the policy of non-interference, he refused any advice. In 1837 a treaty had been negotiated with Nasir-

[1] Governor General's Minute, 18th July, 1855.

ud-daula, King of Oudh, giving the British the right to administer the country, if the misrule continued, but Lord Dalhousie told Wajid Ali, King of Oudh, that this treaty had not been ratified by the Court of Directors, and therefore was not in force. In 1847 Lord Hardinge repeated the previous warnings.

Outram's report was sent to England, and Lord Dalhousie's accompanying despatch proposed four alternatives to the Home Government.

Alternatives proposed by Lord Dalhousie.

1. The king may be required to abdicate the sovereign power he has abused, and to consent to the incorporation of Oudh with the territories of the British Crown.

2. He may be permitted to retain his royal titles and position, but may be required to vest the whole civil and military administration of his kingdom in the government of the East India Company for ever, or (3) for a time only.

4. He may be invited to place the administration of the country in the hands of the Resident, to be carried out by the officers of the king, aided by selected British officers.[1]

Sir Barnes Peacock, the Legal Member of Council, minuted as follows: "I would not place the residue of the revenues of Oudh at the disposal of the East India Company, but would leave it to be disposed of entirely for the benefit of the people." [2]

The orders of the Home Government for absolute annexation reached Lord Dalhousie on the 2nd January, 1856.

Proclamation of Annexation.

The Proclamation of Annexation was issued on

[1] Governor General's Minute, 18th July, 1855.

[2] Minute of Sir Barnes Peacock, 22nd September, 1855.

4th February, 1856. It commenced with a reference to the Treaty of 1801, and to the useless warnings of Lord William Bentinck and Lord Hardinge. It next mentioned the most prominent abuses of Oudh, that power is entrusted to unworthy hands, that revenue is exacted without reference to past or present engagements, and that the king's troops are defrauded of their pay and allowed to plunder the villagers for their support. The treaty of 1801 was declared null and void, because the Government of Oudh has not fulfilled its engagements. The British Government must either desert the people of Oudh or protect them, and, for their protection, the Government of Oudh was declared vested in the East India Company for ever.

LORD CANNING.

Instructions of the Government of India to the Chief Commissioner General, Sir James Outram, February, 1856.

The Chief Commissioner was instructed to give such assurances and hold out such advantages as will tend to reconcile the minds of influential persons in Oudh to the intended transfer of the powers of government. He was also to take every means to give employment to natives of the province, and to hold every encouragement to them to accept it. He was to employ in the Oudh irregular force and the military and district police as many soldiers of the king's army as were qualified. The district officers were to settle the land revenue for three years certain, with the parties actually in possession of the soil, but without any recognition, either formal or indirect, of their proprietary right. The assessments were to be as moderate and equable as possible.

Lord Dalhousie's anticipation.

Lord Dalhousie anticipated that "millions of God's creatures would draw freedom and happiness from the change." This prophecy was not fulfilled. The people preferred a tyranny which originated from themselves, to the severe and impartial justice of the alien rule of the British, and the fear of the repetition of the precedent of Oudh was one of the chief causes which brought about the Indian Mutiny.

Insufficient realisation of the promises of the British Government.

Outram resigned the Chief Commissionership on the ground of ill-health at the end of April, 1856, and after his departure, all the beneficent and conciliatory measures promised were suspended. The Sepoys of the king's army and retainers of the royal family were, as far as possible, enlisted in the new local regiments and the police, and pensions given to the remainder who had twenty-five years' service and gratuities to the others of less service, but a large percentage of those who lost their employment by the Annexation of Oudh received no consideration whatever. The Inam Commission to enquire into the rights of landholders was needlessly severe, the settlement of the land revenue was made with the cultivators direct, and the Talukdars or revenue contractors were considered to be possessed of no rights, which were not capable of strict legal proof. The person of the Raja of Tulseepur, a prominent Talukdar, was seized as being a revenue defaulter. The allowances to the members of the royal family and the stipendiaries of the King of Oudh were withheld. Ex-officials were denied employment. The surplus of the revenues of Oudh, instead of being spent on the benefit of the people, were merged in the general revenues of India. General unrest followed, and

FORT OF BHARTPUR.

Fazl Ali, the Maulavi of Fyzabad, rose against the British Government, but his rising was repressed by Sir Henry Lawrence, the conciliator of the Punjab, who became Chief Commissioner in March, 1857. He announced that the terms of the Proclamation of 1856 would be adhered to; that those at that time in actual possession of estates and property should remain in possession for the three years originally notified, and that all classes, chiefs as well as peasants, should have justice secured to them, and be protected and assured in the enjoyment of their rights. By these declarations, Lawrence temporarily allayed the agitation which prevailed.

Death of the Peshwa Baji Rao.

The Peshwa Baji Rao died, but his pension was not continued to his adopted son, Dhundhu Pant, also called Nana Sahib, who was, however, allowed to succeed to the Peshwa's private property. The Nana thought himself ill-used, and his disloyalty was fanned by an "England-returned" Mahomedan named Azimullah. He affected, however, to be friendly to the English.

Renewal of the East India Company's Charter, 1853. Lieutenant-Governor of Bengal appointed, 1854.

In 1854 a separate Lieutenant-Governor, Sir Frederick Halliday, was appointed for Bengal. Lieutenant-Governors were appointed for the Panjab in 1859, and for Burma in 1897. It was arranged at the same time that the Civil Service of India should be recruited by competition instead of nomination.

Administrative improvements.

Under Dalhousie, railways (the E.I.R. from Calcutta to Raneeganj, and in the Bombay Presidency the line, about 87 miles long, from Bombay to a point beyond Kalyan, and the Madras Railway from Madras to Arcot) and the Ganges (1854) and Bari Doab Irrigation Canals were opened, metalled roads laid down, and telegraphs and the half-anna postage were first introduced.

Educational measures.

A despatch on Education in 1854 from Sir Charles Wood, who held the office of President of the Board of Control, constituted a Department of Public Instruction in India. An attempt was first made to spread the benefit of education by means of the Indian vernaculars, and to minimise the cost to Government of schools by a system of grants-in-aid supplemented by local subscriptions.

CHAPTER VII.

INDIAN MUTINY. ESTABLISHMENT OF THE QUEEN'S GOVERNMENT IN INDIA AND THE VICEROYALTY.

Lord Canning, 1856-61.

LORD DALHOUSIE was succeeded as Governor-General by Lord Canning, 1856-61.

War in Persia, 1856-57.

The war with Persia was caused by the aggression of the Persians upon Northern Afghanistan and Herat. An English expedition was landed at Mohammerah on the shores of the Persian Gulf, and a peace was made by which the Persians agreed to give up all interference in Afghanistan. This attack upon a Mahomedan country was a cause of disaffection among the Indian Mahomedans.

The Indian Mutiny, 1857-58.

The Indian Mutiny, 1857-58. Causes:

1. Laxity of discipline among the Sepoys, and the sense of power engendered among them by their superiority in numbers to the British troops. The British army in India was at this time largely reduced in numbers owing to the Crimean War. There were 45,322 white troops to 233,000 Indian troops.

2. Rumours of defeats suffered by England in the Crimean War.

3. The majority of Sepoys in the Bengal army

were Brahmins; this similarity of caste facilitated combination among the mutinous Hindu regiments.

4. Disaffection among the Sepoys owing to their having to serve in distant and uncongenial countries, such as Afghanistan and Burma. To reach Burma they had to cross the sea, which is for Brahmins contrary to caste. Enlistment for "general service" and the enforcement of the obligation upon the troops to go anywhere they were sent, were very unpopular.

5. Distrust of the intentions of the English Government, and the belief that they wished to annex all the Native States. A large number of the Sepoys in the Bengal army came from Oudh, and their position was in many ways injuriously affected by the annexation. Before the annexation the Sepoys enjoyed priority for their cases in Oudh Law Courts, and could always appeal for the Resident's assistance. They had now lost all these privileges.

6. Dread of forcible conversion to Christianity, a belief which was furthered by the issue of the cartridges for the new Enfield rifle, which were greased with pig's lard. The interference with native customs shown in the laws authorising widow re-marriage, and exempting converts from Hinduism from the forfeiture of property imposed by Hindu law, accentuated this dread.

7. The attraction of a great number of officers away from their regiments to civil employ in Non-Regulation Provinces, and to various Staff appointments, deprived the native troops of their best officers.

8. The policy of centralisation compelled commanding officers of native regiments to refer questions to army headquarters for orders, instead of settling them

themselves by the despotic authority they formerly possessed.

Both these last two causes materially prejudiced discipline.

The Sikhs of the Panjab and the Goorkhas rendered most valuable aid at the siege of Delhi. The Madras and Bombay armies remained faithful. The Mutiny was essentially a military movement, and, except in Oudh, received no support from the people, nor, with very few exceptions, from the native princes or higher classes. The Mutiny broke out at Meerut on the 10th May, 1857, and spread rapidly to Delhi, Lucknow, Bareilly, Aligarh, Cawnpur, and other places. It was fortunate for the English that the self-assertion of the Moghal party and the proclamation of the restoration of the Delhi empire prevented the Mahrattas and Rajputs from participating in the rebellion, as they foresaw no advantage to themselves in upsetting the British rule merely to restore the Mahomedans to power. The English formed the siege of Delhi on the 8th of June, and captured it on the 14th of September. Major-General John Nicholson, whose administration of the districts of Bannu and Peshawar caused him to be venerated on the frontier as a demigod ("Nikolseyn"), was in command of the assaulting troops, but was mortally wounded during the attack. This success was mainly owing to the energy of Sir John Lawrence, Lieutenant-Governor of the Panjab, in disarming the native regiments suspected of mutinous tendencies, and in forwarding fresh troops and military supplies to Delhi. The garrison of Cawnpur, under Sir Hugh Wheeler, after standing a siege for twenty days, surrendered to

Self-assertion of the Moghal party.

THE RESIDENCY, LUCKNOW, FROM THE GARRISON CEMETERY.

Nana Sahib. The English were treacherously fired on as they were entering the boats which were to convey them down the Ganges to Allahabad, and the women and children who survived were massacred the day before Havelock's army arrived at Cawnpur.

Sir Henry Lawrence, Chief Commissioner of Oudh, defended the Residency of Lucknow for three months, till the arrival of Havelock and Outram in September, 1857. The relieving force was, however, shut up with the garrison till finally relieved by Sir Colin Campbell in November, 1857. Sir Colin evacuated Lucknow, and the city was not finally taken till March, 1858. It was not till the end of 1858 that the Mutiny was suppressed in Oudh, as the Talukdars, whose proprietary rights, with some few exceptions, had been confiscated by Lord Canning's proclamation of May, 1858, fought desperately.

A Bombay army under Sir Hugh Rose was engaged in the hot weather of 1858 in Central India, against the Rani of Jhansi and Tantia Topi (a Mahratta Brahman). Jhansi had been annexed on the failure of an heir, and the Rani had been harshly treated in having to pay the debts of the late Raja out of her pension. The chief events were the defeat of Tantia Topi's army, which was attempting to relieve Jhansi, on the Betwa, 1st April; the storming of Jhansi, 3rd April; and the storming of Tantia Topi's entrenchments at Gwalior in June, 1858.

Measures of reform on the Queen's assumption of the direct government of India.

In 1858 the "Act for the better Government of India" was passed, which transferred the authority of the East India Company to the Queen. The Queen's authority was to be exercised through a Secretary of State, who was to be assisted by a Council of fifteen members, eight appointed by the Crown and seven elected by the Directors of the East India Company. The Secretary of State can send secret orders to India without consent of his Council, as he inherits the powers of the Secret Committee of Directors, but he cannot sanction expenditure without their consent.

The Queen's assumption of the government of India was notified by a proclamation issued at Lord Canning's Durbar, held at Allahabad, 1st November, 1858. By this proclamation the Queen confirmed all existing dignities, rights, usages, and treaties, declared that no one should be considered debarred from office by reason of his religion or colour, and recognised adoption by the Native Princes, on failure of direct heirs, as conferring upon the adopted heir the right of succession. Lord Canning became the first Viceroy of India.

Lord Canning first Viceroy of India.

THE RESIDENCY, LUCKNOW.

Queen's proclamation.

Mr. James Wilson was brought from England to reorganise the finances of India after the Mutiny.

Mr. James Wilson, Financial Member of Council.

He imposed the Income Tax, 1860, and established the Paper Currency.

Legal reforms.

The Indian Penal Code became law in 1860, and the Codes of Civil and Criminal Procedure in 1861. The Supreme Court and Sadr Diwani Adalat were abolished and replaced by the Calcutta High Court. Non-official members were added to the Viceroy's Council and to the Councils of Madras and Bombay, to which the legislative powers taken away by the Charter Act of 1833 were restored in 1861. A similar Council was established for Bengal in 1862. Additional members might also be nominated for legislation only.

Indian Councils Act, 1861.

Foundation of Indian Universities, 1859.

The Universities of Calcutta, Bombay, and Madras, which were intended to further the advancement of learning, and to mark the possession of proficiency in its various branches by the grant of degrees to all persons found qualified, were founded in the year 1859.

Amalgamation of the East India Company's and Royal Army.

The services of the European troops of the Company's army were transferred to the Queen by Act of Parliament. The officers resented this being done without their consent, and the fierce discontent caused by this measure is sometimes known as the "White Mutiny."

Famine in the United Provinces of Agra and Oudh.

In 1860-61 there was a very severe famine in the United Provinces, and Colonel Baird-Smith pointed out the urgent necessity of good means of communication for the movement of grain. He thus described the economic effect of the want of roads: "So miserable are the means of intercommunication in most of the districts of supply that while in one bazaar famine prices of four rupees per maund might be ruling, in another, not thirty miles off, the price would be but one and a half rupee for the same quantity, yet no flow from the full to the exhausted market could take place, because roads were not in existence, and means of carriage were unknown." This famine may be considered the last which was caused by an actual want of grain.

Policy of the British Government towards the Native States of India.

The express abandonment of Lord Dalhousie's Annexation Policy by the Queen's proclamation of 1858 affords an appropriate opportunity for reviewing the policy pursued by the British Government towards the Native States in India at various epochs in Indian history.

When the British first became a great power in India they kept their territories as far as possible within a ring fence, and pursued a policy of non-interference with the States beyond their borders. This policy was interrupted by the system of subsidiary alliances originated by Lord Wellesley, but non-interference was undoubtedly the favourite system of those who preferred the improvement of trade to the extension of the British power in India.

The treaties of this period were concluded as if between independent nations.

The parties to the—

Treaty of Allahabad, 16th August, 1766,

Treaty of Alliance with the Peshwa and Nizam against Tipu, 1st July, 1790,

Treaty of Bassein, 31st December, 1802,

Treaty of Lahore, 25th April, 1809,

were in a position of equality.

When the British Government was approaching the position of supreme power in India, it no longer treated the Native States on the terms of equality: they were restricted in making war and alliances, and compelled to exclude from their service British subjects, and subjects of States at war with the British Government. This may be called the period of Subordinate Isolation, and the treaties of 1831 and 1837 with the King of Oudh are illustrations of this policy. The Queen's Proclamation of 1858 marks the commencement of the present policy of subordinate alliance, union, and co-operation between the British Government and the Native States. When the British Government was no longer checked by a policy of non-interference from preventing misgovernment in the Native States, it was no longer necessary to resort to annexation in the last resort, and so the proclamation permitted the Native princes freely to adopt sons on the failure of direct heirs. In the event of misgovernment the offender is removed, and the State held in trust till he can be replaced by a better governor. The Native princes are recognised, in Lord Curzon's words, as "colleagues and partners in the task of administration." It has been understood that "it is better patiently to train an Indian prince than to set him aside, and do the work efficiently in his stead."

The last of the Moghal Emperors.

Shah Alam II. died in 1806. Muinuddin, son of Shah Alam II., enjoyed nominal power as Akbar II., 1806-37.

Surajuddin (Mahomed Bahadur Shah II.), was proclaimed Emperor of Delhi during the Indian Mutiny, and died in exile in Rangoon in 1862. He was the last of the Moghal emperors.

CHAPTER VIII.

LATER HISTORY.

Lord Elgin was appointed as Lord Canning's successor. He arrived in India 1862, but died at Dharamsala soon after his arrival, November, 1863. Lord Elgin, 1862-63.

The most important event during his brief tenure of office was the war with the Wahabi fanatics of Sitana, at Umbeyla, on the North-West Frontier, 1863.

Sir John Lawrence.

Lord Elgin was succeeded in 1864 by Sir John Lawrence, 1864-69. Sir John Lawrence, 1864-69.

The insults offered to the British envoy, Mr. Ashley Eden, led to the Bhutan War, and to the annexation of a tract called the Bhutan Dooars, from the river Teesta to the Jaldaka. This tract became a portion of the Jalpaiguri district, and is largely used for growing tea. Bhutan War.

Lord Lawrence was the principal exponent of the policy of "Masterly Inactivity" as a means of Masterly Inactivity.

defence against Russian attack upon India. He considered that the Government of India should hold itself strictly aloof from political complications beyond its own border, and remain quiet behind its Himalayan defences, trusting to difficulties of distance from his base of operations, of transit and of the inclemencies of the climate, to exhaust the enemy's strength. It should reserve all its strength to attack the enemy when they have struggled through the Himalayan defiles. Following Lord Lawrence's example, the Panjab Government long contented itself with maintaining its own frontier intact, and leaving the tribes beyond it severely alone, unless they raided British territory too much, when punitive expeditions were undertaken against them.

The Forward Policy of Frontier Politics.

The Forward Policy was first formally enunciated by Lord Lytton's Government in 1879, which laid it down that "we shall consider it from the first incumbent upon the Government to prevent at any cost, within this outlying country, the political predominance of any other power." It was determined to acquire "through the ruler of Kashmir the power of making such political and military arrangements as will effectually close the passes of the Hindu Kush. If we extend, and by degrees, consolidate our influence over the country, and if we resolve that no foreign interference can be permitted on this side of the mountains, or within the drainage system of the Indus, we shall have laid down a natural line of frontier which is distinct, intelligible and likely to be respected." Such a policy was necessitated by the near approach of Russia within striking distance of India, and by the fact that her boundaries are conterminous with those of Afghanistan, for the integrity of which England has become responsible. The great champions of the Forward Policy were Sir Robert Sandeman, the originator of "Spheres of influence" in Beluchistan and Khelat, and Lord Roberts.

Lord Mayo.

Results of the Forward Policy.

The embassies of Sir John Malcolm to Persia and Sir Mountstuart Elphinstone to Afghanistan, the Afghan Wars, the Gilgit, Hunza and Nagar expeditions, and the Durand and Dane embassies, all resulted from this Forward Policy.

The Orissa famine, 1866-67.

The Orissa officials had no experience of famines, and they were consequently unable to recognise the signs of the times and to prepare for the coming scarcity caused by the failure of the rains of 1865. The isolated position of the province, to which there were then no railways, and the coast of which was harbourless and unapproachable on account of the Monsoon, made the importation of food difficult. To these causes the immense loss of life, which in the Orissa famine amounted to about a quarter of the population, or one million people, was due.

Lord Mayo, 1869-72.

Sir John Lawrence's viceroyalty was followed by that of Lord Mayo. Lord Mayo's scheme for the

Decentralisation of the Finances.

Decentralisation of the Finances had for its object the enlargement of the powers and responsibility of the Local Governments in respect to the public expenditure in some of the civil departments. Certain grants were made and certain departments, such as Police, Education, Jails, Roads and Civil Buildings, were made over by the Provincial Contract system which was fixed for five years to be administered by the Local Governments, which would gain by any economy in administration they were able to introduce. In 1877 certain heads of income and expenditure were made over to Local Government to be subject to their exclusive control. In this year the Internal Customs Line was abolished.

Durbar at Umballa, March, 1869.

Lord Mayo held a Durbar at Umballa, in which he recognised Sher Ali, youngest son of Dost Mahomed, who had conquered his brothers Afzal Khan and Azim Khan, as Amir of Afghanistan.

Lord Northbrook, 1872-76.

Lord Mayo was murdered at the Andamans on the 8th February, 1872, and was succeeded by the Earl of Northbrook, 1872-76.

Behar famine. Assam a separate province. Visit of the Prince of Wales to India. Other Royal visits.

The chief events of Lord Northbrook's viceroyalty were the famine of 1873-74, in Behar; the formation of Assam into a separate province, under a Chief Commissioner, 1874; the dethronement of Mulhar Rao, Gaekwar of Baroda, for attempting to poison the Resident, Colonel Phayre; and the visit of the Prince of Wales to India in the cold weather of 1875-76. The precedent thus set has been happily followed by the visit to India of the Prince's son and his wife exactly thirty years after, in the cold weather of 1905-06. His Majesty George V., accompanied by his Queen, again visited India in the cold weather of

1911-12. It is an absolutely unprecedented occurrence for the reigning monarch of England to visit India. It is to be hoped that this happy event will bring about the many beneficial consequences anticipated from it.

Lord Lytton, 1876-80. The Queen proclaimed Empress of India.

Lord Lytton succeeded Lord Northbrook in 1876. Lord Lytton held a Durbar at Delhi on the 1st January, 1877, at which the Queen was proclaimed Empress of India.

Southern India famine.

Second Afghan War, 1878-80.

Lord Lytton's viceroyalty was chiefly remarkable for the famine in Southern India, 1876-77, in which the mortality was over five million lives, and the Second Afghan War, 1878-80. The Amir Sher Ali ordered the English envoy, Sir Neville Chamberlain, to be refused permission to pass by the fort of Ali Masjid in the Khyber Pass, but he received the Russian envoy, General Stolietoff, at Kabul with all honour.

QUEEN VICTORIA.

Yakub Khan, Amir of Afghanistan.

Treaty of Gundamuk, 1879.

Lord Lytton declared war, and three armies advanced on Kabul through the Khyber, the Kuram, and the Bolan Passes. Sher Ali fled to Turkistan, and died there. His son, Yakub Khan, was recognised as Amir, and concluded the Treaty of Gundamuk, by which he agreed to receive a British Resident in Kabul, and to cede to the English the

Kuram and Pishin valleys. In addition to the annexation of these districts, the Khan of Khelat was declared under British protection, and the province of British Beluchistan was thus formed.

British Beluchistan.

Sir Louis Cavagnari was appointed Resident in Kabul, but he and his escort were massacred in a sudden rising. The war broke out again, and Lord Roberts gained the victory of Charasiab outside Kabul on the 6th October, and made his formal entry into the Bala Hissar on the 12th, but was besieged in the Sherpur cantonments by the Afghans, December, 1879. Yakub Khan was subsequently deported to India. In 1880, a British force was defeated at Maiwand, near Kusk-i-Nakkud, 27th July, by Ayub Khan, brother of Yakub Khan; but Lord Roberts made his famous march of 313 miles from Kabul to Kandahar in twenty-two days, and defeated Ayub Khan outside Kandahar, 1st September. In 1880, on the return of a Liberal Ministry under Mr. Gladstone to power, Lord Lytton resigned. He was succeeded by Lord Ripon, 1880-84. Lord Ripon acknowledged Abdur Rahman Khan, son of Afzal Khan (second son of Dost Mahomed), as Amir of Afghanistan, and withdrew all the British troops from the country. England's gains may be thus summed up: she replaced Afghanistan as the dominant power in the Khyber pass, the Kuram valley was annexed, and Quetta, with the districts of Pishin and Sibi, were ceded by the Khan of Khelat. Ten years afterwards the annexation of the Zhob valley followed. Abdur Rahman reigned undisturbed till October, 1901, when he died, and was peacefully succeeded by his son Habibullah.

Lord Ripon, 1880-84.

Abdur Rahman.

England's territorial gains from the Afghan War.

Lord Ripon in 1882 repealed the Vernacular Press Act passed by his predecessor, which placed the native vernacular press under the control of a Press Commissioner.

Repeal of the Vernacular Press Act, 1882.

In 1884 Lord Ripon's government abolished the Import Duties, excepting those on salt and liquors, and thereby gave an especial impetus to the Manchester trade in cotton goods in India.

Abolition of the Import Duties, 1884.

LORD RIPON.

Lord Ripon's Education Commission enquired into the question how far the education policy of the Government of India was in accordance with Sir Charles Wood's despatch of 1854.

Education Commission.

The Criminal Procedure Amendment Act, 1884 (or Ilbert Bill, so called from the Legal Member who introduced it), proposed to give Indian Magistrates who belonged to the Indian Civil Service, jurisdiction over Europeans in the Mofussil. The bill excited furious opposition, and a compromise was arrived at by which Europeans could in all cases claim to be tried by a jury with a majority of Europeans.

Ilbert Bill, 1884.

The Local Self-Government Act relieved the district magistrates of much of the burden of district administration, and constituted District Boards, partly elected and partly nominated, to undertake the administration of the Road Cess, Primary

Local Self-Government Act, 1885.

and Middle schools, Sanitation, Dispensaries and Vaccination.

Lord Dufferin Viceroy, 1884-88.

Lord Ripon was succeeded as Viceroy by Lord Dufferin, 1884-88. When Lord Dufferin assumed office, war seemed imminent between Russia and Afghanistan, and England as the ally of Afghanistan.

Russian complications. Frontier Commission.

A Boundary Commission was appointed of Russian and English officers, to delimitate the boundary between Russia and Afghanistan. In 1873 the Oxus was agreed on by England and Russia as the boundary between Russia in Asia and Afghanistan, but a dispute arose whether the Aksu, which is the northern, or the Panja, which is the southern branch of the Oxus, was meant. Whilst the Commission was engaged in its labours the attack by the Russians upon the Afghans at Penjdeh nearly precipitated war, but the Frontier Commission persevered, and the ratification of the frontier which they laid down is an important step towards the prevention of future misunderstandings. Lord Dufferin's reception of the Amir Abdur Rahman in Durbar at Rawalpindi proclaimed to the world the fact that England had guaranteed the frontier of Afghanistan against external aggression.

LORD DUFFERIN.

The Penjdeh incident.

The Rawalpindi Durbar, 1885.

Increase of the army in India.

After the alarm of war with Russia in 1885, the army in India was increased by 10,000 British and 20,000 native troops. The expenses thus caused necessitated a revival of the Income Tax, first imposed in 1869. In 1885 Lord Dufferin took a step which had an important influence in confirming the loyalty of the native princes. He restored to Scindia the fortress of Gwalior, which had been held by British troops since the Mutiny.

Annexation of Upper Burma.

Theebaw, king of Burma, was believed to be intriguing with the French, and no redress could be obtained for his oppression of British merchants. After this, when he, without any reason, declared the property of the Bombay-Burma Trading Corporation forfeited, war was declared. General Prendergast occupied Mandalay; Theebaw and his queen, Supaylat, were deported to Ratnagiri in the Bombay Presidency, and Upper Burma was annexed by proclamation, January, 1887. The Chief Commissionership of Burma was raised to a Lieutenant-Governorship in 1897.

Indian National Congress.

The first Indian National Congress was held at Bombay in 1885. Its object was to bring before the notice of Government, in a constitutional manner, the wishes and feelings of the educated classes. The increased measure of self-government allowed by the Morley Reforms is largely the work of the Congress.

Queen's Jubilee, 1887.

The Queen's Jubilee, or the fiftieth anniversary of her accession to the throne, was celebrated in 1887. Her Diamond Jubilee followed in 1897.

Lord Lansdowne Viceroy, 1888-93.

Lord Dufferin was succeeded as Viceroy by Lord Lansdowne, 1888-93.

Thibetan complications.

The Bengal Government had long been anxious to open up trade with Thibet, and in 1886 an expedition under Mr. Colman Macaulay, Secretary to the Bengal Government, was about to start to Lhasa on a mixed political and scientific mission. This was abandoned out of deference to Chinese susceptibilities, and to secure Chinese co-operation in Burma.

Lord Lansdowne.

The Thibetans invaded Sikkim and fortified a post at Lingtu, commanding the trade route through the Jeylap Pass, and the Sikkim Raja permanently absented himself from Sikkim and betook himself to the Chumbi Valley in Thibet.

On the 24th September, 1888, the Thibetans were severely defeated at Gnatong, and pursued as far as Rinchingong in the Chumbi Valley. The Anglo-Chinese Treaty of 1890 recognised the British protectorate over Sikkim, and a British Political Agent has since then been Resident at Guntak. A trading mart was established at Yatung on the Thibetan frontier.

Manipur taken under British management.

In 1892 the Raja of Manipur murdered the Chief Commissioner of Assam and his party. He was dethroned and deported to the Andamans, and the country was taken under British management till the minor Raja, who was appointed from a collateral branch of the reigning family, should attain his majority.

In this year a Commission enquired into the administration of the Government Opium Department. In deference to pressure exerted in Parliament, and conditionally upon the adoption of a similar policy in China, the Government of India has agreed to limit the cultivation of the opium poppy, and to reduce and gradually put an end to the production of opium in India for the Chinese market.

Opium Commission, 1893.

Lord Lansdowne's viceroyalty was the period of the first application of the "Sphere of Influence" policy to the tribes on the North-West Frontier, beyond the British frontier. This merely meant that the British Government claimed to control their foreign relations, without any right to interfere with their internal concerns, and to exercise at all times the right of free access through their territories. In 1893 Sir Mortimer Durand, the Foreign Secretary, was sent on a mission to the Amir, Abdur Rahman, to settle which of the tribes in the "No man's land," between British and Afghan territories, should come under Afghan and which under British influence.

"Spheres of Influence."

In 1892 the number of non-official members in the Imperial and Provincial Legislative Councils was increased, and the Universities and other public bodies were allowed to nominate members. The Councils were allowed to discuss the Imperial and Provincial Budgets, but no resolutions might be moved or divisions taken. Questions were permitted to be asked by the members on subjects of general public interest. This was the first

Re-constitution of the Legislative Councils.

recognition of the elective principle in the Indian Government.

Age of Consent Bill.

Lord Lansdowne's Government incurred some unpopularity by interference with the Hindu custom of infant marriage, and by raising the age at which Hindu girls could be legally married.

Anti-Cow-killing agitation.

The latter part of Lord Lansdowne's administration was marked by Hindu riots to prevent the killing of cows by Mahomedans and Europeans. These riots were promoted by associations called Gorakshini Sabhas, and were manifestations of the general feeling of unrest prevalent in the country.

Imperial Service Corps.

The question of the armies of the Native States came up for consideration in Lord Lansdowne's time. It was resolved to reduce their numbers, but to make those who were kept really good soldiers fit to take their place in line with British troops. They were to be called the Imperial Service Corps.

Currency. Closing of the Mints to Free Coinage.

In 1893, in consequence of the fall in the exchange value of silver, the purchasing power of the rupee with reference to gold declined, and Lord Lansdowne's Government closed the Indian Mints to the free coinage of silver. The object of this was that, when no new coins could be minted, those already in existence should acquire an additional value, as they grew less in number, over and above their metallic value as silver. In 1899 English sovereigns were made legal tender in India at the rate of one sovereign for fifteen rupees.

Lord Elgin, 1893-98.

Lord Lansdowne was succeeded by Lord Elgin, 1893-98.

The Chitral Expedition of 1895.

Chitral is a State to the north-east of Kashmir, which commands the passes of the Hindu Kush mountain range, and the establishment of a British

Agency there was part of the policy of extending British political influence beyond the actual limits of the frontier. In March, 1895, the British Agent was besieged in the fort of Chitral by one of the claimants to the Mehtarship, or chief authority in Chitral, and his ally, Umra Khan, chief of Jandul. On the 3rd April, Sir Robert Lowe's force, advancing from Peshawar, forced the Malakand Pass and the passages of the Swat and Panjkora rivers. Meanwhile Colonel Kelly, advancing from Gilgit and overcoming the greatest physical difficulties in the mountain defiles, succeeded in relieving Chitral, which was permanently occupied by troops, and a road made to it from Peshawar.

LORD ELGIN.

Pamir Delimitation.

The final step in the delimitation of the Russo-Afghan frontier was taken, the boundary was laid down in the region of the Pamirs to the north-east of Afghanistan, and the Afghans agreed to retire to the south bank of the Panja branch of the Oxus, which was fixed as the frontier. In 1896 the boundary between Afghanistan and Persia was delimited. By the Anglo-Russian Convention of 1907 Russia recognised Afghanistan as outside its sphere of political influence.

War on the North-West Frontier, and the Tirah Expedition, 18

The war on the North-West Frontier, in which the British Government was opposed by a most formidable combination of border tribes, was undoubtedly the result of the Forward Policy, and of the Durand Agreement of 1893, which aimed at marking out clearly the spheres of influence of the Amir and the British Government respectively. The tribes, through whose territory the road from Peshawar to Chitral runs, believed that the British Government had treacherously broken their promise not to permanently occupy the country. The attack by the Waziris upon the British force in the Tochi valley was the signal for hostilities, and the attack on the Malakand garrison by the tribesmen of Swat and Buner followed. The next incident was the attack by the Afridis on the Khyber Pass, and that of the Orakzais on the British forts on the Samana range.

It was resolved to punish the Afridis for their attack on the Khyber Pass by an expedition to "lift the purdah of Tirah," that is, to penetrate to the Afridi headquarters to the north-west of Peshawar on the Tirah plateau, which had remained before unvisited by any European foe. The expedition penetrated to Bagh, the centre of Afridi intrigue, and returned down the Bara and Mastura valleys to Peshawar.

Re-imposition of import duties.

An import duty of 5 per cent. was imposed on all articles, except cotton, in March, 1894, and in December, 1894, cotton fabrics and yarns were included, but a countervailing excise duty was placed upon the products of Indian mills which could compete with those of Lancashire. In connection with this

"Mandate" Theory.

legislation, Lord Elgin broached the "Mandate"

theory that the Viceroy and the members of his Council must obey the decision of the Secretary of State or resign. The cotton import duty and the corresponding excise duty were reduced in 1896 to $3\frac{1}{2}$ per cent. This excise duty was levied on all the cotton products of Indian mills, whether competing with those of Lancashire or not.

The famine of 1897.

The other important events of Lord Elgin's viceroyalty were the famine in Behar, Central Bengal, the North-West Provinces, the Southern Panjab, Rajputana, the Central Provinces, Berar, and the Deccan districts belonging to both the Madras and Bombay Presidencies; and the appearance of plague in India.

LORD CURZON.

The Plague.

The Plague is believed to have been imported into India from Hong-Kong, and first appeared in India at Bombay in September, 1896. It caused a great loss of life in Western India, Mysore and the Panjab, but, though it appeared in Calcutta in 1899, it fortunately has been less virulent in Bengal than in Western India.

Lord Curzon, 1898.

Frontier policy.

Lord Curzon succeeded Lord Elgin in 1898. He made an entirely new departure in frontier policy by withdrawing British troops from the isolated frontier posts, and replacing them by tribal levies. He formed the North-West Frontier, including the four Trans-Indus districts of Peshawar, Kohat, Bannu, and Dera Ismail Khan, with the tribal territory beyond their limits, and the six Political Agencies of Dir, Swat, Chitral, the Khyber, the Tochi Valley, and Wano, into a province by itself, separate from the Panjab Administration, and directly subordinate to the Government of India. The object of this policy was to bring the frontier and the tribes in the British sphere of influence beyond it more directly under the supervision of the Supreme Government.

The famine of 1900-1901.

The famine that Lord Curzon had to face was the worst in Indian history. Never before had one famine followed another in so short a time as two years. The maximum of persons ever likely to be in receipt of famine relief at one time was estimated by the Famine Commission of 1878 at four and a half millions, but in July, 1900, there were six million persons famine-stricken. The Central Provinces, Bombay, Deccan, Berar, Rajputana, and the Southern Panjab were stricken with famine for the second time in two years, and the fertile district of Gujrat was affected for the first time in the memory of man.

Indian Famines.

The first notice of a famine in India is found in the Jatakas:[1] "Now at this time there was a drought in the kingdom of Kalinga, the corn grew not and there was a great famine, and men, being unable to live, used robbery." Again, in 1289, there was a terrible famine in Northern India, of which a contemporary chronicler speaks thus: "In the Siwalik hills, the dearth was greatly felt. The Hindus of that country came into Delhi with their

[1] Jatakas XXII., Number 347.

families twenty or thirty of them together, and drowned themselves in the Ganges." Up to 1853, famines were caused by the actual want of grain; after 1853, there has always been grain in some part of India, but the high prices caused by the difficulty of transporting it to where the crops had failed have caused famines. Before 1853 the famines were grain famines; in modern times the famines may be more properly described as caused by want of money to defray high prices.

In addition to the famines mentioned, the following are worthy of notice:

1781-82. Famine was rife near Madras owing to the Mysore War.

1783. The famine of Sambat, 1840, hence called *chalisa*, affected an area from the Karumnasa to the Sutlej.

1790-92. A famine occurred in the Southern Mahratta country called the Doji Bara or Skull Famine.

1803-04. There was famine in the United Provinces which was brought about by the Second Mahratta War.

1837-38. There was famine in the United Provinces and the Panjab. When grain at Agra was selling at 11 seers to the rupee, it was selling in the adjoining province of Malwa at from 50 to 60 seers to the rupee, thus illustrating the difficulty in the time of famine caused by the want of transport facilities.

Lord Curzon's policy.

Lord Curzon took a new departure in famine policy, by not requiring every irrigation enterprise, which is undertaken as an insurance against famine, always to return a profit to Government, and by allowing that there may be protective irrigation as well as protective railways.

Railways, however, have not been neglected. During the five years, 1899-1903, 4,916 miles of line were constructed, as compared with 3,536 miles under Lord Elgin and 3,928 miles under Lord Lansdowne. The total number of miles open in 1905 was 27,577.

Member of Council for Commerce and Industry.

Lord Curzon showed his interest in commerce and industry by creating a special department, under a Member of Council, to deal with them.

Restrictions placed upon the alienation of land.

In connection with the protective measures taken against famine, it is important to ensure that the land should remain in the hands of those who are able to make the best use of it. This consideration led Lord Curzon's Government to place restrictions on the power of the peasantry of the Deccan and the Panjab to alienate their lands for debt.

Incidence of the Land Revenue.

The theory of the land revenue is that, taking one year with another, it should not be excessive, and that the profits of a good year should make up for any losses caused by the deficiency of the crops in a bad year. It is not a tax, but a share in the Rent due to the State as supreme landlord. The question, whether the burden of the land revenue is heavier than it should be, is naturally important in connection with famines. In 1902 the Government of India issued a detailed Resolution showing that in provinces where the revenue is received direct from the landlords the limit of 50 per cent. of their net receipts is uniformly observed, the only exception being the Central

Resolution of the Government of India on the moderation of the Land Revenue.

Provinces, the revenue of which is between 50 and 75 per cent. of the rental, and that, in rayatwari provinces, the State is actually taking less than one-fifth of the gross produce. It is not proved that the areas most highly assessed to the land tax have suffered most from famine. Under Akbar the proportion of the gross produce of the land taken as revenue was 33 per cent., under the Mahrattas never less than 50 per cent., under the old native rulers of Bengal 54 per cent., and under the Sikhs in the Panjab 40 to 50 per cent. These amounts were, however, levied in kind, and if the cultivator suffered from unfavourable seasons, or had his crops devastated by a foreign enemy, the Government suffered with him. Whatever happened the cultivator had usually enough to live on and enough grain for sowing in the next season. The British Government takes a much smaller amount, not more than from 3 to 8 per cent. of the gross produce on the average. In the fertile tracts of the Panjab the assessment amounts to 17 per cent., in Gujrat—the garden of India—to 20 per cent. These amounts are, however, fixed in advance and must be paid in cash, be the season bad or good. The theory of the British Land Revenue system is that the profits of good years should reimburse the losses of bad. Practically, these profits are seldom or never saved by the cultivator, but are always swallowed up by the money-lender, to whom the cultivator must always have recourse for cash to pay his land revenue assessment. In order to make the system of land revenue collection more elastic, suspensions and remissions of land revenue are sometimes given, when a cause like famine prevents the revenue being paid, and in tracts, where the cultivation is insecure, the assessment is sometimes allowed to fluctuate with the crop. The revenue collection is, as far as possible, adjusted in accordance with the variations in the circumstances of the people, and in cases of local deterioration from causes like continual malarial fever or earthquake, the assessments are sometimes reduced.

Certain improvements in the method of levying the land tax have been made. Agricultural improvements affected by the rayats' own capital are not assessed, and prospective assets are no longer taken into consideration. Large enhancements, which are often the necessary result of long-term settlements, are imposed according to a progressive and graduated scale. A system of Co-operative Banks has been established, which borrow money on the joint and several security of their members. By their means it is hoped to reduce the power of the money-lenders.

Co-operative Banks.

Death of Queen Victoria.

Queen Victoria died amidst the lamentations of her subjects on the 22nd January, 1901, and was succeeded by the Prince of Wales as Edward the Seventh.

The Boer War.

The Boer War in South Africa broke out in 1899, and India played an important part in it by sending some thousands of British troops who could be spared from India, and who gave most material aid in the defence of Natal.

Expedition to China, 1900.

In the next year, during the Boxer rising in China, a force mostly consisting of Indian Native troops was sent from India, and took part in the relief of the Legations besieged in Pekin.

Education.

Education occupied a prominent place among the subjects which Lord Curzon took in hand during his viceroyalty. His educational policy was summarised in the Resolution of the Government of India, 11th March, 1904. The most important changes introduced were the abolition of primary examinations, and the substitution of general efficiency for payment by results, as the standard by which primary schools are in future to be estimated. Vernacular education, both primary and secondary, has been reformed on modern lines, by the introduction of an adaptation of the Kindergarten system. Nature study and hand and eye training have been introduced, and "the science of common life" is practically taught.

The University Commission was appointed to consider how far the teaching, as distinct from the merely examining function of the Indian Universities, could be improved. The Commission reported that, owing to the gradual cheapening of University education, more persons had been induced to take advantage of it than were intellectually qualified to profit by their studies. The raising of the college fees, the discontinuance of the affiliation of colleges which do not teach the full graduate course, the introduction of a system of college inspection, and of more stringent affiliation rules for the future were therefore recommended. The number of members in each Senate was also to be diminished, so as to ensure that only those really interested in education were members. Lord Curzon found it expedient to limit the freedom formerly allowed to Local Governments in interpreting the orders of the Government of India on Education. A Director-General of Education was appointed to ensure that the Education

Policy of each Local Government should be animated "by community of principle and of aim." The Director-General has now been replaced by a Member of the Viceroy's Council in special charge of Education.

Effect of Education.

English education has, to a considerable extent, furthered the growth of a spirit of nationality in India, the bond of union being the common use of the English language. It has endowed the people of India with a sense of their own capabilities, and has impelled them, legitimately enough, to seek a larger share in the government of their own country. The product of the Indian schools and colleges is much larger than can be provided with appointments in Government service, and in the discontent of those left outside, is a very real political danger. It is unreasonable, however, to say that Government should not have educated these students, because it could not provide for them. It is in the additional employment to be provided by the increased development of the natural resources of the country that the remedy for this difficulty is to be found.

Police Commission.

The report of the Police Commission, which recommended a substantial increase in the pay and improvement in the prospects of all ranks, and the opening of a career in the police to natives of India by the institution of a new class of officers to be called deputy superintendents, has been adopted by Government.

Remission of taxation.

In 1903, for the first time for twenty years, the burden of taxation was lightened by the levying of the Salt Tax at Rs. 2 instead of Rs. 2.8 per maund, and the raising of the minimum annual income, exempted from Income Tax, from Rs. 500 to Rs. 1000.

Lord Curzon understood that one reason why famines bear so hardly upon the population is that agriculture is the one great industry in India. For this reason he welcomed the investment of capital in various sorts of non-agricultural enterprises, he improved the means of railway communication with the coal-mining centres, he subsidised the schemes for the application of modern science to the needs of the tea and indigo planters, he held the Delhi Durbar Exhibition of Indian Art, and he appointed a Member of Council for Commerce and Industry. **Trade.**

The consideration of Lord Curzon's Foreign Policy divides itself naturally into two heads, the policy of his Government towards foreign nations beyond the Indian borders, and his policy towards the independent and feudatory States of India. He checked the French attempt to obtain a coaling station at Muscat on the Persian Gulf. He made a judicious attempt to extend British influence and trade by carrying the Quetta railway as far as Nushki on the Beluchistan border, and protecting the caravan route from thence to Seistan. In the cold weather of 1903-04 Lord Curzon visited the Persian Gulf, escorted by an imposing naval force, in order to revive and strengthen the friendly disposition of the inhabitants of the territories bordering on the Gulf towards the English. **Foreign policy.**

The Thibetan expedition of 1904 was necessitated by the neglect of the Thibetans to carry out the obligations imposed upon them by the Treaty of 1890. The expedition dictated terms of peace in Lhasa, and, as a security for the performance of these terms, the Chumbi Valley remained in the occupation of **Thibetan Expedition of 1904.**

British troops till the indemnity was paid. This indemnity was subsequently paid by China, and the term of British occupation of the Chumbi Valley was thus materially reduced.

Delhi Durbar 1903.

Within India itself, the principal event was the Delhi Durbar of 1903, when the whole of India acknowledged "its loyalty to a common head, its membership of the same body politic, and its citizenship of the same Empire," which is the only bond of union for "its divisions of race, and class, and custom, and creed." The policy of confidence in the Native States, which led to the establishment of the Imperial Service Corps, was extended by Lord Curzon, who provided, in the Imperial Cadet Corps, a military career for high-born native youths. Other important events were the deposition of the Maharajah of Panna for misconduct, and the Berar Treaty with the Nizam. The old arrangement was that the surplus revenues of the Province, less the cost of administration, should be handed over to the Nizam. The Province is now to be permanently leased to the Indian Government in return for an annual payment of twenty-five lacs of rupees and a lump sum of forty-one lacs.

Imperial Cadet Corps.

Berar Treaty with the Nizam.

Extension of Lord Curzon's term of office for two years.

In 1904 the Home Government paid Lord Curzon the unique compliment of extending his term of office for two years, on the ground that "questions relating to railways, irrigation, famine administration, and police had all been investigated, and it seemed disadvantageous that the Viceroy, who had himself initiated these investigations, should quit office before they were dealt with."

In 1904 Lord Curzon returned to England on leave

for six months, and Lord Ampthill, Governor of Madras, officiated as Viceroy. On Lord Curzon's return to India, the most important topics with which he dealt were the Partition of Bengal, and the abolition of the Dual Control of the Indian Army, a question which was the eventual cause of his resignation.

The Partition of Bengal.

The Partition came into force on the 16th of October, 1904. By it the Bengal Commissioners' Divisions of Chittagong, Dacca, and Rajshahi (with the exception of Darjiling), the district of Maldah, and Assam, were formed into a new Province called "Eastern Bengal and Assam," of which Mr. J. B. Fuller, Chief Commissioner of Assam, was made the first Lieutenant-Governor. The district of Sambalpur, in the Central Provinces, on the ground that Oriya was the language used in it, was handed over to the old Province of Bengal, and incorporated with the Orissa Division. The reason that actuated the Government of India in making this change was that the old Province of Bengal was too large a charge to be efficiently administered by one Lieutenant-Governor.

Abolition of the Dual Control of the Indian army.

Lord Kitchener, the Commander-in-Chief, had protested against the system by which his proposals were criticised by the Military Member of Council. Lord Curzon and the whole of the Viceroy's Council, except Lord Kitchener, were in favour of the maintenance of the present system, but the Secretary of State overruled them in favour of the Commander-in-Chief.

A compromise was arranged, but Lord Curzon's recommendation for filling up the office of Military

Member was not accepted by the Secretary of State, and the new system seemed to unduly depreciate the position of that officer, and to deprive the Viceroy of the advantage of having a second military adviser to appeal to. Lord Curzon was therefore unable to accept the new arrangement, and resigned. He left India, after welcoming the Prince and Princess of Wales on their arrival at Bombay in November, 1905, and was succeeded as Viceroy by the Earl of Minto, late Viceroy and Governor-General of Canada.

BIBLIOGRAPHY.

C. R. Wilson, 'Early Records of the English in India.'

E. T. Oaten, 'European Travellers in India in the 15th, 16th, and 17th Centuries.'

Sir Alfred Lyall, 'British Dominion in India.'

Dr. Bousteed, 'Echoes of Old Calcutta.'

E. A. Cotton, 'Old Calcutta.'

Talboys Wheeler, 'Annals of Old Madras.'

Anderson, 'English in Western India.'

Mir Gholam Husain, 'Seir Mutaqherin.'

Wilks, 'History of Mysore.'

Sir Fitzjames Stephen, 'Nuncomar and Impey.'

Sir Fitzjames Stephen, 'The Rohilla War.'

Beveridge, 'Hastings and Nuncomar.'

Warren Hastings, 'Rulers of India.'

G. W. Forrest, 'State Papers of Warren Hastings.'

Cornwallis, 'Rulers of India.'

Cornwallis, 'Despatches.'

Todd, 'Rajasthan.'

'Annals of Mewar,' being selections from Todd's 'Rajasthan,' abridged and edited by C. H. Payne, M.A.

Dalhousie, 'Rulers of India.'

General Macleod Innes, 'Defence of Lucknow.'

APPENDIX.

DATES OF INDIAN HISTORY.

Empires and Dynasties.	Dates.	Chief Events.
	2800—2000 B.C.	Aryan settlement in Northern India.
	2000—1400 B.C.	Vedic Age.
	1400—1000 B.C.	Epic Age.
	1000—250 B.C.	Rationalistic Age.

Ancient Indian Dated History, 664 B.C. to 766 A.D.

Empires and Dynasties.	Dates.	Chief Events.
Saisunaga (Magadha), 664—371 B.C.	599—527	Vardhamana Mahavira, founder of Jainism.
	557—477	Gautama Buddha.
	515—509	Darius Hystaspes on the Indus.
Nanda (Magadha), 371—322	327—325	Alexander in India.
	326	Defeat of Paurava at the battle of the Jhelum.
Mauryan Empire, 322—184	322—297	Chandra Gupta Maurya (Sandracottos).
	305	War with Seleucus Nikator.
	291—273	Bindusara Amitraghata (Amitracrates).
	273—232	Asoka.
	257—242	Buddhist Edicts.
	256—	Greek kingdom of Bactria.
	208 B.C.–249 A.D.	Andhras (Satakarna or Satavahana dynasty) in the Deccan.
Sunga (Northern India), 184—72 B.C.		Pushyamitra's *asvamedha*.
		Brahmanic reaction against Buddhism.
	165—140	The Yuechi tribes break out of China and expel the Sakas who invade Bactria.

ANCIENT INDIAN DATED HISTORY, 664 B.C. TO 766 A.D —*Continued*

EMPIRES AND DYNASTIES.	DATES.	CHIEF EVENTS.
Sunga (Northern India), 184—72 B.C.	140	Mithridates of Parthia invades Bactria and drives the Sakas into North-Western India, where they set up Kshatrapas in Saurashtra, Mathura, and Taxila.
	126	Sakas, Greco-Bactrians, Parthians, and Yuechi (Kushans) in Bactria and North-Western India.
	155—153	Menander, the Greek king of Kabul and the Panjab, mentioned in the Milindapanha, invades India.
Kushan Empire (Purushapura Peshawar), 45—250 A.D approximately.	45—85 A.D.	Kadphises I.
	85—120	Kadphises II.
	120—150	Kanishka.
Andhras (the Deccan)	208 B.C.–249 A.D.	
	113 A.D —134	Gautamiputra Satakarna Nahapana, founder of the line of Mahakshatrapas.
	126	Chashtana Mahakshatrapa.
	134 A D.—152	Sri Pulumayu (Siro Polemios).
	139	Jain scriptures reduced to writing.
	150	Sivaskanda Varman Pallava's *asvamedha*, South Indian dated history.
Mahakshatrapa (the Deccan), 150 A D.—388	150—161	Rudradaman Mahakshatrapa.
	226—250	Disappearance of Kushans, Parthians, and Andhras.
	249	Rise of the Kalachuris of Chedi (Haihaya).
	290	Rise of the Guptas.
	300	Vigorous revival of Hinduism revision of the Puranas.
Gupta Empire, A.D. 319—520	319—326	Chandra Gupta I
	326—375	Samudra Gupta.
	375—413	Chandra Gupta II. (Vikramaditya, Bikramajit, Raja Bikram).
	375	Kalidasa.
	399—414	Fa Hian in India.
	430	White Huns (Epthalites) in North-Western India.

ANCIENT INDIAN DATED HISTORY, 664 B.C. TO 766 A.D.—*Continued.*

EMPIRES AND DYNASTIES.	DATES.	CHIEF EVENTS.
Gupta Empire, A.D. 319—520	470—513	Toramana at Sakala.
	435—800	Gurjara (Gujar dynasty at Broach (Gujrat)
	490	Chalukyas of Badami (Deccan).
	495	Valabhis of Gujrat. First Hindu dynasty of Sind.
White Huns, Epthalites (N. India), 430—528	515—528	Mihiragula expelled from dominions by Rajput combination.
	540	Death of Mihiragula in Kashmir.
Rajput (N. India)	528—550	Yasodharmadeva of Malwa.
	533	Yasodharmadeva's great victory over the Huns at Korur.
Harshavardhana of Thanesvar and Kanauj (N. India), 585—666	600	Revival of Saiva Hinduism in S. India. The Tevaram collection of Tamil hymns.
	606—648	Harshavardhana (Srikantha, Siladitya II.).
	609—642	Pulakesin II. (Satyasraya) Chalukya.
	615—1127	Eastern Chalukyas of Vengi.
Valabhis (Deccan), 495—766	625	Embassy of Khusru II. of Persia to Pulakesin II.
Chalukyas of Badami (Deccan and S. India), 550—754	636	Arabs appear on West Coast of India.
	640—650	Tamil irruptions into Ceylon under Narasimhavarman Pallava.
	711—712	Arab conquest of Sind.
	735	Capture of Chitor by Sisodia Rajputs.
	747	Rise of the Rashtrakutas under Dantidurga.
	757—888	Rahtors of Gujrat.

MEDIAEVAL HINDU INDIA, 766—1193.

EMPIRES AND DYNASTIES.	DATES.	CHIEF EVENTS.
Rashtrakuta (Deccan and S. India), 747—982	774	Jewish colony at Cochin. Jewish pilgrims are said to have arrived as early as A.D. 68.
	780—820	Sankarcharjya, Saivite religious reformer.
	794—814	Govind III., patronage of Digambar Jains.

MEDIAEVAL HINDU INDIA, 766—1193.—*Continued.*

EMPIRES AND DYNASTIES.	DATES.	CHIEF EVENTS.
Rashtrakuta (Deccan and S India), 747—982	815—973	Rise of Rajput States.
	831—1289	Chandel Rajputs of Bundelkund.
	953—999	Dhangadeva Chandela.
	840—1161	Palas (Bengal).
	1000—1300	Paramara (or Pawar) Rajputs of Malwa.
	1010—1062	Raja Bhoj.
	950—1193	Chauhan Rajputs of Ajmere and Delhi.
Chalukyas of Kalyan, 973—1183	1040—1069	Somesvara I., Chalukya.
	1076—1127	Vikramaditya VI. (Vikramanka) Chalukya.
Kalachuri of Chedi (North-Eastern India), 875—1300	1042—1063	Karnadeva Kalachuri
	825	Conversion to Mahomedanism of Cheruman Perumal, last Chera king of Malabar.
	962—1181	Ghaznavide dynasty.
	1001—1026	Fifteen raids of Mahmud of Ghazni.
	980—1053	Revival of Buddhism in Thibet, by Atisa.
Cholas (S. India), 900—1250	979—1002	Rajaraja Chola the Great.
	1076—1108	Kulottunga Chola I.
	1086	General revenue survey of Chola dominions.
	1048—1310	Hoysala Ballal Rajputs of Dwarasamudra (Hallabid, Mysore).
	1127	Ramanuja, Vaishnavite religious reformer.
	1097—1187	Rise of Rajput States.
	1097—1193	Gaharwars of Kanauj.
	1150—1325	Kakatiyas of Warangal.
	1187—1309	Yadavas of Deogiri.
	1193	Defeat of Prithviraj Chauhan by Mahomed Ghori.

MEDIAEVAL MAHOMEDAN INDIA, 1193—1526.

Delhi ruled from Ghor	1193—1205	Mahomed Ghori (Mahomed bin Sam) Muizuddin, Sahibuddin.
	1204—1261	Venetian trade with India after capture of Constantinople by the Crusaders.

MEDIAEVAL MAHOMEDAN INDIA, 1193—1526.—*Continued*

EMPIRES AND DYNASTIES.	DATES.	CHIEF EVENTS.
Slave Sultans of Delhi, 1206—1293	1206—1210	Kutubuddin Aibak, slave of Mahomed Ghori.
	1210—1230	Shamsuddin (Iyaltimish) (Altamsh), slave of Kutubuddin Aibak.
	1221	First appearance of the Mongols in the Panjab.
	1292	Mongols invade India.
	1266—1287	Ghiasuddin Balban, son of slave of Mahomed Ghori.
	1282—1338	His son founds the Balban dynasty of Bengal.
Khilji Sultans of Delhi, 1290—1320	1296—1316	Alauddin Khilji, extension of Mahomedan power to the South.
	1309—1312	Malik Kafur, slave eunuch, and general, raids S. India.
	1318—1320	The slave minister Malik Khusru; reign of terror in Delhi terminated by Malik Khusru's murder, 1320.
Tughlak Sultans of Delhi, 1320—1414 (Northern India).	1325—1351	Mahomed Tughlak.
	1351—1388	Firoz Shah Tughlak.
	1335—1370	Local Mahomedan dynasties.
	1335—1586	Kashmir.
	1417—1467	Zainulabdin, "But Shikast" (iconoclast).
	1339—1493	Iliyas Shahi, Bengal.
	1438—1460	Mahmud Shah, Iliyas Shahi I. (Bengal).
	1446	Mahmud Shah, Iliyas Shahi I. founds Gaur and Tanda.
Bahmani of Kulburga (Deccan), 1347—1525	1422—1535	Ahmad Shah Bahmani founds Bidar in the Deccan (1428).
Vijaynagar Empire (S. India), 1336—1563	1354—1379	Bukka Rai I. of Vijaynagar.
	1379—1406	Harihara
Sultans of Delhi, Said, 1414—1451; Lodi (Afghan), 1451—1526	1414—1421	Said Khizr Khan.
	1451—1489	Bahlul Lodi.
	1489—1517	Sikundar Lodi.
Sharqi Sultans of Jaunpur, 1394—1493	1401—1440	Ibrahim Shah of Jaunpur.
Gujrat (Deccan), 1396 – 1583	1396—1411	Muzaffar Shah of Gujrat.
	1411—1422	Ahmad Shah of Gujrat.
Habshi dynasty (Bengal) 1487—1493	1398	Invasion of India and sack of Delhi by Timur.

MEDIAEVAL MAHOMEDAN INDIA, 1193—1526.—*Continued.*

EMPIRES AND DYNASTIES.	DATES.	CHIEF EVENTS.
Hussain-Shahi (Bengal), 1493—1576	1453	Turks capture Constantinople. Venetian monopoly of trade with the East.
	1469—1485	Medieval religious reformers.
	1469—1538	Guru Nanak (Sikhs).
	1479	Vallabha.
	1480—1518	Kabir.
	1485—1527	Chaitanya.
	1485—1512	Rise of the Five Shahi dynasties of the Deccan.
	1485—1588	Imad of Berar.
	1490—1595	Nizam of Ahmadnagar.
	1490—1661	Adil of Bijapur.
	1492—1609	Barid of Bidar.
	1512—1672	Qutub of Golkonda.
	1497—1499	Voyage of Vasco da Gama to India.
	1500	First Portuguese settlement at Cochin.
	1506—1518	Alphonso de Albuquerque Viceroy of Portuguese India.

MODERN INDIA FROM 1526.

EMPIRES AND DYNASTIES.	DATES.	CHIEF EVENTS.
Moghal Empire, 1526—1774	1526—1530	Baber.
	1526	First battle of Panipat.
	1530—1556	Humayun.
	1539—1545	Sher Shah, Sur.
	1542	Francis Xavier, Jesuit missionary at Goa.
	1556—1605	Akbar.
	1556	Second battle of Panipat.
	1563	Battle of Tallikota.
	1569	Foundation of Fatehpur Sikri
	1578	Rise of Wodeyar dynasty of Mysore.
	1582	Todar Malla's Financial Settlement of revenues of Moghal empire.
	1581	Turkey and Levant Companies formed.
	1589	Fitch, Newberry and Leedes arrive at Akbar's court.

MODERN INDIA FROM 1526.—*Continued.*

EMPIRES AND DYNASTIES.	DATES.	CHIEF EVENTS.
Moghal Empire, 1526—1774	1587	Drake's capture of the San Philippe. English gain better knowledge of the value of the Indian trade.
	1600	Queen Elizabeth's Charter to the East India Company.
	1612	Factory at Surat.
	1617	Scotch East India Company.
	1595—1599	First Dutch voyage to the Far East.
	1602	Dutch East India Company. Dutch establish themselves in Ceylon.
	1605—1627	Jahangir.
	1611	Jahangir marries Nur Jahan.
	1612	Danish East India Company.
	1616	Danish factory at Tranquebar.
	1615	French East India Company.
	1662	Compagnie des Indes.
	1667	French at Cochin.
	1674	French at Pondicherry.
	1620	Shahji Bhonsla; commencement of Mahratta power.
	1627—1658	Shah Jahan.
	1631	Death of Mumtaz Mahal.
	1632—1645	Building of Taj Mahal in honour of Mumtaz Mahal.
	1640—1690	Foundations of English power.
	1639	English at Madras.
	1640	English occupy Hughli.
	1665	Bombay.
	1690	Calcutta.
	1645	Imperial patent to trade.
	1658—1707	Aurangzeb Alamgir.
	1659	Sivaji Bhonsla, extension of Mahratta power.
	1664	Sivajee assumes title of king.
	1677	Levy of chauth.
	1681	Rise of the Siddis of Jinjira and of the Sawants of Wadi.
	1697	European piracy in the Indian Ocean.
	1718	Rise of the Angria pirates of Gheriah.
	1702—1708	United East India Company.

MODERN INDIA FROM 1526.—*Continued.*

EMPIRES AND DYNASTIES.	DATES.	CHIEF EVENTS.
Moghal Empire, 1526—1774	1714—1727	Austrian Ostend East India Company.
	1731	Swedish East India Company.
	1706	First Protestant missionaries, who are Danes in Tranquebar.
	1726	First British missionaries at Madras.
	1797	Rajput league against the Moghals. Rise of the Mahratta Confederacy. Commencement of the break up of the Moghal empire.
	1710—1739	Local Mahomedan powers.
	1710	Nawabs of the Karnatic.
	1712	Syeds of Barha.
	1723	Nizams of Hyderabad.
	1724	Nawabs of Oudh.
	1727	Rohilla Afghans.
	1739	Nawabs of Bengal.
	1714—1759	Mahratta States.
	1714	Peshwas of Poona.
	1727	Gaekwars of Baroda.
	1732	Holkars of Indore.
	1739	Bhonslas of Nagpur.
	1759	Scindias of Gwalior.
	1738—1739	Invasion of Nadir Shah; sack of Delhi.
	1748 1751	Invasions of Ahmad Shah Abdali of Afghanistan.
	1757 1761	Mahrattas defeated at third battle of Panipat, 1761.
	1749—1761	Rise of Hyder Ali of Mysore.
	1781	Outbreak of Second Mysore War, 1782. Death of Hyder Ali.
	1751—1767	Clive's Indian career.
	1751	Defence of Arcot.
	1756	Siege of Calcutta by Suraj-ud-daula.
	1757	Battle of Plassey.
	1759—1761	Destruction of French power in India.
	1763	Sir Hector Munro's victory of Buxar.

Modern India from 1526.—*Continued.*

Empires and Dynasties.	Dates.	Chief Events.
Moghal Empire, 1526—1774	1765	Shah Alam grants to the English the Dewani of Bengal, Behar, and Orissa.
	1787	Goorkhas overrun Nepal.
East India Company's rule. Governors-General, 1774—1858	1774—1785	Warren Hastings, first Governor-General.
	1774	British Parliament passes Regulating Act.
	1786—1795	Warren Hastings's Impeachment.
	1782—1799	Tipu Sahib of Mysore.
	1786—1793	Lord Cornwallis.
	1793	Permanent Revenue Settlement in Bengal.
	1798—1805	Lord Wellesley.
	1798—1839	Ranjit Singh in the Panjab.
	1803	Second Mahratta War Victories. Lake at Delhi and Laswaree. Wellesley at Assaye, Asirgarh, and Argaon. Harcourt at Katak. Woodington at Baroda. Monson at Aligarh.
	1804	Lake's victory at Dig.
	1807—1813	Lord Minto.
	1809	Treaty of Amritsar.
	1811	Treaty of Tilsit between France and Russia. Commencement of "Russian scare." Lord Hastings.
	1814—1816	Goorkha War.
	1816—1818	Mahratta (Third War), Rohilla and Pindaree campaigns.
	1823—1828	Lord Amherst.
	1824—1826	First Burmese War; Assam, Arracan and Tenasserim annexed.
	1828—1835	Lord William Bentinck.
	1829	Interference with native customs. Suppression of Thuggee and Sati.
	1830	Suppression of female infanticide.
	1836—1842	Lord Auckland.

MODERN INDIA FROM 1526.—*Continued.*

EMPIRES AND DYNASTIES.	DATES.	CHIEF EVENTS.
East India Company's rule. Governors-General, 1774—1858	1838—1842	First Afghan War.
	1842—1844	Lord Ellenborough.
	1844	Battle of Meanee. Annexation of Sind. War with Scindia. Battles of Maharajpur and Punniar.
	1844—1848	Lord Hardinge.
	1845—1846	First Sikh War.
	1845	Battles of Mudki and Firozshah.
	1846	Battles of Aliwal and Sobraon.
	1848—1856	Lord Dalhousie.
	1848—1849	Second Sikh War. Battles of Chilianwala and Gujrat. Annexation of the Panjab. "Doctrine of Lapse," annexation of Jhansi, Satara, and Nagpur.
	1856	Annexation of Oudh on the ground of misgovernment.
	1854	General education introduced.
British Empire. Viceroys from 1858. Direct Government of the Crown	1856—1862	Lord Canning.
	1857—1859	Indian Mutiny and its suppression.
	1858	Act for the Better Government of India passed by British Parliament. Direct government of India assumed by the Crown.
	1858	Lord Canning, first Viceroy. Allahabad Durbar. Queen's Proclamation. Doctrine of Lapse no longer enforced. Indian princes to have right of adoption, on failure of direct offspring.
	1876—1880	Lord Lytton.
	1877	Proclamation of the Queen as Empress of India at the Delhi Durbar.
	1878—1880	Second Afghan War.
	1884—1888	Lord Dufferin.
	1885—1889	Third Burmese War. Annexation of Upper Burma.
	1910	Lord Hardinge.

MODERN INDIA[1] FROM 1526.—*Continued.*

EMPIRES AND DYNASTIES.	DATES.	CHIEF EVENTS.
British Empire. Viceroys from 1858. Direct Government of the Crown	1911	King and Queen present in India at Delhi Durbar, and King George crowned Emperor of India. Imperial capital at Delhi.

INDEX

D

H

I

O.

P.

S